The Random House

Thesaurus

A Dictionary
of Synonyms
and Antonyms

The Random House Thesaurus

A Dictionary of Synonyms and Antonyms

Edited by

Laurence Urdang

RANDOM HOUSE
New York

Latest printing 1981

Library of Congress Catalog Card Number: 60-5553
Manufactured in the United States of America.

In Other Words . . .

Judicious use of this book will more than treble the average person's potential vocabulary. Over 80,000 synonyms and antonyms have been listed in categories which are numbered to correspond with the senses in which they are most commonly used, based on scientific frequency counts. The arrangement within the entries proper varies: if the entry word is a "strong" one, synonyms will be entered in order of decreasing intensity (synonyms for **oblivious** run the gamut from *heedless* to *negligent*), and if "weak," in order of increasing "strength." Also, informal words have their synonyms given in the order of increasing formality (**coast** synonyms run from *shore* to *littoral*), while formal word synonyms go in the opposite direction.

The numerical order of the synonym lists corresponds to that of the definitions in *The American College Dictionary*. Thus, for the entry *trust*, the synonyms given for number **1.** are those which are equated to the most common sense in which the word is used, "reliance on the integrity, justice, etc. of a person, or in some quality or attribute of a thing; confidence." Similarly, synonyms under following numbers correspond to meanings of decreasing frequency. Of course, there won't always be as many synonym lists as there are numbered definitions either because there may be no synonyms for certain meanings or because the dictionary distinguishes finer shades of meaning than are possible in a dictionary of synonyms.

ANTONYMS are provided only for appropriate words which have antonyms. Only a few are provided in each case, but to find more, the user need only look up the synonym entries provided for the antonyms listed.

A Word of Caution

The most important word of caution for the user of this dictionary is to remember that there is *no true synonym* for any word in English. Each word has its own set of meanings, but its use must always be appropriate to the context in which it appears. Thus no one would write "We spent the day on the littoral" instead of "We spent the day at the beach, at the shore, etc." If a selected synonym is unfamiliar, *look up the word in a good dictionary* where it will often be shown used in a sample sentence or phrase. It is only in this way that you can derive the greatest amount of use and benefit from *The Random House Thesaurus: A Dictionary of Synonyms and Antonyms.*

Abbreviations Used in this Book

adj.—adjective
adv.—adverb
conj.—conjunction
n.—noun
prep.—preposition
v.—verb
Ant.—antonym

The Random House

Thesaurus

A Dictionary of Synonyms and Antonyms

A

abandon, *v.* **1.** leave, forsake, desert, relinquish, evacuate, drop, discard, cast off, quit, vacate. **2.** resign, retire, quit, abjure, forswear, withdraw, forgo. **3.** abdicate, waive, give up, yield, surrender, resign, cede, renounce, repudiate.
Ant. keep, maintain; pursue.

abandoned, *adj.* **1.** forsaken, left, deserted, relinquished, dropped, discarded, cast off, cast aside, cast out, rejected, demitted, sent down. **2.** unrestrained. **3.** wicked, depraved, unprincipled, sinful, corrupt, licentious, amoral, profligate, vicious, dissolute, shameless; shameful, immoral, incorrigible, impenitent, graceless, irreclaimable, reprobate, demoralized, vice-ridden.
Ant. virtuous, honest, good, righteous.

abase, *v.* lower, reduce, humble, degrade, downgrade, demote; disgrace, dishonor, debase, take down, humiliate.
Ant. elevate, exalt, honor.

abash, *v.* shame, embarrass, mortify, disconcert, discompose, confound, confuse; cow, humble, humiliate, discountenance, affront.

abate, *v.* **1.** lessen, diminish, reduce, discount, decrease, lower, slow. **2.** deduct, subtract, remit, rebate, allow, discount. **3.** omit, eliminate, disallow. **4.** (*law*) suppress; suspend, extinguish; annul; remove, disallow, nullify, repress. **5.** diminish, lessen, decrease, lower, slow, subside, decline, sink, wane, ebb, slack off, slacken, fade, fade out, fade away.
Ant. increase, intensify.

abatement, *n.* **1.** alleviation, mitigation, lessening, let-up, diminution, decrease, slackening. **2.** suppression, termination, ending, end, cessation. **3.** subsidence, decline, sinking, way, ebb, slack, fade-out, fading.
Ant. intensification, increase.

abbreviate, *v.* shorten, abridge, reduce, curtail, cut, contract, compress; crop, dock, pare down, prune, truncate; condense, digest, epitomize, abstract.
Ant. lengthen, expand.

abbreviation, *n.* shortening, abridgment, compendium, reduction, curtailment, cut, contraction, compression; truncation; condensation, digest, epitome, brief, essence, heart, core, soul.
Ant. lengthening, expansion.

abdicate, *v.* renounce, disclaim, disavow, disown, repudiate; resign, retire, quit, relinquish, abandon, surrender, cede, give up, waive.
Ant. commit.

abdication, *n.* renunciation, disclaimer, disavowal, repudiation, resignation, retirement, quittance; abandonment, surrender, cession, waiver.

Ant. commitment.

abdomen, *n.* **1.** stomach, belly, visceral cavity, viscera, paunch. **2.** (*slang*) pot, guts, gut, potbelly, corporation, alderman, beerbarrel.

abduct, *v.* kidnap, carry off, bear off, capture, carry away, ravish, steal away, run away *or* off with, seize, rape.

abduction, *n.* kidnaping, capture, ravishment, deprehension, seizure, rape.

abductor, *n.* kidnaper, captor, ravisher, seizer, rapist.

abecedarian, *n.* **1.** beginner. —*adj.* **2.** alphabetical. **3.** primary, basic, rudimentary.

aberrant, *adj.* **1.** straying, stray, deviating, deviate, wandering, errant, erring, devious, erratic, rambling, diverging, divergent. **2.** abnormal, irregular, unusual, odd, eccentric, peculiar, exceptional, weird, queer, curious, singular, strange; unconforming, nonconforming, anomalous.

Ant. direct.

aberration, *n.* **1.** wandering, straying, deviation, rambling, divergence, departure. **2.** strangeness, abnormality, abnormity, oddness, anomaly, irregularity, eccentricity; peculiarity, curiosity, oddity. **3.** unsoundness, illusion, hallucination, delusion, *lapsis mentis.*

abet, *v.* aid, assist, help, support, back, succor, sustain; countenance, sanction, uphold, second, condone, approve, favor; encourage, promote, conduce, advocate, advance, further, subsidize.

Ant. hinder.

abeyance, *n.* suspension, suspense, inactivity, hiatus, recess, deferral, intermission, interregnum, dormancy, quiescence.

Ant. operation, action.

abhor, *v.* hate, detest, loathe, abominate, despise, regard with repugnance, execrate, view with horror, shrink from, shudder at, bear malice *or* spleen.

Ant. love.

abhorrence, *n.* hate, hatred, loathing, execration, odium, abomination, aversion, repugnance, revulsion, disgust, horror, antipathy, detestation, animosity, enmity.

Ant. love.

abhorrent, *adj.* **1.** hating, loathing, loathsome, execrating, execratory, antipathetic, detesting, detestable. **2.** horrible, horrifying, shocking, disgusting, revolting, sickening, nauseating, repugnant, repulsive, odious; hateful, detestable, abominable, invidious. **3.** remote, far, distant, removed.

Ant. amiable, lovable.

abide, *v.* **1.** remain, stay, wait, wait for, tarry, sojourn. **2.** dwell, reside, live, inhabit, tenant, stay. **3.** remain, continue, endure, last, persist, persevere, remain steadfast *or* faithful *or* constant, go on, keep on. **4.** stand by, support, second; await *or* accept the consequences of. **5.** await, attend, wait for. **6.** stand one's ground against, await *or* sustain defiantly. **7.** put up with, stand, suffer, brook, allow, tolerate, bear, endure.

ability, *n.* **1.** power, proficiency, expertness, dexterity, capacity, ableness, capability, knack, facility, competency, competence, enablement; puissance, prepotency. **2.** faculty, talent, aptitude, skill, skillfulness, aptness, ingenuity.
Ant. inability.

abject, *adj.* **1.** humiliating, disheartening, debasing, degrading. **2.** contemptible, despicable, scurvy, hateful; base, mean, low, vile, groveling, corrupt; faithless, treacherous, perfidious, dishonorable, inglorious, dishonest, false, fraudulent; disgraceful, ignominious, discreditable.
Ant. supercilious; exalted.

able, *adj.* **1.** qualified, fit, fitted, competent, capable, apt. **2.** talented, accomplished, gifted, endowed; skilled, clever, adroit, expert, ingenious, skillful, proficient, versed.
Ant unable, incompetent, inept.

abnormal, *adj.* nonconforming, nonconformant, irregular, erratic, anomalous, unusual, unnatural, queer, odd, peculiar, aberrant, eccentric, weird, curious, strange, singular, idiosyncratic.
Ant. normal, regular.

abnormality, *n.* abnormity, irregularity, unconformity, anomaly, peculiarity, aberrance, idiosyncrasy, singularity, curiosity; malformation, monstrosity.
Ant. regularity, normality.

abolish, *v.* suppress, put an end to, cease, void, annul, invalidate, nullify, cancel, revoke, rescind, repeal, eradicate, stamp out, annihilate, extirpate, destroy, do away with, abrogate, obliterate, erase, extinguish, put out, eliminate.
Ant. establish.

abolition, *n.* destruction, annihilation, extirpation, abrogation, obliteration, eradication, elimination, extinction; annulment, nullification, invalidation, cancellation, revocation, repeal.
Ant. establishment.

abominable, *adj.* detestable, hateful, loathsome, abhorrent, odious, contemptible, despicable, scurvy; horrible, horrifying, disgusting, nauseating, sickening, revolting, repugnant, obnoxious, foul, noxious.
Ant. likable, admirable, delightful.

abominate, *v.* abhor, regard with aversion, detest, hate, loathe, execrate, contemn, despise, regard with repugnance, view with horror, shrink from, shudder at, bear malice *or* spleen.
Ant. like, love, enjoy.

abomination, *n.* **1.** hatred, loathing, abhorrence, detestation, revulsion, loathsomeness, odiousness, odium; aversion. **2.** vice, sin, impurity, corruption, wickedness, evil, viciousness, depravity, immorality, amorality, profligacy, defilement, pollution, filth.

abortive, *adj.* **1.** failing, unsuccessful, miscarrying, immature, premature. **2.** undeveloped, underdeveloped, rudimentary, primitive. **3.** (*medicine*) abortifacient. **4.** (*pathology*) short, mild, without symptoms. *Ant.* consummate.

abound, *v.* prevail, teem, swarm, be very prevalent, pour, stream, shower. *Ant.* want, need, lack.

about, *prep.* **1.** of, concerning, in regard to, respecting, with regard *or* respect *or* reference to, relating *or* relative to. **2.** connected with, in connection with, relating *or* relative to. **3.** near, around, round, not far from, close to. **4.** near, close to, approximately, almost. **5.** around, circling, encircling, inclosing, enclosing, surrounding. **6.** on one's person, having, in one's possession. **7.** on the point of, ready, prepared. **8.** here and there, in, on, hither and yon, to and fro, back and forth, hither and thither. —*adv.* **9.** near, approximately, nearly, almost, well-nigh. **10.** nearby, close, not far, around. **11.** on every side, in every direction, all around, everywhere, every place, all over. **12.** half round, reversed, backwards, opposite direction. **13.** to and fro, back and forth, hither and thither, hither and yon, here and there. **14.** in succession, alternately, in rotation.

above, *adv.* **1.** overhead, aloft, on high, atop, on top of. **2.** higher, beyond, over, superior, surpassing. **3.** before, prior, earlier, sooner, previous, first. **4.** in heaven, on high, *in excelsis.* —*prep.* **5.** over, in a higher place than, higher than, superior to. **6.** more, greater than, more than, exceeding. **7.** superior to, beyond, surpassing. —*adj.* **8.** supra, said, written, mentioned previously, foregoing, preceding.

aboveboard, *adv.* **1.** in open sight, without tricks, without disguise, openly, overtly, candidly, honestly, frankly, sincerely, guilelessly, unequivocally, unequivocatingly. —*adj.* **2.** open, candid, overt, honest, frank, sincere, guileless, unequivocal, unequivocating. *Ant.* underhand, treacherous, seditious.

abrade, *v.* wear off, wear down, scrape off; erode, wear away, rub off.

abrasion, *n.* **1.** sore, scrape, cut, scratch. **2.** friction, abrading, rubbing, erosion, wearing down, rubbing off.

abreast, *adv., adj.* side by side, alongside, equal, aligned, in alignment.

abridge, *v.* **1.** condense, digest, scale down, reduce, epitomize, abstract. **2.** curtail, reduce, lessen, diminish, contract. **3.** deprive, cut off, dispossess, divest. *Ant.* expand, extend.

abridgment, *n.* **1.** condensation, shortening, digest, epitome, curtailment, reduction, abbreviation, contraction, retrenchment, compression; compendium, synopsis, abstract, abstraction, summary, syllabus, brief, outline, précis. **2.** dispossession, limitation. *Ant.* expansion, extension, enlargement.

abroad, *adv.* **1.** overseas, beyond the sea, away. **2.**

out-of-doors, outside, out of the house. **3.** astir, in circulation, bruited about. **4.** broadly, widely, expansively, at large, everywhere, ubiquitously, in all directions. **5.** untrue, wide of the truth.
Ant. here, domestically.

abrogate, *v.* abolish, cancel, annul, repeal, disannul, revoke, rescind, nullify, void, invalidate.
Ant. ratify, establish.

abrogation, *n.* abolition, cancellation, annulment, repeal, disannulment, revocation, rescission, nullification, invalidation.
Ant. establishment.

abrupt, *adj.* **1.** sudden, unceremonious, short, precipitous, hasty, blunt, curt, brusque, uncomplaisant; rude, rough, discourteous, inconsiderate, boorish. **2.** discontinuous, spasmodic, uneven. **3.** steep, precipitous, acclivitous, craggy.
Ant. gradual, slow, deliberate.

abscond, *v.* depart suddenly, depart secretly, steal away, sneak off *or* out, decamp, run away, run off, escape, flee, fly, bolt.
Ant. remain.

absence, *n.* **1.** want, lack, need, deficiency, defect. **2.** non-appearance.
Ant. presence.

absent, *adj.* **1.** away, out, not in, not here, not present, off. **2.** lacking, missing, not present, away. —*v.* **3.** stay away, keep away.
Ant. present.

absent-minded, *adj.* forgetful, preoccupied, abstracted, oblivious, inattentive, wandering, withdrawn; musing, in a brown study, dreaming, day-dreaming.
Ant. attentive.

absolute, *adj.* **1.** complete, whole, entire, perfect, free from imperfection, ideal. **2.** pure, unmixed, unadulterated, sheer, unqualified. **3.** unqualified, utter, total, entire, unconditional, unrestricted, unlimited, unbound, unbounded. **4.** arbitrary, despotic, autocratic, dictatorial, tyrannous, tyrannical, imperious, Nazi, Fascist, Fascistic. **5.** uncompared, categorical, certain, unquestionable, unequivocal. **6.** positive, affirmative, unquestionable, indubitable, certain, sure, unequivocal, unequivocating, firm, definite.
Ant. mixed; relative.

absolutely, *adv.* **1.** completely, wholly, entirely, unqualifiedly, definitely, unconditionally. **2.** positively, affirmatively, unquestionably, definitely, unequivocally, indubitably, really, without doubt, beyond doubt.

absolve, *v.* **1.** acquit, exonerate, free from blame, exculpate, excuse, forgive, pardon, clear, release, liberate, set free, free, disentangle, discharge, loose, rid. **2.** set free, loose, release, liberate, exempt. **3.** pardon, excuse, forgive.
Ant. blame, censure.

absorb, *v.* **1.** swallow, consume, assimilate, amalgamate, devour, engulf, ingurgitate; destroy. **2.** engross, occupy.

abstinence, *n.* **1.** abstemiousness, sobriety, soberness, teetotalism, moderation, temperance. **2.** self-restraint, forbearance, avoidance, self-denial, nonindulgence.
Ant. indulgence.

abstract, *adj.* **1.** apart, special, unrelated, separate, isolated. **2.** theoretical, unpractical. **3.** abstruse, difficult, deep, complex, complicated. **4.** (*art*) nonrepresentational, unrealistic, unphotographic. —*n.* **5.** summary, digest, epitome, abridgment, synopsis, compendium, condensation, brief; syllabus, outline, précis; gist, substance. **6.** essence, distillation, condensation, substance; core, heart, idea. —*v.* **7.** draw away, take away, remove, distill; separate, fractionate. **8.** divert, disengage. **9.** steal, purloin, rob, pilfer, shoplift, hijack. **10.** separate, consider apart, isolate, dissociate; disjoin, disunite. **11.** summarize, epitomize, distill, abridge, abbreviate, outline, condense, edit, digest.
Ant. concrete; interpolate.

absurd, *adj.* ridiculous, preposterous, foolish, inane, asinine, stupid, unwise, false, unreasonable, irrational, incongruous, self-contradictory.
Ant. sensible, rational.

abundance, *n.* **1.** overflow, plenty, copiousness, fertility, profusion, plenteousness, prodigality, extravagance, oversupply, flood. **2.** fulness, generosity, large-heartedness. **3.** affluence, wealth.
Ant. lack, need, paucity.

abundant, *adj.* abounding, teeming, thick, plentiful, plenteous, flowing, copious, profuse, overflowing, rich, replete.
Ant. sparse, scarce, poor.

abuse, *v.* **1.** misuse, misapply, mistreat, misemploy, misappropriate; desecrate, profane, prostitute; deceive, betray, seduce, subvert. **2.** maltreat, ill-use, injure, harm, hurt. **3.** revile, malign, vilify, vituperate, berate, rate, rail at, upbraid, scold, carp at, inveigh against, reproach; traduce, slander, defame, denounce, asperse, calumniate, disparage; satirize, lampoon. —*n.* **4.** misuse, misapplication, mistreatment, misemployment, misappropriation; desecration, profanation, prostitution; deception, betrayal, seduction, subversion. **5.** censure, adverse criticism, blame, condemnation, hostile condemnation; denunciation, vilification, malignment, vituperation, invective, slander, defamation, aspersion, calumniation, curse, disparagement; contumely, scorn, reproach, opprobrium. **6.** offense, crime, corruption.
Ant. esteem; praise, acclaim.

academic, *adj.* **1.** college, collegiate, university. **2.** unscientific, literary, lettered, scholastic, unprofessional. **3.** theoretical, unpractical, impractical. **4.** conventional, formal.

Ant. illiterate.

accept, *v.* **1.** receive, take. **2.** admit, agree to, accede to, acquiesce in, assent to, approve, allow, concede, acknowledge. **3.** resign oneself to, accommodate oneself to, yield, consent. **4.** believe, acknowledge. **5.** understand, construe, interpret. **6.** receive, acknowledge.
Ant. reject.

accident, *n.* **1.** mischance, misfortune, disaster, calamity, catastrophe, casualty, mishap, misadventure, contingency. **2.** fortuity, chance.
Ant. intent, calculation.

accidental, *adj.* **1.** casual, fortuitous, undesigned, unplanned, contingent. **2.** nonessential, incidental, subsidiary, secondary, dispensable, expendable, adventitious.
Ant. planned, designed, essential.

accommodate, *v.* **1.** oblige, serve; aid, assist, help, abet. **2.** provide, supply, furnish, minister to. **3.** furnish room for, board, entertain. **4.** make suitable, suit, fit, adapt. **5.** bring into harmony, adjust, reconcile, compose, harmonize. **6.** contain, hold. **7.** conform, agree, concur, assent.
Ant. inconvenience, incommode.

accompany, *v.* **1.** go along, attend, join, escort, convoy, wait on. **2.** coexist with, consort with. **3.** associate with, consider together with, couple with.
Ant. desert, abandon, forsake.

accomplice, *n.* associate, partner, confederate, accessory.

accomplish, *v.* **1.** fulfill, complete, achieve, execute, do, carry out, perform, finish, attain, consummate, culminate, dispatch, effect, effectuate, perfect, realize. **2.** succeed in, be successful with *or* in, triumph over, win over. **3.** equip, supply, furnish, provide.
Ant. foil.

accomplishment, *n.* **1.** fulfillment, completion, effecting, execution. **2.** achievement, success, consummation. **3.** attainment, acquirement, acquisition, proficiency.
Ant. failure.

accord, *v.* **1.** agree, assent, concur, correspond, be harmonious *or* in harmony, harmonize. **2.** adapt, accommodate, reconcile, suit, fit. **3.** grant, concede, yield, give up *or* in, allow, deign, vouchsafe.
Ant. conflict, disagree.

accordingly, *adv.* **1.** correspondingly, conformably, agreeably. **2.** in due course, consequently, hence, therefore, thus, so, wherefore.

account, *n.* **1.** narrative, narration, recital, report, history, chronicle, journal, anecdote, description, story, expose, tale. **2.** explanation, elucidation. **3.** explication, clearing up, exposition. **4.** reason, consideration, motive, excuse, purpose. **5.** consequence, importance, value, consideration, worth, distinction, repute, reputation. **6.** estimation, judgment, consideration, regard. **7.** profit, advantage, benefit. **8.** statement, ledger, inventory, register, score, book, books. **9.** record, ledger; balance. —*v.* **10.** give an explanation for, explain, elucidate. **11.** make excuse for, give reasons for, answer, reply. **12.** explain, explicate. **13.** cause death *or* capture for. **14.** count, reckon, estimate, consider, regard, judge, deem, rate, assess, hold, see, view, look upon. **15.** assign to, impute to, blame, credit, accuse.

accurate, *adj.* correct, exact, precise, careful, true, unerring.
Ant. inaccurate.

accuse, *v.* **1.** arraign, indict, charge, incriminate, impeach. **2.** blame, inculpate, charge, involve, point to.
Ant. exonerate.

accustomed, *adj.* **1.** customary, habitual, usual, characteristic, familiar, common. **2.** wont, used to, in the habit of.
Ant. unused, unaccustomed.

ache, *v.* **1.** suffer, hurt, suffer pain. —*n.* **2.** pain, continued *or* dull pain, agony.

achieve, *v.* **1.** carry through, accomplish, consummate, complete, effect, execute, do, perform, realize, reach. **2.** gain, obtain, acquire, procure, secure, get, attain, realize, win. **3.** effect, result.
Ant. fail.

achievement, *n.* **1.** exploit, feat, deed. **2.** accomplishment, realization, attainment, consummation.
Ant. failure.

acid, *adj.* **1.** vinegary. **2.** sour, tart, biting, ill-natured, ill-tempered, sarcastic, sardonic, scornful.
Ant. sweet, mild.

acknowledge, *v.* **1.** admit, confess, own, declare, grant, concede, give in, allow, agree. **2.** realize, recognize. **3.** accept, receive, allow. **4.** appreciate, be grateful for, express gratitude for. **5.** reply to, receive, indorse, admit *or* certify receipt of.

acquaintance, *n.* **1.** associate, companion, friend. **2.** personal knowledge, familiarity.

acquiesce, *v.* assent, accede, comply, agree, concur, consent, bow, submit, yield, resign *or* reconcile oneself, rest, be satisfied *or* content (with).
Ant. protest, object.

acquire, *v.* **1.** appropriate, gain, win, earn, attain; take over, take possession of, procure, secure, obtain, get. **2.** accomplish, achieve.
Ant. forfeit.

acquit, *v.* **1.** absolve, exonerate, exculpate, pardon, excuse, forgive. **2.** release *or* discharge, liberate, set free. **3.** settle, pay, fulfill.
Ant. convict, condemn.

act, *n.* **1.** feat, exploit, achievement, transaction, accomplishment, performance. **2.** deed, performance. **3.** decree, edict, law, statute, judgment, resolve, award. **4.** record, deed, enactment, ordinance. **5.** turn, routine, performance, stint. —*v.* **6.** exert energy *or* force, operate, function, perform, do, work. **7.** function, be active, substitute (for). **8.** produce an effect, operate, be efficient *or* effective *or* efficacious. **9.** behave, perform, conduct *or* deport *or* comport oneself. **10.** pretend, sham, dissemble, feign, fake, do imitations, dissimulate, play. **11.** play parts, do imitations *or* impersonations. **12.** represent, impersonate, imitate, play the part of. **13.** feign, counterfeit, fake, imitate. **14.** behave as, play the part of.

action, *n.* **1.** movement, work, performance, moving, working, performing, operation. **2.** deed, act. **3.** (*plural*) conduct, behavior. **4.** energetic activity. **5.** exertion, energy, effort. **6.** gesture. **7.** mechanism, contrivance, apparatus. **8.** skirmish, brush, affair, encounter, meeting, engagement, conflict, combat, fight, battle. **9.** (*law*) proceeding, process, case, suit, lawsuit.
Ant. lethargy, inactivity.

active, *adj.* **1.** acting, moving, working, operative **2.** busy, energetic, strenuous, vigorous, animated, enterprising, efficient, fervent, earnest, eager, diligent, industrious, hard-working, untiring, indefatigable, assiduous; engaged, occupied, consumed with. **3.** nimble, sprightly, agile, alert, smart, quick, spirited, brisk, supple, lively. **4.** practical, working, applicable, applied. **5.** (*commerce*) busy, profitable; interest-bearing. **6.** (*medicine*) effective, productive.
Ant. inactive, lazy.

actual, *adj.* **1.** true, genuine, real, veritable, palpable, tangible, certain, positive, absolute, sure, categorical, decided, definite, determinate, substantial. **2.** now existing, present, here and now.
Ant. unreal, untrue, fake.

acute, *adj.* **1.** pointed, cuspidate, aciform, acicular, acuminate, sharp, sharpened. **2.** intense, poignant, touching; severe, fierce, violent, distressing, crucial, sudden, piercing, penetrating. **3.** sharp, penetrating, perceptive, keen, astute, discerning, intelligent, perspicacious, sharp-witted, shrewd, clever, knowing, wise, sage, sagacious, sapient; smart, bright, ingenious. **4.** sensitive, keen. **5.** alt, high, intense.
Ant. blunt.

adapt, *v.* suit, adjust, modify, fit, reconcile, accommodate, prepare, conform, make conformable *or* suitable, qualify, compose.

add, *v.* **1.** unite, annex, connect, affix, join; append, attach, supplement, increase, make an addition to, augment, adjoin, tack on. **2.** total, tot, sum, aggregate.
Ant. subtract, deduct.

addition, *n.* **1.** uniting, adding, joining. **2.** summing up. **3.** increase, increment, enlargement, aggrandizement, accession; supplement, appendix, accessory, adjunct, attachment, addendum, appendage.
Ant. deduction, subtraction.

address, *n.* **1.** discourse, lecture, speech, oration. **2.** location, post office. **3.** residence, domicile, abode, habitation, lodging, dwelling, home quarters, house. **4.** manner, bearing. **5.** skillful management, skill, art, adroitness, cleverness, tact, ingenuity, technique, dexterity, ability. —*v.* **6.** direct (speech or writing to), speak to; accost. **7.** invoke, appeal to, apply to.

adequate, *adj.* commensurate, equal, suitable, fit for; satisfactory, competent, sufficient, enough; capable.
Ant. inadequate, insufficient.

adhere, *v.* **1.** stick fast, cleave, cling to, stick, hold, cohere. **2.** be devoted, identify, be attached, be a follower, be faithful, be true. **3.** hold closely *or* firmly to.
Ant. separate.

adherent, *n.* **1.** supporter, follower, partisan, disciple; devoté, fan, aficionado. —*adj.* **2.** clinging, adhering, sticking, cleaving.
Ant. recreant, deserter.

adjacent, *adj.* near, close, contiguous, adjoining, juxtaposed, neighboring, nearby, touching.
Ant. distant.

adjoining, *adj.* bordering, contiguous, adjacent, near *or* close *or* next to, touching.
Ant. distant.

adjourn, *v.* **1.** suspend (*for a day*), postpone, interrupt, put off, defer, delay, prorogue. **2.** postpone, defer, transfer.
Ant. convene; begin.

adjunct, *n.* **1.** addition, appendix, supplement, attachment. **2.** aide, attaché, subordinate, accessory.

adjust, *v.* **1.** fit, make correspondent *or* conformable to, adapt, accommodate, suit. **2.** regulate, set, repair, fix; change, alter. **3.** arrange, rectify, reconcile, settle. **4.** adapt oneself, make oneself suitable *or* suited for.

administer, *v.* **1.** manage, conduct, control, execute; rule, govern; direct, superintend, oversee, supervise. **2.** dispense, distribute, supply, job, furnish, contribute. **3.** give, dispense, apply, dose, deal out, dole out. **4.** tender, offer, proffer; impose. **5.** provide aid, contribute assistance. **6.** (*law*) act as executor; act as administrator.

admirable, *adj.* estimable, praiseworthy, fine, rare, excellent.
Ant. abhorrent.

admiration, *n.* wonder, awe, pleasure, approbation, delight, esteem; liking, affection, regard.
Ant. abhorrence, disgust, hatred.

admire, *v.* esteem; revere, venerate; like, delight in.
Ant. detest, hate.

admission, *n.* **1.** entrance, introduction, access, admittance, entrée, ticket, pass, Annie Oakley, key, shibboleth. **2.** confession, acknowledgment, allowance, concession.
Ant. rejection.

admit, *v.* **1.** allow to enter, grant *or* afford entrance to,

let in, afford access to, receive. **2.** permit, allow, agree to, concede, bear. **3.** acknowledge, own, avow, confess. **4.** permit entrance, give access. **5.** grant permission, be capable of.
Ant. reject.

admittance, *n.* **1.** entrance, admission, introduction. **2.** access, reception.

admonish, *v.* **1.** caution, advise, warn, counsel. **2.** rebuke, censure, reprove. **3.** recall to duty, remind, notify, make aware, apprise, acquaint, inform.

ado, *n.* activity, bustle, fuss, flurry, to-do, commotion, babble, stir, tumult, confusion, upset, excitement, hubbub, noise, turmoil, bother, pother.
Ant. serenity, calm.

adolescent, *adj.* **1.** immature, youthful, young. *—n.* **2.** youth, teen-ager, minor.
Ant. adult.

adore, *v.* idolize, worship, love; respect, honor, esteem, reverence, revere, venerate, idolize.
Ant. abhor, detest, abominate, hate.

adorn, *v.* **1.** embellish, add luster to. **2.** decorate, enhance, beautify, deck, bedeck, ornament, trim, bedizen, array.
Ant. disfigure, deface.

adroit, *adj.* expert, ingenious, skillful, dexterous, clever, resourceful, ready, quick, apt, adept.
Ant. clumsy, maladroit.

adult, *adj.* **1.** mature, grown up, full-grown, ripe, of age. *—n.* **2.** grown-up, man, woman.
Ant. immature, adolescent.

advance, *v.* **1.** move *or* set *or* push *or* bring forward, further, forward. **2.** propose, bring to view *or* notice, adduce, propound, offer, allege. **3.** improve, further, forward, promote, strengthen. **4.** promote, elevate, dignify, exalt. **5.** increase, raise the price of, augment. **6.** update, accelerate, quicken, hasten, speed up, bring forward. **7.** furnish *or* supply on credit, lend, loan. **8.** move *or* go forward, proceed, move on. **9.** improve, progress, make progress, grow, increase, flourish, rise, thrive. **10.** rise, increase, appreciate. *—n.* **11.** moving forward, progress, procedure, way; march, procession. **12.** advancement, promotion, improvement, advance, rise. **13.** overture, proposal, proposition; tender, offer, proffer, offering. **14.** price rise, raise, rise, increase. *—adj.* **15.** going before, preceding, precedent. **16.** beyond, ahead, before; prepublication.
Ant. retreat.

advantage, *n.* **1.** favorable opportunity *or* state *or* circumstance *or* means *or* situation, vantage point, superiority, superior condition. **2.** benefit, avail, gain, profit, value; return, dividend; utility, usefulness, expediency, use, service. **3.** superiority, ascendancy, pre-eminence. **4.** behalf, vantage; privilege, prerogative, convenience, accommodation. *—v.* **5.** be of

service to, serve, avail, benefit, profit, help, aid, yield profit *or* gain to.
Ant. disadvantage.

adversary, *n.* **1.** antagonist, opponent, enemy, foe. **2.** contestant, litigant, opponent. **3.** Satan, the Devil, the Evil One, the Prince of Darkness, Beelzebub, the Tempter.
Ant. ally, compatriot, friend.

adverse, *adj.* **1.** antagonistic, contrary, opposite, conflicting, opposed, hostile, against, con, contra, inimical, unfriendly. **2.** unfavorable, unlucky, unfortunate; calamitous, disastrous, catastrophic. **3.** opposite, confronting, opposed, facing, vis-à-vis, face-to-face.
Ant. favorable, beneficial.

adversity, *n.* calamity, distress, catastrophe, disaster; bad luck, misfortune, misery, trouble, affliction, wretchedness.
Ant. happiness, wealth.

advice, *n.* **1.** admonition, warning, caution, counsel, opinion, recommendation, guidance, suggestion, persuasion, urging, exhortation. **2.** communication, information, news, report, intelligence, tidings, word, notice, notification.

advisable, *adj.* **1.** expedient, advantageous, politic, proper, fit, suitable, desirable, correct, prudent, sensible, common-sense, judicious. **2.** receptive, open to suggestion *or* advice.

advise, *v.* **1.** give counsel to, counsel, admonish, caution, warn, recommend to. **2.** suggest, recommend. **3.** inform, notify, apprise, acquaint. **4.** take counsel, confer, deliberate, discuss, consult. **5.** give advice, offer counsel.

advocate, *v.* **1.** plead in favor of, support, urge, argue for, speak for, recommend. —*n.* **2.** lawyer, attorney, counselor, counselor-at-law, counsel, barrister, solicitor; intercessor. **3.** defender, vindicator, espouser, upholder, supporter, maintainer, promoter, patron, friend.
Ant. oppose; opponent.

aesthete, *n.* dilettante, connoisseur, virtuoso, expert, discriminator, collector.

affable, *adj.* courteous, urbane, debonair, suave, civil, approachable, polite, friendly, cordial, pleasant, amiable, obliging, gracious; benign, mild, easy, casual, social.
Ant. discourteous, boorish, reserved.

affect, *v.* **1.** effect, exert influence on, accomplish, bring about, influence, sway, act on; modify, alter, transform, change. **2.** move, impress, touch, stir, overcome. **3.** pretend, feign, fake, assume, adopt. **4.** imitate, act, mimic. **5.** use, adopt, prefer, choose, select. **6.** profess, pretend.

affectation, *n.* pretension, airs, mannerisms, pose, artificiality, pretense, affectedness, unnaturalness, insincerity.

Ant. sincerity.

affected, *adj.* assumed, pretended, feigned.
Ant. sincere, genuine.

affecting, *adj.* touching, pathetic, piteous, moving, impressive.

affection, *n.* **1.** attachment, liking, friendliness, amity, fondness, devotion, friendship, tenderness, endearment, heart, love. **2.** feeling, inclination, partiality, proclivity, disposition, predisposition, bent, bias. **3.** (*pathology*) disease, disorder, affliction, malady, ailment, illness, complaint.
Ant. abhorrence.

affectionate, *adj.* tender, loving, fond, attentive, attached, devoted, warm, kind, sympathetic.
Ant. apathetic.

affirm, *v.* **1.** state, assert, aver, maintain, declare, asseverate, depose, testify, say, pronounce. **2.** establish, confirm, ratify, approve, indorse.
Ant. deny.

affliction, *n.* **1.** pain, distress, grief, adversity, misfortune, trial, mishap, trouble, tribulation, calamity, catastrophe, disaster. **2.** sickness, loss, calamity, persecution, suffering, misery, woe, depression, wretchedness, heartbreak; plague, scourge, epidemic.
Ant. relief.

affluent, *adj.* **1.** abounding, rich, wealthy, opulent. **2.** abundant, free-flowing, teeming. —*n.* **3.** tributary, feeder.
Ant. poor; scarce.

affront, *n.* **1.** offense, slight, disrespect, insult, impertinence, contumely, scorn, indignity, abuse, outrage, injury. **2.** shame, disgrace, degradation. —*v.* **3.** offend, insult, slight, abuse, outrage. **4.** shame, disgrace, discountenance, confuse, confound, disconcert, abash. **5.** confront, encounter, face, meet.
Ant. compliment.

afraid, *adj.* scared, fearful, alarmed, frightened, terrified, disquieted, shocked, apprehensive, timid, cowardly, pusillanimous, timorous, shy, cautious, overcautious.
Ant. bold, sanguine, confident.

age, *n.* **1.** period, life, duration. **2.** maturity, years of discretion. **3.** old age, decline. **4.** era, epoch, time, date, period. —*v.* **5.** grow old, mature, ripen.
Ant. youth.

aged, *adj.* **1.** old, ancient, decrepit, elderly. **2.** old, of the age of.
Ant. young.

aggravate, *v.* worsen, make severe, intensify, heighten, increase, make serious *or* grave.
Ant. assuage, improve, better.

aggregate, *adj.* **1.** added, combined, total, complete. —*n.* **2.** sum, mass, assemblage, total, gross, body, amount. —*v.* **3.** bring together, assemble, collect, amass, accumulate, gather. **4.** amount to, add up to. **5.** combine into a mass, form a collection.

Ant. particular.

aggressive, *adj.* **1.** pugnacious, attacking, offensive, assaulting, militant, assailing. **2.** energetic, vigorous, pushing, enterprising, assertive, determined, forward.
Ant. retiring, bashful, shy.

agile, *adj.* quick, light, nimble, sprightly, active, lively, brisk, ready, smart, alert, spry.
Ant. awkward.

agitate, *v.* **1.** shake *or* move briskly, disturb, toss, jar. **2.** move to and fro. **3.** disturb, ruffle, stir *or* work up, perturb, excite, fluster. **4.** discuss, debate, controvert, campaign *or* argue for, dispute. **5.** plan, devise; revolve *or* turn over in the mind, cogitate, consider, deliberate. **6.** arouse public interest, ferment, disturb, rouse.
Ant. tranquilize.

agitation, *n.* **1.** agitating, shaking, jarring, disturbing. **2.** disturbance, excitement, turmoil, tumult, storm; unrest, disquiet; struggle, conflict; perturbation, flurry, ado, to-do. **3.** urging, persistence; debate, discussion, dispute, argument, campaign.
Ant. serenity, calm, tranquillity.

agony, *n.* **1.** pain, distress, suffering, torment, torture, rack; throe, paroxysm, spasm, seizure, pang; ache. **2.** excitement, suspense, anguish, torment, torture.
Ant. comfort.

agree, *v.* **1.** assent, yield, consent, accede, concede, acquiesce, allow, comply. **2.** harmonize, concur, unite, accord, combine. **3.** come to an agreement *or* arrangement *or* understanding, compromise, arrive at a settlement. **4.** accord, correspond, compare favorably, coincide, conform, tally, match, stand up, suit. **5.** be applicable *or* appropriate *or* similar, resemble. **6.** make *or* write a contract *or* bargain, contract, stipulate, bargain. **7.** concede, grant, allow, let, permit.
Ant. disagree.

agreement, *n.* **1.** agreeing, being in concord. **2.** bargain, contract, compact, understanding, arrangement, deal. **3.** unanimity, harmony, accord, concord, settlement, treaty, pact, word, conformity, unity, uniformity.
Ant. disagreement.

aid, *v.* **1.** support, help, succor, assist, serve, abet, back, second; spell, relieve. **2.** promote, facilitate, ease, simplify. **3.** be of help, give help *or* assistance. **—*n.*** **4.** help, support, succor, assistance, service, furtherance; relief, charity. **5.** assistant, helper, supporter, servant, aide, aide-de-camp.
Ant. hinder, obstruct; obstacle, obstruction.

ailing, *adj.* sickly, sick, ill, unwell.
Ant. healthy, well.

aim, *v.* **1.** direct, point, give direction to. **2.** direct, point. **3.** strive, try, purpose. **—*n.*** **4.** direction, sighting. **5.** target, object, end. **6.** purpose, end, object, goal; intent, intention, reason; design, scheme.

air, *n.* **1.** atmosphere. **2.** breeze, breath, zephyr, wind. **3.** circulation, publication, publicity. **4.** character, complexion, appearance, impression, aspect, look, mien; manner, demeanor, attitude, conduct, carriage, behavior, deportment, bearing. **5.** affectation, haughtiness. **—***v.* **6.** ventilate. **7.** expose, display.

alarm, *n.* **1.** fear, apprehension, fright, consternation, terror, panic, dismay. **2.** alarum, tocsin, distress-signal, siren. **—***v.* **3.** terrify, frighten, scare, startle; appall, shock; dismay, daunt.
Ant. calm, comfort.

alert, *adj.* **1.** attentive, vigilant, watchful, aware, wary, observant, circumspect, heedful, cautious, on the lookout, on the qui vive. **2.** nimble, brisk, lively, quick, active, agile, sprightly, spirited. **—***n.* **3.** vigilance, caution, wariness. **4.** air-raid alarm. **—***v.* **5.** prepare for action, warn.
Ant. asleep, listless.

alien, *n.* **1.** stranger, foreigner, immigrant. **—***adj.* **2.** strange, foreign. **3.** adverse, hostile, opposed, unfriendly, differing, unallied, unconnected, separate.
Ant. native, friendly.

alive, *adj.* **1.** existing, living, breathing, quick. **2.** unextinguished, operative, functioning. **3.** lively, active, alert. **4.** swarming, thronged, aswarm.
Ant. dead.

allay, *v.* quiet, appease, moderate, soothe, soften, assuage, alleviate, lighten, lessen, mitigate, mollify, temper, relieve, ease.
Ant. aggravate.

allege, *v.* **1.** declare, affirm, attest, state, asseverate, assert, aver. **2.** plead, advance.
Ant. deny.

allegiance, *n.* duty, obligation, faithfulness, loyalty, fealty, fidelity; homage.
Ant. treason, treachery.

alleviate, *v.* ease, lessen, diminish, quell, abate, mitigate, lighten, relieve, assuage, allay, mollify.
Ant. aggravate, intensify.

alley, *n.* back street, lane, byway, street.

alliance, *n.* **1.** association, coalition, combination, bloc, partnership, affiliation, connection, federation, confederacy, confederation, league, union, treaty, pact, compact. **2.** marriage, intermarriage, relation, relationship. **3.** affinity.

allot, *v.* **1.** divide, distribute, parcel out, apportion, assign, deal out, dole out, mete out, deal, dispense, measure out. **2.** appropriate, allocate, set apart, appoint.

allow, *v.* **1.** let, permit, grant. **2.** grant, yield, cede, relinquish, give. **3.** admit, acknowledge, concede, own, confess. **4.** set apart, abate, deduct, remit. **5.** bear, suffer, tolerate, put up with.
Ant. forbid, prohibit; refuse.

allowance, *n.* **1.** allotment, stipend. **2.** deduction, discount, rebate, tret. **3.** acceptance, admission, concession, acknowledgment. **4.** sanction, tolerance, leave, permission, license, permit, authorization, authority, approval, approbation, imprimatur, sufferance.

ally, *v.* **1.** unite, unify, join, confederate, combine, connect, league, marry, wed. **2.** associate, relate. **3.** join, unite. —*n.* **4.** associate, partner, friend, confederate, aide, accomplice, accessory, assistant, abettor; colleague, coadjutor, auxiliary.
Ant. enemy, foe, adversary.

almost, *adv.* nearly, well-nigh, somewhat, toward, towards.

alone, *adj.* apart, lone, lonely, lonesome, single, solitary, desolate, isolated, enisled, unaccompanied, solo.
Ant. together, accompanied.

also, *adv.* in addition, too, further, likewise, besides, moreover, furthermore.

alter, *v.* **1.** modify, adjust, change, permute, vary. **2.** castrate, spay. **3.** differ, vary, change.
Ant. preserve, keep.

alternate, *v.* **1.** reciprocate. **2.** act *or* follow reciprocally, interchange successively. —*adj.* **3.** reciprocal, successive, in turn, one after another. —*n.* **4.** substitute, stand-in.

alternative, *n.* **1.** choice, option, selection, course, other. —*adj.* **2.** mutually exclusive (*choice between two things*).

although, *conj.* though, even though, notwithstanding, even if, albeit.

altitude, *n.* height, elevation.

always, *adv.* **1.** all the time, uninterruptedly, perpetually, everlastingly, eternally, forever, continually, ever, evermore, forevermore, unceasingly. **2.** every time.
Ant. never.

amateur, *n.* dilettante, tyro, novice, nonprofessional, neophyte, greenhorn.
Ant. professional, expert.

amaze, *v.* astound, dumfound, surprise, astonish, stagger; stupify, bewilder, confuse, perplex, daze.

ambiguous, *adj.* **1.** equivocal, doubtful, dubious, unclear, uncertain, vague, indistinct, indeterminate; deceptive. **2.** difficult, obscure, unclassifiable, anomalous. **3.** puzzling, enigmatic, problematic.
Ant. explicit, clear.

ambition, *n.* **1.** aspiration, enterprise, yearning, longing. **2.** energy.
Ant. satisfaction.

ambitious, *adj.* **1.** aspiring, enterprising. **2.** eager, desirous, emulous. **3.** showy, pretentious, ostentatious.
Ant. apathetic; humble.

ameliorate, *v.* improve, better, amend, raise, elevate, promote.
Ant. aggravate.

amiable, *adj.* **1.** gracious, agreeable, kind-hearted. **2.** kind, friendly, amicable.
Ant. hostile.

amid, *prep.* among, amidst, amongst, surrounded by.

among, *prep.* amid, between, surrounded by.

amorous, *adj.* **1.** loving, amatory, tender. **2.** enamored, in love, fond of, ardent, tender, passionate, impassioned, erotic, filled with desire, lustful, libidinous.
Ant. indifferent, cold.

ample, *adj.* **1.** large, spacious, extensive, vast, great, capacious, roomy, broad, wide. **2.** liberal, generous, free, abundant, copious, abounding, unrestricted, rich, lavish, inexhaustible, plenteous, plentiful, overflowing, full, bountiful, exuberant.
Ant. insufficient, meager, scanty, sparse.

amplify, *v.* **1.** enlarge, extend, greaten, expand, widen, broaden, develop, augment, dilate, magnify. **2.** exaggerate, overstate, blow up.
Ant. abridge, abbreviate.

amuse, *v.* entertain, divert, please, charm, cheer, enliven.
Ant. bore.

amusing, *adj.* **1.** entertaining, diverting, pleasing, charming, cheering, lively. **2.** comical, comic, droll, risible, laughable, delightful, mirth-provoking, funny, farcical, ludicrous, ridiculous.
Ant. boring, tedious.

ancestral, *adj.* hereditary, inherited, patrimonial.

ancestry, *n.* **1.** pedigree, descent, stock, genealogy. **2.** family, house, race, line, lineage.
Ant. posterity, descendants.

ancient, *adj.* **1.** old, primitive. **2.** old, aged, antique, antiquated, old-fashioned, out-of-date; antediluvian, prehistoric, of yore.
Ant. new, modern.

anger, *n.* **1.** displeasure, resentment, exasperation, wrath, ire, fury, indignation, rage, choler, bile, spleen. **—*v.* 2.** displease, vex, irritate, arouse, nettle, exasperate, infuriate, enrage, incense, madden.
Ant. patience.

angry, *adj.* indignant, resentful, irate, incensed, enraged, wrathful, wroth, infuriated, furious, mad, passionate, inflamed; provoked, irritated, nettled, galled, chafed, piqued.
Ant. patient, calm.

anguish, *n.* **1.** pain, pang, suffering, distress, agony, torment, torture, rack. **—*v.* 2.** agonize, distress, torture.
Ant. comfort.

angular, *adj.* **1.** with angles *or* corners. **2.** bony, gaunt, skinny, cadaverous. **3.** awkward, stiff, unbending.
Ant. curved; plump; graceful.

animal, *n.* **1.** creature. **2.** beast, brute, monster.

—*adj*. **3.** living, sentient. **4.** carnal, fleshly, unspiritual, physical; beastly, brutal.
Ant. human, man; spiritual.

animate, *v*. **1.** vivify, enliven, vitalize, quicken. **2.** invigorate, encourage, inspire, inspirit, hearten, energize, fortify, stimulate, arouse, waken. **3.** refresh, exhilarate, buoy up, excite, fire, heat, urge, provoke, incite, kindle, prompt. —*adj*. **4.** alive, lively, vigorous.
Ant. thwart; inanimate, sluggish.

animation, *n*. liveliness, vivacity, spirit, life, vigor, energy; enthusiasm, ardor, exhilaration, cheerfulness, sprightliness, buoyancy, airiness.
Ant. sluggishness.

announce, *v*. proclaim, publish, declare, report, set forth, promulgate, publicize.
Ant. suppress.

annoy, *v*. molest, harry, hector, badger, tease, irk, pester, harass, bother, worry, trouble, irritate, chafe, fret, disturb, disquiet.
Ant. comfort, soothe.

answer, *n*. **1.** reply, response, retort, rejoinder. **2.** solution. **3.** defense, plea. —*v*. **4.** reply, make reply *or* response, respond, rejoin. **5.** be responsible *or* liable *or* accountable. **6.** pass, serve, do suit; suffice, be sufficient. **7.** conform, correspond, be correlated. **8.** reply to, respond to. **9.** serve, suit, satisfy, fulfill. **10.** discharge (a responsibility, debt, etc.). **11.** conform *or* correspond to, be similar *or* equivalent to. **12.** atone for, make amends for.
Ant. ask, question; differ.

antagonist, *n*. opponent, adversary, rival, competitor, contestant, enemy, foe.
Ant. ally, friend.

anticipate, *v*. **1.** foresee, expect, foretaste, forecast. **2.** expect, await, wait for. **3.** preclude, obviate, prevent. **4.** forestall, antedate. **5.** accelerate, precipitate.
Ant. close, terminate; slow.

antipathy, *n*. **1.** repugnance, dislike, aversion, disgust, abhorrence, hatred, detestation, hate, loathing, horror. **2.** contrariety, opposition.
Ant. attraction, sympathy, love.

antique, *adj*. **1.** ancient, old, archaic, bygone; antediluvian. **2.** early, old. **3.** antiquated, old-fashioned, out-of-date, obsolescent, obsolete, passé, demoded, démodé. —*n*. **4.** objet d'art, bibelot, curio, rarity.
Ant. modern, new.

anxiety, *n*. **1.** apprehension, fear, foreboding; worry, distress, uneasiness, disquietude, disquiet; trouble, pain. **2.** solicitous desire, eagerness.
Ant. security, certainty.

anxious, *adj*. concerned, worried, apprehensive, uneasy.
Ant. secure, certain, sure, confident.

apartment, *n.* compartment, suite *or* set of rooms, flat, tenement.

apathetic, *adj.* unfeeling, passionless, emotionless, indifferent, unconcerned, impassive, stoical, cool, cold, uninterested, phlegmatic, dull, lifeless, flaccid, obtuse, sluggish, torpid, callous, cold-blooded, insensible, soulless.
Ant. alert, emotional, sensitive.

ape, *v.* imitate, mimic, counterfeit, copy, affect.

apex, *n.* tip, point, vertex, summit, top, pinnacle, zenith; acme, climax.

apology, *n.* **1.** excuse, plea, explanation, reparation. **2.** defense, justification, vindication. **3.** poor substitute, makeshift.

appall, *v.* frighten, horrify, terrify, dismay, daunt, shock, petrify.
Ant. activate, innervate.

apparel, *n.* **1.** clothes, dress, garb, attire, raiment, costume, garments, habiliments, vesture, vestments, robes, rig, accouterments, trappings, outfit, equipment. **2.** aspect, guise. **—***v.* **3.** dress, clothe, garb, attire; equip, rig, outfit, accouter; adorn, ornament, array, deck out.

apparent, *adj.* **1.** plain, clear, open, evident, obvious, conspicuous, patent, unquestionable, unmistakable, manifest. **2.** seeming, ostensible, unreal, specious, quasi, superficial, external. **3.** visible, open, in sight, perceptible, detectable, discernible. **4.** entitled.
Ant. concealed, obscure; real.

apparition, *n.* **1.** specter, vision, illusion, phantom, wraith, spirit, sprite, ghost, phantasm, shade, chimera. **2.** appearance, appearing, manifestation, phenomenon.

appeal, *n.* **1.** entreaty, request, petition, prayer, supplication, invocation. **2.** application, suit, solicitation. **3.** attraction. **—***v.* **4.** entreat, supplicate, petition, ask, request. **5.** resort.

appear, *v.* **1.** become visible, come into sight *or* view, emerge, crop up, arise, turn up, see the light. **2.** have an appearance, seem, look, show, have the appearance. **3.** be obvious *or* manifest *or* clear.
Ant. disappear.

appearance, *n.* **1.** form, being, apparition; arrival, coming, advent. **2.** aspect, mien, guise, air, expression, look; manner, demeanor, presence. **3.** show, seeming, semblance, face, pretense, pretext, colors.

appease, *v.* **1.** pacify, quiet, soothe, calm, placate, tranquilize, mollify, alleviate, mitigate, temper, allay, assuage, ease, abate, lessen; still, hush, lull; keep down, quell, subdue. **2.** satisfy, fulfill, propitiate. **3.** conciliate, propitiate, win over, make amends, accede to the demands of, make favorable.
Ant. aggravate, perturb; dissatisfy.

appendix, *n.* appendage, supplement, addendum, adjunct, appurtenance, addition, extra; enhancement, corrigendum, excursus.

appetite, *n.* **1.** hunger, desire, longing, craving, thirst. **2.** demand. **3.** propensity, liking, relish, gusto, zest, zeal.
Ant. renunciation, anorexia.

applause, *n.* hand-clapping, shouting; approval, acclamation, approbation, acclaim, plaudit, laurel.
Ant. disapproval, condemnation.

appliance, *n.* **1.** instrument, apparatus, device, tool, appurtenance; adjunct, expedient, means, way, resource. **2.** application, use, practice, exercise.

applicable, *adj.* fit, suitable, suited, relevant, apt, fitting, befitting, proper, apropos, germane, pertinent, pointed.
Ant. inept.

application, *n.* **1.** applying, appliance, utilization, use, practice. **2.** usability, utility, relevance, aptness, aptitude, suitability, pertinence. **3.** request, petition, solicitation, appeal. **4.** attention, persistent effort, assiduity, industry, persistence, perseverence.
Ant. inattention, laziness.

apply, *v.* **1.** lay on, place on *or* upon. **2.** use, employ, put to use, effect, utilize. **3.** devote, prescribe, dedicate, assign, appropriate, allot. **4.** have a bearing, refer, be pertinent, hold true *or* good, be appropriate, impinge. **5.** ask, petition, sue, entreat, solicit, appeal.
Ant. neglect.

appoint, *v.* **1.** nominate, assign, name, elect, select, set apart, designate, point out, allot, destine. **2.** constitute, ordain, establish, prescribe, direct, require, command, order, decree, impose *or* insist on. **3.** fix, settle, determine, aggree on *or* upon. **4.** equip, rig, outfit, accouter, furnish, supply; apparel; decorate.
Ant. dismiss; strip.

appointment, *n.* **1.** appointing, designating, designation, place, installation. **2.** office, post, station, sinecure, position. **3.** engagement, agreement, arrangement, assignation, rendezvous, tryst.

apportion, *v.* divide, allot, distribute, assign, allocate, appoint, partition, measure, mete, dole out, deal, dispense, parcel out.

appreciate, *v.* **1.** esteem, prize, value, estimate *or* rate highly. **2.** be aware *or* conscious of, detect. **3.** raise the value of. **4.** rise *or* increase in value.
Ant. disparage; scorn.

apprehension, *n.* **1.** anticipation, anxiety, misgiving, dread, fear, alarm; worry, uneasiness, suspicion, distrust, mistrust. **2.** understanding, intelligence, reason. **3.** view, opinion, idea, belief, sentiment. **4.** arrest, seizure, capture.
Ant. confidence, composure; release.

apprise, *v.* inform, tell, advise, give notice to, acquaint, notify, disclose to.

appropriate, *adj.* **1.** fitting, suitable, suited, apt, befitting, meet, felicitous, proper, opportune, apropos, seemly, due, becoming, germane, pertinent, to the point. **2.** proper, individual, unique, sui generis.

—*v.* **3.** set apart, direct, assign, apportion, allocate; adopt, take as one's own.
Ant. inappropriate, inept.

approve, *v.* **1.** commend, praise, recommend, appreciate, value, esteem, prize. **2.** sanction, authorize, confirm, endorse, ratify, validate, uphold, support, sustain.
Ant. disapprove.

apt, *adj.* **1.** inclined, disposed, prone, liable. **2.** likely. **3.** clever, bright, intelligent, brilliant, ingenious; adroit, handy, dexterous, skillful, expert. **4.** appropriate, suited, pertinent, relevant, fit, fitting, apt, befitting, meet, germane, applicable, apropos, felicitous.
Ant. inapt, indisposed, malapropos.

aptitude, *n.* **1.** tendency, propensity, predilection, proclivity, inclination, bent, gift, genius, talent, knack, faculty. **2.** readiness, intelligence, cleverness, talent; understanding, ability, aptness. **3.** fitness, suitability, applicability.

arbitrary, *adj.* **1.** discretionary. **2.** capricious, uncertain, unreasonable, willful, fanciful, whimsical. **3.** uncontrolled, unlimited, unrestrained; absolute, despotic, dictatorial, totalitarian, tyrannical, imperious, overbearing, peremptory, domineering; Fascistic, undemocratic.
Ant. relative.

archaic, *adj.* old, ancient, antiquated, antique, old-fashioned, out-of-date.
Ant. modern, up-to-date.

archetype, *n.* model, form, pattern, prototype, example, type, paragon, ideal.

ardent, *adj.* **1.** passionate, glowing, fervent, fervid, intense, eager, sanguine, enthusiastic, zealous; vehement, forceful, impassioned, strenuous. **2.** glowing, flashing, flushed. **3.** hot, burning, fiery.
Ant. cool, apathetic.

ardor, *n.* **1.** warmth, fervor, fervency, eagerness, zeal, passion, enthusiasm. **2.** fire, burning, heat, warmth, glow.
Ant. indifference.

arduous, *adj.* **1.** laborious, hard, difficult, toilsome, onerous, burdensome, wearisome, exhausting, Herculean. **2.** energetic, strenuous; fatiguing. **3.** steep, high, acclivitous. **4.** severe, unendurable.
Ant. easy.

argue, *v.* **1.** debate, discuss, reason, plead, hold. **2.** contend, dispute. **3.** reason upon, contest, controvert, debate, discuss, dispute. **4.** maintain, support, contend. **5.** persuade, drive, convince. **6.** show, indicate, prove, imply, infer, betoken, evince, denote.
Ant. agree.

argument, *n.* **1.** controversy, dispute, debate, discussion. **2.** reasoning, reason, proof, ground, evidence. **3.** fact, statement; theme, thesis, topic, subject, mat-

ter. **4.** summary, abstract, epitome, outline, précis.
Ant. agreement.

arid, *adj.* **1.** dry, moistureless, desert, parched; barren, infertile. **2.** dull, lifeless, uninteresting, dry, empty, jejune.
Ant. wet, damp.

aroma, *n.* **1.** perfume, odor, scent, fragrance, bouquet, redolence. **2.** subtle quality, spirit, essence, characteristic, air; suggestion, hint.
Ant. stench.

arouse, *v.* **1.** animate, stir, rouse, awaken; inspirit, inspire, excite, incite, provoke, instigate, stimulate, warm, kindle, fire. **2.** awaken, get up, arise.
Ant. alleviate, calm, mitigate.

arrange, *v.* **1.** order, place, adjust, array, group, sort, dispose, classify, class, rank, distribute. **2.** settle, determine, establish, adjust. **3.** prepare, plan, contrive, devise, concoct, organize. **4.** (*music*) adapt, adjust. **5.** settle, agree, come to terms. **6.** prepare, adjust, adapt, make preparations *or* plans.
Ant. disarrange, disorder, disturb.

array, *v.* **1.** arrange, order, range, marshal, rank, place, dispose, draw up. **2.** clothe, apparel, dress, attire, equip, accouter, rig, outfit; deck, bedeck, ornament, trim, decorate, garnish, adorn. —*n.* **3.** order, arrangement, disposition; allotment. **4.** display, show, exhibit, exhibition, showing, demonstration. **5.** attire, dress, clothes, raiment, apparel, garments; panoply.
Ant. disarray.

arrest, *v.* **1.** seize, apprehend, capture, catch, take, trap, take into custody, take prisoner. **2.** catch, fix, secure, rivet, engage, capture, occupy, attract. **3.** stop, check, bring to a standstill, stay, hinder, deter, obstruct, delay, interrupt, restrain, hold, withhold. —*n.* **4.** detention, custody, imprisonment, apprehension, capture. **5.** seizure, capture, rape. **6.** stoppage, halt, stay, staying, check, hindrance, obstruction, deterrent, detention, restraint, delay, interruption.
Ant. release; activate, animate; continue.

arrival, *n.* **1.** advent, coming. **2.** reaching, attainment. **3.** arriver, comer.
Ant. departure.

arrive, *v.* come, reach a point, attain, attain a position of success.
Ant. depart; fail.

arrogance, *n.* haughtiness, overbearing, pride, insolence, disdain, effrontery, superciliousness, scorn, contumely, self-confidence, self-importance, conceit, egotism, hauteur.
Ant. humility.

arrogant, *adj.* presumptuous, haughty, imperious, supercilious, assuming, proud, insolent, scornful, contumelious, overbearing, overweening, conceited, egotistic, egotistical.
Ant. humble, self-effacing.

art, *n.* **1.** trade, craft; skill, adroitness, dexterity, aptitude, ingenuity, knack, cleverness. **2.** cunning, craft, guile, deceit, duplicity, wiliness, dishonesty, artfulness.

artifice, *n.* **1.** ruse, device, subterfuge, wile, machination, expedient, trick, stratagem. **2.** craft, trickery, guile, deception, deceit, art, cunning, artfulness, fraud, duplicity, double-dealing. **3.** skillful, apt *or* artful contrivance.

artist, *n.* **1.** artisan, painter, sculptor, sketcher. **2.** actor, actress, thespian, singer, artiste. **3.** designer, artificer, workman. **4.** trickster, designer, contriver.

artless, *adj.* ingenuous, naive, unsophisticated, natural, simple, guileless, open, frank, plain, unaffected, candid, honest, sincere, true, truthful, trusting, trustful, unsuspicious, unsuspecting; unskillful, rude, crude.
Ant. cunning, sly, crafty.

ascend, *v.* **1.** mount, rise, climb *or* go upward, soar, climb, arise. **2.** tower. **3.** climb, mount, scale, go *or* get up.
Ant. descend; fall.

ascertain, *v.* determine, establish, define, pinpoint, fix, certify, settle, verify; learn, find out, discover, uncover, get at.
Ant. guess, assume.

ascribe, *v.* attribute, impute, refer, assign, charge.

ashamed, *adj.* **1.** abashed, humiliated, mortified, shamefaced, embarrassed, confused. **2.** unwilling, restrained.
Ant. vain, arrogant; willing.

ask, *v.* **1.** put a question to, interrogate, question, inquire of. **2.** inquire, seek information. **3.** request, solicit, petition, sue, appeal, seek, beseech, implore, beg, supplicate, entreat. **4.** demand, expect, require, exact, call for. **5.** invite, call in. **6.** make inquiry, inquire, question. **7.** request, petition, sue, appeal, pray, beg.
Ant. answer; refuse, decline.

aspect, *n.* **1.** appearance, look, attitude, situation, condition. **2.** countenance, expression, mien, visage; air. **3.** view, viewpoint, point of view, attitude, outlook, prospect, direction, bearing.

aspire, *v.* desire, long, yearn.

assail, *v.* assault, set *or* fall upon, attack; abuse, impugn, maltreat, asperse, malign.

assassinate, *v.* murder, kill, blight, destroy, slay, despatch.

assault, *n.* **1.** assailing, attack, onslaught, onset, combat, invasion, aggression; threat. —*v.* **2.** attack, assail, storm, charge, invade; threaten.

assemble, *v.* **1.** bring together, gather, congregate, collect, convene, convoke, summon, call, call together. **2.** put together, manufacture, connect, set up. **3.** meet, convene, congregate, gather, gather together, come together.
Ant. disperse.

assembly, *n.* **1.** company, assemblage, throng, mob,

gathering, convention, congress, convocation, meeting, meet. **2.** congress, legislature, parliament, lower house, conclave, synod, council, diet.

assent, *v.* **1.** acquiesce, accede, concur, agree, fall in, consent, admit, yield, allow. —*n.* **2.** agreement, concurrence, acquiescence, consent, allowance, approval, concord, accord, approbation.
Ant. refuse, deny, dissent.

assert, *v.* **1.** declare, asseverate, affirm, maintain, aver, say, pronounce, allege, avow. **2.** maintain, defend, uphold, support, vindicate, claim, emphasize. **3.** press, make felt, emphasize.
Ant. controvert, contradict, deny.

assertion, *n.* allegation, statement, asseveration, avowal, declaration, claim, affirmation, predication, vindication, defense, maintenance, emphasis, support.
Ant. denial, contradiction.

assiduous, *adj.* constant, unremitting, continuous, applied, industrious, untiring, tireless, persistent, persisting, devoted, zealous, studious, attentive, diligent, solicitous, sedulous.
Ant. random, casual, lazy.

assign, *v.* **1.** distribute, allot, apportion, allocate, measure, appropriate. **2.** appoint, designate, specify; fix, determine, pinpoint. **3.** ascribe, attribute, refer, adduce, allege, advance, show, offer, bring up *or* forward.

assist, *v.* help, support, aid, sustain, patronize, befriend, further, second, abet, back, speed, promote, serve, succor, relieve, spell.
Ant. impede, obstruct, hinder.

associate, *v.* **1.** connect, link. **2.** join, affiliate, team up with. **3.** unite, combine, couple. **4.** unite, combine. **5.** fraternize, consort, keep company. —*n.* **6.** acquaintance, consort, comrade, fellow, companion, friend, mate, peer, compeer, equal. **7.** confederate, accomplice, ally, partner, colleague, fellow.
Ant. dissociate, alienate; adversary, opponent.

association, *n.* **1.** organization, alliance, union, guild, society, club, fraternity, sorority, lodge; company, corporation, firm, partnership; set, coterie, clique, band. **2.** companionship, intimacy, fellowship, friendship. **3.** connection, combination.

assume, *v.* **1.** suppose, presuppose, take for granted, infer. **2.** undertake, take on, take upon oneself. **3.** pretend, feign, affect, simulate, counterfeit, put on. **4.** appropriate, arrogate, usurp.

assumption, *n.* **1.** supposition, presupposition, assuming, presumption, taking for granted; hypothesis, conjecture, guess, postulate, theory. **2.** arrogance, presumption, effrontery, forwardness, insolence, hauteur, haughtiness, superciliousness, lordliness, stateliness, pride, conceit.

assurance, *n.* **1.** declaration, avowal, asseveration, averment, deposition. **2.** pledge, warranty, surety, guaranty, oath. **3.** confidence, firmness, trust, cer-

tainty. **4.** courage, bravery, self-reliance, self-confidence, intrepidity, sang-froid. **5.** boldness, impudence, presumption, arrogance, effrontery, rudeness, impertinence, nerve, cheek.
Ant. denial; distrust, uncertainty; cowardice, diffidence.

astonish, *v.* amaze, strike with wonder, surprise, astound, shock, startle; daze, stun, stupefy, confound, stagger, overwhelm.

astringent, *adj.* **1.** (Medical) contracting, constrictive, styptic, binding. **2.** stern, severe, austere, sharp, harsh, rigorous, hard, unrelenting.

astute, *adj.* keen, shrewd, cunning, artful, crafty, sly, wily, penetrating, eagle-eyed, sharp, quick, perspicacious, ingenious, intelligent, sagacious, discerning.
Ant. ingenuous, naive, candid, unsophisticated; dull.

asylum, *n.* **1.** hospital, institute, retreat, sanitarium. **2.** refuge, haven, preserve, reserve, sanctuary, shelter, retreat.

atheist, *n.* agnostic, disbeliever, nonbeliever, infidel, skeptic, doubter, heathen, pagan, gentile.
Ant. theist.

atom, *n.* iota, jot, dot, whit, tittle, scintilla, mote; indivisible particle.

atrocious, *adj.* **1.** wicked, cruel, heinous, flagitious, monstrous, felonious, flagrant, grievous, outrageous, diabolical, devilish, infernal, hellish. **2.** bad, tasteless, execrable, detestable, abominable.
Ant. kind, benevolent; good, praiseworthy.

attach, *v.* **1.** fasten to, affix, join, cement, connect, subjoin, append, add, tack on, annex. **2.** go with, accompany. **3.** associate, attribute, assign. **4.** attract, charm, endear, enamour, captivate, engage, bind. **5.** adhere, pertain, belong, obtain.
Ant. detach, separate; repel.

attachment, *n.* **1.** affection, friendship, regard, admiration, fondness, liking, love, devotion; assiduity, bent, predilection. **2.** tie, fastening, junction, connection. **3.** device, apparatus, adjunct.
Ant. detachment, separation.

attack, *v.* **1.** assail, assault, molest, threaten, interfere with, storm, charge, oppugn, engage in battle, set upon. **2.** criticize, impugn, censure, blame, abuse. **3.** affect. **4.** begin hostilities. —*n.* **5.** onslaught, assault, offense, onset, encounter, aggression.
Ant. defend; defense.

attain, *v.* **1.** reach, achieve, accomplish, effect, secure, gain, procure, acquire, get, obtain, win. **2.** arrive at, reach.
Ant. fail.

attempt, *v.* **1.** try, undertake, seek, make an effort, essay. **2.** attack, assault, assail. —*n.* **3.** trial, essay, effort, endeavor, enterprise, undertaking. **4.** attack, assault.
Ant. accomplish, attain.

attend, *v.* **1.** be present at, frequent. **2.** accompany, go with, escort. **3.** minister to, serve, wait on. **4.** tend, take charge of. **5.** heed, listen to, pay attention to, respect. **6.** be present. **7.** pay attention, pay respect, give heed, listen. **8.** apply oneself. **9.** take care *or* charge. **10.** depend, rely. **11.** wait on, serve, minister.

attendant, *n.* **1.** escort, companion, comrade, follower; servant, waiter, valet, footman, lackey, flunky, menial, slave. **2.** attender, frequenter. **3.** concomitant, accompaniment, consequence. —*adj.* **4.** present, in attendance, accompanying, concomitant, consequent.

attention, *n.* **1.** attending. **2.** care, consideration, observation, heed, regard, mindfulness, notice, watchfulness, alertness. **3.** civility, courtesy, homage, deference, respect, politeness, regard. **4.** (*plural*) regard, court, courtship, suit, devotion, wooing.
Ant. inattention.

attentive, *adj.* **1.** observant, regardful, mindful, heedful, thoughtful, alive, alert, awake, on the qui vive; wary, circumspect, watchful, careful. **2.** polite, courteous, respectful, deferential, assiduous.
Ant. inattentive, unwary; discourteous.

attitude, *n.* **1.** position, disposition, manner, bearing mien, pose. **2.** position, posture.

attract, *v.* **1.** draw, cause to approach, magnetize **2.** draw, invite, allure, win, engage, captivate, endear enamor, charm.
Ant. repel, repulse.

attribute, *v.* **1.** ascribe, impute. —*n.* **2.** quality, character, characteristic, property, mark; peculiarity quirk.

audacious, *adj.* **1.** bold, daring, spirited, adventurous fearless, intrepid, brave, courageous, dauntless, venturesome, undaunted, valiant. **2.** reckless, bold, impudent, presumptuous, assuming, unabashed, unashamed, shameless, flagrant, insolent, impertinent, brazen, forward.
Ant. cowardly, contumelious, feckless.

augment, *v.* **1.** enlarge, extend, increase, swell, bloat. **2.** increase.
Ant. reduce, abate.

austere, *adj.* **1.** harsh, hard, stern, strict, forbidding, severe, formal, stiff, inflexible, rigorous, uncompromising, relentless, stringent, restrictive. **2.** grave, sober, serious. **3.** simple, severe, without ornament, plain. **4.** rough, harsh, sour, astringent, acerb, bitter.
Ant. soothing, flexible; kind; sweet.

austerity, *n.* severity, harshness, strictness, asceticism, rigor, rigidity, rigorousness, stiffness, inflexibility.
Ant. lenience, flexibility.

authentic, *adj.* **1.** reliable, trustworthy, veritable, true, accurate, authoritative. **2.** genuine, real, true, unadulterated, pure, uncorrupted.
Ant. unreliable, inaccurate; sham, fraudulent, corrupt.

authoritative, *adj.* **1.** official, conclusive, unques-

tioned, authentic. **2.** impressive, positive; peremptory, dogmatic, authoritarian, dictatorial, imperious, arrogant, autocratic.
Ant. unofficial; servile.

authority, *n.* **1.** control, influence, command, rule, sway, power, supremacy. **2.** expert, adjudicator, arbiter, judge, sovereign. **3.** statute, law, rule, ruling. **4.** warrant, justification, permit, permission, sanction, liberty, authorization. **5.** testimony, witness.

authorize, *v.* **1.** empower, commission, allow, permit, let. **2.** sanction, approve. **3.** establish, entrench. **4.** warrant, justify, legalize, support, back.
Ant. forbid, prohibit.

automatic, *adj.* **1.** self-moving, self-acting, mechanical. **2.** involuntary, uncontrollable.
Ant. manual; deliberate, intentional.

auxiliary, *adj.* **1.** supporting, helping, helpful, aiding, assisting, abetting. **2.** subsidiary, subordinate, secondary, ancillary, additional. —*n.* **3.** helper, aide, ally, assistant, confederate.
Ant. chief, main.

available, *adj.* **1.** accessible, ready, at hand, handy, usable, of use *or* service, serviceable; suitable, fit, appropriate, fitting, befitting. **2.** valid, efficacious, profitable, advantageous.
Ant. unavailable; unbecoming; invalid, unprofitable.

avenge, *v.* revenge, vindicate, take vengeance, exact satisfaction for.
Ant. forgive, pardon.

average, *n.* **1.** mean, mean proportion, median. **2.** mediocrity. —*adj.* **3.** mean, medial, normal, intermediate, middle; mediocre, middling, ordinary, passable, tolerable, satisfactory. —*v.* **4.** reduce to a mean, equate; proportion. **5.** show *or* produce a mean.

averse, *adj.* disinclined, reluctant, unwilling, loath, opposed.
Ant. inclined, disposed.

aversion, *n.* repugnance, disgust, antipathy, loathing, detestation, hate, hatred, abhorrence; dislike, distaste, objection, disinclination, unwillingness, reluctance.
Ant. predilection, liking; favor.

avoid, *v.* keep away from *or* clear of, shun, evade, escape, elude, fight shy of, eschew.
Ant. confront, face.

await, *v.* **1.** wait for, look for, expect. **2.** attend, be in store for, be ready for. **3.** wait.

aware, *adj.* cognizant *or* conscious (of), informed, mindful, apprised.
Ant. unaware, oblivious.

awe, *n.* **1.** reverence, respect, veneration; dread, fear, terror. —*v.* **2.** solemnize; daunt, cow, frighten, intimidate.
Ant. contempt, irreverence; scorn.

awkward, *adj.* **1.** clumsy, bungling, unskillful, inexpert, gauche, inept, maladroit. **2.** ungraceful, un-

gainly, unwieldy, unmanageable, coarse, rude, crude, wooden, stiff, constrained, gawky, unrefined, unpolished, rough. **3.** hazardous, dangerous. **4.** trying, embarrassing.
Ant. deft, adroit, adept; graceful, refined, polished.

B

back, *n.* **1.** rear, posterior, end. —*v.* **2.** support, sustain, second, aid, abet, favor, assist; countenance, allow, side with, endorse, stand by. **3.** reverse, move *or* push backward. **4.** retire, retreat, withdraw, go backward. —*adj.* **5.** hind, posterior, rear; remote, frontier, unpopulated.
Ant. front, fore, face.

backward, *adv.* **1.** rearward, back foremost, retrogressively, behind. —*adj.* **2.** reversed, returning. **3.** behind, late, slow, tardy, behindhand. **4.** reluctant, hesitant, bashful, wavering, disinclined, timid, retired. **5.** slow, retarded, undeveloped, underdeveloped, ignorant.
Ant. forward; precocious.

bad, *adj.* **1.** evil, wicked, ill, corrupt, base, depraved, unprincipled, immoral, disingenuous, rascally; mischievous, sinful, criminal, dishonest, villainous, baneful; deleterious, pernicious, harmful, hurtful, injurious, detrimental. **2.** defective, worthless, poor, inferior, imperfect; incompetent, ill-qualified, inadequate. **3.** incorrect, faulty. **4.** invalid, unsound. **5.** sick, ill. **6.** regretful, sorry, contrite, wretched, upset. **7.** unfavorable, unfortunate, adverse, unlucky, unhappy. **8.** offensive, disagreeable, painful, mean, abominable. **9.** vile, wretched, shabby, scurvy. **10.** severe, serious. **11.** rotten, decayed.
Ant. good.

bag, *n.* **1.** pouch, receptacle, sack, reticule, wallet. **2.** handbag, purse, moneybag. —*v.* **3.** catch, net, trap, entrap, kill.

balance, *n.* **1.** scales. **2.** equilibrium, equilibration, symmetry, equipoise, equality. **3.** poise, composure, self-control, equilibrium, equipoise, self-possession. **4.** counterpoise, equalizer, stabilizer. —*v.* **5.** weigh, compare, equilibrate, estimate, assay. **6.** counterpoise, counterbalance, offset, counteract, neutralize, countervail, compensate, allow for, make up for. **7.** proportion, equalize, square, adjust.

ball, *n.* **1.** sphere, globe, orb. **2.** bullet, shot, missile, projectile. **3.** dance, assembly, dancing-party.

ban, *v.* **1.** prohibit, interdict, outlaw, forbid, proscribe, taboo. —*n.* **2.** prohibition, interdiction, interdict, taboo, proscription. **3.** anathema, curse, malediction, excommunication, denunciation.

Ant. permit, allow; permission, blessing.

band, *n.* **1.** company, party, troop, crew, gang, group; body; clique, coterie, set, society, association, sodality, horde, host, assembly. **2.** strip, fillet, belt, tag, strap, cincture, girdle; (*heraldry*) bend. **3.** cord, fetter, shackle, manacle, bond, chain. **—***v.* **4.** unite, confederate. **5.** stripe; mark, tag, identify.

banish, *v.* **1.** exile, expel, expatriate, deport, ostracize, outlaw. **2.** send *or* drive *or* put away, exclude, expel, dismiss, dispel.

Ant. admit, receive.

bank, *n.* **1.** pile, heap, embankment, mount, knoll, hillock, hill, tumulus, dike. **2.** slope, shore, acclivity, shoal, ridge. **3.** row, ridge, tier, course. **—***v.* **4.** embank, border, bound, rim, edge, dike.

banter, *n.* **1.** badinage, joking, jesting, pleasantry, persiflage; mockery, ridicule, derision. **—***v.* **2.** tease, twit, make fun of; ridicule, deride, mock, jeer, chaff.

bar, *n.* **1.** rod, pole. **2.** obstruction, hindrance, deterrent, stop, impediment, obstacle, barrier, barricade. **3.** ridge, shoal, reef, sand-bank, bank, sand-bar, shallow. **4.** counter; saloon, café, bistro, nightclub, cocktail lounge. **5.** lawyers, the legal fraternity; tribunal, judgment-seat, court. **6.** stripe, band. **—***v.* **7.** hinder, obstruct, deter, stop, impede, barricade, prevent, prohibit, restrain. **8.** exclude, shut out, eliminate, block, except.

Ant. suffer, allow, permit.

barbarian, *n.* **1.** savage, philistine, alien, brute, boor, ruffian. **—***adj.* **2.** rude, uncivilized, savage, primitive, barbaric, barbarous, rough, crude, coarse, untutored, ignorant, uncultivated, unlettered. **3.** cruel, ferocious, wild, feral, inhuman, brutal, harsh, harsh-sounding, raucous.

Ant. cosmopolite; refined, civilized, cultivated; kind.

bare, *adj.* **1.** naked, nude, uncovered, unclothed, undressed, exposed, unprotected, unsheltered, unshielded, open. **2.** unfurnished, undecorated, plain, stark, mean, poor, destitute, meager, unadorned, bald, empty, barren. **3.** simple, sheer, mere, alone, sole, just. **4.** unconcealed, undisguised, unreserved, conspicuous, obvious, glaring, evident, palpable. **—***v.* **5.** disclose, denude, lay open, expose.

Ant. covered, dressed.

bargain, *n.* **1.** compact, agreement, stipulation, arrangement, contract, convention, concord, concordat, treaty, stipulation, transaction. **2.** good purchase, buy. **—***v.* **3.** contract, agree, stipulate, covenant, transact. **4.** trade, sell, transfer.

barren, *adj.* **1.** sterile, unprolific, childless, infecund, unfruitful, infertile, unproductive, poor, bare. **2.** uninteresting, dull, stupid; uninstructive, unsuggestive, ineffectual, ineffective.

Ant. fertile; interesting, effectual.

barricade, *n.* **1.** barrier, obstruction, bar. **—***v.* **2.** obstruct, block, bar, shut in, stop up, fortify.

barrier, *n.* bar, obstruction, hindrance, barricade, stop, impediment, obstacle, restraint; fence, railing, stockade, palisade, wall; limit, boundary.

barter, *v.* trade, exchange, traffice, bargain; sell.

base, *n.* **1.** bottom, stand, rest, pedestal, understructure, substructure, foot, basis, foundation, ground, groundwork; principle. **2.** fundamental part, ingredient, element. **3.** station, goal, starting-point, point of departure. —*adj.* **4.** (morally) low, despicable, contemptible, mean-spirited, mean, degraded, degrading, selfish, cowardly. **5.** servile, lowly, slavish, menial, beggarly, abject, sordid, ignoble. **6.** poor, inferior, cheap, tawdry, worthless; debased, counterfeit, fake, spurious, shabby, coarse. **7.** unrefined, plebeian, vulgar, lowly, humble, unknown, baseborn; impure, corrupted, corrupt, vile, venal. **8.** scandalous, shameful, disreputable, disgraceful, discreditable, dishonorable, infamous, notorious. —*v.* **9.** found, rest, establish, ground.
Ant. top, peak; moral, virtuous; good, valuable; refined, pure; honorable.

bashful, *adj.* diffident, shy, abashed, timid, timorous, coy, sheepish, modest, self-effacing, embarrassed, shamefaced, ashamed.
Ant. arrogant, immodest.

basis, *n.* bottom, base, foundation.

batter, *v.* beat, pound, belabor, smite, pelt; bruise, wound; break, shatter, shiver, smash, destroy, demolish, ruin.

battle, *n.* **1.** action, skirmish, campaign, contest, conflict, engagement, military engagement, *or* encounter. **2.** warfare, combat, war, fight. —*v.* **3.** strive, struggle, fight, combat, war, contest, conflict.

beach, *n.* **1.** coast, seashore, littoral, shore, strand, sands, margin, rim. —*v.* **2.** run ashore, strand, put aground.

beam, *n.* **1.** girder. **2.** ray, pencil, streak, gleam, suggestion, hint, glimmer. —*v.* **3.** shine, gleam, glisten, glitter, radiate. **4.** smile, grin.

bear, *v.* **1.** support, hold up, uphold, sustain. **2.** carry, transport, convey, waft; conduct, guide, take. **3.** thrust, drive, force, push, press. **4.** render, give, yield, afford, produce. **5.** transmit, utter, spread, broadcast, advertise, exhibit, show, demonstrate. **6.** sustain, endure, suffer, undergo, tolerate, brook, abide, put up with, stand, stand for, submit to; allow, admit, permit, admit of, hold up under, be capable of. **7.** maintain, keep up, carry on. **8.** entertain, harbor, cherish. **9.** give birth to, bring forth. **10.** confirm, prove. **11.** hold, remain firm. **12.** be patient. **13.** tend, relate, be pertinent, concern, affect, refer. **14.** act, operate, take effect, work succeed.

bearing, *n.* **1.** carriage, posture, manner, mien, deportment, demeanor, behavior, conduct, air. **2.** relation, connection, dependency, reference, application. **3.** direction, course, aim.

beat, *v.* **1.** hit, pound, strike, thrash, belabor, batter, knock, thump, drub, maul, baste, pommel, thwack, whack, punch, cudgel, cane, ship, flog, lash, buffet. **2.** break, forge, hammer. **3.** conquer, subdue, overcome, vanquish, overpower, defeat, checkmate. **4.** excel, outdo, surpass. **5.** throb, pulsate. **6.** win, conquer. —*n.* **7.** stroke, blow. **8.** pulsation, throb, tattoo, rhythm.

beautiful, *adj.* handsome, comely, seemly, attractive, lovely, pretty, fair, fine, elegant, beauteous, graceful, pulchritudinous.
Ant. ugly; inelegant, ungraceful.

beauty, *n.* **1.** loveliness, pulchritude, elegance, grace, gracefulness, comeliness, seemliness, fairness, attractiveness. **2.** belle. **3.** grace, charm, excellence, attraction.
Ant. ugliness; witch; gracelessness.

because, *conj.* as, since, for, inasmuch as, for the reason that.

becoming, *adj.* **1.** attractive, comely, neat, pretty, graceful. **2.** fit, proper, apt, suitable, appropriate, meet, right, correct, decorous, congruous, fitting, seemly.
Ant. unbecoming, ugly; unfit, inappropriate, indecorous.

bedim, *v.* darken, dim, obscure, cloud, becloud.
Ant. brighten.

befitting, *adj.* fitting, proper, suitable, seemly, appropriate, becoming, fit, apt.
Ant. unbecoming, improper, unsuitable, inappropriate.

beg, *v.* ask for, entreat, pray, crave, implore, beseech, importune, petition, sue, request, supplicate, sue for, solicit.

begin, *v.* **1.** commence, start, initiate, inaugurate, institute, enter upon, set about. **2.** originate, create; arise.
Ant. end, conclude, die.

beginning, *n.* **1.** initiation, inauguration, inception, start, commencement, outset, rise, onset, arising, emergence. **2.** source, birth, origin, rise, first cause.

begrudge, *v.* envy, grudge, covet.

beguile, *v.* **1.** mislead, delude, charm, cheat, deceive, befool. **2.** divert, charm, amuse, entertain, cheer, solace.

behave, *v.* conduct oneself, act, deport *or* comport oneself, demean oneself, acquit oneself.
Ant. misbehave.

behavior, *n.* demeanor, conduct, manners, deportment, bearing, carriage, mien, air.
Ant. misbehavior.

belief, *n.* **1.** opinion, view, tenet, doctrine, dogma, creed. **2.** certainty, conviction, assurance, confidence, persuasion, believing, trust, reliance. **3.** credence, credit, acceptance, assent.

belt, *n.* **1.** girth, girdle, cinch, cincture, zone. **2.** band, zone, strip, stripe, stretch. —*v.* **3.** gird, girdle, surround, encircle.

bend, *v.* **1.** curve, crook, bow, deflect, draw, flex. **2.** cause to yield, subdue, persuade, influence, mold. dispose, bias, incline, direct, turn. **3.** stoop, bow, **4.** yield, submit, bow, stoop, kneel, give way, acquiesce, agree. **5.** crook, deflect, deviate, swerve, diverge, incline. —*n.* **6.** curve, crook, bow, rib, elbow, turn, angle, curvature, turning.

beneficial, *adj.* salutary, wholesome, serviceable, useful, favorable, helpful, profitable, advantageous.
Ant. unwholesome, unfavorable, disadvantageous.

benevolent, *adj.* kind, kindly, well-disposed, kind-hearted, humane, tender, tender-hearted, unselfish, generous, liberal, obliging, benign, benignant, charitable, philanthropic, altruistic.
Ant. cruel, selfish, egotistical.

bent, *adj.* **1.** curved, crooked, hooked, bowed, flexed, deflected. **2.** determined, set on, resolved, fixed on. —*n.* **3.** inclination, leaning, bias, tendency, propensity, proclivity, disposition, turn, penchant, predilection, partiality, liking, fondness, proneness.
Ant. straight; undecided; disinclination.

beseech, *v.* **1.** implore, beg, entreat, pray, petition, obsecrate, obtest, supplicate, importune, adjure. **2.** solicit, ask, entreat, beg, implore, importune, crave.

beset, *v.* **1.** assail, harass, surround, encompass, encircle, enclose, besiege, beleaguer. **2.** set, bestud, stud, decorate, ornament, embellish, garnish.

besides, *adv.* **1.** moreover, in addition, furthermore, else, otherwise, too, also, yet, further. —*prep.* **2.** over and above, in addition to, except, other than, save, distinct from.

betray, *v.* **1.** deliver, expose, give up, uncover, reveal. **2.** be unfaithful to, be a traitor to, deceive, be disloyal to, disappoint. **3.** show, exhibit, display, manifest, indicate, imply, betoken, evince, expose, uncover, reveal.
Ant. protect, safeguard.

better, *adj.* **1.** more good; more useful, more valuable; more suitable, more appropriate, more fit, more applicable. **2.** larger, greater, bigger. —*v.* **3.** improve, amend, ameliorate, meliorate, emend; advance, promote; reform, correct, rectify. **4.** improve upon, surpass, exceed.
Ant. worse; worsen.

bewilder, *v.* confuse, perplex, puzzle, mystify; confound, nonplus, astonish, daze, stagger, befog, muddle.

bewitch, *v.* throw a spell over, charm, enchant, captivate, transport, enrapture, fascinate, hypnotize.

bias, *n.* **1.** prejudice, inclination, preconception, predilection, prepossession, proclivity, propensity, proneness, partiality, predisposition, bent, leaning, tendency. —*v.* **2.** prejudice, warp, predispose, bend, influence, incline, dispose.
Ant. justness, impartiality.

bid, *v.* **1.** command, order, direct, charge, require, enjoin, summon. **2.** greet, wish, say. **3.** offer, propose, tender, proffer. —*n.* **4.** offer, proposal, proffer.
Ant. forbid, prohibit, enjoin.

big, *adj.* **1.** large, great, huge, bulky, massive, immense, tremendous, capacious, gigantic, extensive. **2.** pregnant, with child, enceinte. **3.** filled, teeming, overflowing, productive. **4.** important, consequential, haughty, proud, arrogant, pompous, swelling, swollen, inflated, tumid, self-important, conceited, self-sufficient, bombastic, boastful. **5.** generous, big-hearted, kindly.
Ant. small; trivial, nugatory.

bill, *n.* **1.** account, reckoning, score, charges, invoice, statement. **2.** bulletin, handbill, notice, advertisement, broadside, poster, placard, announcement, throw-away, circular. **3.** beak, nib, neb, mandible.

bind, *v.* **1.** band, bond, tie, make fast, fasten, secure, gird, attach. **2.** encircle, border; confine, restrain, restrict. **3.** engage, obligate, oblige. **4.** indenture, apprentice.
Ant. untie, unbind.

birth, *n.* **1.** act of bearing, bringing forth, parturition. **2.** lineage, extraction, parentage, descent, ancestry, line, blood, family, race. **3.** origin, beginning, rise, nativity.
Ant. death, end.

bit, *n.* **1.** particle, speck, grain, mite, crumb, iota, jot, atom, scintilla, tittle, whit, fragment. **2.** bridle, curb, control, rein, check, checkrein, restrainer.

bite, *v.* **1.** gnaw, chew, champ; nip, rip, rend, tear. **2.** cut, pierce; sting, burn, cause to smart. **3.** corrode, erode, eat away. **4.** cheat, deceive, defraud, dupe, trick, gull, make a fool of, cozen, outwit, fool, bamboozel, inveigle, mislead, beguile. —*n.* **5.** nip, sting, cut. **6.** food, snack; morsel, mouthful.

bitter, *adj.* **1.** harsh, acrid, biting. **2.** grievous, distasteful, painful, distressing, intense, sore, poignant, sorrowful, calamitous. **3.** piercing, stinging, biting, nipping. **4.** harsh, sarcastic, caustic, cutting, acrimonious, acerbate, severe, stern, sardonic, scornful, sneering. **5.** fierce, cruel, savage, mean, merciless, ruthless, relentless, virulent, dire.
Ant. sweet.

black, *adj.* **1.** dark, dusky, sooty, inky, ebon, sable, swart, swarthy. **2.** soiled, dirty, dingy, dusky, stained. **3.** gloomy, sad, dismal, sullen, hopeless, dark, depressing, doleful, funereal, sombre, mournful, forbidding, disastrous, calamitous. **4.** amoral, evil, wicked, sinful, fiendish, inhuman, devilish, diabolic, infernal, monstrous, atrocious, horrible, outrageous, heinous, flagitious, nefarious, treacherous, traitorous, infamous, villainous. **5.** ruined, desolate, empty. —*n.* **6.** Negro, Negrito, Papuan, Melanesian; blackamoor, moor; native, aborigine.

Ant. white; clean, pure, undefiled; happy; good, upright, Caucasian.

blackguard, *n.* churl, scoundrel, scamp, rascal, rapscallion, rogue, roué, devil, rake, wastrel, villain.
Ant. hero, protagonist.

blame, *v.* **1.** reproach, reprove, reprehend, censure, condemn, find fault, criticize, disapprove. *—n.* **2.** censure, reprehension, condemnation, stricture, disapproval, disapprobation, reproach, reproof, animadversion. **3.** guilt, culpability, fault, wrong, misdeed, misdoing, shortcoming, sin, defect, reproach.
Ant. credit, honor.

blameless, *adj.* irreproachable, guiltless, unimpeachable, faultless, innocent, inculpable, not guilty, undefiled, unsullied, unspotted, spotless, unblemished.
Ant. guilty, culpable; sullied, besmirched.

blanch, *v.* whiten, bleach, etiolate, pale, fade.
Ant. darken, blacken.

bland, *adj.* **1.** gentle, agreeable, affable, friendly, kindly, mild, amiable; suave, urbane, mild-mannered; complaisant, self-satisfied. **2.** soft, mild, balmy, soothing, nonirritating.
Ant. cruel, unfriendly; boorish, crude; irritable, irksome.

blank, *adj.* **1.** unmarked, void, empty, unadorned, undistinguished. **2.** amazed, astonished, nonplussed, astounded, confused, dumfounded, disconcerted. **3.** complete, utter, pure, simple, unadulterated, unmixed; perfect, entire, absolute, unmitigated, unabated, unqualified, mere. *—n.* **4.** space, line, area; form; void, vacancy, emptiness.
Ant. distinguished, marked; blasé; impure; significant.

blasphemy, *n.* profanity, cursing, swearing, impiousness, sacrilege.
Ant. reverence, piety.

blast, *n.* **1.** wind, squall, gust, gale, blow, storm. **2.** blare, peal, clang. **3.** explosion, outburst, burst, outbreak, discharge. *—v.* **4.** blow, toot, blare. **5.** wither, blight, kill, shrivel. **6.** ruin, destroy, annihilate. **7.** explode, burst, split.

blaze, *n.* **1.** fire, flame, holocaust, inferno; glow, gleam, brightness; outburst. *—v.* **2.** burn, shine, flame, flare up, flicker.

bleach, *v.* **1.** whiten, blanch, etiolate, pale. *—n.* **2.** whitener.
Ant. blacken, darken.

blemish, *v.* **1.** stain, sully, spot, taint, injure, tarnish, mar, damage, deface, impair. *—n.* **2.** stain, defect, blot, spot, speck, disfigurement, flaw, taint, fault.
Ant. purify; purity, immaculateness.

blend, *v.* **1.** mingle, combine, coalesce, mix, intermingle, commingle, amalgamate, unite, compound. *—n.* **2.** mixture, combination, amalgamation.
Ant. separate, precipitate.

blind, *adj.* **1.** sightless, stone-blind, purblind. **2.** ignorant, undiscerning, unenlightened, benighted. **3.**

irrational, uncritical, indiscriminate, headlong, rash, heedless, careless, thoughtless, unreasoning, inconsiderate. **4.** hidden, concealed, obscure, remote, dim, confused, dark. **5.** closed, dead-end, shut. —*n.* **6.** curtain, shade, blinker, blinder, screen, cover. **7.** hiding place, ambush. **8.** cover, decoy, ruse, stratagem, pretense, pretext.
Ant. discerning, enlightened; rational, discriminating; open.

blink, *v.* **1.** wink, nictitate. **2.** flicker, flutter, twinkle. **3.** ignore, overlook, disregard, evade, avoid, condone. —*n.* **4.** wink, twinkle; glance, glimpse, peep, sight.

bliss, *n.* blitheness, happiness, gladness, joy, transport, rapture, ecstasy.
Ant. misery, unhappiness, dejection.

blithe, *adj.* joyous, merry, gay, glad, cheerful, happy, mirthful, sprightly, lighthearted, buoyant, lively, animated, elated, vivacious, joyful, blithesome.
Ant. unhappy, miserable, cheerless.

block, *n.* **1.** mass. **2.** blockhead, dolt, idiot, imbecile, simpleton, fool, dunce. **3.** mold. **4.** blank. **5.** pulley, tackle, sheave. **6.** obstacle, hindrance, impediment, blocking, blockade, obstruction, stoppage, blockage, jam. —*v.* **7.** mold, shape, form. **8.** obstruct, close, hinder, deter, arrest, stop, blockade, impede, check.
Ant. genius; encourage, advance, continue.

bloody, *adj.* **1.** bloodstained, sanguinary, ensanguined, gory. **2.** murderous, cruel, bloodthirsty, savage, barbarous, ferocious, homicidal, inhuman, ruthless.

bloom, *n.* **1.** flower, blossom, efflorescence. **2.** freshness, glow, flush, vigor, prime. —*v.* **3.** flourish, effloresce; glow.

blot, *n.* **1.** spot, stain, inkstain, erasure, blotting, blotch, obliteration, blur. **2.** blemish, reproach, stain, taint, dishonor, disgrace, spot. —*v.* **3.** spot, stain, bespatter; sully, disfigure, deface. **4.** darken, dim, obscure, eclipse, hide, overshadow. **5.** destroy, annihilate, obliterate, efface, erase, expunge, rub out, cancel, strike out, eliminate.

blow, *n.* **1.** stroke, buffet, thump, thwack, rap, slap, cuff, box, beat, knock. **2.** shock, calamity, reverse, disaster, misfortune, affliction. **3.** attack. **4.** blast, wind, gale, gust. **5.** blossom, flower, bloom. —*v.* **6.** pant, puff, wheeze. **7.** blossom, bloom, flower.

blue, *n.* **1.** azure, cerulean, sky-blue, sapphire. **2.** prude, censor, pedant. —*adj.* **3.** depressed, dismal, unhappy, morose, gloomy, doleful, melancholy, dispiriting, dispirited, dejected, sad, glum, downcast, crestfallen, despondent. **4.** prudish, moral, rigid, unbending, righteous, puritanical, self-righteous, severe, rigorous. **5.** obscene, lewd, lascivious, licentious, indecent, risque, ribald, irreverent, scurrilous, suggestive, immoral, amoral.
Ant. happy, mirthful.

bluff, *adj.* **1.** abrupt, unconventional, blunt, direct, frank, open, honest, hearty, rough, crude. **2.** steep,

precipitous, abrupt. —*n.* **3.** cliff, headland, hill, bank. **4.** fraud, deceit, lie, dissembling. —*v.* **5.** mislead, defraud, deceive, lie, dissemble, fake.
Ant. suave, diplomatic, tactful; gradual; plain.

blunt, *adj.* **1.** rounded, not sharp, dull. **2.** abrupt, bluff, brusque, curt, short, obtuse, difficult, gruff, uncourtly, uncivil, rough, harsh, uncourteous, discourteous, rude, impolite. **3.** slow, dull, dimwitted, dullwitted, stupid, thick, stolid. —*v.* **4.** dull, obtund. **5.** numb, paralyze, deaden, stupify, make insensible.
Ant. sharp, acute; courteous, civil, polite; quick, alert.

boast, *v.* **1.** exaggerate, brag, vaunt, swagger, crow. —*n.* **2.** bragging, rodomontade, swaggering, braggadocio.
Ant. depreciate, belittle.

body, *n.* **1.** carcass, corpse, cadaver. **2.** trunk, torso. substance, matter, bulk, main part; fuselage, hull, **3.** collection, group; company, party, band, coterie, society, clique, set; association, corporation. **4.** consistency, density, substance, thickness.
Ant. spirit, soul.

boil, *v.* **1.** seethe, foam, forth, churn, stew, simmer, rage. —*n.* **2.** ebullition. **3.** furuncle, pustule.

boisterous, *adj.* rough, noisy, loud, clamorous, roaring, unrestrained, wild, tumultuous, turbulent, violent, impetuous, stormy, tempestuous, uproarious, obstreperous, roistering, vociferous.
Ant. calm, serene, pacific.

bold, *adj.* **1.** fearless, courageous, brave, intrepid, daring, dauntless, valorous, valiant, heroic, manly, doughty, undaunted, hardy, spirited, mettlesome, gallant, stout-hearted, resolute. **2.** forward, brazen, brassy, presumptuous, shameless, insolent, impudent, immodest, defiant, over confident, saucy, pushing. **3.** conspicuous, prominent, obvious, evident. **4.** steep, abrupt, precipitous.
Ant. cowardly, timorous, timid; backward, shy; inconspicuous; gradual.

bond, *n.* **1.** binder, fastener, fastening, band, cord, ligature, ligament, link, rope. **2.** tie, connection, link, attraction, attachment, union. **3.** bondsman, security, ward, promise; promissory note; obligation, contract, compact. **4.** (pl.) chains, fetters, captivity, constraint, restriction, bondage; prison, imprisonment. —*v.* **5.** mortgage. **6.** cement, glue.

bondage, *n.* slavery, indenture, servitude, serfdom, thraldom, captivity, imprisonment, confinement.
Ant. freedom.

bonus, *n.* bounty, premium, reward, honorarium, gift, subsidy; dividend, perquisite.

border, *n.* **1.** side, edge, margin; orphrey; periphery, circumference, lip, brim, verge, brink. **2.** frontier, limit, confine, boundary. —*v.* **3.** bound, limit, confine; adjoin.

bore, *v.* **1.** perforate, drill, pierce. **2.** weary, fatigue,

tire, annoy. —*n.* **3.** caliber, hole. **4.** tidal wave, eagre.
Ant. amuse.

bosom, *n.* **1.** breast, heart, affection. —*adj.* **2.** intimate, close, confidential.

bother, *v.* **1.** annoy, pester, worry, trouble, plague, tease, harass, vex, harry; molest, disturb. **2.** bewilder, confuse.
Ant. solace, comfort.

bottom, *n.* **1.** base, foot. **2.** underside. **3.** foundation, base, basis, groundwork. **4.** seat, buttocks. —*adj.* **5.** fundamental, basic, elementary; undermost, lowest.
Ant. top; superficial, superfluous.

bough, *n.* branch, limb, arm, shoot.

bound, *v.* **1.** leap, jump, spring. **2.** rebound, ricochet. —*n.* **3.** (*usually plural*) limit, confine, boundary, verge, border. —*adj.* **4.** constrained; destined for, tending, going.
Ant. free.

bounty, *n.* **1.** generosity, munificence, charity, liberality, beneficence. **2.** gift, award, present, benefaction. **3.** reward, premium, bonus.

bow, *v.* **1.** stoop, bend, buckle, give way. **2.** yield, submit. **3.** subdue, crush, depress, cast down. **4.** curve, bend, inflect. —*n.* **5.** front, forepart, prow.

brace, *n.* **1.** clasp, clamp, vise. **2.** stay, support, prop, strut. **3.** bitstock. **4.** couple, pair. —*v.* **5.** fasten firmly, strengthen, support, back up, fortify, prop, steady. **6.** tighten, tauten, make tense. **7.** stimulate, strengthen, fortify.

brag, *v., n.* boast, rodomontade, bluster.
Ant. depreciate.

brains, *n.* understanding, intelligence, mind, intellect, sense, reason; capacity.
Ant. stupidity.

branch, *n.* **1.** bough, limb, arm, shoot, offshoot. **2.** limb, offshoot, ramification, arm. **3.** section, subdivision, department; member, portion, part; article. **4.** tributary, feeder. —*v.* **5.** divide, subdivide, diverge, ramify.

bravado, *n.* boasting, swaggering, braggadocio, pretense, brag, bluster, bombast.
Ant. shame, modesty.

brave, *adj.* **1.** courageous, fearless, gallant, confident, cool, chivalrous, impetuous, dashing, intrepid, daring, dauntless, doughty, bold, valiant, heroic, manly, hard, mettlesome, stout-hearted. **2.** fine, showy, effective, brilliant; gay; debonair. —*n.* **3.** warrior (*esp. American Indian*). —*v.* **4.** face, defy, challenge, dare.
Ant. cowardly, fearful; craven, pusillanimous.

bravery, *n.* boldness, courage, intrepidity, daring, prowess, heroism, pluck, gallantry, spirit, audacity, nerve, mettle, fearlessness, spunk, valor.
Ant. cowardice.

brawl, *n.* **1.** quarrel, squabble, argument, spat, wrangle, fend, disagreement, dispute, fracas, disturbance, disorder, row, tumult, clamor, rumpus, fray, fight, affray, altercation, mêlée, riot. —*v.* **2.** quarrel, squabble, argue, wrangle, fend, disagree, dispute, fight, bicker.

brazen, *adj.* **1.** brassy. **2.** bold, forward, shameless, impudent, insolent, immodest, defiant.
Ant. shy, diffident, modest.

breach, *n.* **1.** break, rupture, fracture, crack, gap, fissure, rift, rent, opening, chasm. **2.** infraction, violation, infringement. **3.** alienation, disaffection, falling out, misunderstanding; split, rift, schism, severance, separation; dissension, disagreement, difference, variance, quarrel, dispute.
Ant. observance.

break, *v.* **1.** fracture, crush, shatter, splinter, shiver, smash, batter, demolish, destroy. **2.** contravene, transgress, disobey, violate, infringe, infract. **3.** dissolve, annul, negate, dismiss. **4.** lacerate, wound, cut, injure, harm, hurt. **5.** interrupt, suspend, disrupt, stop; abbreviate, curtail. **6.** end, overcome. **7.** exceed, outdo, surpass, beat. **8.** disclose, open, unfold, divulge. **9.** ruin, bankrupt, make bankrupt. **10.** impair, weaken, enfeeble, enervate; dispirit. **11.** tame, make obedient. **12.** discharge, degrade, cashier, demote. **13.** shatter, shiver; burst. **14.** dissolve, separate, split. **15.** escape, break loose. **16.** dawn, open, appear. **17.** decline, weaken. —*n.* **18.** disruption, separation, rent, tear, rip rift, schism, severance, split; breach, gap, fissure, crack, chasm, rupture, fracture. **19.** suspension, stoppage, stop, caesura, hiatus, interruption, lacuna, pause, discontinuity.
Ant. repair.

breaker, *n.* wave, comber, surge, white-cap, roller; bore, eagre.

breed, *v.* **1.** beget, bear, bring forth, conceive, give birth to, produce, engender, father, mother. **2.** propagate, procreate, originate, create, beget, occasion, generate. **3.** raise, rear, bring up, nurture; train, educate, discipline, instruct, teach, school. **4.** grow, develop, flourish, arise, rise. —*n.* **5.** race, lineage, strain, family, pedigree, line, extraction, stock, progeny. **6.** sort, kind, species, class, denomination, order, rank, character, nature, description.

breeze, *n.* wind, air, blow, zephyr.
Ant. calm.

brevity, *n.* **1.** shortness, briefness. **2.** conciseness, compactness, condensation, succinctness, pithiness; terseness, curtness.
Ant. lengthiness.

bridle, *n.* **1.** curb, restraint, check, control, governor. —*v.* **2.** restrain, check, curb, control, govern. **3.** bristle, ruffle.
Ant. freedom; decontrol.

brief, *adj.* **1.** short, short-lived, fleeting, transitory, ephemeral, transient, temporary. **2.** concise, suc-

cinct, pithy, condensed, compact, laconic; curt, short, terse, abrupt. —*n.* **3.** outline, précis, synopsis, summary, epitome, syllabus, abstract, abridgment, conspectus, compendium, breviary. —*v.* **4.** abstract, summarize, outline, epitomize, abridge, abbreviate.
Ant. long, tedious, boring.

bright, *adj.* **1.** radiant, radiating, refulgent, resplendent, effulgent, lucent, lustrous, glowing, beaming, lambent, splendid, brilliant, shining, irradiant, gleaming, luminous; scintillating, sparkling, twinkling, glistening, glistering, shimmering, coruscating, glittering; flashing, flaming, blazing; shiny, sheeny, glossy, burnished; vivid, light, sunny, fulgid, fulgent. **2.** clear, transparent, pellucid, translucent, lucid, limpid, unclouded, crystal, cloudless, lambent. **3.** illustrious, distinguished, glorious, famous, golden, silver. **4.** quick-witted, intelligent, keen, discerning, acute, ingenious, sharp, clever. **5.** lively, animated, cheerful, merry, happy, sprightly, light-hearted, gay, vivacious, genial, pleasant. **6.** favorable, auspicious, propitious, promising, encouraging, inspiriting, inspiring, enlivening, exhilarating.
Ant. dull; opaque, dense; undistinguished, ignominous; slow, stupid; laconic, doleful, melancholy; unfavorable, discouraging.

brilliance, *n.* **1.** brightness, splendor, luster, refulgence, effulgence, radiance, brilliancy; sparkle, glitter, glister, gleam. **2.** excellence, distinction, eminence, renown, prominence, preeminence, singularity, fame, illustriousness.
Ant. dullness; notoriety, oblivion.

brim, *n.* rim, edge, border; orphrey; periphery, circumference, bound, brink, lip.
Ant. center.

bring, *v.* **1.** take along, conduct, convey, lead, fetch, guide, convoy, accompany, transport, carry. **2.** lead, induce, prevail upon, draw.
Ant. remove, withdraw.

brisk, *adj.* **1.** active, lively, energetic, peart, quick, nimble, agile, alert, spry, on the qui vive, spirited, bright, vivacious. **2.** sharp, stimulating, acute. **3.** effervescent, bubbly, bubbling.
Ant. slow, lethargic; dull; flat.

brittle, *adj.* fragile, frail, breakable, frangible.
Ant. supple, flexible, elastic.

broad, *adj.* **1.** wide. **2.** large, extensive, vast, spacious, ample. **3.** diffused, diffuse, open, full. **4.** liberal, large, big, tolerant, open-minded, hospitable. **5.** main, general, chief, important, obvious. **6.** plain, clear, bold, plain-spoken, open, unconfined, free, unrestrained. **7.** rough, coarse, countrified, unrefined, vulgar, indecent, indelicate, gross.
Ant. narrow; penurious, stingy; refined, cultivated, decent.

brood, *n.* **1.** offspring, litter, young, progeny, issue. **2.** breed, kind, sort, line, lineage, stock, family, strain.

species, class, order. —*v*. 3. incubate, sit. 4. dwell on, ponder, ruminate over, meditate on. 5. sit, hatch, set. 6. rest. 7. meditate morbidly.

brook, *n*. 1. stream, rivulet, run, runnel, runlet, streamlet, rill, burn, branch. —*v*. 2. bear, suffer, tolerate, allow, stand, endure, abide, put up with, submit to.

brother, *n*. fellow man, fellow countryman, kinsman, associate; sibling.

brownie, *n*. goblin, fairy, elf, pixie, leprechaun, nix, nixie, sprite, imp.

brush, *n*. 1. encounter, brief encounter, meeting; engagement, affair, contest, collision, action, fight, battle, skirmish, struggle, conflict. 2. bushes, scrub, thicket, copse, shrubs, bracken, brake.

brusque, *adj*. abrupt, blunt, rough, unceremonious, bluff, gruff, ungracious, uncivil, discourteous, impolite, rude, crude, curt.
Ant. courteous, courtly, polished, refined, gentle.

brutal, *adj*. 1. savage, cruel, inhuman, ruthless, pitiless, unfeeling, barbarous, barbarian, uncivilized, ferocious, brutish, barbaric, truculent. 2. crude, coarse, gross, harsh, rude, rough, uncivil, ungracious, impolite, unmannerly, ungentlemanly, brusque. 3. irrational, unreasoning, brute, unthinking. 4. bestial, beastly, animal, carnal.
Ant. kind, sensitive; artistic; gracious, rational, sensible; human.

brute, *n*. 1. beast, quadruped. 2. barbarian. —*adj*. 3. animal, brutish, irrational, unreasoning. 4. savage, cruel, brutal. 5. sensual, carnal.
Ant. human; kind; spiritual.

building, *n*. edifice, structure, construction, erection.

bulk, *n*. 1. size, magnitude, mass, volume, dimensions. 2. greater part, majority, most; body, mass. —*v*. 3. grow, swell, bulge, expand, enlarge, aggrandize.

bulky, *adj*. massive, ponderous, unwieldy, clumsy, cumbersome; great, big, large, huge, vast.
Ant. small, delicate.

bunch, *n*. 1. cluster; group, lot, bundle, batch, collection. 2. knob, lump, protuberance.

bundle, *n*. 1. bunch. 2. parcel, pack, package, packet.

burden, *n*. 1. load, weight. 2. encumbrance, impediment, grievance, trial. 3. substance, core, point, essence, epitome, central idea, tenor, drift. 4. refrain, chorus. —*v*. 5. load, overload, oppress.
Ant. disburden.

burn, *v*. 1. flame. 2. tingle, be hot, glow. 3. consume, scorch, sear, singe, char, toast, brown, tan, bronze. —*n*. 4. brook, rivulet, rill, run, runnel, streamlet, runlet.

burst, *v*. 1. explode, crack, blow up, split. 2. rend, tear, break. —*n*. 3. explosion. 4. spurt, outpouring, gust.
Ant. implode.

bury, *v*. 1. inter, entomb, inhume, inearth. 2. sink.

3. cover, hide, conceal, secrete, shroud, enshroud.
Ant. disinter; rise; uncover.

business, *n.* **1.** occupation, trade, craft, metier, profession, calling, employment, vocation, pursuit. **2.** company, concern, enterprise, corporation, firm, partnership. **3.** affair, matter, concern, transaction. **4.** commerce, trade, traffic. **5.** function, duty, office, position.

busy, *adj.* **1.** engaged, occupied, diligent, industrious, employed, working, assiduous, active, sedulous, hard-working. **2.** active, brisk, bustling, spry, agile, nimble. **3.** officious, meddlesome, prying.
Ant. indolent, unoccupied, lazy.

but, *conj.* **1.** however, nevertheless, yet, further, moreover, still. **2.** excepting, save, except. **—***prep.* **3.** excepting, except, save, excluding. **—***adv.* **4.** only, just, no more than.

butcher, *n.* **1.** meat dealer. **2.** slaughterer, meat-dresser. **3.** murderer, slayer, killer, assassin, cut-throat, thug. **—***v.* **4.** kill, slaughter. **5.** slaughter, massacre, murder, kill, assassinate. **6.** bungle, botch, fail in.

buy, *v.* **1.** purchase. **2.** hire, bribe, corrupt.
Ant. sell.

byword, *n.* **1.** slogan, motto. **2.** proverb, maxim, apothegm, aphorism, saw, adage, saying. **3.** epithet.

C

cabin, *n.* **1.** hut, shanty, shack, cot, cottage, shed, hovel. **—***v.* **2.** cramp, confine, enclose, restrict.

calamity, *n.* affliction, adversity, ill fortune, misery, bad luck, distress, trouble, evil, hardship, trial, reverse, mischance, mishap, blow, misfortune, disaster, catastrophe, cataclysm.
Ant. fortune, blessing, boon.

calculate, *v.* **1.** count, figure, reckon, cast, estimate, weigh, deliberate, compute, rate. **2.** suit, adapt, fit, adjust.
Ant. assume, guess.

calculation, *n.* **1.** computation, figuring, reckoning, estimate, estimation. **2.** estimate, forecast, expectation, prospect, anticipation. **3.** forethought, planning, circumspection, caution, wariness, foresight, cautiousness, discretion, prudence, deliberation.
Ant. guess, assumption.

call, *v.* **1.** cry out. **2.** announce, proclaim. **3.** awaken, waken, rouse, wake up, arouse. **4.** summon, invite, send for. **5.** convoke, convene, call together, assemble, muster. **6.** telephone, ring up. **7.** name, give a name to, label, term, designate, style, dub, christen, entitle, nominate, denominate. **8.** reckon, consider, estimate, designate. **9.** shout, cry, voice. **10.** visit, stop. **—*n.*** **11.** shout, cry, outcry. **12.** summons, signal; invitation, bidding; appointment. **13.** need, occasion; demand, claim, requisition.

callous, *adj.* **1.** hard, hardened, inured, indurated. **2.** unfeeling, insensible, blunt, apathetic, unimpressible, indifferent, unsusceptible, obtuse; dull, sluggish, torpid, slow.
Ant. soft; sensitive; alert.

calm, *adj.* **1.** still, quiet, smooth, motionless, tranquil, unruffled, mild, peaceful. **2.** tranquil, peaceful, serene, self-possessed, cool, collected, unruffled, composed, undisturbed, sedate, aloof. **—*n.*** **3.** stillness, serenity, calmness, quiet, smoothness, tranquillity, peacefulness, aloofness, self-possession, composure, repose, equanimity. **—*v.*** **4.** still, quiet, tranquilize, pacify, smooth, appease, compose; allay, assuage, mollify, soothe, soften.
Ant. perturbed; tempestuous; excite, agitate.

can, *v.* **1.** know how to, be able to, have the ability *or* power *or* right *or* qualifications *or* means to. **—*n.*** **2.** tin, container.

cancel, *v.* **1.** cross out, delete, dele, erase, expunge, obliterate, blot out, efface, rub out. **2.** void, annul, countermand, revoke, rescind, counterbalance, compensate for, allow for.
Ant. ratify.

candid, *adj.* **1.** frank, open, outspoken, sincere, ingenious, naive, artless, honest, plain, guileless, straightforward, aboveboard, free, honorable. **2.** impartial, honest, just, fair, unprejudiced, unbiased. **3.** white, clear, pure, unadulterated, lucid, transparent, pellucid, lucent.
Ant. concealed, hidden, wily, deceitful; biased, prejudiced; turgid, cloudy, dull, impure.

canon, *n.* **1.** rule, law, standard, formula. **2.** criterion, principle, standard.

capable, *adj.* **1.** able, competent, efficient, intelligent, clever, skillful, ingenious, sagacious, gifted, accomplished. **2.** fitted, adapted, suited, qualified. **3.** susceptible, open, admitting, allowing, permitting, permissive.
Ant. incapable.

capacious, *adj.* spacious, roomy, ample, large, broad, comprehensive, wide.
Ant. confining, narrow.

capacity, *n.* **1.** cubic contents, volume, magnitude, dimensions, amplitude. **2.** ability, power, aptitude, faculty, wit, genius, aptness, bent, forte, leaning, propensity, ableness, talent, discernment; caliber, cleverness, skill, skillfulness, competency, competence readiness, capability. **3.** position, relation, function, sphere, area, province; office, post, charge, responsibility.
Ant. incapacity, incompetence.

capital, *n.* **1.** metropolis, seat. **2.** wealth, principal,

investment, worth, resources, assets, stock. —*adj.* **3.** principal, first, important, chief, prime, primary, major, leading, cardinal, essential, vital. **4.** excellent, first-rate, splendid, fine. **5.** large-size, upper case. **6.** fatal, serious.
Ant. trivial, unimportant.

capsize, *v.* overturn, upset.
Ant. right.

captivate, *v.* charm, enthrall, enchant, fascinate, hypnotize, bewitch, enamor, win, catch.
Ant. repel, repulse.

captivity, *n.* bondage, servitude, slavery, thralldom, serfdom, subjection; imprisonment, confinement, incarceration.
Ant. freedom.

capture, *v.* **1.** seize, take prisoner, catch, arrest, snare, apprehend, grab, nab; imprison, incarcerate. —*n.* **2.** arrest, seizure, apprehension, catch.
Ant. release.

carcass, *n.* **1.** body, corpse, cadaver. **2.** framework, skeleton.

care, *n.* **1.** worry, anxiety, concern, solicitude, trouble. **2.** heed, caution, pains, anxiety, regard, attention, vigilance, carefulness, solicitude, circumspection, alertness, watchfulness, wakefulness. **3.** burden, charge, responsibility. —*v.* **4.** have concern *or* regard, be solicitous *or* anxious, worry, be troubled. **5.** like, be inclined *or* disposed *or* interested.

careful, *adj.* **1.** cautious, circumspect, watchful, wakeful, vigilant, guarded, chary, discreet, wary, suspicious, prudent, tactful; trustworthy. **2.** painstaking, meticulous, discerning, exact, thorough, concerned, scrupulous, finical, conscientious, attentive, heedful, thoughtful.
Ant. careless.

careless, *adj.* **1.** inattentive, incautious, unwary, unthoughtful, forgetful, remiss, negligent, neglectful, unmindful, heedless, reckless, indiscreet, thoughtless, unconcerned. **2.** negligent, inaccurate, inexact. **3.** unconsidered; inconsiderate.
Ant. careful.

cargo, *n.* freight, load, burden, lading.

caricature, *n.* **1.** burlesque, exaggeration, travesty, take-off, parody, farce, satire, lampoon, cartoon. —*v.* **2.** burlesque, exaggerate, travesty, parody, take off, satirize, lampoon.

carnal, *adj.* **1.** human, temporal, worldly, mundane, earthly, unregenerate, natural, unspiritual. **2.** sensual, fleshly, bodily, animal. **3.** lustful, impure, gross, lecherous, worldly, lascivious, salacious, libidinous, concupiscent, lewd, lubricious, wanton, lubricous.
Ant. spiritual, moral, intellectual.

carriage, *n.* **1.** vehicle, cart, wagon, conveyance; dogcart, brougham, hansom, victoria, calash, buckboard, carry-all, shay, sulky, surrey. **2.** bearing, manner, mien, deportment, behavior, conduct, demeanor.

carry, *v.* **1.** convey, bear, transport; transmit, transfer, take, bring. **2.** bear, support, sustain, stand, suffer. **3.** lead, impel, drive, conduct, urge. **4.** effect, accomplish, gain, secure, win, capture.

case, *n.* **1.** instance, example, illustration, occurrence. **2.** state, circumstance, situation, condition, contingency; plight, predicament. **3.** patient; action, suit, lawsuit, cause, process, trial. **4.** receptacle, box, container, chest, folder, envelope, sheath. **5.** frame, framework.

cast, *v.* **1.** throw, fling, hurl, deposit, propel, put, toss, pitch, shy, sling, pitch. **2.** throw off, shed, slough, put off, lay aside. **3.** direct, turn, cause to fall, throw, shed, impart. **4.** throw out, send forth, hurl, toss. **5.** throw down, defeat, overwhelm. **6.** part with, lose. **7.** set aside, throw aside, discard, reject, dismiss, disband. **8.** emit, eject, vomit, spew forth, puke. **9.** bestow, confer. **10.** arrange, plan out, allot, apportion, appoint, assign. **11.** mold, form, found. **12.** compute, calculate, reckon; forecast, fortell. **13.** ponder, consider, contrive, devise, plan. **14.** throw. **15.** calculate, add. **16.** consider; plan, scheme. —*n.* **17.** throw, fling, toss. **18.** fortune, lot. **19.** appearance, form, shape, mien, demeanor. **20.** sort, kind, style. **21.** tendency, inclination, turn, bent, trend, air. **22.** turn, twist; warp. **23.** tinge, tint, hue, shade, touch; dash, trace, hint, suggestion. **24.** computation, calculation, addition. **25.** forecast, conjecture, guess.

castle, *n.* **1.** fortress, citadel, stronghold. **2.** palace, chateau, mansion. **3.** (*Chess*) rook.

casual, *adj.* **1.** unexpected, fortuitous, unforeseen, chance, accidental. **2.** unpremeditated, offhand, unintentional. **3.** careless, negligent, unconcerned. **4.** irregular, occasional, random.
Ant. premeditated, deliberate, calculated; careful; regular, routine.

catalogue, *n.* list, roll, roster, register, record, inventory.

catastrophe, *n.* disaster, mishap, cataclysm, calamity, misfortune, mischance; end, dénouement, finale; upshot, conclusion, windup, termination.
Ant. triumph.

catch, *v.* **1.** capture, apprehend, arrest. **2.** ensnare, entrap, deceive, entangle. **3.** surprise, detect, take unawares. **4.** strike, hit. **5.** lay hold of, grasp, seize, snatch, grip, entangle, clutch. **6.** captivate, charm, enchant, fascinate, win, bewitch. —*n.* **7.** capture, apprehension, arrest, seizure. **8.** ratchet, bolt. **9.** take.
Ant. release.

cause, *n.* **1.** occasion, reason, ground, grounds, basis; motive, determinant, incitement, inducement. **2.** purpose, object, aim, end. —*v.* **3.** bring about, effect, determine, make, produce, create, originate, occasion, give rise to.

caution, *n.* **1.** prudence, discretion, circumspectness, watchfulness, circumspection, heed, care, wariness,

heedfulness, vigilance, forethought, providence. **2.** warning, admonition, advice, injunction, counsel. **—*v*. 3.** warn, admonish, advise, enjoin, counsel, forewarn.
Ant. carelessness.

cautious, *adj*. prudent, careful, heedful, watchful, discreet, wary, vigilant, alert, provident, chary, circumspect, guarded.
Ant. careless, heedless, indiscreet.

cavity, *n*. hollow, hole, void.

cease, *v*. **1.** stop, desist, stay. **2.** terminate, end, culminate. **3.** discontinue, end.
Ant. start, begin; continue, persist.

cede, *v*. yield, resign, surrender, relinquish, abandon, give up; make over, grant, transfer, convey.
Ant. persist, maintain.

celebrate, *v*. **1.** commemorate, honor, observe. **2.** proclaim, announce. **3.** praise, extol, laud, glorify, honor, applaud, commend. **4.** solemnize, ritualize.

celebrated, *adj*. famous, renowned, well-known, disdinguished, illustrious, eminent, famed.
Ant. obscure, unknown.

censure, *n*. **1.** condemnation, reproof, disapproval, disapprobation, blaming, criticism, blame, reproach, reprehension, rebuke, reprimand, stricture, animadversion. **—*v*. 2.** criticize, disapprove, condemn, find fault with. **3.** reprove, rebuke, reprimand, reprehend, chide, blame, reproach.
Ant. praise, commend.

center, *n*. **1.** middle, midst. **2.** pivot, hub, point, axis.
Ant. brim, edge.

ceremony, *n*. rite, ritual, formality, observance.
Ant. informality.

certain, *adj*. **1.** confident, sure, assured, convinced, satisfied, indubitable, indisputable, unquestionable, undeniable, incontestable, irrefutable, unquestioned, incontrovertible, absolute, positive, plain, patent, obvious, clear. **2.** sure, inevitable, infallible, unfailing. **3.** fixed, agreed upon, settled, prescribed, determined, determinate, constant, stated, given. **4.** definite, particular, special, especial. **5.** unfailing, reliable, trustworthy, dependable, trusty.
Ant. uncertain; unclear, unsure; unsettled; indefinite; fallible, unreliable.

certainty, *n*. **1.** unquestionableness, inevitability, certitude, assurance, confidence, conviction. **2.** fact, truth.
Ant. doubt, uncertainty.

champion, *n*. **1.** winner, victor, hero. **2.** defender, protector, vindicator. **3.** fighter, warrior. **—*v*. 4.** defend, support, maintain, fight for, advocate.
Ant. loser; oppose.

chance, *n*. **1.** fortune, fate, luck, accident, fortuity, hap. **2.** possibility, contingency, probability. **3.** opportunity, opening, occasion. **4.** risk, hazard, peril,

danger, jeopardy. —*v.* **5.** happen, occur, befall, take place. —*adj.* **6.** casual, accidental, fortuitous.
Ant. necessity, inevitability; surety.

change, *v.* **1.** alter, make different, turn, transmute, transform, vary, modify. **2.** exchange, substitute, convert, shift, replace; barter, trade, commute. **3.** interchange. —*n.* **4.** variation, alteration, modification, deviation, transformation, transmutation, mutation, conversion, transition. **5.** substitution, exchange. **6.** variety, novelty, innovation, vicissitude.
Ant. remain, endure; immutability.

character, *n.* **1.** individuality, personality. **2.** feature, trait, characteristic. **3.** nature, quality, disposition, mien, constitution, cast. **4.** name, reputation, repute. **5.** status, capacity. **6.** symbol, mark, sign, letter, figure, emblem.

characteristic, *adj.* **1.** typical, distinctive, discrete, special, peculiar, singular. —*n.* **2.** feature, quality, trait, peculiarity, mark, attribute, property.

charge, *v.* **1.** load, lade, burden, freight. **2.** command, enjoin, exhort, order, urge, bid, require. **3.** impute, ascribe. **4.** blame, accuse, indict, arraign, impeach, inculpate, incriminate, involve, inform against, betray. **5.** attack, assault, set on. —*n.* **6.** load, burden, cargo, freight. **7.** duty, responsibility, commission, office, trust, employment. **8.** care, custody, superintendence, ward, management. **9.** command, injunction, exhortation, order, direction, mandate, instruction, precept. **10.** accusation, indictment, imputation, allegation, crimination, incrimination. **11.** price, cost. **12.** tax, lien, cost, expense, encumbrance, outlay, expenditure, liability, debt. **13.** onset, attack, onslaught, assault, encounter.

charitable, *adj.* **1.** generous, open-handed, liberal, beneficient, benign, kind, benignant, benevolent, bountiful, lavish. **2.** broad-minded, liberal, lenient, considerate, mild, kindly.
Ant. mean, stingy; narrow-minded, inconsiderate.

charm, *n.* **1.** attractiveness, allurement, fascination, enchantment, bewitchment, spell, witchery, magic, sorcery. **2.** trinket, bauble, jewelry; amulet. —*v.* **3.** enchant, fascinate, captivate, catch, entrance, enrapture, transport, delight, please; attract, allure, enamor, bewitch; ravish.
Ant. revulsion; disgust.

chart, *n.* map, plan.

charter, *n.* **1.** privilege, immunity, guaranty, warranty. —*v.* **2.** lease, hire, rent, let.

chary, *adj.* **1.** careful, wary, cautious, circumspect. **2.** shy, bashful, self-effacing. **3.** fastidious, choosy, particular. **4.** sparing, stingy, frugal.
Ant. careless.

chaste, *adj.* virtuous, pure, moral, decent, undefiled, modest, continent; clean, elevated, unsullied; unaf-

fected, simple, subdued, neat, straight, honest; refined, classic, elegant.
Ant. sinful, impure, immodest; unrefined, coarse, inelegant.

chasten, *v.* discipline, punish, chastise, restrain, subdue, humble.
Ant. indulge, humor.

cheap, *adj.* **1.** inexpensive, low-priced. **2.** paltry, common, mean, low, lowly, poor, inferior, base.
Ant. dear, expensive, costly; exceptional, extraordinary, elegant.

cheat, *n.* **1.** fraud, swindle, deception, trick, imposture, wile, deceit, artifice, chicanery, stratagem, hoax, imposition, snare, trap, pitfall, catch. **2.** swindler, imposter, trickster, sharper, cheater, dodger, charlatan, fraud, fake, phony, mountebank, rogue, knave. —*v.* **3.** deceive, defraud, trick, victimize, mislead, dupe, gudgeon, cog, gull, cozen, outwit, bamboozle, delude, hoodwink, beguile, inveigle, swindle, con entrap, hoax, ensnare, fool, cajole; dissemble.

check, *v.* **1.** stop, halt, delay, arrest. **2.** curb, restrain, control, repress, chain, bridle, hinder, hobble, obstruct, curtail. **3.** investigate, verify, assess, test, measure, examine, compare. **4.** agree, correspond. **5.** pause, stop. —*n.* **6.** restraint, curb, bridle, bit, hindrance, obstacle, obstruction, impediment, control, bar, barrier, restriction, damper, interference, deterrent, repression. **7.** rebuff, arrest, stoppage, cessation, repulse, halt. **8.** ticket, receipt, coupon, tag, counterfoil, stub.
Ant. continue, advance, foster, support.

cheer, *n.* **1.** encouragement, comfort, solace. **2.** gladness, gaiety, animation, joy, mirth, glee, merriment, cheerfulness. **3.** food, provisions, victuals, repast, viands. —*v.* **4.** gladden, enliven, inspirit, exhilarate, animate, encourage. **5.** shout, applaud, acclaim, salute.
Ant. derision; misery; discourage, deride; boo, hiss.

cheerful, *adj.* **1.** cheery, gay, blithe, happy, lively, spirited, sprightly, joyful, joyous, mirthful, buoyant, gleeful, sunny, jolly. **2.** pleasant, bright, gay, winsome, gladdening, cheery, cheering, inspiring, animating. **3.** hearty, robust, ungrudging, generous.
Ant. miserable; unpleasant; stingy, mean.

cherish, *v.* **1.** foster, harbor, entertain, humor, encourage, indulge. **2.** nurse, nurture, nourish, support, sustain, comfort. **3.** treasure, cling to, hold dear.
Ant. abandon, scorn.

chide, *v.* **1.** scold, fret, fume, chafe. **2.** reprove, rebuke, censure, criticize, scold, admonish, upbraid, reprimand, blame, reprehend.
Ant. praise, commend.

chief, *n.* **1.** head, leader, ruler, chieftain, commander. —*adj.* **2.** principal, most important, prime, first, supreme, leading, paramount, great, grand, cardinal, master; vital, essential.

Ant. follower, disciple; unimportant, trivial, trifling; secondary.

chiefly, *adv.* mostly, principally, mainly, especially, particularly, eminently.
Ant. last, lastly.

childish, *adj.* childlike, puerile, infantile, young, tender; weak, silly, simple, ingenuous, guileless, trusting, confident.
Ant. adult, sophisticated.

chill, *n.* **1.** cold, coldness, frigidity. **2.** shivering, ague. **3.** depression, damp. —*adj.* **4.** chilly, cool, unfriendly, depressing, discouraging, bleak. —*v.* **5.** cool, freeze; depress, discourage, deject, dishearten.
Ant. warm.

choice, *n.* **1.** selection, choosing, election, option, alternative, preference. —*adj.* **2.** worthy, excellent, superior, fine, select, rare, uncommon, valuable, precious.

choose, *v.* select, elect, prefer, pick, cull.

chop, *v.* cut, mince.

chronic, *adj.* **1.** inveterate, constant, habitual, confirmed, hardened. **2.** perpetual, continuous, continuing, unending, never-ending, everlasting.
Ant. fleeting, temporary.

chuckle, *v., n.* laugh, giggle, titter.
Ant. cry, sob.

circle, *n.* **1.** ring, periphery, circumference, perimeter. **2.** ring, circlet, crown. **3.** compass, area, sphere, province, field, region, bounds, circuit. **4.** cycle, period, series. **5.** coterie, set, clique, society, club, company, class, fraternity. **6.** sphere, orb, globe, ball. —*v.* **7.** surround, encircle, encompass, round, bound, include. **8.** orbit, circuit, revolve.

circuit, *n.* **1.** course, tour, journey, revolution, orbit. **2.** circumference, perimeter, periphery, boundary, compass. **3.** space, area, region, compass, range, sphere, province, district, field.

civil, *adj.* polite, courteous, courtly, gracious, complaisant, respectful, deferential, obliging; affable, urbane, debonair, chivalrous, gallant, suave; refined, well-mannered, well-bred, civilized.
Ant. uncivil, discourteous; rude; ill-mannered, unrefined.

claim, *v.* **1.** demand, require, ask, call for, challenge. **2.** assert, maintain, uphold. —*n.* **3.** demand, request, requirement, requisition, call. **4.** right, title, privilege, pretension.

clamor, *n.* **1.** shouting, uproar, outcry, noise, hullabaloo. **2.** vociferation. —*v.* **3.** vociferate, cry out, shout. **4.** importune, demand noisily.
Ant. quiet, serenity, taciturnity.

clandestine, *adj.* secret, private, concealed, hidden, sly, underhand.
Ant. open, candid, aboveboard.

clash, *v.* **1.** clang, crash, clap, dash, clatter, clank. **2.** collide. **3.** conflict, struggle, disagree, interfere,

content. —*n.* **4.** collision. **5.** conflict, opposition, disagreement, interference, struggle, contradiction.
Ant. harmony, agreement.

clasp, *n.* **1.** brooch, pin, clip, hook, fastening, catch, hasp. **2.** embrace, hug, grasp. —*v.* **3.** clip. **4.** grasp, grip, clutch. **5.** embrace, hug, clutch, grasp, fold.

clean, *adj.* **1.** unsoiled, unstained, clear, unblemished, pure, flawless, spotless, unsullied, neat, immaculate. **2.** pure, purified, unmixed, unadulterated, clarified. **3.** uncontaminated, not radioactive. **4.** clear, readable, legible. **5.** unsullied, undefiled, moral, innocent, upright, honorable, chaste. **6.** neat, trim, shapely, graceful, delicate, light. **7.** adroit, deft, dextrous. **8.** complete, perfect, entire, whole, unabated, unimpaired. —*adv.* **9.** cleanly, neatly. **10.** wholly, completely, perfectly, entirely, altogether, fully, thoroughly, in all respects, out and out. —*v.* **11.** scour, scrub, sweep, brush, wipe, mop, dust, wash, rinse, lave, cleanse, deterge, purify, clear; decontaminate.
Ant. dirty, contaminated; radioactive; impure, immoral; clumsy, awkward.

cleanse, *v.* clean.
Ant. soil.

clear, *adj.* **1.** unclouded, light, bright, pellucid, limpid, diaphanous, crystalline, transparent, luminous. **2.** bright, shining, lucent. **3.** perceptible, understood, distinct, intelligible, orotund, comprehensible, lucid, plain, perspicuous, conspicuous, obvious. **4.** distinct, evident, plain, obvious, apparent, manifest, palpable, patent, unmistakable, unequivocal, unambiguous, indisputable, undeniable, unquestionable. **5.** convinced, certain, positive, definite, assured, sure. **6.** innocent, pure, not guilty, unsullied, irreproachable, unblemished, clean, unspotted, unadulterated, moral, undefiled, virtuous, immaculate, spotless. **7.** serene, calm, untroubled, fair, cloudless, sunny. **8.** unobstructed, open, free, unimpeded, unhindered, unhampered, unencumbered, unentangled. **9.** smooth, clean, even, regular, unblemished. **10.** emptied, empty, free, rid. **11.** limitless, unlimited, unqualified, unequivocal, boundless, free, open. **12.** net. —*adv.* **13.** clearly. —*v.* **14.** clarify, purify, refine, clean, cleanse. **15.** acquit, absolve, exonerate, vindicate, excuse, justify. **16.** extricate, disentangle, disabuse, rid, disencumber, disengage. **17.** liberate, free, emancipate, set free, disenthrall, loose, unchain, unfetter, let go.
Ant. cloudy, dim, obscure; indistinct, unclear; equivocal, doubtful; guilty, culpable; troubled, disturbed, perturbed, obstructed; limited, confined.

clearly, *adv.* definitely, distinctly, evidently, plainly, understandably, obviously, certainly, surely, assuredly, entirely, completely, totally.
Ant. confusedly, indefinitely; partly.

cleft, *n.* split, fissure, crack, crevice, cleaving, cleavage, rift, breach, break, fracture, cranny, gap, chasm.

Ant. joint, link.

clemency, *n.* mildness, mercy, lenience, leniency, forbearance, compassion, tenderness, kindness, kindliness, gentleness, mercifulness.
Ant. severity, austerity, cruelty, mercilessness.

clever, *adj.* **1.** bright, quick, able, apt, smart, intelligent, expert, gifted, talented, ingenious, quick-witted. **2.** skillful, adroit, dextrous, nimble, agile, handy.
Ant. dull, slow, dimwitted; clumsy, awkward, maladroit.

climb, *v.* **1.** mount, ascend, scale, surmount. **2.** rise, arise. **—***n.* **3.** ascent, climbing, scaling, rise.
Ant. descend; descent.

cloister, *n.* monastery, nunnery, convent, abbey, priory.

close, *v.* **1.** stop, obstruct, shut, block, bar, stop up, clog, choke. **2.** enclose, cover in, shut in. **3.** bring together, join, unite. **4.** end, terminate, finish, conclude, cease, complete. **5.** terminate, conclude, cease, end. **6** come together, unite, coalesce, join. **7.** grapple, fight. **—***adj.* **8.** shut, tight, closed, fast, confined. **9.** enclosed, shut in. **10.** heavy, unventilated, muggy, oppressive, uncomfortable, dense, thick. **11.** secretive, reticent, taciturn, close-mouthed, silent, uncommunicative, incommunicative, reserved, withdrawn. **12.** parsimonious, stingy, tight, closefisted, penurious, niggardly, miserly, mean. **13.** scarce, rare. **14.** compact, condensed, dense, thick, solid, compressed, firm. **15.** near, nearby, adjoining, adjacent, neighboring, immediate **16.** intimate, confidential, attached, dear, devoted. **17.** strict, searching, minute, scrupulous, exact, exacting, accurate, precise, faithful, nice. **18.** intent, fixed, assiduous, intense, concentrated, earnest, constant, unremitting, relentless, unrelenting. **—***n.* **19.** end, termination, conclusion. **20.** junction, union, coalescence, joining.
Ant. open.

clothes, *n.* clothing, attire, raiment, dress, garments, vesture, habit, costume, garb, vestments, habiliments, accouterments.

cloud, *n.* **1.** fog, haze, mist, vapor. **2.** host, crowd, throng, multitude, swarm, horde, army. **—***v.* **3.** becloud, bedim, shadow, overshadow, obscure, shade.
Ant. clarify.

cloudy, *adj.* **1.** overcast, shadowy, clouded, murky, lowering, gloomy, cloudy, dismal, depressing, sullen **2.** obscure, indistinct, dim, blurred, blurry, unclear, befogged, muddled, confused, dark, turbid, muddy, opaque.
Ant. clear; distinct.

club, *n.* **1.** stick, cudgel, bludgeon, blackjack, billy; bat. **2.** society, organization, association, circle, set, coterie, clique, fraternity, sorority.

clumsy, *adj.* **1.** awkward, unskillful, ungainly, lumbering, ungraceful, lubberly. **2.** unhandy, maladroit,

unskillful, inexpert, bungling, ponderous, heavy, heavy-handed, inept.
Ant. adroit, clever, dexterous.

coarse, *adj.* **1.** impure, base, common, inferior, faulty, crude, rude, rough. **2.** indelicate, unpolished, uncivil, impolite, gruff, bluff, boorish, churlish. **3.** gross, broad, indecent, vulgar, crass, ribald, lewd, lascivious, amoral, immoral, dirty.
Ant. pure, refined; civil, civilized, cultivated; decent, decorous.

coast, *n.* shore, seashore, strand, beach, seaside, seacoast, littoral.

coax, *v.* wheedle, cajole, beguile, inveigle, persuade, flatter.
Ant. force, bully; deter.

coherence, *n.* **1.** cohesion, union, connection. **2.** connection, congruity, consistency, correspondence, harmony, harmoniousness, agreement, unity, rationality.
Ant. incoherence.

cold, *adj.* **1.** chilly, chill, cool, frigid, gelid, frozen, freezing. **2.** dead. **3.** impassionate, unemotional, unenthusiastic, passionless, apathetic, unresponsive, unsympathetic, unaffected, stoical, phlegmatic, unfeeling, unsusceptible, unimpressible, unimpressed, cool, sluggish, torpid, indifferent, cold-blooded, unconcerned, heartless, unperturbed, imperturbable. **4.** polite, formal, reserved, unresponsive, unfriendly, inimical, hostile. **5.** calm, deliberate, depressing, dispiriting, disheartening, uninspiring, spiritless, unaffecting, dull. **6.** faint, weak. **7.** bleak, raw, cutting, nipping, arctic, polar, frosty, icy, wintry, chill, chilly. —*n.* **8.** chill, shivers, ague.
Ant. warm, hot.

collect, *v.* gather, assemble, amass, accumulate, aggregate, scrape together.
Ant. strew, broadcast, spread.

collection, *n.* **1.** set, accumulation, mass, heap, pile, hoard, store, aggregation. **2.** contribution, alms.

colloquial, *adj.* conversational, informal.
Ant. formal.

column, *n.* pillar, shaft, stele, pilaster.

combat, *v.* **1.** fight, contend, battle, oppose, struggle, contest, war, resist, withstand. —*n.* **2.** fight, skirmish, contest, battle, struggle, conflict, war, brush, affair, encounter, engagement.
Ant. support, defend.

combination, *n.* **1.** conjunction, association, union, connection, coalescence, blending. **2.** composite, compound, mixture, amalgamation, amalgam. **3.** alliance, confederacy, federation, union, league, coalition, association, society, club; cartel, combine, monopoly; conspiracy, cabal.

combine, *v.* **1.** unite, join, conjoin, associate, coalesce, blend, mix, incorporate, involve, compound, amalgamate. —*n.* **2.** combination (def. 3.).
Ant. dissociate, separate.

comfort, *v.* **1.** soothe, console, relieve, ease, cheer, pacify, calm, solace, gladden, refresh. **—*n.* 2.** relief, consolation, solace, encouragement.
Ant. agitate, discommode, incommode; discomfort, discouragement.

command, *v.* **1.** order, direct, bid, demand, charge, instruct, enjoin, require. **2.** govern, control, oversee, manage, rule, lead, preside over; dominate, overlook. **3.** exact, compel, secure, demand, require, claim. **—*n.* 4.** order, direction, bidding, injunction, charge, mandate, behest, commandment, requisition, requirement, instruction, dictum. **5.** control, mastery, disposal, ascendency, rule, sway, superintendence, power, management, domination.
Ant. obey.

commence, *v.* begin, open, start, originate, inaugurate, enter upon *or* into.
Ant. end, finish, terminate.

commend, *v.* **1.** recommend, laud, praise, extol, applaud, eulogize. **2.** entrust.
Ant. censure, blame; distrust.

commendation, *n.* **1.** recommendation, praise, approval, approbation, applause; medal. **2.** eulogy, encomium, panegyric, praise.
Ant. censure, blame.

comment, *n.* **1.** explanation, elucidation, expansion, criticism, critique, note, addendum, annotation, exposition, commentary. **2.** remark, observation, criticism. **—*v.* 3.** remark, explain, annotate, criticize.

commerce, *n.* **1.** interchange, traffic, trade, dealing, exchange, business. **2.** intercourse, conversation, converse, intimacy.

commercial, *adj.* **1.** mercantile, trafficking. **—*n.* 2.** advertisement.

common, *adj.* **1.** mutual. **2.** joint, united. **3.** public, communal. **4.** notorious. **5.** widespread, general, ordinary, universal, prevalent, popular. **6.** familiar, usual, customary, frequent, habitual, everyday. **7.** hackneyed, trite, stale, commonplace. **8.** mean, low, mediocre, inferior. **9.** coarse, vulgar, ordinary, undistinguished, ill-bred.
Ant. exceptional, singular, extraordinary, separate; unfamiliar, strange.

commonplace, *adj.* **1.** ordinary, uninteresting. **2.** trite, hackneyed, common, banal, stereotyped. **—*n.* 3.** cliché, bromide.
Ant. extraordinary, original.

commotion, *n.* **1.** tumult, disturbance, perturbation, agitation, disorder, pother, bustle, ado, turmoil, turbulence, riot, violence. **2.** sedition, insurrection, uprising, revolution.
Ant. peace, calm, serenity.

communicate, *v.* **1.** impart, transmit; give, bestow. **2.** divulge, announce, declare, disclose, reveal, make known.
Ant. withhold, conceal.

community, *n.* **1.** hamlet, town, village, city. **2.** public, commonwealth, society. **3.** agreement, identity, similarity, likeness. *—adj.* **4.** common, joint, cooperative.

compact, *adj.* **1.** dense, solid, firm, tightly packed, condensed. **2.** concise, pithy, terse, laconic, short, sententious, succinct, brief, pointed, meaningful. *—v.* **3.** condense, consolidate, compress. **4.** stabilize, solidify. *—n.* **5.** covenant, pact, contract, treaty, agreement, bargain, entente, arrangement, convention, concordat.
Ant. diverse, dispersed.

companion, *n.* **1.** associate, comrade, partner, fellow, mate. **2.** assistant; nurse, governess.

company, *n.* **1.** group, band, party, troop, assemblage, body, unit. **2.** companionship, fellowship, association, society. **3.** assembly, gathering, concourse, crowd, circle, set, congregation. **4.** firm, partnership, corporation, concern, house, syndicate, association.

compare, *v.* **1.** liken, contrast. **2.** vie, compete, equal, resemble.

compartment, *n.* division, section, apartment, cabin, roomette.

compassion, *n.* sorrow, pity, sympathy, feeling, ruth, mercy, commiseration, kindness, kindliness, tenderness, heart, tender-heartedness, clemency.
Ant. mercilessness, indifference.

compassionate, *adj.* pitying, sympathetic, tender, kind, merciful, tender-hearted, kindly, clement, gracious, benignant, gentle.
Ant. merciless, pitiless, harsh, cruel, mean.

compel, *v.* **1.** force, drive, coerce, constrain, oblige, commit, impel, motivate, necessitate. **2.** subdue, subject, bend, bow, overpower. **3.** unite, drive together, herd.
Ant. coax.

compensate, *v.* **1.** counterbalance, counterpoise, offset, countervail, make up for. **2.** remunerate, reward, pay, recompense, reimburse. **3.** atone, make amends.

compensation, *n.* **1.** recompense, remuneration, payment, amends, reparation, indemnity, reward. **2.** atonement, requital, satisfaction, indemnification.

compete, *v.* contend, vie, contest, rival, emulate, oppose, dispute, strive, cope, struggle.
Ant. support.

competent, *adj.* **1.** fitting, suitable, sufficient, convenient, adequate, qualified, fit, apt, capable, proficient. **2.** permissible, allowable,
Ant. incompetent, inapt.

competitor, *n.* opponent, contestant, rival, antagonist.
Ant. ally, friend.

complain, *v.* grumble, growl, murmur, whine, moan, bewail, lament, bemoan.

complement, *v.* **1.** complete, supplement, add to, round out. *—n.* **2.** supplement.

complete, *adj.* **1.** whole, entire, full, intact, unbroken,

unimpaired, undivided, one, perfect, developed, unabated, undiminished, fulfilled. **2.** finished, ended, concluded, consummated, done, consummate, perfect, thorough; through-and-through, dyed-in-the-wool. —*v.* **3.** finish, end, conclude, consummate, perfect, accomplish, do, fulfill, achieve, effect, terminate, close.
Ant. incomplete; unfinished; begin, commence, initiate.

complex, *adj.* **1.** compound, composite, complicated, mixed, mingled. **2.** involved, complicated, intricate, perplexing, tangled. —*n.* **3.** complexus, net, network, complication, web, tangle.
Ant. simple; simplex.

compliment, *n.* **1.** praise, commendation, admiration, tribute, honor, eulogy, encomium, panegyric. **2.** regard, respect, civility; flattery. —*v.* **3.** commend, praise, honor, flatter. **4.** congratulate, felicitate.
Ant. insult, injury; decry, disparage.

comply, *v.* acquiesce, obey, yield, conform, consent, assent, agree, accede, concede.
Ant. refuse.

component, *adj.* **1.** composing, constituent. —*n.* **2.** element, ingredient, part.
Ant. complex.

composed, *adj.* calm, tranquil, serene, undisturbed, peaceful, cool, placid, pacific, unruffled, sedate, unperturbed, self-possessed, controlled, imperturbable, quiet.
Ant. upset, perturbed, disturbed, disquieted.

composite, *adj., n.* compound, complex.
Ant. divers.

composure, *n.* serenity, calm, calmness, tranquillity, equability, peacefulness, quiet, coolness, equanimity, self-possession.
Ant. agitation.

comprehend, *v.* **1.** understand, conceive, know, grasp, see, discern, imagine, perceive. **2.** include, comprise, embrace, take in, embody, contain.

comprehensive, *adj.* comprehending, inclusive, broad, wide, large, extensive, sweeping.
Ant. limited.

compress, *v.* **1.** condense, squeeze, constrict, contract, press, crowd. —*n.* **2.** pad, bandage.
Ant. spread, stretch.

comprise, *v.* include, comprehend, contain, embrace, embody; consist *or* be composed of.
Ant. exclude.

compulsory, *adj.* **1.** compelling, coercive, constraining. **2.** compelled, forced, obligatory, arbitrary, binding, necessary, unavoidable, inescapable, ineluctable.
Ant. free, unrestrained, unrestricted.

compute, *v.* reckon, calculate, estimate, count, figure.

conceal, *v.* **1.** hide, secrete, cover, put away, bury, screen. **2.** keep secret, hide, disguise, dissemble.
Ant. reveal.

conceit, *n.* **1.** self-esteem, vanity, amour-propre, egotism, complacency. **2.** fancy, imagination, whim, notion, vagary; thought, idea, belief, conception.
Ant. humility, modesty.

conceited, *adj.* vain, proud, egotistical, self-important, self-satisfied, smug, complacent, self-sufficient.
Ant. humble, modest, shy, retiring.

conceive, *v.* **1.** imagine, create, ideate, think. **2.** understand, apprehend, comprehend.

concentrate, *v.* **1.** focus, condense. **2.** intensify, purify, clarify.
Ant. dissipate, disperse.

concern, *v.* **1.** affect, touch, interest, relate to, engage, involve, include. **2.** disquiet, trouble, disturb. —*n.* **3.** business, affair, interest, matter. **4.** solicitude, anxiety, care, worry, burden, responsibility. **5.** relation, bearing, appropriateness, consequence. **6.** firm, company, business, establishment, corporation, partnership, house.
Ant. exclude; calm; unconcern, indifference.

conciliate, *v.* **1.** placate, win over, soothe, propitiate, appease. **2.** reconcile, pacify.
Ant. alienate, antagonize.

conciseness, *n.* brevity, laconicism, summary, terseness, pithiness, sententiousness.
Ant. diversity.

conclusion, *n.* **1.** end, close, termination, completion, ending, finale. **2.** summing up, summation. **3.** result, issue, outcome. **4.** settlement, arrangement, wind-up. **5.** decision, judgment, determination. **6.** deduction, inference.
Ant. beginning, commencement.

concur, *v.* **1.** agree, consent, coincide, harmonize. **2.** cooperate, combine, help, conspire, contribute.
Ant. disagree.

condemn, *v.* **1.** blame, censure, disapprove. **2.** doom, find guilty, sentence, damn.
Ant. liberate, release, exonerate.

condense, *v.* compress, concentrate, consolidate, contract; abridge, epitomize, digest, shorten, abbreviate, reduce, diminish, curtail.
Ant. expand.

condescend, *v.* deign, stoop, descend, degrade oneself.

condition, *n.* **1.** state, case, situation, circumstance, conjuncture, circumstances. **2.** requisite, prerequisite, requirement, contingency, consideration, proviso, provision, stipulation, *sine qua non.* —*v.* **3.** determine, limit, restrict.

conduct, *n.* **1.** behavior, demeanor, action, actions, deportment, bearing, carriage, mien, manners. **2.** direction, management, execution, guidance, leadership, administration. **3.** guidance, escort, leadership, convoy, guard. —*v.* **4.** behave, deport, act, bear. **5.** direct, manage, carry on, supervise, regulate, administrate, administer, execute, guide, lead. **6.** lead, guide, escort, convoy.

confederation, *n.* alliance, confederacy, league, federation, union, coalition.

confer, *v.* **1.** bestow, give, donate, grant, vouchsafe, allow, promise. **2.** compare. **3.** consult together, discuss, deliberate, discourse, parley, converse, advise, talk.

conference, *n.* meeting, interview, parley, colloquy, convention, consultation.

confess, *v.* acknowledge, avow, own, admit, grant, concede; declare, aver, confirm.

confidence, *n.* **1.** trust, belief, faith, reliance, dependence. **2.** self-reliance, assurance, boldness, intrepidity, self-confidence, courage,
Ant. distrust, mistrust; modesty.

confident, *adj.* sure, bold, believing, assured, self-assured, certain, positive, convinced; brave, intrepid.
Ant. shy, modest, diffident.

confidential, *adj.* **1.** secret, restricted, private. **2.** familiar, trusted, trusty, trustworthy, faithful, honorable, honest.

confine, *v.* **1.** enclose, bound, circumscribe, circle, encircle, limit, bind, restrict. **2.** immure, imprison, incarcerate. —*n.* **3.** (*usually plural*) bounds, boundary, perimeter, periphery, limits; frontiers, borders.

confirm, *v.* **1.** make certain *or* sure, assure, corroborate, verify, substantiate, authenticate. **2.** make valid *or* binding, ratify, sanction, approve, validate, bind. **3.** make firm, strengthen, settle, establish, fix, assure.

conflict, *v.* **1.** collide, clash, oppose, vary with, interfere. **2.** contend, fight, combat, battle. —*n.* **3.** battle, struggle, encounter, contest, collision, fight; siege, strife; contention, controversy, opposition, variance. **4.** interference, discord, disunity, disharmony, inconsistency, antagonism.
Ant. harmony.

conform, *v.* **1.** comply, yield, agree, assent, harmonize. **2.** tally, agree, correspond, square. **3.** adapt, adjust, accommodate.
Ant. disagree, dissent.

confuse, *v.* **1.** jumble, disorder, disarrange, disturb, disarray. **2.** confound, mix, mix up, intermingle, mingle. **3.** perplex, mystify, nonplus, bewilder, astonish, surprise, disarm, shock, disconcert, embarrass, disturb. **4.** disconcert, abash, mortify, shame, confound.
Ant. enlighten.

confusion, *n.* **1.** perplexity, embarrassment, surprise, astonishment, shock, bewilderment, distraction. **2.** disorder, disarray, disarrangement, jumble, mess, turmoil, chaos, tumult, furor, commotion, ferment, agitation, stir. **3.** embarrassment, abashment, shamefacedness, shame, mortification.
Ant. enlightenment; clarity.

congenial, *adj.* sympathetic, kindred, similar, friend-

ly, favorable, genial; agreeable, pleasing, pleasant, complaisant, suited, adapted, well-suited, suitable, apt, proper.
Ant. unsympathetic, disagreeable; unsuitable.

congress, *n.* meeting, assembly, conference, council, convention.

conjecture, *n.* **1.** hypothesis, theory, guess, surmise, opinion, supposition, inference, deduction. —*v.* **2.** conclude, suppose, assume, presume, suspect, surmise, hypothesize, theorize, guess.
Ant. determine, ascertain.

conjoin, *v.* associate, unite, join, combine, connect.
Ant. disjoin, dissociate.

connect, *v.* join, unite, link, conjoin, couple, associate, combine; cohere.
Ant. disconnect, disjoin.

connection, *n.* **1.** junction, conjunction, union, joining, association, alliance, dependence, interdependence. **2.** link, yoke, connective, bond, tie, coupling. **3.** association, relationship, affiliation, affinity. **4.** circle, set, coterie, acquaintanceship. **5.** relation, relative, kinsman; kin, kith.
Ant. disjunction, dissociation.

conquer, *v.* **1.** win, gain. **2.** overcome, subdue, vanquish, overpower, overthrow, subjugate, defeat, master, subject, beat, rout, crush, reduce. **3.** surmount, overcome, overwhelm.
Ant. surrender, submit, give up, yield.

conquest, *n.* **1.** captivation, seduction, enchantment. **2.** vanquishment, victory, triumph. **3.** subjugation, overthrow, defeat, mastery, subjection, rout.
Ant. surrender.

conscientious, *adj.* just, upright, honest, straightforward, incorruptible, faithful, careful, particular, painstaking, scrupulous, exacting, demanding; devoted, dedicated.
Ant. dishonest, corrupt, unscrupulous.

conscious, *adj.* **1.** awake, aware, sentient, knowing, cognizant, percipient, intelligent. **2.** sensible, sensitive, felt; rational, reasoning. **3.** deliberate, intentional, purposeful.
Ant. unconscious.

consecrate, *v.* **1.** sanctify, hallow, venerate, elevate. **2.** devote, dedicate.
Ant. desecrate.

consecutive, *adj.* successive, continuous, regular, uninterrupted.
Ant. alternate, random.

consent, *v.* **1.** agree, assent, permit, allow, let, concur, yield, comply, accede, acquiesce. —*n.* **2.** assent, acquiescence, permission, compliance, concurrence, agreement. **3.** accord, concord, agreement, consensus.
Ant. refuse, disagree; dissent.

consequence, *n.* **1.** effect, result, outcome, issue, upshot, sequel, event, end. **2.** importance, significance, moment, weight, concern, interest. **3.** distinction, importance, singularity, weight.

consider, *v.* **1.** contemplate, meditate, reflect, ruminate, ponder, deliberate, weigh, revolve, study, think about. **2.** think, suppose, assume, presume. **3.** regard, respect, honor.
Ant. ignore.

considerate, *adj.* thoughtful, kind, charitable, patient, concerned, well-disposed.
Ant. inconsiderate.

consideration, *n.* **1.** considering, meditation, reflection, rumination, deliberation, contemplation, attention, advisement, regard. **2.** regard, account. **3.** recompense, payment, remuneration, fee, compensation, pay. **4.** thoughtfulness, sympathy, kindness, kindliness, patience, concern. **5.** importance, consequence, weight, significance, moment, interest. **6.** estimation, esteem, honor.

consistent, *adj.* **1.** agreeing, concordant, compatible, congruous, consonant, harmonious, suitable, apt, conformable, conforming. **2.** constant, faithful, assiduous, unwavering.
Ant. inconsistent.

consolation, *n.* comfort, solace, relief, encouragement.
Ant. discomfort, discouragement.

console, *v.* comfort, solace, cheer, encourage, soothe, relieve, calm.
Ant. aggravate, agitate, disturb.

consonant, *n.* **1.** sonorant, fricative, stop, continuant. —*adj.* **2.** in agreement, concordant, consistent, harmonious, compatible, congruous, conformant, suitable.
Ant. vowel; discordant, inconsistent.

conspicuous, *adj.* **1.** visible, manifest, noticeable, clear, marked, salient, discernible, perceptible, plain, open, apparent. **2.** prominent, outstanding, obvious, striking, noteworthy, attractive, eminent, distinguished, noted, celebrated, illustrious.
Ant. unclear, imperceptible; undistinguished, trifling.

conspire, *v.* **1.** complot, plot, intrigue, cabal, contrive, devise. **2.** combine, concur, cooperate.

constancy, *n.* firmness, fortitude, resolution, determination, inflexibility, decision, tenacity, steadfastness, faithfulness, fidelity, fealty, devotion, loyalty; regularity, stability, immutability, uniformity, permanence, sameness.
Ant. randomness, faithlessness, irregularity, instability.

constant, *adj.* **1.** invariable, uniform, stable, unchanging, fixed, immutable, invariable, unvarying, permanent. **2.** perpetual, unremitting, uninterrupted, continual, recurrent, assiduous, unwavering, unfailing, persistent, persevering, determined. **3.** steadfast, faithful, loyal, stanch, true, trusty, devoted, steady, resolute, firm, unshaking, unshakable, unwavering, unswerving, determined.

Ant. inconstant, variable, random, unstable, changeable; sporadic; unsteady, wavering.

consternation, *n.* amazement, dread, dismay, bewilderment, awe, alarm, terror, fear, panic, fright, horror.

Ant. composure, equanimity.

constrain, *v.* **1.** force, compel, oblige, coerce. **2.** confine, check, bind, restrain, curb.

Ant. liberate, free.

constrict, *v.* compress, contract, shrink, cramp, squeeze, bind, tighten.

Ant. unbind, untie.

construct, *v.* build, frame, form, devise, erect, make, fabricate, raise.

Ant. raze.

consult, *v.* confer, deliberate.

consume, *v.* **1.** destroy, expend, use up, use, exhaust, spend, waste, dissipate, squander, eat up, devour. **2.** be absorbed *or* engrossed.

consummate, *v.* **1.** complete, perfect, fulfill, accomplish, achieve, finish, effect, execute, do. *—adj.* **2.** complete, perfect, done, finished, effected, fulfilled, excellent, supreme.

Ant. imperfect, unfinished, base.

contagious, *adj.* **1.** communicable, infectious, catching. **2.** noxious, pestilential, poisonous, deadly, foul.

contain, *v.* hold, accommodate, include, embody, embrace.

contaminate, *v.* defile, pollute, sully, stain, soil, tarnish, taint, corrupt, befoul, besmirch, infect, poison, vitiate.

contemplate, *v.* **1.** look at, view, observe, regard, survey. **2.** consider, reflect upon, meditate on, study, ponder, deliberate, think about, revolve. **3.** intend, mean, purpose, design, plan.

contemplative, *adj.* reflective, meditative, thoughtful, studious, musing.

Ant. inattentive.

contemporary, *adj.* coexisting, coeval, contemporaneous.

Ant. antecedent; succeeding.

contempt, *n.* **1.** scorn, disdain, derision, contumely. **2.** dishonor, disgrace, shame.

Ant. respect, reverence; honor.

contemptible, *adj.* despicable, mean, low, miserable, abject, base, vile.

Ant. splendid, admirable.

contemptuous, *adj.* disdainful, scornful, sneering, insolent, arrogant, supercilious, haughty.

Ant. humble, respectful.

contend, *v.* **1.** struggle, strive, fight, battle, combat, vie, compete, rival. **2.** debate, dispute, argue, wrangle. **3.** assert, maintain, claim.

content, *adj.* **1.** satisfied, contented, sanguine. **2.** assenting, acceding, resigned, willing, agreeable. *—v.* **3.** appease, gratify, satisfy.

Ant. dissatisfy.

contention, *n.* **1.** struggling, struggle, strife, discord, dissention, quarrel, disagreement, squabble, feud; rupture, break, falling out; opposition, combat, conflict, competition, rivalry, contest. **2.** disagreement, dissension, debate, wrangle, altercation, dispute, argument, controversy.

Ant. agreement.

contentment, *n.* happiness, satisfaction, content, ease.

Ant. misery.

contest, *n.* **1.** struggle, conflict, battle, combat, fight, encounter. **2.** competition, contention, rivalry, match, tournament, tourney, game. **3.** strife, dispute, controversy, debate, argument, altercation, quarrel, contention. **—***v.* **4.** struggle, fight, compete, contend, vie, combat, battle. **5.** argue against, dispute, controvert litigate, debate, oppose, contend against. **6.** doubt, question, challenge, dispute. **7.** rival, strive, compete, vie, contend for.

continual, *adj.* unceasing, incessant, ceaseless, uninterrupted, unremitting, constant, continuous, unbroken, successive, perpetual, unending, habitual, permanent, everlasting, eternal; recurrent, recurring, frequentative, repeated, repetitious, repetitive.

Ant. periodic, sporadic.

continue, *v.* **1.** keep on, go onward *or* forward, persist, persevere. **2.** last, endure, remain, persist. **3.** remain, abide, tarry, stay, rest. **4.** persist in, extend, perpetuate, prolong, carry on, maintain, retain; carry over, postpone, adjourn.

Ant. cease, interrupt.

contract, *n.* **1.** agreement, compact, bargain, covenant, arrangement, pact, convention, concordat, treaty, stipulation. **—***v.* **2.** draw together, compress, concentrate, condense, reduce, lessen, shorten, narrow, shrivel, shrink. **3.** elide, abbreviate, apocopate, abridge, epitomize.

Ant. disperse, spread.

contradict, *v.* deny, gainsay, dispute, controvert, impugn, challenge, assail.

Ant. corroborate, support.

contradictory, *adj.* contrary, opposed, opposite, opposing, antagonistic, irreconcilable, paradoxical, inconsistent, contrary.

Ant. corroborative.

contrary, *adj.* **1.** opposite, opposed, contradictory, conflicting, discordant, counter, opposing. **2.** untoward, unfavorable, adverse, unfriendly, hostile, oppugnant, antagonistic, disagreeable, irreconcilable. **3.** perverse, self-willed, intractable, obstinate, refractory, headstrong, stubborn, pig-headed, contumacious.

Ant. obliging, compliant, tractable.

contrast, *v.* **1.** oppose, compare, differentiate, discriminate, distinguish, set off. **—***n.* **2.** opposition, comparison, differentiation, difference, discrimination, contrariety.

contrive, *v.* plan, devise, invent, design, hatch, brew, concoct, form, make; plot, complot, conspire, scheme; manage, effect.

control, *v.* **1.** dominate, command, manage, govern, rule, direct, reign over. **2.** check, curb, hinder, restrain, bridle, constrain. **3.** test, verify, prove. *—n.* **4.** regulation, domination, command, management, direction, government, rule, reign, sovereignty, mastery, superintendence.

controversy, *n.* dispute, contention, debate, disputation, disagreement, altercation; quarrel, wrangle, argument.
Ant. concord, agreement, accord.

convene, *v.* **1.** assemble, meet, congregate, collect, gather. **2.** convoke, summon.
Ant. disperse, adjourn.

convenient, *adj.* **1.** suited, fit, appropriate, suitable, adapted, serviceable, well-suited, favorable, easy, comfortable, agreeable, helpful, advantageous, useful. **2.** at hand, accessible, handy.
Ant. inconvenient.

convention, *n.* **1.** assembly, conference, convocation, meeting. **2.** agreement, contract, compact, pact, treaty. **3.** agreement, consent. **4.** custom, precedent.

conventional, *adj.* **1.** formal, conforming, conformant. **2.** accepted, usual, habitual, customary, regular, common.
Ant. unconventional, unusual.

conversant, *adj.* **1.** familiar, versed, learned, skilled, practiced, well-informed, proficient. **2.** acquainted, associating.
Ant. unfamiliar, ignorant.

converse, *v.* **1.** talk, chat, speak, discuss, confabulate. *—n.* **2.** discourse, talk, conversation, discussion, colloquy. **3.** opposite, reverse, transformation.

convert, *v.* **1.** change, transmute, transform, proselyte, proselytize. *—n.* **2.** proselyte, neophyte, disciple.
Ant. renegade, recreant.

convey, *v.* **1.** carry, transport, bear, bring, transmit, lead, conduct. **2.** communicate, impart.

convince, *v.* persuade, satisfy.

convoy, *v.* **1.** accompany, escort, attend. *—n.* **2.** escort, guard, attendance, protection.
Ant. desert.

cool, *adj.* **1.** cold. **2.** calm, unexcited, unmoved, deliberate, composed, collected, self-possessed, unruffled, sedate, undisturbed, placid, quiet, dispassionate, unimpassioned. **3.** frigid, distant, superior, chilling, freezing, apathetic, repellent. **4.** indifferent, lukewarm, unconcerned, cold-blooded. **5.** audacious, impudent, shameless. *—v.* **6.** allay, calm, moderate, quiet, temper, assuage, abate, dampen.
Ant. warm, tepid, lukewarm, hot.

copious, *adj.* abundant, large, ample, plentiful, overflowing, profuse, rich, full, plenteous.
Ant. scarce, scanty, meager.
copy, *n.* **1.** transcript, reproduction, imitation, carbon, duplicate, facsimile. **2.** original, manuscript, pattern, model, archetype. —*v.* **3.** imitate, duplicate, transcribe.
Ant. original.
corporal, *adj.* corporeal, bodily, physical, material.
Ant. spiritual.
corpse, *n.* body, remains, carcass.
correct, *v.* **1.** set right, rectify, amend, emend, reform, remedy, cure. **2.** admonish, warn, rebuke, discipline, chasten, punish, castigate. —*adj.* **3.** factual, truthful, accurate, proper, precise, exact, faultless, perfect, right, true.
Ant. ruin, spoil; incorrect, wrong.
correspond, *v.* **1.** conform, agree, harmonize, accord, match, tally, concur, coincide, fit, suit. **2.** communicate.
Ant. differ, diverge.
corrode, *v.* **1.** eat, gnaw, consume, erode, wear away. **2.** impair, deteriorate. **3.** canker, rust, crumble.
corrupt, *adj.* **1.** dishonest, venal, false, untrustworthy, bribable. **2.** debased, depraved, base, perverted, wicked, sinful, evil, dissolute, profligate, abandoned, reprobate. **3.** putrid, impure, putrescent, rotten, contaminated, adulterated, tainted, corrupted, spoiled, infected. —*v.* **4.** bribe, lure, entice, demoralize, lead astray. **5.** pervert, deprave, debase, vitiate. **6.** infect, taint, pollute, contaminate, adulterate, spoil, defile, putrefy.
Ant. honest; honorable; pure, unspoiled, unadulterated; purify.
corruption, *n.* **1.** perversion, depravity, abandon, dissolution, sinfulness, evil, immorality, wickedness, profligacy. **2.** dishonesty, baseness, bribery. **3.** decay, rot, putrefaction, putrescence, foulness, pollution, defilement, contamination, adulteration.
Ant. righteousness; honesty; purity.
cost, *n.* **1.** price, charge, expense, expenditure, outlay. **2.** sacrifice, loss, penalty, damage, detriment, suffering, pain.
costly, *adj.* valuable, dear, high-priced, sumptuous, expensive, precious, rich, splendid.
Ant. cheap.
coterie, *n.* society, association, set, circle, clique, club, brotherhood, fraternity.
cottage, *n.* cabin, lodge, hut, shack, cot, shanty.
Ant. palace, castle.
counsel, *n.* **1.** advice, opinion, instruction, suggestion, recommendation, caution, warning, admonition. **2.** consultation, deliberation, forethought. **3.** purpose, plan, design, scheme. **4.** lawyer, solicitor, barrister, advocate, counselor, adviser.
countenance, *n.* **1.** aspect, appearance, look, expres-

sion, mien. **2.** face, visage, physiognomy. **3.** favor, encouragement, aid, assistance, support, patronage, sanction, approval, approbation. —*v.* **4.** favor, encourage, support, aid, assist, abet, patronize, sanction, approve.
Ant. condemn, prohibit.

counteract, *v.* neutralize, counterbalance, annul, countervail, offset, contravene, thwart, oppose, resist, hinder, check, frustrate, defeat.
Ant. cooperate.

counterfeit, *adj.* **1.** spurious, false, fraudulent, forged. **2.** sham, pretended, feigned, simulated, fraudulent, false, mock, fake, unreal, ersatz. —*n.* **3.** imitation, forgery, falsification, sham. —*v.* **4.** imitate, forge, copy, fake, falsify. **5.** resemble. **6.** simulate, feign, sham, pretend. **7.** feign, dissemble.
Ant. genuine.

countryman, *n.* **1.** compatriot, fellow citizen. **2.** native, inhabitant. **3.** rustic, farmer, peasant, husbandman.
Ant. alien, foreigner.

couple, *n.* **1.** pair, duo, duet, yoke, brace, two, span. —*v.* **2.** fasten, link, join, unite, associate, pair, conjoin, connect.
Ant. separate, disjoin.

courage, *n.* fearlessness, dauntlessness, intrepidity, fortitude, pluck, spirit, heroism, daring, audacity, bravery, mettle, valor, hardihood, bravado, gallantry, chivalry.
Ant. cowardice.

course, *n.* **1.** advance, direction, bearing. **2.** path, route, channel, way, road, track, passage. **3.** progress, passage, process. **4.** process, career, race. **5.** conduct, behavior, deportment. **6.** method, mode, procedure. **7.** sequence, succession, order, turn, regularity. **8.** range, row, series, layer, order. —*v.* **9.** chase, pursue, follow, hunt. **10.** run, race.

courteous, *adj.* civil, polite, well-mannered, well-bred, urbane, debonair, affable, gracious, courtly, respectful, obliging.
Ant. discourteous, rude, curt, brusque.

cover, *v.* **1.** overlay, overspread, envelop, enwrap, clothe, invest. **2.** shelter, protect, shield, guard, defend. **3.** hide, screen, cloak, conceal, disguise, secrete, veil, shroud, mask, enshroud. **4.** include, comprise, provide for, take in, embrace, contain, embody, comprehend. **5.** suffice, defray, offset, compensate for, counterbalance. —*n.* **6.** lid, top, case, covering, tegument, integument. **7.** protection, shelter, asylum, refuge, concealment, guard, defense. **8.** woods, underbrush, covert, shrubbery, growth, thicket, copse. **9.** veil, screen, disguise, mask, cloak.
Ant. uncover; exposure.

covet, *v.* desire, envy, long for.
Ant. relinquish, renounce.

coward, *n.* **1.** poltroon, cad, dastard, milksop. **—***adj.* **2.** timid, cowardly.

cowardice, *n.* poltroonery, dastardliness, pusillanimity, timidity.
Ant. boldness, bravery, temerity.

cowardly, *adj.* craven, poltroon, dastardly, pusillanimous, recreant, timid, timorous, faint-hearted, white-livered, lily-livered, chicken-hearted, yellow, fearful, afraid, scared.
Ant. brave, bold, valiant.

coxcomb, *n.* dandy, fop, dude, exquisite, beau, popinjay, jackanapes.

coy, *adj.* retiring, diffident, shy, self-effacing, bashful, modest, shrinking, timid, demure.
Ant. bold, pert, brazen, arch.

crack, *v.* **1.** snap. **2.** break, snap, split; crackle, craze. **—***n.* **3.** snap, report. **4.** break, flaw, split, fissure, cleft, chink, breach, crevice, cranny, interstice.

craft, *n.* **1.** skill, ingenuity, dexterity, talent, ability, aptitude, expertness. **2.** skill, art, artfulness, craftiness, subtlety, artifice, cunning, deceit, guile, shrewdness, deceitfulness, deception. **3.** handicraft, trade, art, vocation, metier, calling. **4.** boat, vessel, ship; aircraft, airplane, plane.

craftsman, *n.* artisan, artificer, mechanic, handicraftsman, workman.
Ant. bungler, shoemaker.

crafty, *adj.* skillful, sly, cunning, deceitful, artful, wily, insidious, tricky, designing, scheming, plotting, arch, shrewd.
Ant. gullible, naive.

cram, *v.* stuff, crowd, pack, compress, squeeze, overcrowd, gorge, glut, press.

cranky, *adj.* **1.** ill-tempered, cross, crotchety, cantankerous, perverse. **2.** eccentric, queer, odd, strange, peculiar, curious. **3.** shaky, unsteady, loose, disjointed, out of order, broken. **4.** bent, twisted, crooked.
Ant. amiable, good-natured; firm; solid.

crash, *v.* **1.** break, shatter, shiver, splinter, dash, smash. **—***n.* **2.** falling, collapse, depression, failure, ruin.

crave, *v.* **1.** long for, desire, want, yearn *or* hunger for. **2.** require, need. **3.** beg for, beseech, entreat, implore, solicit, supplicate.
Ant. relinquish, renounce.

craven, *adj.* cowardly.
Ant. brave, bold, intrepid, fearless.

crazy, *adj.* **1.** demented, insane, mad, deranged, crazed, lunatic, cracked. **2.** rickety, shaky, tottering, doddering, loose. **3.** weak, infirm, confused, impaired.
Ant. sane, well-balanced; firm; strong.

create, *v.* **1.** produce, originate, invent, cause, occasion. **2.** make, constitute.

credit, *n.* **1.** belief, trust, confidence, faith, reliance, credence. **2.** influence, authority, power. **3.** trust-

worthiness, credibility. **4.** repute, estimation, character; reputation, name, esteem, regard, standing, position, rank, condition; notoriety. **5.** commendation, honor, merit. **6.** acknowledgment, ascription. —*v.* **7.** believe, trust, confide in, have faith in, rely upon.
Ant. discredit.

creditable, *adj.* praiseworthy, meritorious, estimable, reputable, honorable, respectable.
Ant. disreputable, dishonorable.

credulous, *adj.* believing, trusting, trustful, unsuspecting, gullible.
Ant. incredulous, cautious, wary.

crime, *n.* offense, wrong, sin; infraction, violation, breach, misdemeanor, tort, felony: trespassing, breaking and entering, theft, robbery, assault, battery, statutory rape, rape, embezzlement, slander, libel, treason, manslaughter, murder.

criminal, *adj.* **1.** felonious, unlawful, illegal, nefarious, flagitious, iniquitous, wicked, sinful, wrong. —*n.* **2.** convict, malefactor, evildoer, transgressor, sinner, culprit, delinquent, offender, felon; crook, hoodlum, gangster.

cripple, *v.* disable, maim, weaken, impair, break down, ruin, destroy.

crisis, *n.* climax, juncture, exigency, strait, pinch, emergency.

criterion, *n.* standard, rule, principle, measure, parameter, touchstone, test, proof.

critic, *n.* **1.** reviewer, censor, judge, connoisseur. **2.** censurer, carper, faultfinder.

critical, *adj.* **1.** captious, carping, censorious, faultfinding, caviling, severe. **2.** discriminating, tasteful, judicial, fastidious, nice, exact, precise. **3.** decisive, climacteric, crucial, determining, momentous, important. **4.** dangerous, perilous, risky, suspenseful, hazardous, precarious, ticklish.
Ant. unimportant, superficial, trivial.

criticism, *n.* **1.** censure, faultfinding, stricture, animadversion, reflection. **2.** review, critique, comment.

crooked, *adj.* **1.** bent, curved, winding, devious, sinuous, flexuous, serpentine. **2.** deformed, misshapen, disfigured, twisted, awry, askew, crippled. **3.** dishonest, unscrupulous, knavish, tricky, fraudulent, dishonorable, unlawful, illegal, deceitful, insidious, crafty, treacherous.
Ant. straight; honest, upright.

crop, *n.* **1.** harvest, produce, yield. **2.** craw, stomach. —*v.* **3.** cut, cut short, clip, lop, mow.

cross, *n.* **1.** opposing, thwarting, opposition, frustration. **2.** trouble, misfortune, misery, burden. —*v.* **3.** intersect, traverse. **4.** oppose, thwart, frustrate, baffle, contradict, foil. **5.** interbreed, mongrelize. —*adj.* **6.** petulant, fractious, irascible, waspish, crabbed, cranky, curmudgeonly, churlish, sulky, cantankerous, ill-natured, peevish, sullen, ill-tempered, in-

temperate, impatient, complaining, snappish, irritable, fretful, moody, touchy, testy, unpleasant, unkind, mean, angry, spiteful, resentful, gloomy, glowering, morose, sour.
Ant. supporting; aid, support; complaisant, amenable, agreeable, sweet.

crowd, *n.* **1.** throng, multitude, swarm, company, host, horde, herd. **2.** masses, proletariat, plebians, rabble, mob, people, populace. *—v.* **3.** assemble, throng, swarm, flock together, herd. **4.** push, shove, cram, pack, press, squeeze, cramp, force.

crude, *adj.* **1.** unrefined, unfinished, unprepared, coarse, raw. **2.** unripe, immature, undeveloped. **3.** unpolished, unfinished, incomplete, coarse, boorish, uncouth, rough, rude, clumsy, awkward. **4.** undisguised, blunt, bare, rough, direct.
Ant. refined; aged, mature, ripe; complete, perfect; indirect, subtle.

cruel, *adj.* **1.** barbarous, bloodthirsty, sanguinary, ferocious, fell, merciless, unmerciful, relentless, implacable, pitiless, distressing, ruthless, truculent, brutal, savage, inhuman, brutish, barbarian, unmoved, unfeeling, unrelenting. **2.** severe, hard, bitter.
Ant. kind, benevolent, beneficial.

cruelty, *n.* harshness, brutality, ruthlessness, barbarity, inhumanity, atrocity.
Ant. kindness, benevolence.

crush, *v.* **1.** squeeze, press, bruise, crumple, rumple, wrinkle, compress. **2.** break, shatter, pulverize, granulate, powder, mash, smash, crumble, disintegrate. **3.** put down, quell, overpower, subdue, overwhelm, overcome, quash, conquer, oppress.

cry, *v.* **1.** lament, grieve, weep, bawl, sorrow, sob, shed tears, bewail, bemoan, squall, blubber, whimper, mewl, pule, wail. **2.** call, shout, yell, yowl, scream, exclaim, ejaculate, clamor, roar, bellow, vociferate. **3.** yelp, bark, bellow, hoot. *—n.* **4.** shout, scream, wail, shriek, screech, yell, yowl, roar, whoop, bellow. **5.** exclamation, outcry, clamor, ejaculation. **6.** entreaty, appeal. **7.** proclamation, announcement. **8.** weeping, lament, lamentation, tears.
Ant. laugh.

crying, *adj.* **1.** weeping, wailing. **2.** flagrant, notorious, demanding, urgent, important, great, enormous.
Ant. laughing; nugatory, trifling.

cunning, *n.* **1.** ability, skill, adroitness, expertness. **2.** craftiness, skillfulness, shrewdness, artfulness, wiliness, trickery, finesse, intrigue, artifice, guile, craft, deceit, deceitfulness, slyness, deception. *—adj.* **3.** ingenious, skillful. **4.** artful, wily, tricky, foxy, crafty.
Ant. stupidity, inability; dullness; naive, gullible, dull.

curb, *n.* **1.** restraint, check, control, bridle, rein, checkrein. *—v.* **2.** control, restrain, check, bridle, repress.
Ant. encourage, further, foster.

cure, *n.* **1.** remedy, restorative, specific, antidote. *—v.*

2. remedy, restore, heal, make well *or* whole, mend, repair, correct.

curious, *adj.* **1.** inquisitive, inquiring, prying, spying, peeping, meddlesome, interested. **2.** strange, novel, unusual, singular, rare, foreign, exotic, queer, extraordinary, unique.
Ant. blasé; common, commonplace, usual, customary.

current, *adj.* **1.** present, prevailing, prevalent, general, common, circulating, widespread, popular, rife. **2.** accepted, stylish, in vogue, *à la mode,* fashionable. **—*n.*** **3.** stream, river, tide, course, progress, progression.
Ant. outmoded, uncommon, unpopular.

curse, *n.* **1.** imprecation, execration, fulmination, malediction, oath, denunciation, anathema, ban. **2.** evil, misfortune, calamity, trouble, vexation, annoyance, affliction, torment, bane, thorn, plague, scourge. **—*v.*** **3.** blaspheme, swear, imprecate, execrate, fulminate, damn, denunciate, accurse, maledict, anathematize, denounce, condemn, profane, excommunicate. **4.** doom, destroy, plague, scourge, afflict, trouble, vex, annoy.
Ant. blessing, benediction.

cursed, *adj.* **1.** damned, accursed, banned, blighted. **2.** execrable, damnable, hateful, abominable, villainous.
Ant. blessed.

curt, *adj.* **1.** short, shortened, brief, abbreviated, concise, laconic, blunt, terse. **2.** rude, snappish, abrupt, dry.
Ant. long, drawn-out, lengthy; courteous, courtly.

curtail, *v.* lessen, diminish, decrease, dock, shorten, abbreviate, blunt, abridge.
Ant. extend, expand.

curtain, *n.* **1.** drape, drapery, hanging, portière, lambrequin, valance, blind, shade, shutter, shutters. **2.** cover, concealment.
Ant. window.

cushion, *n.* **1.** pillow, bolster, pad; shock-absorber. **—*v.*** **2.** absorb, check, slow, alleviate, meliorate.

custody, *n.* **1.** keeping, guardianship, care, custodianship, charge, safekeeping, watch, preserving, protection, preservation; possession, ownership, mastery, holding. **2.** imprisonment, confinement.

custom, *n.* **1.** habit, practice, usage, procedure, rule. **2.** rule, convention, form, observance, formality. **3.** tax, duty, impost, tribute, toll. **4.** patronage, customers, patrons, clientele.

customary, *adj.* usual, habitual, wonted, accustomed, conventional, common, regular.
Ant. unusual, rare, uncommon, irregular.

cut, *v.* **1.** gash, slash, slit, lance, pierce, penetrate, incise, wound. **2.** wound, hurt, move, touch, slight, insult. **3.** divide, sever, carve, cleave, sunder, bisect, chop, hack, hew, fell, saw. **4.** lop off, crop. **5.** reap, mow, harvest. **6.** clip, shear, pare, prune. **7.** cross, intersect, transect. **8.** abridge, edit, shorten, abbreviate, curtail. **9.** lower, lessen, reduce, diminish. **10.** dissolve, dilute, thin, water, water down. **11.** facet, make, fashion. **12.** hollow out, excavate, dig. —*n.* **13.** incision, wound, slash, gash, slit; channel, passage, strait. **14.** style, fashion, mode, kind, sort.

cutting, *n.* **1.** root, shoot, leaf, branch, limb. —*adj.* **2.** sharp, keen, incisive, trenchant, piercing. **3.** mordant, mordacious, caustic, biting, acid, wounding, sarcastic, sardonic, bitter, severe.
Ant. dull; kind.

cynical, *adj.* distrustful, pessimistic, sarcastic, satirical, unbelieving, disbelieving, sneering, contemptuous, derisive, cutting, scornful, ridiculing, censorious, captious, waspish, petulant, testy, fretful, touchy, cross, surly, ill-tempered, ill-natured, crusty, cantankerous.
Ant. optimistic, hopeful; good-natured, calm, pleasant.

D

dainty, *adj.* **1.** delicate, beautiful, charming, exquisite, fine, elegant. **2.** toothsome, delicious, savory, palatable, tender, juicy, delectable, luscious. **3.** particular, fastidious, scrupulous. **4.** squeamish, finical, overnice. —*n.* **5.** delicacy, tidbit, sweetmeat.
Ant. clumsy, inelegant; disgusting, distasteful; sloppy.

dally, *v.* **1.** sport, play, trifle, fondle, toy, caress. **2.** waste time, loiter, delay, dawdle.
Ant. hasten, hurry.

damage, *n.* **1.** injury, harm, hurt, detriment, mischief, impairment, loss. —*v.* **2.** injure, harm, hurt, impair, mar.
Ant. improvement; improve, better.

damp, *adj.* **1.** moist, humid, dank, steamy, wet. —*n.* **2.** moisture, humidity, dankness, wet, wetness, dampness, fog, vapor, steam. **3.** dejection, depression, dispiritedness, chill, discouragement, check. —*v.* **4.** dampen, moisten, wet, humidify. **5.** check, retard, slow, inhibit, restrain, moderate, abate, allay, slow, interfere with. **6.** stifle, suffocate, extinguish.
Ant. dry, arid.

danger, *n.* hazard, risk, peril, jeopardy, liability, exposure; injury, evil.
Ant. security, safety.

dare, *v.* venture, hazard, risk, brave, challenge, defy, endanger.

daring, *n.* **1.** courage, adventurousness, boldness, bravery, audacity, intrepidity, heroism. —*adj.* **2.** courageous, venturesome, adventurous, bold, brave, audacious, dauntless, undaunted, intrepid, fearless, valiant, valorous, gallant, chivalrous, doughty, heroic.

Ant. cowardice; timid, cowardly, pusillanimous, fearful.

dark, *adj.* **1.** dim, gloomy, murky, umbrageous, shadowy, penumbral, dusky, unilluminated, unlit, sunless, shady, swarthy, black, pitchy, ebon, Cimmerian. **2.** gloomy, cheerless, dismal, sad, morose, morbid, disheartening, discouraging. **3.** sullen, frowning. **4.** unenlightened, ignorant, untaught, untutored, uneducated, unlettered, benighted, in the dark. **5.** obscure, recondite, abstruse, dim, incomprehensible, unintelligible, occult, cabalistic, mysterious, puzzling, enigmatic, enigmatical, mystic, mystical. **6.** hidden, secret, concealed. **7.** silent, reticent. **8.** infernal, wicked, sinful, nefarious, flagitious, foul, infamous, hellish, devilish, evil, bad, satanic.
Ant. light, fair; cheerful; pleasant; intelligent, educated; clear, intelligible; open, revealed; voluble; heavenly, godly.

dart, *n.* **1.** arrow, barb. **—***v.* **2.** spring, start, dash, bolt, rush, fly, shoot.

dash, *v.* **1.** strike, break; throw, thrust; splash, splatter. **2.** adulterate, mix, deteriorate, mingle. **3.** rush, dart, bolt, fly. **—***n.* **4.** pinch, bit, suggestion, soupçon, hint, touch, tinge, smack, sprinkle, sprinkling. **5.** vigor, spirit, élan, flourish, éclat.

daunt, *v.* **1.** intimidate, overawe, subdue, dismay, frighten, appall. **2.** discourage, dispirit, dishearten, thwart, frustrate.
Ant. encourage, actuate.

dauntless, *adj.* fearless, bold, undaunted, intrepid, brave, courageous, daring, indomitable, unconquerable, valiant, valorous, heroic, chivalrous, doughty, undismayed.
Ant. fearful, cowardly, timid, timorous.

dawn, *n.* **1.** daybreak, sunrise, dawning. **—***v.* **2.** appear, open, begin, break.
Ant. sunset; disappear.

dead, *adj.* **1.** deceased, lifeless, extinct, inanimate, defunct, departed. **2.** insensible, numb, unfeeling, indifferent, cool, cold, callous, obtuse, frigid, unsympathetic, apathetic, lukewarm. **3.** infertile, barren, sterile. **4.** still, motionless, inert, inoperative, useless, dull, inactive, unemployed. **5.** extinguished, out. **6.** complete, absolute, utter, entire, total. **7.** straight, direct, unerring, exact, precise, sure.
Ant. alive, live, animate; fervid, eager, warm, animated; fertile; partial; crooked, indirect, devious.

deadly, *adj.* **1.** fatal, lethal, mortal. **2.** implacable, sanguinary, murderous, bloodthirsty.

deal, *v.* **1.** act, behave. **2.** trade, do business, traffic. **3.** distribute, dole, mete, dispense, apportion, allot, give, assign. **—***n.* **4.** bargain, arrangement, pact, contract. **5.** quantity, amount, extent, degree. **6.** dealing, distribution, share.
Ant. gather, collect.

dear, *adj.* **1.** beloved, loved, precious, darling, esteemed. **2.** expensive, high-priced, costly, high; exorbitant.
Ant. hateful; cheap.

death, *n.* **1.** decease, demise, passing, departure. **2.** stop, cessation, surcease, estoppage, end, finale.
Ant. life.

debar, *v.* **1.** exclude, shut out. **2.** prevent, prohibit, hinder, interdict, outlaw.
Ant. include, welcome; encourage, support.

debase, *v.* **1.** adulterate, corrupt, vitiate, contaminate, pollute, defile, foul, befoul. **2.** lower, depress, reduce, impair, deteriorate, degrade, abase, demean.
Ant. purify; elevate, raise, exalt.

debate, *n.* **1.** discussion, argument, controversy, disputation, dispute, contention. **2.** deliberation, consideration. **—***v.* **3.** discuss, dispute, argue, contend, hold. **4.** deliberate, consider, discuss, argue.
Ant. agreement.

debt, *n.* liability, obligation, duty, due, debit.

decadence, *n.* decline, degeneration, retrogression, decay, fall.
Ant. flourishing, progress.

decay, *v.* **1.** deteriorate, decline, retrogress, degenerate, fall, fall away, wither, perish. **2.** decompose, putrefy, rot, disintegrate. **—***n.* **3.** decline, deterioration, degeneration, decadence, impairment, dilapidation. **4.** decomposition, putrefaction, rotting, rot.
Ant. flourish, grow; progress.

deceit, *n.* **1.** deceiving, concealment, fraud, deception, cheating, guile, hypocrisy, craftiness, slyness, insincerity, disingenuousness. **2.** trick, stratagem, artifice, wile, trickery, chicane, chicanery, device, cozenage. **3.** falseness, duplicity, treachery, perfidy.
Ant. honesty, forthrightness.

deceitful, *adj.* **1.** insincere, disingenuous, false, hollow, empty, deceiving, fraudulent, designing, tricky, wily, two-faced. **2.** misleading, fraudulent, deceptive, counterfeit, illusory, fallacious.
Ant. sincere, honest, forthright; genuine.

deceive, *v.* mislead, delude, cheat, cozen, dupe, gull, fool, bamboozle, hoodwink, trick, double-cross, defraud, outwit; entrap, ensnare, betray.

decent, *adj.* **1.** fitting, appropriate, suited, suitable, apt, proper, fit, becoming. **2.** conformant, tasteful, modest, seemly, proper, decorous.
Ant. indecent, indecorous, improper, unfit, unsuitable.

deception, *n.* **1.** deceiving, guiling. **2.** artifice, sham, cheat, imposture, treachery, subterfuge, stratagem, ruse, hoax, fraud, trick, wile.

deceptive, *adj.* deceiving, misleading, delusive, fallacious, specious, false, deceitful.
Ant. genuine, authentic.

decide, *v.* determine, settle, resolve, purpose, conclude.
Ant. waver, hesitate, vacillate.

decided, *adj.* **1.** unambiguous, unquestionable, definite, unmistakable, undeniable, indisputable, indubitable, certain, sure, emphatic, pronounced, absolute, unequivocal, categorical, incontrovertible. **2.** resolute, determined, resolved, unwavering, unhesitating. *Ant.* undecided, ambiguous, indefinite; irresolute, hesitant.

decisive, *adj.* incontrovertible, firm, resolute, determined, conclusive, final.
Ant. indecisive, irresolute, vacillating, wavering.

deck, *v.* clothe, attire, bedeck, array, garnish, trim, dress, bedizen, adorn, embellish, decorate.
Ant. undress.

declare, *v.* **1.** announce, proclaim, pronounce. **2.** affirm, assert, aver, protest, make known, state, asseverate, utter. **3.** manifest, reveal, disclose, publish.
Ant. deny, controvert; suppress.

decline, *v.* **1.** refuse, avoid, reject, deny. **2.** descend, slope, incline *or* bend downward. **3.** stoop, condescend, lower oneself, abase, debase. **4.** fail, weaken, deteriorate, pale, diminish, degenerate, decay, languish. —*n.* **5.** incline, declivity, slope, hill. **6.** failing, loss, enfeeblement, deterioration, degeneration, enervation, weakening, decay, diminution, lessening, retrogression.
Ant. agree; rise; improve, increase; strengthening.

decompose, *v.* **1.** separate, distill, fractionate, analyze, disintegrate. **2.** rot, putrefy, decay, mould.

decorous, *adj.* proper, decent, seemly, becoming, sedate, conventional, fitting, fit, suitable.
Ant. indecorous, indecent, unseemly, unbecoming, unfit.

decorum, *n.* etiquette, politeness, politesse, manners, manner, behavior, comportment, deportment, decency, propriety, dignity.
Ant. indecency, impropriety.

decrease, *v.* **1.** diminish, lessen, abate, fall off, decline, contract, dwindle, shrink, wane, ebb, subside. —*n.* **2.** abatement, diminution, reduction, decline, wane, subsidence, falling-off, contraction, shrinking, dwindling, lessening, ebb, ebbing.
Ant. increase.

decrepit, *adj.* weak, feeble, enfeebled, infirm, aged, superannuated, effete, broken down.
Ant. sturdy, strong.

decry, *v.* disparage, censure, belittle, discredit, depreciate, condemn.
Ant. praise, laud, commend.

deduct, *v.* subtract, remove, detract, withdraw.
Ant. add.

deed, *n.* act, performance, exploit, achievement, action, feat.

deem, *v.* judge, regard, think, consider, hold, believe, account, count, suppose.

deep, *adj.* **1.** recondite, abstruse, abstract, difficult, profound, mysterious, obscure, unfathomable. **2.** grave, serious, grievous. **3.** absorbing, absorbed, involved, intense, heartfelt, great, extreme. **4.** pene-

trating, intelligent, bright, cunning, sagacious, wise, discerning, astute, shrewd, artful. **—*n.* 5.** ocean, sea, abyss.
Ant. shallow.

deface, *v.* mar, disfigure, deform, spoil, soil, injure, harm; blot out, efface, obliterate, erase, eliminate.
Ant. beautify.

defeat, *v.* **1.** overcome, conquer, overwhelm, vanquish, subdue, overthrow, subjugate, suppress, rout, check. **2.** frustrate, thwart, foil, baffle, disconcert, unnerve, balk. **—*n.* 3.** overthrow, vanquishment, downfall, rout. **4.** frustration, bafflement.
Ant. yield, surrender, submit.

defect, *n.* **1.** blemish, flaw, fault, shortcoming, imperfection, mar, blotch, scar, blot, foible, weakness. **2.** deficiency, want, lack, destitution. **—*v.* 3.** desert, abandon, revolt, rebel, betray.
Ant. sufficiency, perfection; support.

defective, *adj.* imperfect, incomplete, faulty, deficient, insufficient, inadequate.
Ant. perfect, complete, adequate.

defend, *v.* **1.** guard, garrison, fortify, shield, shelter, screen, preserve, protect, keep, watch over, safeguard, secure. **2.** uphold, maintain, assert, justify, plead, espouse, vindicate.
Ant. attack.

defer, *v.* delay, postpone, put off, prevent, adjourn; procrastinate.
Ant. speed, expedite.

defiant, *adj.* antagonistic, insubordinate, contumacious, refractory, recalcitrant, rebellious, insolent, resistant; daring, courageous, brave, bold.
Ant. friendly, amiable; cowardly.

definite, *adj.* **1.** defined, determined, specific, particular, exact, fixed, precise, determinate. **2.** certain, clear, express, sure.
Ant. indefinite, undetermined, indeterminate; uncertain, unclear.

deform, *v.* misshape, deform, disfigure, deface, efface, mar, spoil, ruin; transform.

deformed, *adj.* malformed, misshapen, crippled, disfigured.

defy, *v.* challenge, resist, dare, brave, flout, scorn, despise.
Ant. encourage, support, help.

degradation, *n.* humiliation, disgrace, debasement, dishonor, degeneration, decline, decadence, degeneracy, perversity.
Ant. exaltation.

degrade, *v.* **1.** demote, depose, downgrade, lower, break, cashier. **2.** debase, deprave, lower, abase, vitiate, deteriorate. **3.** humiliate, dishonor, disgrace, discredit.
Ant. exalt.

dejected, *adj.* depressed, dispirited, disheartened, low-

spirited, discouraged, despondent, downhearted, sad, unhappy, miserable.
Ant. happy, cheerful, lighthearted.

delay, *v.* **1.** put off, defer, postpone, procrastinate. **2.** impede, slow, retard, hinder, detain, stop, arrest. **3.** linger, loiter, tarry. —*n.* **4.** delaying, procrastination, loitering, tarrying, dawdling, stay, stop. **5.** deferment, postponement, respite, deferring.
Ant. expedite, hasten, speed.

delegate, *n.* **1.** representative, deputy, envoy, ambassador, legate. —*v.* **2.** depute, entrust, commission.

delete, *v.* cancel, strike *or* take out, dele, erase, expunge, eradicate, remove, efface, blot out.

deleterious, *adj.* injurious, hurtful, harmful, pernicious, destructive, deadly, lethal; noxious, poisonous.
Ant. salutary, beneficial, advantageous.

deliberate, *adj.* **1.** weighed, considered, studied, intentional, purposive, purposeful, premeditated, voluntary, willful. **2.** careful, slow, unhurried, leisurely, methodical, thoughtful, circumspect, cautious, wary. —*v.* **3.** weigh, consider, ponder over, reflect, think, ruminate, meditate. **4.** consult, confer.
Ant. haphazard, unintentional; careless, unwary, incautious.

delicate, *adj.* **1.** fine, dainty, exquisite, nice, fragile, graceful, elegant, choice. **2.** fine, slight, subtle. **3.** tender, fragile, frail, dainty, slight, weak, slender, sensitive, frangible. **4.** critical, precarious. **5.** scrupulous, careful, painstaking, exact, exacting, precise, accurate. **6.** discriminating, fastidious, careful, demanding.
Ant. rude, crude; blunt; rough, insensitive, unbreakable; careless.

delicious, *adj.* pleasing, luscious, palatable, savory, dainty, delicate.
Ant. unpleasant, bitter, acrid, unpalatable.

delight, *n.* **1.** enjoyment, pleasure, transport, delectation, joy, rapture, ecstasy. —*v.* **2.** please, satisfy, transport, enrapture, enchant, charm, ravish.
Ant. disgust, revulsion, displeasure; displease.

delightful, *adj.* pleasing, pleasant, pleasurable, enjoyable, charming, enchanting, agreeable, delectable, rapturous.
Ant. unpleasant, disagreeable, revolting, repellent.

deliver, *v.* **1.** give up, surrender, hand over, transfer, give over, yield, resign, cede, grant, relinquish. **2.** give forth, emit, cast, direct, deal, discharge. **3.** utter, pronounce, announce, proclaim, declare, communicate, publish, impart, promulgate, advance. **4.** set free, liberate, release, free, emancipate. **5.** redeem, rescue, save, release, extricate, disentangle.
Ant. limit, confine.

delude, *v.* mislead, deceive, beguile, cozen, cheat, dupe, gull, defraud, trick.
Ant. enlighten.

deluge, *n.* inundation, flood, downpour, overflow, cataclysm, catastrophe.

delusion, *n.* illusion, deception, trick, fancy, fallacy, error, mistake, hallucination.

demand, *v.* **1.** claim, require, exact, ask for, call for, challenge. **2.** ask, inquire. **—***n.* **3.** claim, requisition, requirement. **4.** inquiry, question, asking, interrogation.
Ant. waive, relinquish.

demolish, *v.* ruin, destroy, put an end to, lay waste, raze, level.
Ant. construct, build, create.

demur, *v.* **1.** object, take exception, raise *or* make objection; refuse. **—***n.* **2.** objection, hesitation, refusal.
Ant. agree, accede, consent.

demure, *adj.* **1.** prudish, prim, overmodest, priggish. **2.** sober, modest, serious, sedate, decorous, coy.
Ant. licentious, immodest; indecorous.

denounce, *v.* **1.** condemn, assail, censure, attack, stigmatize, blame, brand, label. **2.** inform against, accuse, denunciate, give away.
Ant. commend, exonerate.

deny, *v.* **1.** dispute, controvert, oppose, gainsay, contradict. **2.** reject, renounce, abjure, disavow. **3.** refuse, repudiate, disown.
Ant. concede, agree, concur; accept; receive.

depart, *v.* **1.** go away, start, set out, leave, quit, retire, withdraw, absent, go. **2.** turn aside, diverge, deviate, vary. **3.** die, pass on *or* away.
Ant. arrive; converge.

depict, *v.* **1.** represent, portray, paint, limn, delineate, sketch, reproduce, draw. **2.** describe.

deplore, *v.* grieve, regret, lament, bemoan, bewail, mourn.
Ant. boast.

deposit, *v.* **1.** place, put, lay down, lay. **2.** throw down, drop, precipitate. **3.** bank, save, store, hoard; secure. **—***n.* **4.** sediment, deposition, precipitate; silt, mud, slime, sand, alluvium; snow, rain, sleet, hail. **5.** coating; lode, vein.

depot, *n.* station, terminal; storehouse, warehouse, depository.

depraved, *adj.* corrupt, perverted, corrupted, immoral, wicked, evil, sinful, iniquitous, profligate, debased, dissolute, reprobate, degenerate, licentious, lascivious, lewd.
Ant. upright, honest; honorable, decorous, modest.

depress, *v.* **1.** dispirit, deject, oppress, dishearten, discourage, dampen, chill, sadden. **2.** reduce, weaken, dull, lower. **3.** devalue, cheapen. **4.** humble, humiliate, abase, debase, degrade, abash.
Ant. inspirit, encourage; elevate; gladden.

depressed, *adj.* dejected, downcast, sad, unhappy, miserable, morose, saddened, blue, despondent, melancholy, gloomy, morbid.

Ant. happy, cheerful.

deprive, *v.* dispossess, bereave, strip, divest, disallow, deny.
Ant. endow.

dereliction, *n.* neglect, negligence, delinquency, fault, abandonment, desertion, renunciation.

descent, *n.* **1.** falling, fall, sinking, descending. **2.** inclination, declination, slope, declivity, grade, decline. **3.** extraction, lineage, derivation, parentage, genealogy. **4.** incursion, attack, assault, raid, foray.
Ant. ascent, rise.

describe, *v.* narrate, account, recount, tell, relate; delineate, portray, characterize, limn, represent, depict.

desert, *n.* **1.** waste, wilderness. *—adj.* **2.** desolate, barren, forsaken, wild, uninhabited. *—v.* **3.** abandon, forsake, leave behind, give up, relinquish, leave, quit, renounce.

design, *v.* **1.** plan, devise, project, contrive. **2.** intend, purpose, mean, propose. **3.** sketch, draw, delineate. *—n.* **4.** plan, scheme, proposal, proposition, project. **5.** sketch, plan, drawings, blueprint, outline, draught. **6.** end, intention, purpose, intent, aim, object. **7.** meaning, purport, drift.
Ant. achieve, execute, accomplish; execution; accident, fortuity, chance.

designing, *adj.* contriving, scheming, sly, artful, cunning, tricky, wily, crafty, deceitful, treacherous, arch, Machiavellian, astute, unscrupulous.
Ant. open, candid, frank, honest, guileless, artless, naive.

desire, *v.* **1.** wish *or* long for, crave, want, wish, covet, fancy. **2.** ask, request, solicit. *—n.* **3.** longing, craving, yearning, wish, need, hunger, appetite, thirst. **4.** request, wish, aspiration. **5.** lust.
Ant. abominate, loathe, abhor.

desolate, *adj.* **1.** barren, laid waste, devastated, ravaged, scorched, destroyed. **2.** deserted, uninhabited, desert, lonely, alone, lone, solitary, forsaken, lonesome. **3.** miserable, wretched, unhappy, sad, woeful, woebegone, disconsolate, inconsolable, forlorn, lost, cheerless. **4.** dreary, dismal, wild. *—v.* **5.** lay waste, devastate, ravage, ruin, sack, destroy, despoil. **6.** depopulate. **7.** sadden, depress. **8.** forsake, abandon, desert.
Ant. fertile; populous, crowded; happy, delighted; cultivated; build, create; cheer.

despair, *n.* hopelessness, desperation, despondency, discouragement, gloom, disheartenment.
Ant. encouragement, hope, optimism.

desperate, *adj.* **1.** reckless, despairing, rash, headlong, frantic. **2.** hopeless, serious, grave, dangerous. **3.** wretched, forlorn, hopeless, desolate. **4.** extreme, excessive, great, heroic, prodigious, foolhardy.
Ant. careful; hopeful.

despicable, *adj.* despisable, contemptible, vile, base, worthless, mean, abject, low, pitiful.
Ant. lovable, likable, worthy.

despise, *v.* contemn, scorn, disdain, spurn.
Ant. love, like, admire.

despite, *prep.* notwithstanding, in spite of.

despondency, *n.* depression, dejection, discouragement, melancholy, gloom, desperation, despair, sadness, blues.
Ant. elation, joy, happiness.

despondent, *adj.* desponding, depressed, dejected, discouraged, disheartened, downhearted, melancholy, sad, blue, dispirited, hopeless, low-spirited.
Ant. elated, joyful, happy.

destiny, *n.* fate, karma, kismet, lot, fortune, future, doom, destination.

destitute, *adj.* needy, poor, indigent, penniless, impoverished, poverty-stricken.
Ant. affluent, rich, opulent.

destroy, *v.* **1.** smash, dash, demolish, raze, spoil, consume, level, ruin, waste, ravage, devastate, desolate, lay waste. **2.** end, extinguish, extirpate, annihilate, eradicate, slay, kill, uproot. **3.** nullify, invalidate.
Ant. create; originate, start.

destruction, *n.* **1.** extinction, extermination, desolation, devastation, ruin, eradication. **2.** demolition, annihilation, murder, slaughter, death, massacre, genocide. **3.** plague, shipwreck, holocaust.
Ant. birth, origin; creation.

destructive, *adj.* **1.** ruinous, baleful, pernicious, mischievous, deleterious, fatal, deadly, lethal. **2.** extirpative, eradicative.
Ant. salutary; creative.

detain, *v.* **1.** delay, arrest, retard, stop, slow, stay, check, keep. **2.** restrain, confine, arrest. **3.** keep back, withhold, retain.
Ant. promote, encourage; advance.

detect, *v.* discover, catch, expose, descry, find, find out, ascertain, learn, hear of, hear.

deter, *v.* discourage, restrain, dissuade, hinder, prevent, stop.
Ant. encourage, further, contine.

determine, *v.* **1.** settle, decide, conclude, adjust. **2.** conclude, ascertain, verify, check, certify. **3.** fix, decide, establish, condition, influence, resolve. **4.** impel, induce, lead, incline.

determined, *adj.* stanch, resolute, unflinching, firm, inflexible, rigid, rigorous, unfaltering, unwavering.
Ant. irresolute, vacillating, wavering, faltering, flexible.

detest, *v.* abhor, hate, loathe, abominate, execrate, despise.
Ant. love, like.

detestable, *adj.* abominable, hateful, execrable, loathsome, vile, odious, abhorred, abhorrent, despicable.
Ant. lovable, likable.

detraction, *n.* detracting, disparagement, belittling, defamation, vilification, calumny, abuse, slander, aspersion, depreciation.
Ant. praise, commendation.

detriment, *n.* loss, damage, injury, hurt, harm, impairment, disadvantage, prejudice.
Ant. advantage, profit.

devastate, *v.* ravage, lay waste, desolate, destroy, strip, pillage, plunder, sack, spoil, despoil.
Ant. build, erect, create.

development, *n.* **1.** expansion, growth, elaboration, progress, increase. **2.** opening, disclosure, developing, unfolding, maturing, maturation. **3.** community, project, housing project.
Ant. deterioration, decadence, degeneration.

deviate, *v.* **1.** depart, swerve, digress, diverge, part, wander, veer, err, stray. **2.** turn aside, avert.
Ant. converge.

device, *n.* **1.** invention, contrivance, gadget. **2.** plan, scheme, project, design, expedient. **3.** wile, ruse, artifice, shift, trick, stratagem, evasion, maneuver. **4.** design, figure, emblem, trademark, badge, logotype, colophon, symbol, crest, seal. **5.** motto, slogan, legend. **6.** (*plural*) will, desire, inclination, bent, abilities, aptitudes.

devilish, *adj.* satanic, diabolic, diabolical, demoniac, infernal, Mephistophelian, fiendish, hellish.
Ant. good, fine, upstanding, righteous, godly.

devise, *v.* order, arrange, plan, think out, contrive, invent, prepare, concoct, scheme, project, design.
Ant. disorder, disarrange.

devote, *v.* assign, apply, consign, give up, dedicate, consecrate.
Ant. resign, relinquish.

devotion, *n.* **1.** dedication, consecration. **2.** attachment, affection, love. **3.** devotedness, zeal, ardor, eagerness, earnestness. **4.** (*theology*) religion, religiousness, piety, faith, devoutness, sanctity, saintliness, godliness.

devout, *adj.* **1.** pious, devoted, religious, worshipful, holy, saintly. **2.** earnest, sincere, hearty, serious, honest.
Ant. atheistic, agnostic; insincere, scornful.

dexterous, *adj.* skillful, adroit, deft, handy, nimble, clever, expert, apt, ready, quick, able.
Ant. clumsy, awkward, maladroit, unapt.

dialect, *n.* **1.** provincialism, idiom, localism, jargon, patois, variant. **2.** branch, sub-family, sub-group. **3.** language, tongue, speech.

diction, *n.* phraseology, wording, style, usage, grammar, language; distinctness, enunciation, pronunciation.

die, *v.* **1.** decease, pass away *or* on, perish, expire, depart. **2.** cease, end, vanish, disappear. **3.** weaken, fail, subside, fade, sink, faint, decline, wither, decay. **—***n.* **4.** cube, block. **5.** stamp.

difference, *n.* **1.** discrepancy, disparity, dissimilarity, inconsistency, unlikeness, variation, diversity, imbalance, disagreement, inequality, dissimilitude, divergence, contrast, contrariety. **2.** discrimination, distinction.
Ant. similarity; agreement.

different, *adj.* **1.** differing, unlike, diverse, divergent, altered, changed, contrary, contrasted, deviant, deviating, variant. **2.** sundry, divers, miscellaneous, various, manifold.
Ant. similar, like; uniform, identical.

differentiate, *v.* **1.** set off, distinguish, alter, change. **2.** distinguish, discriminate, separate, contrast.
Ant. group together.

difficult, *adj* **1.** hard, arduous. **2.** obscure, complex, intricate, perplexing. **3.** austere, rigid, reserved, forbidding, unaccommodating. **4.** fastidious, particular.
Ant. easy, simple; clear, plain; accommodating; careless, sloppy.

difficulty, *n.* **1.** dilemma, predicament, quandary, fix, exigency, emergency. **2.** trouble, problem. **3.** reluctance, unwillingness, obstinacy, stubbornness. **4.** demur, objection, obstacle.
Ant. ease; willingness.

diffident, *adj.* shy, self-conscious, self-effacing, bashful, abashed, embarrassed, timid, sheepish, modest.
Ant. forward, bold, unabashed.

digest, *v.* **1.** understand, assimilate, study, ponder, consider, contemplate, ruminate over, reflect upon. **2.** arrange, systematize, think over, classify, codify. **—*n.*** **3.** summary, epitome, abstract, synopsis, abridgment, brief, conspectus.
Ant. expand.

digress, *v.* deviate, diverge, wander.

dilate, *v.* expand, spread out, enlarge, engross, widen, extend, swell, distend.
Ant. shrink, constrict.

dilemma, *n.* predicament, problem, question, quandary, difficulty, strait.

diligence, *n.* persistence, effort, application, industry, assiduity, perseverance, assiduousness.
Ant. carelessness, laziness.

diligent, *adj.* industrious, assiduous, sedulous, occupied, busy, constant, attentive, persistent. **2.** painstaking, persevering, indefatigable, untiring, tireless, unremitting, industrious.
Ant. lazy, careless; remiss.

dim, *adj.* **1.** obscure, dark, shadowy, dusky, nebulous, hazy, cloudy, faint, indistinct. **2.** indistinct, unclear, ill-defined, blurred, vague, confused, indefinite. **3.** dull, tarnished, blurred, slow, stupid, dense, foggy. **4.** disparaging, adverse, uncomplimentary. **—*v.*** **5.** darken, cloud, obscure, dull. **6.** blur, dull, fade.
Ant. clear, bright, distinct; definite.

diminish, *v.* lessen, reduce, decrease, subside, ebb,

dwindle, shrink, abate, contract, shrivel up.
Ant. increase.

diminutive, *adj.* little, small, tiny, dwarf, dwarflike dwarfish, minute, microscopic, submicroscopic.
Ant. large, immense.

dip, *v.* **1.** plunge, immerse, dive, duck. **2.** sink, drop, incline, decline, slope downward.
Ant. rise.

diplomatic, *adj.* politic, tactful, artful.
Ant. tactless, rude, naive.

direct, *v.* **1.** guide, advise, regulate, conduct, manage, control, dispose, lead, govern, rule. **2.** order, command, instruct. **3.** point, aim. —*adj.* **4.** straight, undeviating. **5.** immediate, personal, unbroken, simple, evident. **6.** straightforward, downright, plain, categorical, unequivocal, unambiguous, express, open, sincere, outspoken, frank, earnest, ingenuous, obvious, naive.
Ant. divert, mislead; crooked; devious; ambiguous, sly.

dirty, *adj.* **1.** soiled, foul, unclean, filthy, squalid, defiled, grimy. **2.** dirtying, soiling, befouling, besmirching. **3.** vile, mean, base, vulgar, low, groveling, scurvy, shabby, contemptible, despicable. **4.** indecent, obscene, nasty, lascivious, lewd, lecherous, licentious, immoral, amoral. **5.** contaminated, radioactive. **6.** stormy, squally, rainy, foul, sloppy, disagreeable, nasty. **7.** dark-colored, dingy, dull, dark, sullied, clouded.
Ant. clean; elevated, exalted; decent, moral; fair; clear.

disability, *n.* incapacity, disqualification, inability, incompetence, impotence, incapability.
Ant. ability, capacity, capability.

disable, *v.* **1.** weaken, destroy, cripple, incapacitate, enfeeble, paralyze. **2.** disqualify, incapacitate, eliminate.
Ant. strengthen; qualify; include.

disadvantage, *n.* **1.** drawback, inconvenience, hindrance, deprivation. **2.** detriment, hurt, harm, damage, injury, loss, disservice.
Ant. advantage.

disappear, *v.* vanish, fade, cease, pass away, end.
Ant. appear.

disappointment, *n.* **1.** failure, defeat, frustration, unfulfillment. **2.** mortification, frustration, chagrin.
Ant. fulfillment, victory; consummation.

disaster, *n.* misfortune, calamity, mischance, mishap, accident, misadventure, blow, reverse, catastrophe, adversity, affliction.
Ant. luck, fortune.

disband, *v.* break up, disorganize, demobilize, dissolve, disperse, dismiss, scatter, separate.
Ant. organize, unite.

disburse, *v.* spend, pay, expend, lay out.
Ant. bank, save.

discern, *v.* **1.** perceive, see, recognize, notice, apprehend, discover, descry, espy, come upon, behold. **2.** discriminate, distinguish, differentiate, judge.

discharge, *v.* **1.** unload, disburden, relieve, unburden. **2.** remove, send forth, get rid of, expel, eject, emit. **3.** fire, shoot, set off, detonate. **4.** relieve, release, absolve, exonerate, clear, acquit, liberate, set free, free. **5.** fulfill, perform, execute, observe. **6.** dismiss, cashier, fire, remove, expel, send down, break. **7.** pay, honor, disburse, make good on, liquidate, dissolve, settle. —*n.* **8.** emission, ejection, expulsion, removal, evacuation, voiding. **9.** detonation, firing, shooting. **10.** fulfillment, execution, performance, observance.
Ant. load, burden.

disciple, *n.* follower, adherent, supporter; pupil, student, scholar.
Ant. leader; rebel.

discipline, *n.* **1.** training, drill, exercise, instruction, practice. **2.** punishment, chastisement, castigation, correction. **3.** subjection, order, control, regulation, subjugation, government. **4.** rules, regulations. —*v.* **5.** train, exercise, drill, practice, instruct, teach, educate. **6.** punish, correct, chastise, castigate.

disclose, *v.* **1.** reveal, make known, divulge, show, tell, unveil, communicate. **2.** uncover, lay open, expose, bring to light; muckrake.
Ant. conceal, hide; cover.

disconcert, *v.* disturb, confuse, perturb, ruffle, discompose, perplex, bewilder, frustrate, embarrass, abash; disarrange, disorder.
Ant. calm; order, arrange.

disconsolate, *adj.* inconsolable, unhappy, desolate, forlorn, heart-broken, sad, melancholy, dejected, gloomy, miserable, cheerless, sorrowful.
Ant. happy, cheerful, delighted.

discontent, *adj.* **1.** discontented, dissatisfied. —*n.* **2.** discontentment, dissatisfaction, uneasiness, inquietude, restlessness, displeasure.
Ant. contentment; satisfaction, pleasure, ease, restfulness.

discontinue, *v.* put an end to, interrupt, stop, cease, quit; desist.
Ant. continue, further.

discourage, *v.* **1.** dishearten, dispirit, daunt, depress, deject, overawe, cow, awe, subdue, abash, embarrass, dismay, intimidate, frighten. **2.** dissuade, deter, hinder, prevent, obstruct.
Ant. encourage, hearten, embolden.

discouragement, *n.* **1.** depression, dejection, hopelessness, despair. **2.** deterrent, damper, wet blanket, cold water, impediment, obstacle, obstruction.
Ant. encouragement.

discover, *v.* **1.** learn of, ascertain, unearth, determine, ferret out, dig up; find out, detect, espy, descry, discern, see, notice. **2.** originate, bring to light, invent.
Ant. conceal.

discreet, *adj.* wise, judicious, prudent, circumspect,

cautious, careful, heedful, considerate, wary.
Ant. indiscreet, careless, imprudent; incautious, inconsiderate.

discrepancy, *n.* difference, inconsistency, incongruity, disagreement, discordance, contrariety, variance, variation.
Ant. similarity, congruity, consistency, concord, accord, agreement.

discriminate, *v.* **1.** distinguish, set apart, differentiate. —*adj.* **2.** critical, distinguishing, discriminative, discriminatory.
Ant. group, unite; indiscriminate, undistinguished.

discuss, *v.* examine, reason, deliberate, argue, debate, talk over, sift, consider.

disdain, *v.* **1.** contemn, despise, scorn, spurn. —*n.* **2.** contempt, scorn, contumely, contemptuousness, haughtiness, arrogance, superciliousness, hauteur.
Ant. accept, like, love; love, admiration, regard.

disdainful, *adj.* contemptuous, scornful, haughty, arrogant, supercilious, contumelious.
Ant. friendly, amiable, considerate, attentive.

disease, *n.* **1.** morbidity, illness, sickness, ailment, complaint, affection, disorder, malady, abnormality, derangement, distemper, disposition, infirmity.
Ant. health, salubriety.

disfigure, *v.* mar, deface, injure, deform, spoil, ruin, blemish.
Ant. beautify.

disgrace, *n.* **1.** ignominy, shame, dishonor, infamy, disfavor, disapproval, disapprobation, disparagement, stain, taint, notoriety, baseness. **2.** odium, obloquy, degradation, opprobrium, scandal. —*v.* **3.** shame, dishonor, defame, disfavor, humiliate, disapprove, discredit, degrade, debase, stain, sully, taint, tarnish, reproach.

disgust, *v.* **1.** sicken, nauseate, turn one's stomach. **2.** offend, displease, repel, repulse, revolt, abhor, detest. —*n.* **3.** distaste, nausea, loathing, hatred, abhorrence, disrelish. **4.** dislike, detestation, repugnance, aversion, dissatisfaction, antipathy.
Ant. please, delight, attract; relish, liking, love; satisfaction.

disgusting, *adj.* offensive, offending, loathsome, sickening, nauseous, nauseating, repulsive, revolting, odious, hateful, repugnant, foul, abominable, abhorrent, distasteful, detestable.
Ant. delightful, delectable, attractive, beautiful.

dishonest, *adj.* unscrupulous, conniving, corrupt, knavish, thievish, deceitful, treacherous, perfidious; false, fraudulent, counterfeit.
Ant. honest.

dishonorable, *adj.* **1.** ignoble, base, disgraceful, shameful, shameless, false, fraudulent. **2.** infamous, notorious, unscrupulous, unprincipled, disreputable, disgraceful, scandalous, ignominious, discreditable.
Ant. honorable.

disintegrate, *v.* reduce to particles *or* fragments, break up, decay, rot, fall apart, separate.
Ant. integrate.

disinterested, *adj.* unbiased, unprejudiced, unselfish, impartial, fair, generous, liberal.
Ant. biased, prejudiced, illiberal, bigoted, selfish, partial.

dislike, *v.* **1.** have an aversion *or* be averse to, be disinclined *or* reluctant. —*n.* **2.** disrelish, disgust, distaste, repugnance, antipathy, loathing, aversion, antagonism.
Ant. like; relish, delight, delectation.

disloyal, *adj.* unfaithful, false, perfidious, treacherous, traitorous, treasonable, subversive, disaffected, untrue, unpatriotic.
Ant. loyal, faithful, true, honest.

disloyalty, *n.* unfaithfulness, perfidy, treachery, treason, betrayal, disaffection, faithlessness, subversion.
Ant. loyalty, fealty, allegiance.

dismay, *v.* **1.** discourage, dishearten, daunt, appall, terrify, horrify, frighten, scare, intimidate, disconcert, put out, alarm, paralyze. —*n.* **2.** consternation, terror, horror, panic, fear, alarm.
Ant. encourage, hearten, embolden; security, confidence.

dismiss, *v.* release, let go, discharge, discard, reject, set *or* put aside; fire.
Ant. hire, employ.

disobedient, *adj.* insubordinate, contumacious, defiant, refractory, unruly, rebellious, obstinate, stubborn, unsubmissive, uncompliant.
Ant. obedient.

disobey, *v.* transgress, violate, disregard, defy, infringe.
Ant. obey.

disorder, *n.* **1.** disorderliness, disarray, jumble, mess, litter, clutter, disarrangement, confusion, irregularity, disorganization, derangement. **2.** disturbance, tumult, brawl, uproar, fight, unrest, quarrel, bustle, clamor, riot, turbulence. **3.** ailment, malady, derangement, illness, complaint, sickness, disease, indisposition. —*v.* **4.** disarrange, disarray, mess up, disorganize, unsettle, disturb, derange, discompose, upset, confuse, confound.
Ant. order.

disparity, *n.* dissimilarity, inequality, difference, distinction, dissimilitude.
Ant. similarity, equality, similitude.

dispense, *v.* deal, distribute, apportion, allot, dole.

disperse, *v.* **1.** scatter, dissipate, separate. **2.** spread, diffuse, disseminate, broadcast, sow, scatter. **3.** dispel. **4.** vanish, disappear, evanesce.
Ant. unite, combine; appear.

displace, *v.* **1.** misplace, move, dislocate. **2.** replace, remove, depose, oust, dismiss, cashier.

display, *v.* **1.** show, exhibit, demonstrate, make visible,

evince, manifest. **2.** reveal, uncover, betray. **3.** unfold, open out, spread out. **4.** show, flourish, flaunt, parade, show off. **—*n.* 5.** show, exhibition, manifestation. **6.** parade, ostentation, flourish, flaunting.
Ant. conceal, hide; cover.

displeasure, *n.* dissatisfaction, annoyance, disapprobation, disapproval, distaste, dislike; anger, ire, wrath, indignation, vexation; offense.
Ant. pleasure, satisfaction, approval, delight; calm, peace.

disposition, *n.* **1.** temper, temperament, nature, character, humor. **2.** inclination, willingness, bent, tendency, proneness, bias, predisposition, proclivity. **3.** arrangement, order, grouping, location, placement. **4.** settlement, outcome, finale, result, dispensation. **5.** regulation, appointment, management, control, direction. **6.** bestowal, endowment.
Ant. indisposition, unwillingness.

dispute, *v.* **1.** argue, discuss, debate, agitate. **2.** wrangle, contest, quarrel, bicker, spat, squabble, spar, brawl. **3.** oppose, controvert, contradict, deny, impugn. **—*n.* 4.** argumentation, argument, contention, debate, controversy, disputation, altercation, quarrel, wrangle, bickering, spat, squabble, tiff.
Ant. agree, concur; agreement, concurrence.

disregard, *v.* **1.** ignore, neglect, overlook, disobey, pay no attention *or* heed *or* regard to, take no notice of. **2.** slight, insult. **—*n.* 3.** neglect, inattention, inattentiveness, oversight. **4.** disrespect, slight, indifference.
Ant. regard, view, notice, note; attention; respect.

disrespectful, *adj.* discourteous, impolite, rude, crude, uncivil, impudent, impertinent, irreverent.
Ant. respectful, courteous, polite, civil, reverent.

dissatisfaction, *n.* discontent, displeasure, dislike, disappointment, disapproval, disapprobation, uneasiness.
Ant. satisfaction, approval, approbation.

dissent, *v.* **1.** differ, disagree. **—*n.* 2.** difference, dissidence, disagreement, dissatisfaction, opposition, nonconformity, separation.
Ant. agree, concur; agreement, concurrence, satisfaction, unity.

dissipate, *v.* **1.** scatter, disperse, dispel, disintegrate. **2.** waste, squander. **3.** scatter, disappear, vanish, disintegrate. **4.** debauch.
Ant. integrate, unite; appear; join.

dissolve, *v.* **1.** melt, liquefy. **2.** sever, loose, loosen, free, disunite, break up; dismiss, disperse, adjourn. **3.** destroy, dispel, ruin, disintegrate, break down, terminate, end; perish, crumble, die, expire.
Ant. solidify; unite; meet; integrate; originate.

distaste, *n.* dislike, disinclination, aversion, repugnance, disgust, displeasure, dissatisfaction; disrelish.

Ant. taste, delectation, liking, love, satisfaction; relish.

distasteful, *adj.* **1.** disagreeable, displeasing, offensive, repugnant, repulsive, unpleasant. **2.** unpalatable, unsavory, nauseating, loathsome, disgusting, sickening.
Ant. tasteful, agreeable, pleasant, inoffensive; attractive, delightful.

distend, *v.* expand, swell, stretch, dilate, bloat, enlarge.
Ant. contract, shrink, reduce.

distinct, *adj.* **1.** distinguished, distinguishable, different, individual, separate, dividual, various, varied; dissimilar. **2.** definite, well-defined, clear, plain, unmistakable, unconfused.
Ant. indistinct, blurred, same; similar; indefinite, unclear, confused.

distinction, *n.* **1.** difference, differentiation, discrimination. **2.** honor, repute, name, fame, celebrity, renown, importance, note, account, eminence, superiority.
Ant. indifference; similarity; disrepute, dishonor.

distinguish, *v.* **1.** mark, characterize. **2.** discriminate, differentiate, separate, divide, classify, categorize. **3.** discern, recognize, perceive, know, tell. **4.** make prominent *or* conspicuous *or* eminent.

distinguished, *adj.* **1.** conspicuous, marked, extraordinary. **2.** noted, eminent, famed, famous, celebrated, renowned, illustrious. **3.** distingué, refined.
Ant. undistinguished, common; infamous; unknown; unrefined, coarse.

distress, *n.* **1.** pain, anxiety, sorrow, grief, agony, anguish, misery, adversity, hardship, trial, tribulation, suffering, trouble, affliction. **2.** need, necessity, want, privation, deprivation, destitution, poverty, indigence. **—***v.* **3.** trouble, worry, afflict, bother, grieve, pain, make miserable *or* unhappy.
Ant. comfort; fulfillment, opulence; console, mitigate, delight.

distribute, *v.* **1.** deal out, deal, allot, apportion, assign, mete, dole, dispense, give. **2.** disperse, spread, scatter. **3.** divide, separate, classify, categorize, dispose, sort, arrange.
Ant. collect, keep; unite.

distrust, *v.* **1.** doubt, suspect, mistrust. **—***n.* **2.** doubt, suspicion, mistrust, misgiving.
Ant. trust, depend.

disturbance, *n.* **1.** perturbation, agitation, commotion, disorder, confusion, derangement. **2.** disorder, tumult, riot, uproar.
Ant. order, organization; calm, serenity.

diverge, *v.* **1.** branch off, separate, fork, bifurcate, divide. **2.** differ, deviate, disagree, vary.
Ant. converge, unite; agree, concur.

diverse, *adj.* **1.** unlike, dissimilar, separate, different,

disagreeing. **2.** various, varied, multiform, manifold, variant, divergent.
Ant. similar, like.

divert, *v.* **1.** turn aside, deflect. **2.** draw aside *or* away, turn aside, distract. **3.** distract, entertain, amuse, delight, gratify, exhilarate.
Ant. fix; weary, bore, tire.

divest, *v.* **1.** strip, unclothe, denude, disrobe, undress. **2.** strip, dispossess, deprive.
Ant. invest.

divide, *v.* **1.** separate, sunder, cut off, sever, shear, cleave, part. **2.** apportion, share, deal out, partition, distribute, portion. **3.** alienate, disunite, cause to disagree, estrange. **4.** distinguish, classify, sort, arrange, distribute.
Ant. unite; keep, retain; disarrange.

division, *n.* **1.** partition, dividing, separation, apportionment, allotment, distribution, sharing. **2.** mark, boundary, partition, demarcation. **3.** section, part, compartment, partition, segment. **4.** disagreement, dissension, difference, variance, rupture, disunion, discord, breach, rift, estrangement, alienation, feud.
Ant. agreement, union, accord.

divulge, *v.* disclose, reveal, make known, impart, tell, broadcast.
Ant. conceal.

do, *v.* **1.** perform, act. **2.** execute, finish, carry out, conclude, end, terminate, complete. **3.** accomplish, finish, achieve, attain, effect, bring about, execute, carry out. **4.** exert, put forth. **5.** cover, traverse. **6.** serve, suffice for. **7.** behave, proceed, act, fare, manage.

doctrine, *n.* tenet, dogma, theory, precept, belief, principle; teachings.

dodge, *v.* equivocate, quibble, evade, be evasive, elude.

dominant, *adj.* **1.** ruling, governing, controlling, most influential, prevailing, prevalent, common, principal, predominant, paramount, preeminent, outstanding, important, first, ascendant. **2.** commanding, advantageous.
Ant. secondary, disadvantageous.

donation, *n.* gift, contribution, offering, grant, benefaction, boon, largess, present, gratuity.

doom, *n.* **1.** fate, destiny, lot, fortune. **2.** ruin, death. **3.** judgment, decision, sentence, condemnation. —*v.* **4.** destine, predestine, foreordain, decree. **5.** condemn, sentence, ordain.

dormant, *adj.* **1.** asleep, inactive, torpid, quiescent. **2.** quiescent, inoperative, in abeyance, latent, potential, inert, suspended.
Ant. awake, active; operative; kinetic.

doubt, *v.* **1.** distrust, mistrust, suspect, question. **2.** hesitate, waver. —*n.* **3.** undecidedness, indecision, uncertainty, faltering, irresolution, hesitation, hesitancy, vacillation, misgiving, suspense; mistrust, distrust, suspicion.

Ant. trust; decision, certainty, conviction.

doubtful, *adj.* **1.** uncertain, unsure, ambiguous, equivocal, indeterminate, undecided, fifty-fifty. **2.** undetermined, unsettled, indecisive, dubious, enigmatic, problematic, puzzled. **3.** hesitating, hesitant, wavering, irresolute, vacillating, dubious, skeptical, incredulous.
Ant. certain, sure, unambiguous, decided; settled; unhesitating, resolute.

dowdy, *adj.* ill-dressed, frumpy, shabby, old-maidish, old-fashioned.
Ant. fashionable, chic, modish, à la mode.

downhearted, *adj.* dejected, discouraged, depressed, downcast, despondent, disheartened, sad, sorrowful, unhappy, dispirited, crestfallen.
Ant. happy.

drag, *v.* **1.** draw, pull, haul, trail, tug. **2.** trail, linger, loiter, slow.
Ant. drive, push; speed, expedite.

draw, *v.* **1.** drag, haul, pull, tug, tow, lead. **2.** attract, magnetize. **3.** delineate, sketch, draught, depict, trace. **4.** frame, formulate, compose, write, draw up, prepare, form. **5.** suck, inhale, drain. **6.** get, derive, deduce, infer, understand. **7.** produce, bring in, bear. **8.** draw *or* pull out, attenuate; extend, stretch, lengthen. **9.** extract.
Ant. drive, push.

dread, *v.* **1.** fear. *—n.* **2.** terror, fear, apprehension. **3.** awe, reverence, veneration. *—adj.* **4.** frightful, dire, terrible, dreadful, horrible.
Ant. intrepidity, bravery; pleasant, delightful.

dreary, *adj.* **1.** gloomy, dismal, drear, cheerless, chilling, chill, depressing, comfortless. **2.** monotonous, tedious, wearisome, dull, boring, uninteresting, tiresome.
Ant. cheerful, comforting; interesting, engaging.

drench, *v.* steep, wet, soak, ret, saturate.
Ant. dry.

dress, *n.* **1.** costume, frock, gown. **2.** clothing, raiment, garb, attire, apparel, vesture, garments, vestments, clothes, suit, habit, habiliment. **3.** regalia, array, panoply. *—v.* **4.** attire, robe, garb, clothe, array, accouter, apparel, rig, deck out. **5.** trim, ornament, adorn, decorate. **6.** straighten, align. **7.** prepare, fit.
Ant. undress.

drink, *v.* **1.** imbibe, sip, quaff, swallow. **2.** tipple, tope. *—n.* **3.** beverage, potion, liquid refreshment, draft.

drive, *v.* **1.** push, force, impel, propel, send. **2.** overwork, overtask, overburden, overtax. **3.** urge, constrain, impel, compel, force. **4.** go, travel, ride. *—n.* **5.** vigor, pressure, effort, energy.
Ant. curb, restrain.

droll, *adj.* **1.** queer, odd, diverting, amusing, comical, waggish, witty, funny. *—n.* **2.** wag, buffoon, jester,

comedian, clown, zany, punch, merry-andrew. —*v.* **3.** joke, jest, clown.
Ant. common; serious.

droop, *v.* sink, bend, hang down, flag, languish, fail, weaken, decline, faint, wilt, wither, fade.
Ant. rise.

drove, *n.* herd, flock, company, crowd, host, collection.

drudgery, *n.* work, labor.

drunkard, *n.* toper, sot, tippler, drinker, inebriate, dipsomaniac, alcoholic.
Ant. teetotaler, dry.

drunken, *adj.* drunk, sotted, besotted, tipsy, inebriated, intoxicated, befuddled.
Ant. sober.

dry, *adj.* **1.** arid, parched. **2.** wiped *or* drained away, evaporated. **3.** thirsty. **4.** plain, bald, unadorned, unembellished. **5.** dull, uninteresting, dreary, tiresome, boring, tedious, jejune, barren, vapid. **6.** humorous, sarcastic, biting, sardonic, keen, sharp, pointed, sly.
Ant. wet, drenched; interesting, fascinating; dull.

dubious, *adj.* **1.** doubtful, undecided, indeterminate, uncertain, dubitable, fluctuating, wavering. **2.** questionable, equivocal, ambiguous, obscure, unclear.
Ant. definite, incisive, certain; unquestionable, unequivocal, clear.

dull, *adj.* **1.** slow, obtuse, stupid, blunted, unimaginative, sluggish, unintelligent, stolid. **2.** insensible, unfeeling, insensate, apathetic, unimpassioned, lifeless, callous, dead. **3.** listless, spiritless, torpid, inactive, lifeless, inert, inanimate. **4.** boring, depressing, ennuyant, tedious, uninteresting, tiresome, drear, dreary, vapid, wearisome, dry, jejune. **5.** blunt, dulled. —*v.* **6.** blunt, deaden, stupefy, paralyze, obtund, benumb. **7.** depress, dishearten, discourage, dispirit, sadden, deject.
Ant. bright, imaginative, quick; sensitive; spirited, active, animated; interesting; sharp, clever; encourage, inspirit, hearten.

dumb, *adj.* **1.** mute, speechless, silent, voiceless. **2.** stupid.
Ant. voluble, talkative, loquacious.

duplicate, *adj.* **1.** double, twofold. —*n.* **2.** facsimile copy, replica, reproduction, transcript. —*v.* **3.** copy, replicate, reproduce, repeat, double, imitate.
Ant. original.

duplicity, *n.* deceitfulness, deceit, double-dealing, deception, guile, hypocrisy, dissimulation, chicanery, artifice, fraud, dishonesty, perfidy, treachery.
Ant. naivete, honesty, openness, simplicity.

durable, *adj.* lasting, enduring, stable, constant, permanent.
Ant. unstable, temporary, temporal.

dusky, *adj.* **1.** swarthy, dark. **2.** dim, shadowy, murky, cloudy, shady, obscure, clouded, penumbral.
Ant. fair, blond, light; clear, unclouded.

dutiful, *adj.* respectful, docile, submissive, deferential, reverential, obedient.
Ant. disrespectful, disobedient, irreverent.
duty, *n.* **1.** obligation. **2.** office, function, responsibility, service, business. **3.** homage, respect, deference, reverence. **4.** levy, tax, impost, custom, toll excise.
dwarf, *n.* **1.** homunculus, manikin, pygmy, midget, Lilliputian. **2.** runt. —*adj.* **3.** diminutive, tiny, small, little, Lilliputian, stunted, dwarfed, undersized. —*v.* **4.** stunt.
Ant. giant, colossus; huge, gigantic, immense, colossal.
dwell, *v.* **1.** abide, reside, stay, live, inhabit. **2.** continue, perpetuate. **3.** linger, emphasize.
Ant. leave, depart; cease, end, terminate, stop.
dwindle, *v.* diminish, lessen, decline, decrease, wane, shrink, waste away, degenerate, sink, decay.
Ant. increase, grow, wax.

E

earn, *v.* **1.** gain, acquire, win, get, obtain, secure, procure. **2.** merit, deserve.
earnest, *adj.* **1.** sincere, zealous, ardent, eager, fervent, resolute, serious, fervid, determined, purposeful. **2.** deep, firm, stable, intent, steady, faithful, true.
Ant. insincere, apathetic; faithless, unfaithful, wavering.
earth, *n.* **1.** globe, world. **2.** ground, soil, turf, sod, dirt, terra firma.
Ant. heaven; sky.
earthly, *adj.* **1.** terrestrial, worldly, mundane, earthy. **2.** possible, conceivable, imaginable.
Ant. spiritual; impossible, inconceivable.
ease, *n.* **1.** comfort, relaxation, rest, repose, well-being, effortlessness, contentment, happiness. **2.** tranquillity, serenity, calmness, quiet, quietude, peace. **3.** informality, unaffectedness, naturalness, lightness, flexibility, freedom. —*v.* **4.** comfort, relieve, disburden. **5.** tranquilize, soothe, allay, alleviate, mitigate, abate, assuage, lighten, lessen, reduce. **6.** facilitate.
Ant. discomfort, effort; disturbance, perturbation; affection; burden; increase.
easy, *adj.* **1.** facile, light, gentle, moderate. **2.** tranquil, untroubled, comfortable, contented, satisfied, quiet, at rest. **3.** easygoing, compliant, submissive, complying, accommodating, agreeable, yielding. **4.** lenient. **5.** informal, unrestrained, unconstrained, brash, unembarrassed, smooth.
Ant. difficult, hard, immoderate; troubled, disturbed,

uncomfortable, disagreeable, unyielding; restrained, embarrassed.

ebb, *n.* **1.** reflux, regression, regress, retrogression. **2.** decline, decay, deterioration, degeneration, wane. **—***v.* **3.** subside, abate, recede, retire. **4.** decline, sink, wane, decrease, decay, waste *or* fade away.
Ant. flow, neap; wax; increase, swell, well; rise.

economical, *adj.* saving, provident, sparing, thrifty, frugal; stingy, tight, penurious.
Ant. lavish, spendthrift.

economy, *n.* **1.** frugality, thriftiness, thrift, saving. **2.** management, system, method.
Ant. lavishness.

edge, *n.* **1.** border, rim, lip, margin, boundary, verge, brink. **—***v.* **2.** inch, sidle.
Ant. center.

educate, *v.* teach, instruct, school, drill, indoctrinate, train, discipline.

education, *n.* **1.** instruction, schooling, tuition, training. **2.** learning, knowledge, enlightenment, culture.
Ant. illiteracy.

eerie, *adj.* fearful, awesome, weird, uncanny, strange.
Ant. common, ordinary.

effect, *n.* **1.** result, consequence, end, outcome, issue. **2.** power, efficacy, force, validity, weight. **3.** operation, execution; accomplishment, fulfillment. **4.** purport, intent, tenor, significance, signification, meaning, import. **—***v.* **5.** bring about, accomplish, make happen, achieve, do, perform, complete, consummate, bring about, realize.
Ant. cause.

effective, *adj.* **1.** capable, competent, efficient, efficacious, effectual. **2.** operative, in force, active.
Ant. ineffective, incompetent, inefficient, ineffectual; inactive, inoperative.

effectual, *adj.* effective.
Ant. ineffectual.

efficacious, *adj.* effective.
Ant. ineffective.

efficient, *adj.* effective.
Ant. inefficient, ineffective.

effort, *n.* application, endeavor, exertion, nisus, attempt, struggle, striving.
Ant. ease.

egoism, *n.* self-love, egotism, selfishness, self-conceit.
Ant. altruism.

egotism, *n.* self-centeredness, egoism, boastfulness, conceit.
Ant. altruism, modesty.

elaborate, *adj.* **1.** perfected, painstaking, labored, studied; detailed, ornate, intricate, complicated, complex. **—***v.* **2.** produce, develop, work out, refine, improve.
Ant. simple; simplify.

elect, *v.* **1.** select, choose, prefer, pick out. **—***adj.* **2.** select, chosen, choice.

Ant. refuse, reject; spurned.

elegant, *adj.* tasteful, fine, luxurious; refined, polished, cultivated, genteel, courtly, graceful; choice, nice, superior; excellent.
Ant. inelegant, distasteful; unrefined, disgraceful; inferior.

element, *n.* **1.** component, constituent, ingredient, unit, part, essential. **2.** rudiments, principle, basis, basics. **3.** habitat, environment, medium, milieu.
Ant. whole, nonessential; compound.

elementary, *adj.* primary, rudimentary, basic, fundamental, rudimental; uncompounded, simple, uncomplicated.
Ant. advanced, secondary; complex, complicated.

elevate, *v.* raise, lift up, exalt, heighten, increase, intensify, promote, advance, improve, enhance, dignify, refine; animate, cheer.
Ant. lower, debase, decrease; depress.

elevation, *n.* **1.** eminence, height, hill; altitude. **2.** loftiness, grandeur, dignity, nobility, nobleness, refinement, exaltation.
Ant. valley; depths.

eliminate, *v.* get rid of, expel, remove, exclude, reject, omit, ignore.
Ant. include, accept.

elocution, *n.* oratory, declamation, rhetoric.

elucidate, *v.* explain, explicate, clarify, make plain *or* clear.
Ant. becloud, bedim, confuse.

elude, *v.* **1.** avoid, escape, evade, slip away from, shun, dodge. **2.** baffle, confound, foil, thwart, confuse, frustrate, disconcert.
Ant. pursue, follow.

emanate, *v.* emerge, issue, proceed, come forth, originate, arise, spring, flow.

embarrass, *v.* **1.** disconcert, abash, make uncomfortable, confuse, discomfit, discompose, chagrin. **2.** complicate, make difficult, perplex, mystify. **3.** impede, hamper, hinder, annoy, vex, trouble, harass, distress.
Ant. comfort, console; simplify.

embarrassment, *n.* **1.** disconcertment, abashment, perplexity, confusion, discomposure, discomfort, mortification, chagrin. **2.** trouble, annoyance, vexation, distress, harassment, hindrance, deterrent.
Ant. comfort, composure; encouragement.

embellish, *v.* **1.** beautify, ornament, adorn, decorate, garnish, bedeck, embroider. **2.** enhance, embroider, exaggerate about.
Ant. mar, disfigure, deface.

emblem, *n.* token, sign, symbol, figure, image, badge, device, mark.

embrace, *v.* **1.** clasp, hug. **2.** accept, adopt, espouse, welcome, seize. **3.** encircle, surround, enclose, contain. **4.** include, contain, comprise, comprehend, cover, embody.

Ant. exclude.

emerge, *v.* come forth, emanate, issue, spread, stream.
Ant. enter.

emergency, *n.* crisis, straits, urgency, turning-point, exigency, necessity, extremity, pinch, dilemma, quandary.

eminence, *n.* **1.** repute, distinction, prominence, celebrity, renown, conspicuousness, note, fame, rank, position. **2.** elevation, hill, prominence.
Ant. disrepute.

eminent, *adj.* **1.** distinguished, signal, notable, noteworthy, noted, reputable, prominent, celebrated, renowned, outstanding, illustrious, conspicuous, exalted. **2.** lofty, high, prominent, projecting, protruding, protuberant.
Ant. disreputable, commonplace, ordinary; low, debased; inconspicuous.

emit, *v.* **1.** send *or* give forth, discharge, eject, vent, exhale, exude, expel. **2.** issue, circulate, publish.
Ant. inspire, inhale, accept; hide.

emotion, *n.* feeling; sympathy, empathy.
Ant. apathy.

emphatic, *adj.* significant, marked, striking, positive, energetic, forcible, forceful, pronounced, strong, decided, unequivocal, definite.
Ant. insignificant, uncertain, unsure.

empire, *n.* **1.** power, sovereignty, dominion, rule, supremacy, authority. **2.** command, sway, rule, government, control.

employ, *v.* **1.** use, engage, hire, retain, occupy. **2.** use, apply, make use of. **—***n.* **3.** service, employment.

employee, *n.* worker, servant, agent, clerk, wage-earner.
Ant. employer, boss.

empower, *v.* **1.** authorize, warrant, commission, license, qualify, deputize. **2.** enable, permit.

empty, *adj.* **1.** void, vacant, blank, unoccupied, uninhabited. **2.** unsatisfactory, meaningless, superficial, hollow, delusive, vain, ineffectual, ineffective, unsatisfying. **3.** frivolous, foolish. **—***v.* **4.** unload, unburden, pour out, evacuate, drain, discharge.
Ant. full, replete, occupied, inhabited; satisfactory, effectual; serious.

emulation, *n.* competition, rivalry, contention, strife, envy.

enamor, *v.* inflame, captivate, bewitch, charm, fascinate, enchant.

enchant, *v.* fascinate, captivate, charm, enrapture, transport, bewitch, delight.
Ant. bore.

encircle, *v.* surround, encompass, environ, gird, enfold, enclose.

enclose, *v.* surround, encircle, encompass, circumscribe.
Ant. exclude.

encounter, *v.* **1.** meet, confront, face. **2.** contend against, engage with, attack, cope with, compete with. —*n.* **3.** meeting. **4.** battle, combat, conflict.

encourage, *v.* **1.** inspirit, embolden, hearten, stimulate, incite; reassure, assure, console, comfort. **2.** urge, abet, second, support, favor, countenance, advance, foster, promote, aid, help, foment.
Ant. discourage, dispirit.

encroach, *v.* trespass, intrude, invade, infringe.

encumber, *v.* **1.** impede, hamper, retard, embarrass, obstruct, complicate, involve, entangle. **2.** load, oppress, overload, burden.
Ant. disencumber; unload, unburden.

end, *n.* **1.** extremity, extreme. **2.** limit, bound, boundary, termination, tip, terminus. **3.** close, termination, conclusion, finish, outcome, issue, consequence, result, completion, attainment. **4.** finale, conclusion, peroration. **5.** purpose, aim, object, objective, intention, design, intent, drift. —*v.* **6.** terminate, conclude, wind up, finish, complete, close. **7.** stop, cease, discontinue, conclude.
Ant. beginning, start; begin, commence, open; continue.

endeavor, *v.* **1.** attempt, essay, try, make an effort, strive, struggle, labor; seek, aim. —*n.* **2.** exertion, struggle, essay, attempt, trial.

endless, *adj.* limitless, unlimited, vast, illimitable, immeasurable, unending, boundless, infinite, interminable, incessant, unceasing, eternal, continuous, perpetual, everlasting.
Ant. limited, finite.

endow, *v.* equip, invest, clothe, endue, enrich; confer, bestow, give.
Ant. divest.

endowment, *n.* gift, grant, bequest, largess, bounty, present; capacity, talent, faculties, quality, power, ability, aptitude, capability, genius.
Ant. incapacity.

endure, *v.* **1.** sustain, hold out against, undergo, bear, support, suffer, experience. **2.** experience, stand, tolerate, bear, brook, allow, permit, submit. **3.** continue, last, persist, remain.
Ant. fail, subside; refuse; die, perish, fail.

enemy, *n.* foe, adversary, opponent, antagonist.
Ant. friend, ally.

energetic, *adj.* **1.** forcible, vigorous, active. **2.** powerful, effective, effectual, strong, efficacious, potent.
Ant. lazy, inactive; ineffective, impotent, weak.

energy, *n.* activity, exertion, power, force, operation, dynamism, vigor, potency, zeal, push, spirit, animation, life. **2.** force, power, might, efficacy, strength, intensity.
Ant. inertia, inactivity; weakness.

engender, *v.* **1.** produce, cause, give rise to, beget, create, occasion, excite, stir up, incite, generate, breed. **2.** procreate, beget, create, generate, breed.
Ant. terminate; kill.

enigma, *n.* puzzle, riddle, problem, question.
enjoin, *v.* **1.** charge, order, direct, prescribe, bid, command, require. **2.** prohibit, proscribe, interdict, ban, preclude.
Ant. encourage, allow.
enjoyment, *n.* delight, delectation, pleasure, gratification, happiness.
Ant. detestation, abhorrence, displeasure.
enlarge, *v.* extend, augment, amplify, dilate, increase, aggrandize, magnify, expand, greaten.
Ant. limit, decrease, lessen, abate.
enlighten, *v.* illumine, edify, teach, inform, instruct, educate.
Ant. confuse.
enliven, *v.* **1.** invigorate, animate, inspirit, vivify, stimulate, quicken. **2.** exhilarate, gladden, cheer, brighten, inspire, delight.
Ant. dispirit, slow; depress.
enormous, *adj.* **1.** huge, immense, vast, colossal, mammoth, gigantic, prodigious, stupendous, elephantine, monstrous. **2.** outrageous, atrocious, flagitious, depraved, wicked, flagrant, scandalous, egregious.
Ant. small, diminutive, tiny; honorable.
enrage, *v.* infuriate, anger, incense, inflame, provoke, madden, exasperate, aggravate.
Ant. tranquilize, calm, assuage.
ensue, *v.* follow, succeed; issue, arise, result, flow.
Ant. lead; precede.
entangle, *v.* **1.** complicate, ensnare, enmesh, tangle, knot, mat. **2.** embarrass, confuse, perplex, bewilder, involve, ensnare.
Ant. simplify.
enterprise, *n.* **1.** project, plan, undertaking, venture. **2.** boldness, readiness, spirit, energy.
enterprising, *adj.* ambitious, ready, resourceful, adventurous, venturesome, dashing, bold, energetic, spirited, eager, zealous.
Ant. smug, phlegmatic.
entertain, *v.* **1.** divert, amuse, please. **2.** receive, consider, admit. **3.** harbor, cherish, hold.
Ant. bore; refuse, reject; expel.
enthusiasm, *n.* eagerness, earnestness, sincerity, interest, warmth, fervor, zeal, ardor, passion, devotion.
Ant. coolness.
enthusiast, *n.* **1.** zealot, devotee, fan. **2.** zealot, bigot, fanatic.
enthusiastic, *adj.* ardent, zealous, eager, fervent, passionate, vehement, fervid, burning, impassioned.
Ant. blasé, dispassionate, cool, unenthusiastic.
entice, *v.* allure, inveigle, excite, lure, attract, decoy, tempt, seduce, coax, cajole, wheedle, persuade.
Ant. discourage, deter, dissuade.
entire, *adj.* **1.** whole, complete, unbroken, perfect, unimpaired, intact, undiminished, undivided, continuous. **2.** full, complete, thorough, unqualified, unrestricted, unmitigated. **—*n.*** **3.** entirety.

Ant. partial, imperfect, divided; restricted, incomplete.

entitle, *v.* **1.** empower, qualify. **2.** name, designate, call, title, dub.
Ant. disqualify.

entrance, *n.* **1.** entry, ingress, access, entree. **2.** entry, door, portal, gate, doorway, stoa, passage, inlet. **3.** admission, entry, admittance. **—***v.* **4.** enrapture, enchant, charm, delight, transport.
Ant. exit; disenchant.

entreat, *v.* appeal, implore, beg, beseech, obsecrate, obtest, supplicate, crave, solicit, pray, importune, petition, sue.

entreaty, *n.* supplication, appeal, suit, plea, solicitation, petition.

enumerate, *v.* count, name, recount, recapitulate, rehearse, cite.

envelop, *v.* **1.** wrap, cover, enfold, hide, conceal. **2.** surround, enclose, encompass, cover, enfold.

envy, *n.* **1.** jealousy, enviousness, grudge, covetousness. **—***v.* **2.** covet, begrudge, resent.
Ant. generosity.

ephemeral, *adj.* **1.** short-lived, transitory, temporary, fleeting, momentary, brief, evanescent. **—***n.* **2.** will o' the wisp, St. Elmo's fire, corposant, ephemeron.
Ant. concrete, permanent.

epicure, *n.* gastronome, gourmet, epicurean, voluptuary, sensualist, glutton, gourmand.

episode, *n.* occurrence, event, incident, happening.

epoch, *n.* age, era, period, date.

equable, *adj.* even, uniform, tranquil, steady, regular, even-tempered, temperate.
Ant. uneven, irregular, turbulent, intemperate.

equal, *adj.* **1.** proportionate, commensurate, balanced, coordinate, correspondent, equivalent, tantamount, like, alike. **2.** uniform, even, regular, unvarying, invariant. **3.** adequate, sufficient, competent, suitable, fit. **—***n.* **4.** peer, compeer, match, mate, fellow. **—***v.* **5.** match, be commensurate with.
Ant. unequal, disproportionate, incommensurate, dissimilar; uneven, irregular, variable; inadequate, insufficient, unsuitable.

equip, *v.* furnish, provide, fit out, outfit, rig, array, accouter.

equipment, *n.* apparatus, paraphernalia, gear, accouterment.

equivocal, *adj.* **1.** ambiguous, uncertain. **2.** doubtful, uncertain, questionable, dubious, indeterminate.
Ant. unequivocal, certain; definite, unquestionable.

eradicate, *v.* remove, destroy, extirpate, abolish, obliterate, uproot, exterminate, annihilate.
Ant. insert, add; originate, create.

erase, *v.* efface, expunge, cancel, obliterate.
Ant. create.

erect, *adj.* **1.** upright, standing, vertical. **—***v.* **2.** build,

raise, construct, upraise. **3.** set up, found, establish, institute.
Ant. horizontal; raze, destroy; dissolve, liquidate.

erroneous, *adj.* mistaken, incorrect, inaccurate, false, wrong, untrue.
Ant. correct, accurate, true.

error, *n.* **1.** mistake, blunder, slip, oversight. **2.** offense, wrongdoing, fault, sin, transgression, trespass, misdeed, iniquity.

escape, *v.* **1.** flee, abscond, decamp, fly, steal away, run away. **2.** shun, fly, elude, evade, avoid. —*n.* **3.** flight; release.

escort, *n.* **1.** convoy, guard, guide, protection, safeguard, guidance. —*v.* **2.** conduct, usher, guard, guide, convoy, accompany, attend.

especially, *adv.* particularly, chiefly, principally, unusually, significantly, prominently, signally, specially, markedly.

espy, *v.* catch sight of, descry, discover, perceive, make out.
Ant. overlook.

essential, *adj.* **1.** indispensable, necessary, vital, fundamental, rudimentary, elementary, basic, inherent, intrinsic, important. —*n.* **2.** necessity, basic, element.
Ant. dispensable, unnecessary, unimportant.

establish, *v.* **1.** set up, found, institute, form, organize, fix, settle, install. **2.** verify, substantiate, prove. **3.** appoint, ordain, fix, enact, decree.
Ant. liquidate, dissolve; disprove.

esteem, *v.* **1.** prize, value, honor, revere, respect, appreciate, estimate, regard. —*n.* **2.** respect, regard, favor, admiration, honor, reverence, veneration. **3.** estimation, valuation, estimate, appreciation.
Ant. disregard; disrespect, disfavor; depreciation.

estimable, *adj.* respectable, reputable, worthy, deserving, meritorious, good, excellent.
Ant. disreputable, unworthy, bad, inferior.

estimate, *v.* **1.** judge, compute, reckon, gauge, count, assess, value, evaluate, appraise. —*n.* **2.** judgment, calculation, valuation, estimation, opinion, computation.

estimation, *n.* judgment, opinion, appreciation, regard, honor, veneration, esteem, respect, reverence.

eternal, *adj.* **1.** endless, everlasting, infinite, unending, neverending, interminable, unceasing, perpetual, ceaseless, permanent. **2.** timeless, immortal, deathless, undying, imperishable, indestructible.
Ant. transitory, ephemeral; perishable, mortal.

etiquette, *n.* decorum, propriety, code of behavior, convention, dignity.
Ant. impropriety, indignity.

eulogize, *v.* praise, extol, laud, commend, panegyrize, applaud.
Ant. criticize, condemn.

evade, *v.* **1.** escape, elude, escape from, avoid, shun,

sidestep, dodge. **2.** baffle, foil, elude. **3.** prevaricate, equivocate, quibble, fence.
Ant. face, confront.

evaporate, *v.* **1.** vaporize, dehydrate, dry. **2.** disappear, fade, vanish, evanesce.
Ant. condense, sublimate.

evasion, *n.* **1.** avoidance, dodging, escape. **2.** prevarication, equivocation, quibbling, subterfuge, sophistry.

even, *adj.* **1.** level, flat, smooth, plane. **2.** parallel, level. **3.** regular, equable, uniform, steady, well-balanced, in equilibrium, conformant, standard. **3.** commensurate, equal; square, balanced. **4.** calm, placid, tranquil, even-tempered, temperate, composed, peaceful. **5.** fair, just, equitable, impartial. —*adv.* **6.** still, yet; just; fully, quite, completely; indeed. —*v.* **7.** level, smooth; balance, equilibrate, counterpoise.
Ant. uneven, irregular; unsteady; unequal, incommensurate; agitated, intemperate; unfair, unjust, prejudiced, biased.

evening, *n.* eventide, dusk, twilight, gloaming, nightfall, eve, even, sundown.
Ant. dawn, sunrise.

event, *n.* **1.** occurrence, happening, affair, case, circumstance, episode, incident. **2.** result, issue, consequence, outcome.

ever, *adv.* **1.** continuously, eternally, perpetually, constantly, always. **2.** by any chance, at all, at any time.
Ant. never.

everlasting, *adj.* eternal.
Ant. ephemeral, transitory.

evidence, *n.* **1.** ground, grounds, proof, testimony. **2.** indication, sign, signal. **3.** information, deposition, affidavit, exhibit, testimony, proof. —*v.* **4.** make clear, show, manifest, demonstrate.

evident, *adj.* plain, clear, obvious, manifest, palpable, patent, unmistakable, apparent.
Ant. concealed, hidden.

evil, *adj.* **1.** wicked, bad, immoral, amoral, sinful, iniquitous, flagitious, depraved, vicious, corrupt, perverse, wrong, base, vile, nefarious, malicious, malignant, malevolent. **2.** harmful, injurious, wrong, bad, pernicious, destructive, mischief. **3.** unfortunate, disastrous, miserable. —*n.* **4.** wickedness, depravity, iniquity, unrighteousness, sin, corruption, baseness, badness. **5.** harm, mischief, misfortune, disaster, calamity, misery, pain, woe, suffering, sorrow.
Ant. good.

exact, *adj.* **1.** accurate, correct, precise, literal, faithful, close. **2.** strict, rigorous, rigid, unbending, exacting, demanding, severe, scrupulous. **3.** methodical, careful, punctilious, accurate, critical, nice, regular, precise, orderly. —*v.* **4.** call for, demand, require, force, compel. **5.** extort, wrest, wring, extract.

Ant. inexact, inaccurate, imprecise, unfaithful, free; disorderly.

exalt, *v.* **1.** elevate, promote, dignify, raise, ennoble. **2.** praise, extol, glorify, bless. **3.** elate, make proud, please. **4.** stimulate. **5.** intensify.
Ant. lower, debase; damn, condemn; displease.

examination, *n.* **1.** inspection, inquiry, observation, investigation, scrutiny, scanning, inquisition. **2.** test, trial.

examine, *v.* **1.** inspect, scrutinize, search, probe, explore, study, investigate, test. **2.** catechize.

example, *n.* sample, specimen, representative, illustration, case, pattern, model.

exasperate, *v.* irritate, annoy, vex, infuriate, exacerbate, anger, incense, provoke, nettle, needle, enrage, inflame.
Ant. calm, assuage, tranquilize.

exceed, *v.* overstep, transcend, surpass, cap, top, outdo, excel, outstrip, beat.

excel, *v.* surpass, outdo, exceed, transcend, outstrip, eclipse, beat, win over, cap, top.

excellence, *n.* superiority, eminence, preeminence, transcendence, distinction; merit, virtue, purity, goodness, uprightness.
Ant. baseness; inferiority.

excellent, *adj.* good, choice, worthy, fine, first-rate, estimable, superior, better, admirable, prime.
Ant. bad, inferior, base.

except, *prep.* **1.** but, save, excepting, excluding. —*v.* **2.** exclude, leave out, omit, bar, reject.
Ant. including; include, admit.

exceptional, *adj.* unusual, extraordinary, irregular, peculiar, rare, strange, unnatural, anomalous, abnormal, aberrant.
Ant. customary, common, usual, normal, regular, natural.

excess, *n.* **1.** superfluity, superabundance, nimiety, redundancy. **2.** surplus, remainder. **3.** immoderation, intemperance, over-indulgence, dissipation.
Ant. lack, need, want.

excessive, *adj.* immoderate, extravagant, extreme, exorbitant, inordinate, outrageous, unreasonable, disproportionate.
Ant. reasonable, proportionate.

exchange, *v.* **1.** barter, trade, interchange, commute, swap, reciprocate. —*n.* **2.** interchange, trade, traffic, business, commerce, reciprocity, barter. **3.** market, bourse.
Ant. embargo.

exchangeable, *adj.* interchangeable, replaceable, returnable.

excitable, *adj.* emotional, passionate, fiery, quick-tempered, hot-tempered, hasty, irascible, irritable, choleric.
Ant. unemotional, cool, calm, serene, tranquil.

excite, *v.* **1.** stir, arouse, rouse, awaken, stimulate,

animate, kindle, inflame, incite. **2.** stir up, provoke, disturb, agitate, irritate, discompose.
Ant. pacify, calm, soothe.

excited, *adj.* ruffled, discomposed, stormy, perturbed, impassioned, stimulated, brisk, agitated, stirred up, agog, eager, enthusiastic.
Ant. calm, unruffled, composed, pacific.

excitement, *n.* agitation, commotion, ado, to do, perturbation, disturbance.
Ant. serenity, peace.

exclamation, *n.* outcry, ejaculation, interjection, cry, complaint, protest, vociferation, shout, clamor.

exclude, *v.* **1.** bar, restrain, keep out, shut out. **2.** debar, eliminate, expel, eject, reject, prohibit, withhold, except, omit, preclude; proscribe, prevent.
Ant. include; accept.

exclusive, *adj.* **1.** incompatible, excluding, barring. **2.** restrictive, cliquish, snobbish, fastidious. **3.** single, sole, only, special. **4.** select, narrow, clannish, snobbish, selfish, illiberal, narrow, narrow-minded, uncharitable. **5.** fashionable, chic, aristocratic, choice.
Ant. inclusive, including; general; liberal; poor.

excursion, *n.* **1.** journey, tour, trip, jaunt, junket, outing, cruise. **2.** deviation, digression, episode.

excuse, *v.* **1.** forgive, pardon, overlook, acquit, absolve, exonerate, exculpate. **2.** apologize for, exonerate, exculpate, clear, vindicate. **3.** extenuate, palliate, justify. **4.** release, disoblige, free, liberate, disencumber. —*n.* **5.** plea, apology, absolution, justification. **6.** pretext, pretense, subterfuge, evasion, makeshift.
Ant. condemn; oblige, shackle.

execute, *v.* **1.** carry out, accomplish, do, perform, achieve, effect, consummate, finish, complete. **2.** kill, put to death, hang. **3.** enforce, effectuate, administer; sign, seal, and deliver.

exemption, *n.* immunity, impunity, privilege, freedom, exception.
Ant. culpability.

exercise, *n.* **1.** exertion, labor, toil, work, action, activity. **2.** drill, practice, training, schooling, discipline. **3.** practice, use, application, employment, performance, operation. **4.** ceremony, ritual, procedure, observance, service. —*v.* **5.** discipline, drill, train, school. **6.** practice, use, apply, employ, effect, exert. **7.** discharge, perform. **8.** worry, annoy, make uneasy, try, burden, trouble, pain, afflict.
Ant. laziness.

exertion, *n.* effort, action, activity, endeavor, struggle, attempt, strain, trial.

exhaust, *v.* **1.** empty, drain, void. **2.** use up, expend, consume, waste, squander, dissipate, spend, fritter away. **3.** enervate, tire, prostrate, wear out, fatigue, weaken, cripple, debilitate. —*n.* **4.** fumes, smoke, vapor, effluvium.
Ant. fill; use; innervate, invigorate, strengthen.

exhaustion, *n.* weariness, lassitude, weakness, fatigue.
Ant. energy, exhilaration, strength.

exhibit, *v.* **1.** expose, present, display, show, demonstrate, offer. **2.** manifest, display, show, betray, reveal, express, disclose, indicate, evince. —*n.* **3.** exhibition, showing, show, display, demonstration, offering, exposition, manifestation. **4.** evidence, testimony.
Ant. conceal, hide.

exhilarate, *v.* make cheerful *or* merry, cheer, gladden, enliven, inspirit, animate, inspire, elate.
Ant. depress, sadden, deject.

exonerate, *v.* **1.** absolve, exculpate, clear, acquit, vindicate, justify. **2.** relieve, release, discharge, except, exempt, free.
Ant. blame, condemn; imprison.

exorbitant, *adj.* exceeding, excessive, inordinate, extravagant, unreasonable, unconscionable, enormous.
Ant. reasonable, inexpensive.

expand, *v.* increase, extend, swell, enlarge, dilate, distend, inflate, bloat, aggrandize, spread *or* stretch out, unfold, develop.
Ant. contract, shrink.

expect, *v.* look forward to, anticipate, await, hope for, wait for, count on, rely on.

expectation, *n.* expectancy, anticipation, hope, trust, prospect.

expedient, *adj.* **1.** advantageous, fit, suitable, profitable, advisable, proper, appropriate, desirable. —*n.* **2.** device, contrivance, means, resource, shift, resort.
Ant. unsuitable, inapt, undesirable.

expedite, *v.* speed up, hasten, quicken, speed, push, accelerate, hurry, precipitate; dispatch.
Ant. slow.

expedition, *n.* **1.** excursion, journey, voyage, trip, junket, safari. **2.** promptness, speed, haste, quickness, dispatch, alacrity.
Ant. sloth.

expel, *v.* drive *or* force away, drive *or* force out, discharge, eject; dismiss, oust, banish, exile, expatriate, (*British*) send down.
Ant. accept, invite.

expend, *v.* **1.** use, employ, consume, spend, exhaust, use up. **2.** pay out, disburse, spend, lay out.
Ant. waste, squander.

expense, *n.* **1.** cost, charge, price, outlay, expenditure. **2.** loss, injury, harm, debit, detriment.

expensive, *adj.* costly, dear, high-priced.
Ant. inexpensive, cheap, tawdry.

experience, *n.* **1.** undergoing, feeling, encountering. **2.** knowledge, wisdom, sagacity. —*v.* **3.** meet with, undergo, feel, encounter, live through, know, observe; endure; suffer.
Ant. inexperience, naivete.

experienced, *adj.* skilled, expert, veteran, practiced, accomplished, versed, qualified, adroit, adept.

Ant. inexperienced, inexpert, naive, artless, unqualified.

experiment, *n.* **1.** test, trial, examination, proof, assay, procedure. **2.** experimentation, research, investigation. —*v.* **3.** try, test, examine, prove, assay.

expert, *n.* **1.** specialist, authority, connoisseur, master. —*adj.* **2.** trained, skilled, skillful, experienced, proficient, dexterous, adroit, clever, apt, quick.
Ant. butcher, shoemaker, dolt; untrained, inexperienced, maladroit.

explain, *v.* **1.** elucidate, expound, explicate, interpret, clarify, throw light on, make plain *or* manifest. **2.** account for, justify.
Ant. confuse.

explanation, *n.* **1.** explaining, elucidation, explication, exposition, definition, interpretation, description. **2.** meaning, interpretation, solution, key, answer, definition, account, justification.

explicit, *adj.* **1.** clear, unequivocal, express, unambiguous, precise, definite, exact, categorical, determinate. **2.** open, outspoken, definite, unashamed, unabashed.
Ant. unclear, equivocal, ambiguous, indefinite; clandestine, concealed.

exploit, *n.* **1.** deed, feat, accomplishment, achievement. —*v.* **2.** use, utilize, take advantage of.

expose, *v.* **1.** lay open, subject, endanger, imperil, jeopardize. **2.** bare, uncover; exhibit, display. **3.** make known, betray, uncover, unveil, disclose, reveal, unmask, bring to light; muckrake.
Ant. conceal, hide.

exposition, *n.* **1.** exhibit, exhibition, show, demonstration, display, **2.** explanation, elucidation, commentary, treatise, critique, interpretation, exegesis, explication.

exposure, *n.* **1.** exposing; disclosure, unmasking, presentation, display, divulgement, revelation, exposé. **2.** aspect, orientation.
Ant. hiding, concealment.

express, *v.* **1.** utter, declare, state, word, speak, assert, asseverate. **2.** show, manifest, reveal, expose, indicate, exhibit, represent. **3.** indicate, signify, designate, denote. **4.** press *or* squeeze out. —*adj.* **5.** clear, distinct, definite, explicit, plain, obvious, positive, unambiguous, categorical; unsubtle. **6.** special, particular, singular, signal. **7.** faithful, exact, accurate, precise, true, close. **8.** swift, direct, fast, rapid, nonstop. —*n.* **9.** courier, special messenger.
Ant. conceal.

expression, *n.* **1.** utterance, declaration, assertion, statement. **2.** phrase, term, idiom. **3.** language, diction, phraseology, wording, phrasing, presentation. **4.** manifestation, sign. **5.** look, countenance, aspect, air, mien, intonation, tone.
Ant. silence.

expressive, *adj.* **1.** meaning, significant, suggestive,

meaningful, indicative. **2.** lively, vivid, strong, emphatic.
Ant. expressionless, meaningless.

exquisite, *adj.* **1.** dainty, beautiful, elegant, rare, delicate, appealing, charming. **2.** fine, admirable, consummate, perfect, matchless, complete, valuable, precious. **3.** intense, acute, keen, poignant. **4.** sensitive, responsive. **5.** rare, select, choice, excellent, precious, valuable, priceless; vintage. **6.** refined, elegant, delicate, discriminating, polished, debonair.
Ant. ugly, hideous; imperfect, valueless, worthless; dull; vacuous, vapid; common, ordinary; poor, inferior; boorish.

extemporaneous, *adj.* extemporary, extempore, impromptu, improvised, unpremeditated, offhand, off the cuff.
Ant. prepared, premeditated.

extend, *v.* **1.** stretch *or* draw out, attenuate. **2.** lengthen, prolong, protract, continue. **3.** expand, spread out, dilate, enlarge, widen, diffuse, fill out. **4.** hold forth, offer, bestow, grant, give, impart, yield.
Ant. shorten, abbreviate; discontinue; shrink, curtail.

extension, *n.* **1.** stretching, expansion, enlargement, dilation, dilatation, increase. **2.** prolongation, lengthening, protraction, continuation; delay. **3.** extent, limit.
Ant. shrinking, decrease; curtailment.

extensive, *adj.* **1.** wide, broad, large, extended, spacious, ample, vast. **2.** far-reaching, comprehensive, thorough; inclusive.

extent, *n.* space, degree, magnitude, measure, amount, scope, compass, range, expanse, stretch, reach, size; length, area, volume.

exterior, *adj.* **1.** outer, outside, outward, external, outer, superficial. **2.** outlying, extraneous, foreign, extrinsic. —*n.* **3.** outside, face. **4.** appearance, mien, aspect, face.
Ant. interior, inner; important; interior, inside.

exterminate, *v.* extirpate, annihilate, destroy, eradicate, abolish, eliminate.
Ant. create, generate, originate.

extinct, *adj.* **1.** extinguished, quenched, out, put out. **2.** obsolete, archaic. **3.** ended, terminated, over, dead, gone, vanished.
Ant. extant; modern; begun, initiated.

extol, *v.* praise, laud, eulogize, commend, glorify, exalt, celebrate, applaud, panegyrize.
Ant. condemn, damn.

extort, *v.* extract, exact, wrest, wring, blackmail, bleed.

extract, *v.* **1.** draw forth *or* out, get, pull *or* pry out. **2.** deduce, divine, understand. **3.** extort, exact, evoke, educe, draw out, elicit, wrest, wring, bleed. **4.** derive, withdraw, distill. —*n.* **5.** excerpt, quotation, citation, selection. **6.** decoction, distillate, solution.

extraneous, *adj.* external, extrinsic, foreign, alien, adventitious; inappropriate, not germane, not pertinent, nonessential, superfluous.
Ant. internal, intrinsic; appropriate, pertinent, essential, vital.

extraordinary, *adj.* exceptional, special, inordinate, uncommon, singular, signal, rare, phenomenal, remarkable, unusual, egregious, unheard-of.
Ant. ordinary, common, usual, customary.

extravagant, *adj.* **1.** imprudent, wasteful, lavish, spendthrift, prodigal, immoderate, excessive, inordinate, exorbitant. **2.** unreasonable, fantastic, wild, foolish, absurd.
Ant. prudent, thrifty, moderate; reasonable, thoughtful, sensible.

extreme, *adj.* **1.** utmost, greatest, rarest, highest; superlative. **2.** outermost, endmost, ultimate, last, uttermost, remotest. **3.** extravagant, immoderate, excessive, fanatical, uncompromising, radical, outré, unreasonable. **4.** last, final, ultimate. —*n.* **5.** furthest, remotest. **6.** acme, limit, end; extremity.
Ant. reasonable.

extremity, *n.* **1.** terminal, limit, end, termination, extreme, verge, border, boundary, bounds. **2.** utmost, extreme.

exuberance, *n.* exuberancy, superabundance, excess, copiousness, profusion, luxuriance, lavishness, superfluity, redundancy, overflow.
Ant. paucity, lack, need, want.

F

fable, *n.* **1.** legend, tale, apologue, parable, allegory, myth, story. **2.** lie, untruth, falsehood, fib, fiction, invention, fabrication, forgery. —*v.* **3.** lie, fib, fabricate, invent.
Ant. truth, gospel.

fabricate, *v.* **1.** construct, build, frame, erect, make, manufacture. **2.** assemble, put together, erect. **3.** devise, invent, coin, feign; forge, fake.
Ant. destroy, raze.

fabulous, *adj.* **1.** unbelievable, incredible, amazing, astonishing, astounding. **2.** untrue, unreal, unrealistic, invented, fabled, fictional, fictitious, fabricated, coined, made up, imaginary.
Ant. commonplace; real, natural.

face, *n.* **1.** countenance, visage, front, features, look, expression, appearance, aspect, mien; sight, presence. **2.** show, pretense, pretext, exterior. **3.** name, prestige, reputation. —*v.* **4.** meet face to face, confront,

encounter, meet, meet with. **5.** oppose. **6.** cover, veneer.
Ant. back; absence; interior.

facetious, *adj.* amusing, humorous, comical, funny, witty, droll, jocular.
Ant. sad.

factory, *n.* manufactory, mill, workshop, plant.

faculty, *n.* ability, capacity, aptitude, capability, knack, turn, talent.
Ant. inability, incapacity.

fade, *v.* **1.** wither, droop, languish, decline, decay. **2.** blanch, bleach, pale. **3.** disappear, vanish, die out, pass away, evanesce.
Ant. flourish; flush; appear.

fail, *v.* **1.** come short, fall short, disappoint. **2.** fall off, dwindle, pass *or* die away, decline, fade, weaken, sink, wane, give out, cease, disappear. **3.** desert, forsake, disappoint.
Ant. succeed.

failing, *n.* shortcoming, weakness, foible, deficiency, defect, frailty, imperfection, fault, flaw.
Ant. success, sufficiency; strength.

failure, *n.* **1.** unsuccessfulness, miscarriage, abortion, failing. **2.** neglect, omission, dereliction, nonperformance. **3.** deficiency, insufficiency, defectiveness. **4.** decline, decay, deterioration, loss. **5.** bankruptcy, insolvency, failing, bust; dud.
Ant. success; adequacy, sufficiency, effectiveness.

faint, *adj.* **1.** indistinct, ill-defined, dim, faded, dull. **2.** feeble, half-hearted, faltering, irresolute, weak, languid, drooping. **3.** feeble, languid, swooning. **4.** cowardly, timorous, pusillanimous, fearful, timid, dastardly, faint-hearted. **—*v.*** **5.** swoon, pass out, black out. **—*n.*** **6.** swoon, unconsciousness.
Ant. strong; distinct; brave, bold.

fair, *adj.* **1.** unbiased, equitable, just, honest, impartial, disinterested, unprejudiced. **2.** reasonable, passable, tolerable, average, middling. **3.** likely, favorable, promising, hopeful. **4.** bright, sunny, cloudless; fine. **5.** unobstructed, open, clear, distinct, unencumbered, plain. **6.** clean, spotless, pure, untarnished, unsullied, unspotted, unblemished, unstained. **7.** clear, legible, distinct. **8.** light, blond, white, pale. **9.** beautiful, lovely, comely, pretty, attractive, pleasing, handsome. **10.** courteous, civil, polite, gracious. **—*adv.*** **11.** straight, directly. **12.** favorably, auspiciously. **—*n.*** **13.** exhibit, exhibition, festival, kermis.
Ant. unfair.

fairy, *n.* fay, pixy, leprechaun, nix, nixie, brownie, elf, sprite.

faith, *n.* **1.** confidence, trust, reliance, credit, credence, assurance. **2.** belief, doctrine, tenet, creed, dogma, religion, persuasion.
Ant. discredit, distrust.

faithful, *adj.* **1.** strict, thorough, true, devoted. **2.** true, reliable, trustworthy, trusty. **3.** stable, depend-

able, steadfast, stanch, loyal, constant. **4.** credible, creditable, believable, trustworthy, reliable. **5.** strict, rigid, accurate, precise, exact, conscientious, close. —*n.* **6.** believers.
Ant. unfaithful, faithless.

faithless, *adj.* **1.** disloyal, false, inconstant, fickle, perfidious, treacherous. **2.** unreliable, untrustworthy, untrue. **3.** untrusting; unbelieving, doubting. **4.** atheistic, agnostic, heathen, infidel.
Ant. faithful.

false, *adj.* **1.** erroneous, incorrect, mistaken, wrong, untrue, improper. **2.** untruthful, lying, mendacious, untrue. **3.** deceitful, treacherous, faithless, insincere, hypocritical, disingenuous, disloyal, unfaithful, two-faced, inconstant, recreant, perfidious, traitorous. **4.** deceptive, deceiving, misleading, fallacious. **5.** spurious, artificial, bogus, phony, forged, sham, counterfeit. **6.** substitute, *ersatz,* supplementary, stand-in.
Ant. true; genuine.

falsehood, *n.* lie, fib, untruth, distortion, fabrication, fiction.
Ant. truth.

falter, *v.* **1.** hesitate, vacillate, waver, tremble. **2.** stammer, stutter.

fame, *n.* reputation, estimation, opinion, consensus, repute, renown, eminence, celebrity, honor, glory; notoriety.
Ant. infamy, disrepute.

familiar, *adj.* **1.** common, well-known, frequent. **2.** well-acquainted, conversant, well-versed. **3.** easy, informal, unceremonious, unconstrained, free. **4.** intimate, close, friendly, amicable. **5.** presuming, presumptive, unreserved, disrespectful. **6.** tame, domesticated. —*n.* **7.** friend, associate, companion.
Ant. unfamiliar, unknown.

familiarity, *n.* **1.** acquaintance, knowledge, understanding. **2.** intimacy, liberty, freedom, license, disrespect. **3.** informality, unconstraint, freedom.
Ant. unfamiliarity.

famous, *adj.* celebrated, renowned, well-known, famed, notable, eminent, distinguished, illustrious, honored.
Ant. unknown, undistinguished.

fanatical, *adj.* zealous, enthusiastic, visionary, frenzied, rabid.
Ant. apathetic.

fancy, *n.* **1.** imagination, fantasy. **2.** image, conception, idea, thought, notion, impression; hallucination. **3.** caprice, whim, vagary, quirk, humor, crotchet. **4.** preference, liking, inclination, fondness. **5.** judgment, taste, sensitivity, sensitiveness. —*adj.* **6.** fine, elegant, choice. **7.** ornamental, decorated, ornate. **8.** fanciful, capricious, whimsical, irregular, extravagant. —*v.* **9.** picture, envision, conceive, imagine. **10.** like, be pleased with, take a fancy to.
Ant. plain; regular, ordinary; dislike, abhor.

fascinate, *v.* bewitch, charm, enchant, entrance, enrapture, captivate, allure, infatuate, enamor.
Ant. repel, disgust.

fashion, *n.* **1.** custom, style, vogue, mode, fade, rage, craze. **2.** custom, style, conventionality, conformity. **3.** haut monde, beau monde, four hundred, society. **4.** manner, way, mode, method, approach. **5.** make, form, figure, shape, stamp, mold, pattern, model, cast. **6.** kind, sort. —*v.* **7.** make, shape, frame, construct, mold, form. **8.** accommodate, adapt, suit, fit, adjust.

fast, *adj.* **1.** quick, swift, rapid, fleet. **2.** energetic, active, alert, quick. **3.** dissolute, dissipated, profligate, unmoral, wild, reckless, extravagant, prodigal. **4.** strong, resistant, impregnable. **5.** immovable, fixed, secure, steadfast, stanch, firm. **6.** inescapable, inextricable. **7.** tied, knotted, fastened, fixed, tight, close. **8.** permanent, lasting, enduring, eternal. **9.** loyal, faithful, steadfast. **10.** deep, sound, profound. **11.** deceptive, insincere, inconstant, unreliable. —*adv.* **12.** tightly, fixedly, firmly, securely, tenaciously. **13.** quickly, swiftly, rapidly, speedily. **14.** energetically, recklessly, extravagantly, wildly, prodigally.
Ant. slow, lethargic; upright, moral; weak, defenseless; feeble; temporary; disloyal, faithless; shallow; sincere, constant, reliable.

fasten, *v.* make fast, fix, secure, attach, pin, rivet, bind, tie, connect, link, hook, clasp, clinch, clamp, tether.
Ant. loosen, loose, untie.

fat, *adj.* **1.** fleshy, plump, corpulent, obese, adipose, stout, portly, chubby, pudgy. **2.** oily, fatty, unctuous, greasy, pinguid. **3.** rich, profitable, remunerative, lucrative. **4.** fertile, rich, fruitful, productive. **5.** thick, broad, extended, wide. **6.** plentiful, copious, abundant. **7.** dull, stupid, sluggish, coarse.
Ant. thin, skinny, cadaverous; poor; scarce, scanty; barren; clever.

fatal, *adj.* deadly, mortal, lethal; destructive, ruinous, pernicious, calamitous, catastrophic. **2.** fateful, inevitable, doomed, predestined, foreordained, damned.
Ant. lifegiving, constructive; indeterminate.

fate, *n.* **1.** fortune, luck, lot, chance, destiny, karma, kismet, doom. **2.** death, destruction, ruin. —*v.* **3.** predetermine, destine, predestine, foreordain, preordain.

fatherly, *adj.* paternal, protecting, protective; kind, tender, benign.

fatuous, *adj.* stupid, dense, dull, dimwitted, foolish, silly, idiotic.
Ant. clever, bright, intelligent.

fault, *n.* **1.** defect, imperfection, blemish, flaw, failing, frailty, foible, weakness, shortcoming, vice. **2.** error, mistake, slip. **3.** misdeed, sin, transgression, trespass,

misdemeanor, offense, wrong, delinquency, indiscretion, culpability.
Ant. strength.

faulty, *adj.* **1.** defective, imperfect, incomplete, bad. **2.** blameworthy, culpable, reprehensible, censurable.
Ant. perfect, complete, consummate; exonerated, blameless.

favor, *n.* **1.** kindness, good will, benefit, good deed. **2.** partiality, bias, patronage, prejudice. **3.** gift, present. —*v.* **4.** prefer, encourage, patronize, approve, countenance, allow. **5.** facilitate, ease; propitiate, conciliate, appease. **6.** aid, help, support, assist.
Ant. cruelty; disfavor; disapprove, disallow, discourage.

fear, *n.* **1.** apprehension, consternation, dismay, alarm, trepidation, dread, terror, fright, horror, panic. **2.** anxiety, solicitude, concern. **3.** awe, reverence, veneration. —*v.* **4.** be afraid of, apprehend, dread. **5.** revere, venerate, reverence.
Ant. boldness, bravery, intrepidity; security, confidence.

fearless, *adj.* brave, intrepid, bold, courageous, heroic.
Ant. cowardly.

feasible, *adj.* **1.** practicable, workable, possible. **2.** suitable, suited, usable, practical, practicable. **3.** likely, probable.
Ant. unfeasible, impractical, impossible; unsuitable, unsuited; unlikely, improbable.

feast, *n.* **1.** celebration, anniversary, commemoration, ceremony, banquet, fête, entertainment, carousal. **2.** repast, sumptuous repast. —*v.* **3.** eat, gourmandize, glut *or* stuff *or* gorge oneself. **4.** gratify, delight.

feat, *n.* achievement, accomplishment, deed, action, act, exploit.

feature, *n.* characteristic, peculiarity, trait, property, mark.

feeble, *adj.* **1.** weak, feckless, ineffective, ineffectual. **2.** infirm, sickly, debilitated, enervated, declining, frail. **3.** faint, dim, weak.
Ant. strong, effective, effectual; healthy; clear.

feed, *v.* **1.** nourish, sustain, purvey. **2.** satisfy, minister to, gratify, please. **3.** eat. **4.** subsist. —*n.* **5.** fodder, forage, provender, food.
Ant. starve.

feeling, *n.* **1.** consciousness, impression; emotion, passion, sentiment, sensibility; sympathy, empathy. **2.** tenderness, sensitivity, sentiment, sentimentality, susceptibility, pity. **3.** sentiment, opinion, tenor. —*adj.* **4.** sentient, emotional, sensitive, tender; sympathetic. **5.** emotional, impassioned, passionate.
Ant. apathy, coolness; unemotional, insensitive, unsympathetic; cool.

feign, *v.* **1.** invent, concoct, devise, fabricate, forge, counterfeit. **2.** simulate, pretend, counterfeit, affect; emulate, imitate, mimic. **3.** make believe, pretend, imagine.

female, *n.* **1.** woman, girl. —*adj.* **2.** feminine, effeminate, delicate, unmanly, weak, soft, gentle.
Ant. male; masculine, manly.

ferocious, *adj.* fierce, savage, wild, cruel, violent, ravenous, rapacious.
Ant. mild, tame, calm.

fertile, *adj.* productive, prolific, fecund, fruitful, rich, teeming.
Ant. sterile, barren.

fervent, *adj.* fervid, ardent, earnest, warm, heated, hot, burning, glowing, fiery, inflamed, eager, zealous, vehement, impassioned, passionate, enthusiastic.
Ant. cool, apathetic.

fervor, *n.* ardor, intensity, earnestness, eagerness, enthusiasm, passion, fire, heat, vehemence.
Ant. coolness, apathy.

feud, *n.* hostility, quarrel, argument, difference, falling-out.

fiction, *n.* **1.** novel, fantasy. **2.** fabrication, figment, unreality, falsity.
Ant. nonfiction, fact; reality.

fidelity, *n.* **1.** loyalty, faithfulness, devotion, fealty. **2.** accuracy, precision, faithfulness, exactness, closeness.
Ant. disloyalty, unfaithfulness; inaccuracy.

fierce, *adj.* **1.** ferocious, wild, vehement, violent, savage, cruel, fell, brutal, bloodthirsty, murderous, homicidal. **2.** truculent, barbarous, untamed, furious, passionate, turbulent, impetuous.
Ant. tame, domesticated; calm; civilized; cool, temperate.

fiery, *adj.* **1.** hot, flaming, heated, fervent, fervid, burning, afire, glowing. **2.** fervent, fervid, vehement, inflamed, impassioned, spirited, ardent, impetuous, passionate, fierce.
Ant. cool, cold; dispassionate.

fight, *n.* **1.** battle, war, combat, encounter, conflict, contest, scrimmage, engagement, fray, affray, action, skirmish, affair, struggle. **2.** melee, struggle, scuffle, tussle, riot, row, fray. —*v.* **3.** contend, strive, battle, combat, conflict, contest, engage, struggle.

figment, *n.* invention, fiction, fabrication, fable.
Ant. fact, reality.

filthy, *adj.* **1.** dirty, foul, unclean, defiled, squalid. **2.** obscene, vile, dirty, pornographic, licentious, lascivious.
Ant. clean, spotless, immaculate.

final, *adj.* **1.** last, latest, ultimate. **2.** conclusive, decisive.
Ant. prime, primary.

financial, *adj.* monetary, fiscal, pecuniary.

fine, *adj.* **1.** superior, high-grade, choice, excellent, admirable, elegant, exquisite, finished, consummate, perfect, refined, select, delicate. **2.** powdered, pulverized, minute, small, little. **3.** keen, sharp, acute.

4. skilled, accomplished, brilliant. 5. affected, ornate, ornamented, fancy.
Ant. inferior, poor, bad, unfinished; dull; unskilled, maladroit; plain.

finish, *v.* **1.** bring to an end, end, terminate, conclude, close. **2.** use up, complete, consume. **3.** complete, perfect, consummate, polish. **4.** accomplish, achieve, execute, complete, perform, do. *—n.* **5.** end, conclusion, termination, close. **6.** polish, elegance, refinement.
Ant. begin, start, commence; originate, create; beginning.

finished, *adj.* **1.** ended, completed, consummated, over, done, done with; complete, consummate, perfect. **2.** polished, refined, elegant, perfected; trained, experienced, practiced, qualified, accomplished, proficient, skilled, gifted, talented.
Ant. begun; incomplete, imperfect; unrefined, inelegant; inexperienced, unqualified, unskilled, maladroit.

firm, *adj.* **1.** hard, solid, stiff, rigid, inelastic, compact, condensed, compressed, dense. **2.** steady, unshakable, rooted, fast, fixed, stable, secure, immovable. **3.** fixed, settled, unalterable, established, confirmed. **4.** steadfast, unwavering, determined, immovable, resolute, stanch, constant, steady, reliable. *—n.* **5.** company, partnership, association, business, concern, house, corporation.
Ant. flabby, flaccid, elastic, soft; unsteady, unstable; wavering, irresolute, inconstant, unreliable; dissociation.

fix, *v.* **1.** make fast, fasten, pin, attach, tie, secure, stabilize, establish, set, plant, implant. **2.** settle, determine, establish, define, limit. **3.** assign, refer. **4.** repair, mend, correct, emend. *—n.* **5.** predicament, dilemma, plight, spot.
Ant. loosen, loose, detach; unsettle; break.

flame, *n.* **1.** blaze, conflagration, holocaust, inferno, fire. **2.** heat, ardor, zeal, passion, fervor, warmth, enthusiasm. *—v.* **3.** burn, blaze. **4.** glow, burn, warm; shine, flash. **4.** inflame, fire.

flash, *n.* **1.** flame, outburst, flare, gleam, glare. **2.** instant, split second, moment, twinkling, wink. **3.** ostentation, display. *—v.* **4.** glance, glint, glitter, scintillate, gleam. *—adj.* **5.** showy, ostentatious, flashy, gaudy, tawdry, flaunting, pretentious, superficial. **6.** counterfeit, sham, fake, false, fraudulent.

flat, *adj.* **1.** horizontal, level, even, equal, plane, smooth. **2.** low, supine, prone, prostrate. **3.** collapsed, deflated. **4.** unqualified, downright, positive, outright, peremptory, absolute. **5.** uninteresting, dull, tedious, lifeless, boring, spiritless, prosaic, unanimated. **6.** insipid, vapid, tasteless, stale, dead, unsavory. **7.** pointless. *—adv.* **8.** horizontally, levelly. **9.** positively, absolutely, definitely. *—n.* **10.** apartment, suite.
Ant. vertical, upright, perpendicular; doubtful, dubi-

ous; spirited, animated; tasteful, savory; pointed.

flavor, *n.* **1.** taste, savor. **2.** seasoning, extract, flavoring. **3.** characteristic, essence, quality, spirit, soul. **4.** smell, odor, aroma, perfume, fragrance.

flaw, *n.* defect, imperfection, blot, blemish, spot, fault, crack, crevice, breach, break, cleft, fissure, rift, fracture.

flexible, *adj.* **1.** pliable, pliant, flexile, limber, plastic, elastic, supple. **2.** adaptable, tractable, compliant, yielding, gentle.
Ant. inflexible, rigid, solid, firm; intractable, unyielding.

flit, *v.* **fly,** dart, skim along; flutter.

flock, *n.* bevy, covey, flight, gaggle; brood, hatch, litter; shoal, school; swarm; pride; drove, herd, pack; group, company, crowd.

flood, *n.* **1.** deluge, inundation, overflow, flash flood, freshet. *—v.* **2.** overflow, inundate, deluge, flow.

flourish, *v.* **1.** thrive, prosper, be successful, grow, increase, succeed. **2.** luxuriate. **3.** brandish, wave. **4.** parade, flaunt, display, show off, be ostentatious, boast, brag, vaunt. **5.** embellish, adorn, ornament, decorate. *—n.* **6.** parade, ostentation, show, display, dash. **7.** decoration, ornament, adornment, embellishment.
Ant. decline, die, fail; disfigure, mar.

flow, *v.* **1.** gush, spout, stream, spurt, jet, discharge. **2.** proceed, run, pour, roll on. **3.** overflow, abound, teem, pour. *—n.* **4.** current, flood, stream. **5.** stream, river, rivulet, rill, streamlet. **6.** outpouring, discharge, overflowing.

fluctuate, *v.* waver, vacillate, change, vary; wave, undulate, oscillate.

fluent, *adj.* flowing, glib, voluble, copious, smooth.
Ant. terse, curt, silent.

fluid, *n.* **1.** liquid; gas, vapor. *—adj.* **2.** liquid, gaseous.
Ant. solid.

fly, *v.* **1.** take wing, soar, hover, flutter, flit, wing, flap. **2.** elapse, pass, glide, slip.

foe, *n.* enemy, opponent, adversary, antagonist.
Ant. friend, ally, associate.

fog, *n.* **1.** cloud, mist, haze; smog. **2.** cloud, confusion, obfuscation, dimming, blurring, darkening. *—v.* **3.** befog, becloud, obfuscate, dim, blur, darken. **4.** daze, bewilder, befuddle, muddle.
Ant. clarity; clear, brighten; clarify.

foible, *n.* weakness, fault, failing, frailty, defect, imperfection, infirmity.
Ant. strength, perfection.

follow, *v.* **1.** succeed, ensue. **2.** conform, obey, heed, comply, observe. **3.** accompany, attend. **4.** pursue, chase, trail, track, trace. **5.** ensue, succeed, result, come next, arise, proceed.
Ant. lead; order.

follower, *n.* **1.** adherent, partisan, disciple, pupil. **2.** attendant, servant; supporter, retainer, companion, associate.
Ant. leader, teacher; enemy, foe.

food, *n.* provisions, rations, nutrition, nutriment, aliment, bread, sustenance, victuals; meat, viands; diet, regimen, fare, menu.

fool, *n.* **1.** simpleton, dolt, dunce, blockhead, nincompoop, ninny, numskull, ignoramus, booby, sap, dunderhead, dunderpate, idiot. **2.** jester, buffoon, droll, harlequin, zany, clown, merry-andrew. **3.** imbecile, moron, idiot. —*v.* **4.** impose on, trick, deceive, delude, hoodwink, cozen, cheat, gull, gudgeon, hoax, dupe. **5.** joke, jest, play, toy, trifle, dally, idle, dawdle, loiter, tarry.
Ant. genius.

foolish, *adj.* **1.** silly, senseless, fatuous, stupid, inane, dull, vacant, vapid, slow, asinine, simple, witless. **2.** ill-considered, unwise, thoughtless, irrational, imprudent, unreasonable, absurd, ridiculous, nonsensical, preposterous, foolhardy.
Ant. bright, brilliant, clever, intelligent; wise, sage, sagacious.

forbid, *v.* inhibit, prohibit, taboo, interdict, prevent, preclude, stop, obviate, deter, discourage.
Ant. allow, permit, encourage.

force, *n.* **1.** strength, power, impetus, intensity, might, vigor, energy. **2.** coercion, violence, compulsion, constraint, enforcement. **3.** efficacy, effectiveness, effect, efficiency, validity, potency, potential. **4.** effect, operation. —*v.* **5.** compel, constrain, oblige, coerce, necessitate. **6.** drive, propel, impel. **7.** overcome, overpower, violate, ravish, rape.
Ant. weakness, frailty; ineffectiveness, inefficiency.

forecast, *v.* **1.** predict, augur, foretell, foresee, anticipate. **2.** prearrange, plan, contrive, project. **3.** conjecture, guess, estimate. —*n.* **4.** prediction, augury, conjecture, guess, estimate, foresight, prevision, anticipation, forethought, prescience.

foreigner, *n.* alien, stranger, non-native, outsider, outlander.
Ant. native.

foresight, *n.* **1.** prudence, forethought, prevision, anticipation, precaution; forecast. **2.** prescience, prevision, foreknowledge, prospect.

forest, *n.* grove, wood, woods, woodland.
Ant. plain.

forgive, *v.* pardon, excuse; absolve, acquit.
Ant. blame, condemn, censure.

forlorn, *adj.* **1.** abandoned, deserted, forsaken, desolate, alone, lost, solitary. **2.** desolate, dreary, unhappy, miserable, wretched, pitiable, pitiful, helpless, woebegone, disconsolate, comfortless, destitute.
Ant. accompanied; happy, cheerful.

form, *n.* **1.** shape, figure, outline, mold, appearance, cast, cut, configuration. **2.** mold, model, pattern. **3.** manner, style, arrangement, sort, kind, order, type. **4.** assemblage, group. **5.** ceremony, ritual, formula, formality, conformity, rule, convention. **6.** document, paper, application, business form, blank. **7.** method, procedure, system, mode, practice, formula, approach. —*v.* **8.** construct, frame, shape, model, mold, fashion, outline, cast. **9.** make, produce, create, originate. **10.** compose, make up, serve for, constitute. **11.** order, arrange, organize, systematize, dispose, combine. **12.** instruct, teach, educate, discipline, train. **13.** frame, invent, contrive, devise.

formal, *adj.* **1.** academic, conventional, conformal, conforming, conformist. **2.** ceremonial, ceremonious, ritual, conventional. **3.** ceremonious, stiff, prim, precise, punctilious, starched. **4.** perfunctory, external. **5.** official, express, explicit, strict, rigid, rigorous, stodgy. **6.** rigorous, methodical, regular, set, fixed, rigid, stiff.

formidable, *adj.* dread, dreadful, appalling, threatening, menacing, fearful, terrible, frightful, horrible. *Ant.* pleasant, friendly, amiable.

forsake, *v.* **1.** quit, leave, desert, abandon. **2.** give up, renounce, forswear, relinquish, recant, drop, forgo.

fortification, *n.* **1.** fortifying, strengthening, bolstering, arming. **2.** fort, castle, fortress, citadel, stronghold, bulwark, fastness.

fortuitous, *adj.* accidental, chance, casual, incidental. *Ant.* purposeful, intentional.

fortunate, *adj.* lucky, happy, propitious, favorable, advantageous, auspicious; successful, prosperous. *Ant.* unlucky, unfortunate.

forward, *adv.* **1.** onward, ahead, up ahead, in advance, frontward. **2.** out, forth. —*adj.* **3.** well-advanced, up front, ahead. **4.** ready, prompt, eager, willing, sincere, earnest, zealous. **5.** pert, bold, presumptuous, assuming, confident, impertinent, impudent, brazen, flippant. **6.** radical, extreme, unconventional, progressive. **7.** early, premature, future, preliminary. *Ant.* backward.

foster, *v.* **1.** promote, encourage, further, favor, patronize, forward, advance. **2.** bring up, rear, breed, nurse, nourish, sustain, support. **3.** care for, cherish. *Ant.* discourage.

foul, *adj.* **1.** offensive, gross, disgusting, loathsome, repulsive, repellent, noisome, fetid, putrid, stinking. **2.** filthy, dirty, unclean, squalid, polluted, sullied, soiled, tarnished, stained, tainted, impure. **3.** stormy, unfavorable, rainy, tempestuous. **4.** abominable, wicked, vile, base, shameful, infamous, sinful, scandalous. **5.** scurrilous, obscene, smutty, profane, vulgar, low, coarse. **6.** unfair, dishonorable, underhanded, cheating. **7.** entangled, caught, jammed, tangled. —*adv.* **8.** unfairly, foully. —*v.* **9.** soil, defile, sully, stain, dirty, besmirch, smut, taint, pollute, poison. **10.** entangle, clog, tangle, catch. **11.** defile, dishonor, disgrace, shame. *Ant.* delightful, attractive, pleasant; pure; saintly, angelic; fair, honorable; clean, purify; clear; honor.

foundation, *n.* **1.** base, basis, ground, footing. **2.** establishment, settlement; endowment.
Ant. superstructure.

fractious, *adj.* cross, fretful, peevish, testy, captious, petulant, touchy, splenetic, pettish, waspish, snappish, irritable; unruly, refractory, stubborn.
Ant. temperate, kind, even-tempered; amenable, tractable, obedient.

fragrant, *adj.* perfumed, odorous, redolent, sweet-smelling, sweet-scented, aromatic, odoriferous.
Ant. noxious.

frail, *adj.* brittle, fragile, breakable, frangible, delicate, weak, feeble.
Ant. strong, pliant, elastic, unbreakable.

frank, *adj.* **1.** open, unreserved, unrestrained, unrestricted, nonrestictive, outspoken, candid, sincere, free, bold, truthful, uninhibited. **2.** artless, ingenuous, undisguised, avowed, downright, outright, direct. **—***n.* **3.** signature, mark, sign, seal; franchise.
Ant. secretive, restrained, restricted; sly, artful, dissembling.

fraud, *n.* deceit, trickery, duplicity, treachery, sharp practice, breach of confidence, trick, deception, guile, artifice, ruse, stratagem, wile, hoax, humbug.
Ant. honesty.

free, *adj.* **1.** unfettered, independent, at liberty, unrestrained, unrestricted. **2.** unregulated, unrestricted, unimpeded, open, unobstructed. **3.** clear, immune, exempt, uncontrolled, decontrolled. **4.** easy, firm, swift, unimpeded, unencumbered. **5.** loose, unattached, lax. **6.** frank, open, unconstrained, unceremonious, familiar, informal, easy. **7.** loose, licentious, ribald, lewd, immoral, libertine. **8.** liberal, lavish, generous, bountiful, unstinted, munificent, charitable, open-handed. **—***v.* **9.** liberate, set free, release, unfetter, emancipate, manumit, deliver, disenthrall. **10.** exempt, deliver. **11.** rid, relieve, disengage, clear.
Ant. dependent, restrained, restricted; close, obstructed; difficult; unfamiliar; moral, upright; stingy, niggardly; confine, enthrall.

freedom, *n.* **1.** liberty, independence. **2.** immunity, franchise, privilege. **3.** ease, facility. **4.** frankness, openness, ingenuousness. **5.** familiarity, license, looseness, laxity.
Ant. dependence; restriction; difficulty; secrecy; unfamiliarity, restraint.

freight, *n.* **1.** cargo, shipment, load. **2.** freightage, transportation, expressage. **—***v.* **3.** load, lade, burden, charge.

frenzy, *n.* agitation, excitement, paroxysm, enthusiasm; rage, fury, raving, mania, insanity, delirium, derangement, aberration, lunacy, madness.
Ant. calm, coolness; sanity, judgment.

frequently, *adv.* often, many times, repeatedly.
Ant. seldom.

fresh, *adj.* **1.** new, recent, novel. **2.** youthful, healthy,

robust, vigorous, well, hearty, hardy, strong. **3.** refreshing, pure, cool, unadulterated, sweet, invigorating. **4.** inexperienced, artless, untrained, raw, green, uncultivated, unskilled.
Ant. stale, old; impure, contaminated; experienced, skilled.

fret, *v.* **1.** worry, fume, rage. **2.** torment, worry, harass, annoy, irritate, vex, taunt, goad, tease, nettle, needle. **3.** wear away, erode, gnaw, corrode, rust. —*n.* **4.** annoyance, vexation, harassment, agitation, worry, irritation. **5.** erosion, corrosion, eating away, gnawing. **6.** fretwork, ornament.

fretful, *adj.* irritable, peevish, petulant, querulous, touchy, testy, waspish, pettish, splenetic, captious, snappish, short-tempered, ill-tempered.
Ant. calm, even-tempered, temperate, easy-going.

friend, *n.* **1.** companion, crony, chum, acquaintance, intimate, confidant. **2.** well-wisher, patron, supporter, backer, encourager, advocate, defender. **3.** ally, associate, confrère.
Ant. enemy, foe, adversary.

friendly, *adj.* **1.** kind, kindly, amicable, fraternal, amiable, cordial, genial, well-disposed, benevolent, affectionate, kind-hearted. **2.** helpful, favorable, advantageous, propitious.
Ant. unfriendly, inimical; unfavorable.

fright, *n.* dismay, consternation, terror, fear, alarm, panic.
Ant. bravery, boldness.

frighten, *v.* scare, terrify, alarm, appall, shock, dismay, intimidate.

frightful, *adj.* dreadful, terrible, alarming, terrific, fearful, awful, shocking, dread, dire, horrid, horrible, hideous, ghastly, gruesome.
Ant. delightful, attractive, beautiful.

frivolous, *adj.* **1.** unimportant, trifling, petty, paltry, trivial, flimsy. **2.** idle, silly, foolish, childish, puerile.
Ant. important, vital; mature, adult, sensible.

froward, *adj.* perverse, contrary, refractory, obstinate, willful, disobedient, uncooperative, fractious, contumacious, wayward, unmanageable, difficult, defiant, fresh, impudent.
Ant. tractable, lenient, cooperative, easy.

frugal, *adj.* economical, thrifty, chary, provident, saving, sparing, careful; parsimonious, stingy, penurious.
Ant. lavish, wasteful.

fruitful, *adj.* prolific, fertile, fecund, productive, profitable; plentiful, abundant, rich, copious.
Ant. barren, scarce, scanty, unprofitable, fruitless.

fruitless, *adj.* **1.** useless, inutile, unavailing, profitless, ineffectual, unprofitable, vain, idle, futile, abortive. **2.** barren, sterile, unfruitful, unproductive, infecund, unprolific.
Ant. fruitful, useful, profitable, effectual; abundant, fertile.

frustrate, *v.* defeat, nullify, baffle, disconcert, foil, disappoint, balk, check, thwart.
Ant. encourage, foster.

fulfill, *v.* **1.** carry out, consummate, execute, discharge, accomplish, achieve, complete, effect, realize, perfect. **2.** perform, do, obey, observe, discharge. **3.** satisfy, meet, answer, fill, comply with. **4.** complete, end, terminate, bring to an end, finish, conclude.
Ant. fail; dissatisfy; create, originate.

fume, *n.* **1.** smoke, vapor, exhalation, steam. **2.** rage, fury, agitation, storm. —*v.* **3.** smoke, vaporize. **4.** chafe, fret, rage, rave, flare up, bluster, storm.

fun, *n.* merriment, enjoyment, pleasure, amusement, divertissement, sport, diversion, joking, jesting, playfulness, gaiety, frolic.
Ant. misery, melancholy.

fundamental, *adj.* **1.** basic, underlying, principal, main, central, chief, essential, primary, elementary, necessary, indispensable. **2.** original, first. —*n.* **3.** principle, rule, basic law, essence, essential.
Ant. superficial, superfluous, dispensable; last, common; nonessential.

funny, *adj.* amusing, diverting, comical, farcical, absurd, ridiculous, droll, witty, facetious, humorous, laughable, ludicrous, incongruous, foolish.
Ant. sad, melancholy, humorless.

furnish, *v.* **1.** provide, supply; purvey, cater. **2.** appoint, equip, fit up, rig, deck out, decorate, outfit, fit out.

fury, *n.* **1.** passion, furor, frenzy, rage, ire, anger, wrath. **2.** violence, turbulence, fierceness, impetuousness, impetuosity, vehemence. **3.** shrew, virago, termagant, vixen, nag, hag, maenad, bacchante.
Ant. calm, serenity.

fuse, *v.* **1.** melt, liquefy, dissolve, smelt; combine, blend, intermingle, coalesce, intermix, commingle, amalgamate, homogenize, merge. —*n.* **2.** match, fusee, fuze.
Ant. solidify, separate.

fuss, *n.* **1.** activity, ado, bustle, pother, to-do, stir, commotion. —*v.* **2.** bother, annoy, pester.
Ant. inactivity.

futile, *adj.* **1.** ineffective, ineffectual, useless, unsuccessful, vain, unavailing, idle, profitless, unprofitable, bootless, worthless, valueless, fruitless, unproductive. **2.** trivial, frivolous, minor, nugatory, unimportant, trifling.
Ant. effective, effectual, successful; profitable, worthy; basic, important, principal, major.

G

gaiety, *n.* **1.** merriment, mirth, glee, jollity, joyousness, liveliness, sportiveness, hilarity, vivacity, life, cheerfulness, joviality, animation, spirit. **2.** showiness, finery, gaudiness, brilliance, glitter, flashiness, flash.

Ant. sadness, melancholy, misery.

gain, *v.* **1.** obtain, secure, procure, get, acquire, attain, earn, win. **2.** reach, get to, arrive at, attain. **3.** improve, better, progress, advance, forward; near, approach. —*n.* **4.** profit, increase, advantage, advance; profits, winnings.

Ant. lose; worsen; retreat; losses.

gallant, *adj.* **1.** brave, high-spirited, valorous, valiant, chivalrous, courageous, bold, intrepid, fearless, daring. **2.** gay, showy, magnificent, splendid, fine. **3.** polite, courtly, chivalrous, noble, courteous. —*n.* **4.** suitor, wooer, lover, paramour.

Ant. cowardly, fearful; tawdry; impolite, discourteous.

gambol, *v., n.* frolic, spring, caper, romp, dance.

game, *n.* **1.** amusement, pastime, diversion, divertissement, play, sport, contest, competition. **2.** scheme, artifice, strategy, stratagem, plan, plot, undertaking, venture, adventure. **3.** fun, sport, joke, diversion. **4.** prey, quarry. —*adj.* **5.** plucky, brave, bold, resolute, intrepid, dauntless, valorous, fearless, heroic, gallant.

gang, *n.* **1.** band, group, crew, crowd, company, party, set, clique, coterie; horde. **2.** squad, shift, team.

gape, *v.* **1.** yawn. **2.** stare, wonder, gaze. **3.** split, open, dehisce, separate.

garb, *n.* **1.** fashion, mode, style, cut. **2.** clothes, clothing, dress, costume, attire, apparel, habiliments, habit, garments, raiment, vesture. —*v.* **3.** dress, clothe, attire, array, apparel.

garish, *adj.* **1.** glaring, loud, showy, tawdry, gaudy, flashy. **2.** ornate, ornamented, decorated.

Ant. elegant; plain, simple.

garnish, *v.* **1.** adorn, decorate, ornament, embellish, grace, enhance, beautify, trim, bedeck, bedizen, set off. —*n.* **2.** decoration, ornamentation, ornament, adornment, garniture, garnishment.

Ant. strip.

garrulous, *adj.* talkative, loquacious, prating, prattling, wordy, diffuse, babbling, verbose, prolix.

Ant. taciturn, silent, reticent.

gasp, *v.* pant, puff, blow.

gather, *v.* **1.** get together, collect, aggregate, assemble, muster, marshal, bring *or* draw together. **2.** learn, infer, understand, deduce, assume, conclude. **3.** accumulate, amass, garner, hoard. **4.** pluck, garner, reap, harvest, glean, cull, crop. **5.** select, cull, sort, sort out. **6.** grow, increase, accrete, collect, thicken, condense. —*n.* **7.** contraction, drawing together, tuck, pucker, fold, pleat, plait.

Ant. separate, disperse; decrease.

gathering, *n.* **1.** assembly, meeting, assemblage, crowd, convocation, congregation, concourse, company, throng, muster. **2.** selling, boil, abscess, carbuncle, pimple, sore, pustule, tumor.

gaudy, *adj.* showy, tawdry, garish, brilliant, loud, flashy, conspicuous, obvious, vulgar, unsubtle.
Ant. elegant, refined, subtle.

gaunt, *adj.* **1.** thin, emaciated, haggard, lean, spare, skinny, scrawny, lank, angular, raw-boned, meager, attenuated, slender. **2.** bleak, desolate, grim, dreary.
Ant. obese, fat; populous.

gay, *adj.* **1.** joyous, gleeful, jovial, glad, happy, lighthearted, lively, convivial, vivacious, animated, frolicsome, sportive, hilarious, jolly, joyful, merry, goodhumored, expansive, cheerful, sprightly, blithe, airy. **2.** bright, showy, fine, brilliant. **3.** dissipated, licentious, lecherous, dissolute.
Ant. unhappy, miserable; dull; moral, upright.

gaze, *v., n.* stare, gape, wonder.

general, *adj.* **1.** impartial, unparticular, catholic, universal. **2.** common, usual, prevalent, customary, regular, ordinary, popular, nonexclusive, widespread, prevailing. **3.** miscellaneous, unrestricted, unspecialized, nonspecific. **4.** vague, lax, indefinite, ill-defined, inexact, imprecise.
Ant. special, partial; uncommon, unusual, extraordinary; specific; definite, exact, precise.

generally, *adv.* usually, commonly, ordinarily, often, in general.
Ant. especially, particularly, unusually.

generosity, *n.* **1.** readiness, liberality, munificence, charity, bounteousness, bountifulness. **2.** nobleness, disinterestedness, magnanimity.
Ant. stinginess, niggardliness, parsimony.

generous, *adj.* **1.** munificent, bountiful, unselfish, unstinting, liberal, charitable, open-handed, beneficent. **2.** noble, high-minded, magnanimous; large, big. **3.** ample, plentiful, abundant, flowing, overflowing, copious.
Ant. stingy, tightfisted, selfish, niggardly; small, parsimonious; scarce, scanty, barren.

genial, *adj.* **1.** cheerful, sympathetic, cordial, friendly, pleasant, agreeable, kindly, well-disposed, hearty, encouraging. **2.** enlivening, lively, warm, mild.
Ant. unsympathetic, unpleasant, discouraging; cool.

genius, *n.* **1.** capacity, ability, talent, gift, aptitude, faculty, bent. **2.** spirit, guardian angel, genie, jinni.
Ant. inability, incapacity.

gentle, *adj.* **1.** soft, bland, peaceful, clement, moderate, pacific, soothing, kind, tender, humane, lenient, merciful, meek, milk, kindly, amiable, submissive, gentle-hearted, kind-hearted, soft-hearted. **2.** gradual, moderate, temperate, tempered, light, mild. **3.** wellborn, noble, highborn. **4.** honorable, respectable, refined, cultivated, polished, well-bred, polite, elegant, courteous, courtly. **5.** manageable, tractable, tame, docile, trained, peaceable, quiet.
Ant. immoderate, turbulent, unkind, cruel, heartless;

sudden, abrupt; unrefined, unpolished, impolite; intractable, wild, noisy.

get, *v.* **1.** obtain, acquire, procure, secure, gain. **2.** earn, win, gain. **3.** learn, apprehend, grasp. **4.** capture, seize upon. **5.** prepare, get ready. **6.** prevail on *or* upon, persuade, induce, influence, dispose. **7.** beget, engender, generate, breed, procreate. **8.** come to, reach, arrive. **9.** become, grow.
Ant. lose.

ghastly, *adj.* **1.** dreadful, horrible, frightful, hideous, grisly, dismal, terrible, shocking. **2.** pale, deathly, white, wan, cadaverous.
Ant. lovely, attractive, beautiful; ruddy, robust, healthy.

ghost, *n.* **1.** apparition, phantom, spirit, phantasm, wraith, revenant, shade, spook, specter, supernatural being. **2.** shadow, hint, suggestion.

giddy, *adj.* **1.** frivolous, light, impulsive, flighty, unstable, volatile, fickle, irresolute, mutable, changeable, inconstant, unsteady, vacillating. **2.** dizzy, vertiginous, light-headed.
Ant. serious, resolute, constant; sober.

gift, *n.* **1.** donation, present, contribution, offering, boon, alms, gratuity, tip, benefaction, grant, largess, subsidy, allowance, endowment, bequest, legacy, dowry, inheritance, bounty. **2.** talent, endowment, power, faculty, ability, capacity, forte, capability, genius, bent.

gigantic, *adj.* huge, enormous, tremendous, colossal, mammoth, monstrous, elephantine, immense, prodigious, herculean, titanic, cyclopean, vast, extensive, infinite.
Ant. small, tiny, infinitesimal, microscopic.

give, *v.* **1.** deliver, bestow, hand over, offer, vouchsafe, impart, accord, furnish, provide, supply, donate, contribute, afford, spare, accommodate with, confer, grant, cede, relinquish, yield, turn over, assign, present. **2.** enable, assign, award. **3.** set forth, issue, show, present, offer. **4.** assume, suppose, assign. **5.** afford, yield, produce. **6.** perform, make do. **7.** issue, put forth, emit, publish, utter, give out (with), pronounce, render. **8.** communicate, impart, divulge. **9.** draw back, recede, retire, relax, cede, yield, give over, give away, sink, give up. **10.** break down, fail.
Ant. receive.

glad, *adj.* **1.** delighted, pleased, elated, happy, gratified, contented. **2.** cheerful, joyous, joyful, happy, merry, cheery, animated, light.
Ant. miserable, unhappy, sad.

glance, *v.* **1.** glitter, flash, glimpse, gleam, glisten, scintillate, shine. **2.** cast, reflect. **—***n.* **3.** glitter, gleam; glimpse, look.

glare, *n.* **1.** dazzle, flare, glitter, luster, brilliance, sparkle, flash. **2.** showiness. **3.** scowl, glower. **—***v.* **4.** shine, dazzle, gleam. **5.** glower, gloat, scowl.

gleam, *n.* **1.** ray, flash, beam, glimmer, glimmering.

—*v.* **2.** shine, glimmer, flash, glitter, sparkle, beam.

glee, *n.* joy, exultation, merriment, jollity, hilarity, mirth, joviality, gaiety, liveliness, verve, life.
Ant. misery, sadness, melancholy.

glib, *adj.* **1.** fluent, voluble, talkative, ready. **2.** slippery, smooth, facile, artful.
Ant. taciturn, silent, quiet; artless, guileless.

glide, *v., n.* slide, slip, flow.
Ant. stick.

glisten, *v.* glimmer, shimmer, sparkle, shine, gleam, glitter.

gloom, *n.* **1.** darkness, dimness, shadow, shade, obscurity, gloominess. **2.** melancholy, sadness, depression, dejection, despondence.
Ant. brightness, effulgence; joy, glee, happiness.

gloomy, *adj.* **1.** dark, shaded, obscure, shadowy, dim, dusky; dismal, lowering. **2.** depressed, dejected, sad, melancholy, despondent, downcast, crestfallen, downhearted, glum, dispirited, disheartened.
Ant. bright, effulgent, dazzling; happy, delighted, gleeful.

glorious, *adj.* **1.** admirable, delightful. **2.** famous, renowned, noted, celebrated, famed, eminent, distinguished, illustrious.
Ant. horrible; unknown; notorious.

glory, *n.* **1.** praise, honor, distinction, renown, fame, eminence, celebrity. **2.** resplendence, splendor, magnificence, grandeur, pomp, brilliance, effulgence. —*v.* **3.** exult, rejoice, triumph.
Ant. infamy, dishonor; gloom.

gloss, *n.* **1.** luster, sheen, polish, glaze, shine. **2.** front, mien, appearance, pretext, pretence. **3.** explanation, exegesis, critique, comment, note, interpretation, analysis, annotation, commentary. —*v.* **4.** polish, shine, glaze, varnish. **5.** annotate, explain, interpret, analyze.

glossy, *adj.* **1.** lustrous, shiny, shining, glazed, smooth, sleek. **2.** specious, plausible.

gnome, *n.* goblin, troll, sylph, gremlin.

gobble, *v.* gulp, bolt, devour, swallow.

godly, *adj.* pious, saintly, devout, religious, holy, righteous, good.
Ant. ungodly.

good, *adj.* **1.** moral, righteous, religious, pious, pure, virtuous, conscientious, meritorious, worthy, exemplary, upright. **2.** commendable, adroit, efficient, proficient, able, skillful, expert, ready, dexterous, clever, capable, qualified, fit, suited, suitable, convenient. **3.** satisfactory, excellent, exceptional, valuable, precious, capital, admirable, commendable. **4.** well-behaved, obedient, heedful. **5.** kind, beneficent, friendly, kindly, benevolent, humane, favorable, well-disposed, gracious, obliging. **6.** honorable, worthy, deserving, fair, unsullied, immaculate, unblemished, unimpeached. **7.** reliable, safe, trustworthy, honest, competent. **8.** genuine, sound, valid. **9.** agreeable,

pleasant, genial, cheering. **10.** satisfactory, advantageous, favorable, auspicious, propitious, fortunate, profitable, useful, serviceable, beneficial. **11.** ample, sufficient. **12.** full, adequate, all of. **13.** great, considerable, large. —*n.* **14.** profit, worth, advantage, benefit, usefulness, utility, gain. **15.** excellence, merit, righteousness, kindness, virtue. **16.** (*plural*) property, belongings, effects, chattels, furniture. **17.** (*plural*) wares, merchandise, stock, commodities.
Ant. bad.

goodness, *n.* **1.** virtue, morality, integrity, honesty, uprightness, probity, righteousness, good. **2.** kindness, benevolence, generosity, kindliness, benignity, humanity. **3.** excellence, worth, value, quality. **4.** essence, strength.
Ant. evil.

good will, **1.** friendliness, benevolence, favor, kindness. **2.** acquiescence, heartiness, ardor, zeal, earnestness.

gorge, *n.* **1.** defile, pass, cleft, fissure, ravine, notch. **2.** disgust, repulsion, revulsion. —*v.* **3.** stuff, glut, cram, fill. **4.** bolt, gulp, gobble, devour, gormandize.

gorgeous, *adj.* sumptuous, magnificent, splendid, rich, grand, resplendent, brilliant, glittering, dazzling, superb.
Ant. poor; ugly.

gossip, *n.* **1.** scandal, small talk, hearsay, palaver, idle talk, newsmongering. **2.** chatterer, babbler, gabber, nosy Parker. —*v.* **3.** chatter, prattle, prate, palaver, tattle.

govern, *v.* **1.** rule, reign, hold sway, control, command, sway, influence, have control. **2.** direct, guide, restrain, check, conduct, manage, supervise, superintend.
Ant. obey; follow.

gown, *n.* dress, robe, frock, evening gown *or* dress.

grace, *n.* **1.** attractiveness, charm, gracefulness, comeliness, ease, elegance, symmetry, beauty; polish, refinement. **2.** favor, kindness, kindliness, love, good will, benignity, condescension. **3.** mercy, clemency, pardon, leniency, lenity, forgiveness. **4.** love, sanctity, holiness, devoutness, devotion, piety. —*v.* **5.** adorn, embellish, beautify, enhance, deck, decorate, ornament; honor, dignify.
Ant. ugliness; disfavor; condemnation; hate, abhorrence; dishonor, disgrace.

gracious, *adj.* **1.** kind, kindly, benevolent, benign, courteous, polite, courtly, friendly, well-disposed, favorable. **2.** compassionate, tender, merciful, lenient, clement, mild, gentle. **3.** indulgent, beneficent, condescending, patronizing.
Ant. ungracious, unkind, impolite, unfavorable; dispassionate, cool, cruel, inclement.

gradual, *adj.* slow, by degrees, little by little, step by step, moderate, gentle.
Ant. sudden, precipitous, abrupt, immoderate.

grand, *adj.* **1.** imposing, stately, august, majestic, dignified, exalted, elevated, eminent, princely, regal, kingly, royal, great, illustrious. **2.** lofty, magnificent, great, large, palatial, splendid, brilliant, superb, glorious, sublime, noble, fine. **3.** main, principal, chief. **4.** important, distinctive, pretentious. **5.** complete, comprehensive, inclusive, all-inclusive.
Ant. base, undignified; ignoble; secondary; unimportant; incomplete.

grandiloquent, *adj.* lofty, pompous, bombastic, turgid, inflated, declamatory, rhetorical, oratorical, high-flown, pretentious, haughty, highfalutin.
Ant. base, servile, lowly.

grant, *v.* **1.** bestow, confer, award, bequeath, give. **2.** agree *or* accede to, admit, allow, concede, accept, cede, yield. **3.** transmit, convey, transfer. **—*n.* 4.** cession, concession, bequest, conveyance.
Ant. receive.

graphic, *adj.* **1.** lifelike, vivid, picturesque, striking, telling. **2.** diagrammatic, well-delineated, detailed.

grasp, *v.* **1.** seize, hold, clasp, grip, clutch, grab, catch. **2.** lay hold of, seize upon, fasten on; concentrate on, comprehend, understand. **—*n.* 3.** grip, hold, clutches. **4.** hold, possession, mastery. **5.** reach, comprehension, compass, scope.
Ant. loose, loosen; misunderstand.

grateful, *adj.* **1.** appreciative, thankful, obliged, indebted. **2.** pleasing, agreeable, welcome, refreshing, pleasant, gratifying, satisfying, satisfactory.
Ant. ungrateful; unpleasant, disagreeable, unsatisfactory.

gratify, *v.* please, indulge, humor, satisfy.
Ant. displease, dissatisfy.

grave, *n.* **1.** place of interment, tomb, sepulchre, pit, excavation. **—*adj.* 2.** sober, solemn, serious, dignified, sedate, earnest, staid, thoughtful. **3.** weighty, momentous, important, serious, consequential, critical.
Ant. undignified, thoughtless; unimportant, trivial, trifling.

great, *adj.* **1.** immense, enormous, huge, gigantic, vast, ample, grand, large, big. **2.** numerous, countless. **3.** unusual, considerable, important, momentous, serious, weighty. **4.** notable, remarkable, noteworthy. **5.** distinguished, famous, famed, eminent, noted, prominent, celebrated, illustrious, grand, renowned. **6.** consequential, important, vital, critical. **7.** chief, principal, main, grand, leading. **8.** noble, lofty, grand, exalted, elevated, dignified, majestic, august. **9.** admirable, notable.
Ant. small; insignificant; paltry; infamous, notorious; trivial; secondary.

greed, *n.* desire, avidity, avarice, cupidity, covetousness, greediness, voracity, ravenousness, rapacity.
Ant. generosity.

greedy, *adj.* **1.** grasping, rapacious, selfish, avaricious.

2. gluttonous, voracious, ravenous, starved, insatiable. **3.** desirous, covetous, eager, anxious.
Ant. generous, unselfish.

greet, *v.* address, welcome, hail, accost, salute.

grief, *n.* suffering, distress, sorrow, regret, anguish, heartache, woe, misery, sadness, melancholy, moroseness.
Ant. joy, happiness, glee, delight.

grieve, *v.* **1.** lament, weep, mourn, sorrow, suffer, bewail, bemoan. **2.** distress, sadden, depress, agonize, break one's heart, pain.
Ant. delight in.

grievous, *adj.* **1.** distressing, sad, sorrowful, painful, lamentable, regrettable. **2.** deplorable, lamentable, calamitous, heinous, outrageous, flagrant, atrocious, flagitious, dreadful, gross, shameful, iniquitous.
Ant. delighted, happy, joyful; delightful, pleasant, favorable.

grim, *adj.* **1.** stern, unrelenting, merciless, uncompromising, harsh, unyielding. **2.** sinister, ghastly, repellent, frightful, horrible, dire, appalling, horrid, grisly, gruesome, hideous, dreadful. **3.** severe, stern, harsh, hard, fierce, forbidding, ferocious, cruel, savage, ruthless.
Ant. merciful, lenient, sympathetic; wonderful, delightful, pleasant; amenable, genial, congenial, amiable.

grind, *v.* **1.** smooth, sharpen. **2.** bray, triturate, pulverize, powder, crush, comminute, pound. **3.** oppress, torment, harass, persecute, plague, afflict, trouble. **4.** grate, rub, abrade.

grit, *n.* **1.** sand, gravel. **2.** spirit, pluck, fortitude, courage, resolution.

gross, *adj.* **1.** whole, entire, total, aggregate. **2.** glaring, flagrant, outrageous, shameful, heinous, grievous. **3.** coarse, indelicate, indecent, low, animal, sensual, vulgar, broad, lewd. **4.** large, big, bulky, massive, great. **5.** thick, dense, heavy. —*n.* **6.** body, bulk, mass.
Ant. partial, incomplete; delicate, decent; small, dainty.

ground, *n.* **1.** land, earth, soil, mold, loam, dirt. **2.** (*often plural*) foundation, basis, base, premise, motive, reason, cause, consideration, factor, account. **3.** (*plural*) lees, dregs, sediment, silt, deposit. —*v.* **4.** found, fix, settle, establish, base, set. **5.** instruct, train.
Ant. sky, heaven; embellishment.

grow, *v.* **1.** increase, swell, enlarge, dilate, greaten, expand, extend. **2.** sprout, germinate; arise, originate. **3.** swell, wax, extend, advance, improve. **4.** raise, cultivate, produce.
Ant. decrease, shrink; wane, deteriorate.

growl, *v.* **1.** snarl. **2.** grumble, complain, mumble.

growth, *n.* **1.** development, increase, augmentation, expansion. **2.** product, outgrowth, result; produce.

3. (*pathology*) tumor, excrescence. 4. source, production.
Ant. failure, stagnation.

grudge, *n.* 1. malice, ill will, spite, resentment, bitterness, rancor, malevolence, enmity, hatred. —*v.* 2. suffer, yield, submit to. 3. begrudge, envy.
Ant. good will, amiability.

guarantee, *n.* 1. guaranty, warrant, pledge, assurance, promise, surety, security. —*v.* 2. guaranty, secure, insure, warrant.

guard, *v.* 1. protect, keep safe, preserve, save, watch over, shield, defend, shelter. 2. hold, check, watch, be careful. —*n.* 3. protector, guardian, sentry, watchman, defender, sentinel. 4. convoy, escort. 5. defense, protection, shield, bulwark, security, aegis, safety.
Ant. attack, assault; ignore; danger.

guardian, *n.* 1. guard, protector, defender. 2. trustee, warden, keeper.
Ant. assailant.

guess, *v.* 1. conjecture, hazard, suppose, fancy, believe, imagine, think. 2. estimate, solve, answer, penetrate. —*n.* 3. notion, judgment, conclusion, conjecture, surmise, supposition.
Ant. know.

guest, *n.* visitor, company.
Ant. host.

guide, *v.* 1. lead, pilot, steer, conduct, direct, show *or* point the way, escort, instruct, induce, influence, regulate, manage, govern, rule. —*n.* 2. pilot, steersman, helmsman, director, conductor. 3. mark, sign, signal, indication, key, clue.
Ant. follow.

guile, *n.* cunning, treachery, deceit, artifice, duplicity, deception, trickery, fraud, craft, artfulness.
Ant. ingenuousness.

guileless, *adj.* artless, honest, sincere, open, candid, frank, truthful, ingenuous, naive, unsophisticated, simple-minded.
Ant. cunning, sly, deceitful, artful, treacherous.

guilt, *n.* guiltiness, culpability, criminality.
Ant. exoneration.

guiltless, *adj.* innocent, spotless, blameless, immaculate, pure, unsullied, unpolluted, untarnished.
Ant. culpable, guilty, sullied, tarnished.

guise, *n.* appearance, aspect, semblance, form, shape, fashion, mode, manner.

gush, *v.* pour, stream, spurt, flow, spout, flood.

H

habit, *n.* 1. disposition, tendency, bent, wont. 2. custom, practice, way, usage, wont, manner. 3. garb, dress, rig, habiliment. —*v.* **4.** dress, clothe, garb, array, attire, deck out, rig, equip.

habitual, *adj.* confirmed, inveterate, accustomed, customary, usual, common, regular, familiar, ordinary.
Ant. rare, unaccustomed, unusual, uncommon, irregular.

habituate, *v.* accustom, familiarize, acclimate, acclimatize, train, inure, harden, make used (to).

hack, *v.* **1.** cut, notch, chop, hew, mangle. **2.** let, hire, lease, rent. **3.** hackney. —*n.* **4.** cut, notch, gash. **5.** jade, nag. —*adj.* **6.** hired, hackney, mercenary. **7.** hackneyed, trite, clichéd, overdone, old, used, worn out, commonplace, stale, stereotyped; old hat.
Ant. novel, new.

haggard, *adj.* wild-looking, careworn, gaunt, emaciated, drawn, hollow-eyed, meager, spare, worn, wasted.
Ant. hale, hearty, robust.

haggle, *v.* **1.** bargain, chaffer, higgle, palter, negotiate. **2.** wrangle, dispute, cavil, argue. **3.** harass, annoy, vex, tease, worry, badger, bait, fret. **4.** hack, mangle, chop, cut. —*n.* **5.** haggling, wrangle, dispute, argument, disagreement.

hale, *adj.* **1.** robust, healthy, vigorous, sound, strong, hearty. —*v.* **2.** drag, haul, pull, tug, draw.
Ant. haggard, weak, feeble.

half-hearted, *adj.* unenthusiastic, indifferent, uninterested, cold, cool, perfunctory, curt, abrupt, discouraging.
Ant. enthusiastic, eager, encouraging.

hallowed, *adj.* sacred, consecrated, holy, blessed; honored, revered.
Ant. execrative, blasphemous.

hallucination, *n.* illusion, delusion, aberration, phantasm, vision.
Ant. reality.

halt, *v.* **1.** hold, stop, cease, desist. **2.** waver, hesitate.
Ant. continue, persist.

hamlet, *n.* village, community, town, dorp.

hamper, *v.* **1.** impede, hinder, hold back, encumber, prevent, obstruct, restrain, clog. —*n.* **2.** basket; crate.
Ant. further, encourage.

handsome, *adj.* **1.** comely, fine, admirable, good-looking. **2.** liberal, considerable, ample, large, generous, magnanimous. **3.** gracious, generous.
Ant. ugly, unattractive; stingy, penurious, parsimonious.

hang, *v.* **1.** suspend, dangle. **2.** execute, lynch. **3.** drape, decorate, adorn, furnish. **4.** depend, rely, rest; hold fast, cling, adhere. **5.** be doubtful *or* undecided, waver, hesitate, demur, halt. **6.** loiter, linger, hover, float. **7.** impend, be imminent.

happen, *v.* come to pass, take place, occur, chance; befall, betide.

happiness, *n.* good fortune, pleasure, contentment, gladness, bliss, content, contentedness, beatitude, blessedness, delight, joy, enjoyment, gratification, satisfaction.
Ant. misery, dissatisfaction.

happy, *adj.* **1.** joyous, joyful, glad, blithe, merry, cheerful, contented, gay, blissful, delighted, satisfied, pleased, gladdened. **2.** favored, lucky, fortunate, propitious, advantageous, successful, prosperous. **3.** appropriate, fitting, apt, felicitous, opportune, befitting, pertinent.
Ant. unhappy, sad, cheerless, melancholy; unlucky, luckless, unfortunate; inappropriate, inapt.

harangue, *n.* **1.** address, speech, bombast. —*v.* **2.** declaim, address.

harrass, *v.* trouble, harry, raid, molest, disturb, distress; plague, vex, worry, badger, pester, annoy, torment, torture.

harbor, *n.* **1.** haven, port. **2.** shelter, refuge, asylum, protection, cover, sanctuary, retreat. —*v.* **3.** shelter, protect, lodge. **4.** conceal, hide, secrete. **5.** entertain, indulge, foster, cherish.

hard, *adj.* **1.** solid, firm, inflexible, rigid, unyielding, resistant, resisting, adamantine, flinty, impenetrable, compact. **2.** difficult, toilsome, burdensome, wearisome, exhausting, laborious, arduous, onerous, fatiguing, wearying. **3.** difficult, complex, intricate, complicated, perplexing, tough, puzzling. **4.** vigorous, severe, violent, stormy, tempestuous; inclement. **5.** oppressive, harsh, rough, cruel, severe, unmerciful, grinding, unsparing, unrelenting. **6.** severe, harsh, stern, austere, strict, exacting, callous, unfeeling, unsympathetic, impassionate, insensible, unimpressible, insensitive, indifferent, unpitying, inflexible, relentless, unyielding, cruel, obdurate, adamant, hard-hearted. **7.** undeniable, irrefutable, incontrovertible. **8.** unfriendly, unkind; harsh, unpleasant. **9.** unsympathetic, unsentimental, shrewd, hard-headed, callous. **10.** strong, spirituous, intoxicating. —*adv.* **11.** energetically, vigorously, violently. **12.** earnestly, intently, incessantly. **13.** harshly, severely, gallingly, with difficulty. **14.** solid, firm.
Ant. soft; easy; fair; merciful; sympathetic; kind.

harden, *v.* **1.** solidify, indurate, ossify, petrify. **2.** strengthen, confirm, fortify, steel, brace, nerve, toughen, inure; habituate, accustom, season, train, discipline.

hardly, *adv.* **1.** barely, scarcely, nearly. **2.** harshly, severely, roughly, cruelly, unkindly, rigorously.

hardship, *n.* trial, oppression, privation, need, austerity, trouble, affliction, burden, suffering, misfortune, grievance.

hardy, *adj.* **1.** vigorous, hearty, sturdy, hale, robust, stout, strong, sound, healthy. **2.** bold, daring, courageous, brave.

Ant. weak, feeble, unsound, unhealthy; cowardly, pusillanimous.

harm, *n.* **1.** injury, damage, hurt, mischief, detriment. **2.** wrong, evil, wickedness, sinfulness. —*v.* **3.** injure, hurt, damage; maltreat, molest, abuse.
Ant. good.

harmful, *adj.* injurious, detrimental, hurtful, deleterious, pernicious, mischievous.
Ant. beneficial.

harmonious, *adj.* **1.** amicable, congenial, sympathetic. **2.** consonant, congruous, concordant, consistent, correspondent, symmetrical. **3.** melodious, tuneful, agreeable, concordant.
Ant. unsympathetic; discordant, incongruous, asymmetrical; cacophonous, noisy.

harmony, *n.* **1.** agreement, concord, unity, peace, amity, friendship, accord, unison. **2.** congruity, consonance, conformity, correspondence, consistency, congruence, fitness, suitability. **3.** melody, melodiousness, concord, euphony.
Ant. discord, disagreement; nonconformity, unfitness; cacophony, noise.

harry, *v.* **1.** harass, torment, worry, molest, plague, trouble, vex, gall, fret, disturb, harrow, chafe, annoy, pester. **2.** ravage, devastate, plunder, strip, rob, pillage.
Ant. please, delight, enrapture.

harsh, *adj.* **1.** rough; ungentle, unpleasant, severe, austere, brusque, rough, hard, unfeeling, unkind, brutal, cruel, stern, acrimonious, bad-tempered, ill-natured, crabbed, morose. **2.** jarring, unaesthetic, inartistic, discordant, dissonant, unharmonious.
Ant. gentle, pleasant, kind, good-natured; artistic, aesthetic, harmonious.

haste, *n.* **1.** swiftness, celerity, alacrity, quickness, rapidity, dispatch, speed, expedition, promptitude. **2.** need, hurry, flurry, bustle, ado, precipitancy, precipitation.
Ant. sloth.

hasten, *v.* hurry, accelerate, urge, press, expedite, quicken, speed, precipitate, dispatch.

hasty, *adj.* **1.** speedy, quick, hurried, swift, rapid, fast, fleet, brisk. **2.** precipitate, rash, foolhardy, reckless, indiscreet, thoughtless, headlong, unthinking. **3.** quick-tempered, testy, touchy, irascible, petulant, waspish, fretful, fiery, pettish, excitable, irritable, peevish.
Ant. slow, deliberate; discreet, thoughtful; even-tempered, amiable.

hatch, *v.* **1.** incubate, breed, brood. **2.** contrive, devise, plan, plot, concoct, design, scheme, project. **3.** shade, line. —*n.* **4.** brood. **5.** door, cover, deck, hatchway.

hate, *v.* **1.** dislike; detest, abhor, loathe, despise, execrate, abominate. —*n.* **2.** hatred.
Ant. like, love.

hateful, *adj.* detestable, odious, abominable, execrable, loathsome, abhorrent, repugnant, invidious, obnoxious, offensive, disgusting, nauseating, revolting, vile, repulsive.
Ant. lovable, appealing, attractive, likable.

hatred, *n.* aversion, animosity, hate, detestation, loathing, abomination, odium, horror, repugnance.
Ant. attraction, love, favor.

haughty, *adj.* disdainful, proud, arrogant, supercilious, snobbish, lordly, contemptuous.
Ant. humble, shy, self-effacing.

have, *v.* **1.** hold, occupy, possess, own, contain. **2.** get, receive, take, obtain, acquire, gain, secure, procure. **3.** experience, enjoy, suffer, undergo. **4.** permit, allow. **5.** assert, maintain, hold, aver, state, asseverate, testify.

havoc, *n.* devastation, ruin, destruction, desolation, waste, damage.

hazard, *n.* **1.** danger, peril, jeopardy, risk. **2.** chance, hap, accident, luck, fortuity, fortuitousness. **3.** uncertainty, doubt. **—***v.* **4.** venture, offer. **5.** imperil, risk, endanger.
Ant. safety, security; certainty, surety.

haze, *n.* **1.** vapor, dust, mist, cloud, fog, smog. **2.** obscurity, dimness, cloud, vagueness. **—***v.* **3.** torment, torture, abuse, trick.
Ant. clearness, clarity.

head, *n.* **1.** command, authority. **2.** commander, director, chief, chieftain, leader, principal, commander in chief, master. **3.** top, summit, acme. **4.** culmination, crisis, conclusion. **5.** cape, headland, promontory, ness. **6.** source, origin, rise, beginning, headwaters. **7.** froth, foam. **—***adj.* **8.** front, leading, topmost, chief, principal, main, cardinal, foremost, first. **—***v.* **9.** lead, precede, direct, command, rule, govern. **10.** outdo, excel, surpass, beat.

headstrong, *adj.* willful, stubborn, obstinate, intractable, self-willed, dogged, pig-headed, froward.
Ant. amenable, tractable, genial, agreeable.

heal, *v.* **1.** cure, remedy, restore. **2.** amend, settle, harmonize, compose, soothe. **3.** cleanse, purify, purge, disinfect.
Ant. discompose; soil, pollute, infect.

healthy, *adj.* **1.** healthful, hale, sound, hearty, well, robust, vigorous, strong. **2.** nutritious, nourishing, salubrious, salutary, hygienic, invigorating, bracing, wholesome.
Ant. unhealthy, ill, sick, weak; unwholesome, enervating.

heap, *n.* **1.** mass, stack, pile, accumulation, collection. **—***v.* **2.** pile *or* heap up, amass, accumulate. **3.** bestow, confer, cast.

hear, *v.* **1.** listen, perceive, attend. **2.** regard, heed, attend.

heat, *n.* **1.** warmth, caloricity, caloric, hotness. **2.** warmth, intensity, ardor, fervor, zeal. **3.** passion,

ardor, flush, fever, excitement, impetuosity, vehemence, violence. —*v.* **4.** stimulate, warm, stir, animate, arouse, excite, rouse.
Ant. coolness; phlegm; cool, discourage.

heathen, *n.* **1.** gentile, pagan. —*adj.* **2.** gentile, pagan, heathenish, irreligious, unenlightened, barbarous.
Ant. Christian.

heave, *v.* **1.** raise, lift, hoist, elevate. **2.** pant, exhale, breathe. **3.** vomit, retch. **4.** rise, swell, dilate, bulge, expand.

heavenly, *adj.* **1.** blissful, beautiful, divine, seraphic, cherubic, angelic, saintly, sainted, holy, beatific, blessed, beatified, glorified. **2.** celestial.
Ant. hellish, satanic, diabolical, devilish.

heavy, *adj.* **1.** weighty, ponderous, massive. **2.** burdensome, harsh, oppressive, depressing, onerous, distressing, severe, grievous, cumbersome. **3.** broad, thick, coarse, blunt. **4.** serious, intense, momentous, weighty, important, pithy, concentrated. **5.** trying, difficult. **6.** depressed, serious, grave, sorrowful, gloomy, mournful, melancholy, morose, morbid, dejected, sad, disconsolate, crushed, despondent, heavy-hearted, downcast, crestfallen, downhearted. **7.** overcast, cloudy, lowering, oppressive, gloomy. **8.** clumsy, slow. **9.** ponderous, dull, tedious, tiresome, wearisome, burdensome, boring, lifeless. **10.** thick, unleavened, dense, concentrated.
Ant. light.

heed, *v.* **1.** pay *or* give attention to, consider, regard, notice, mark, observe, obey. —*n.* **2.** attention, notice, observation, consideration, care, caution, heedfulness, watchfulness, vigilance.
Ant. disregard, ignore.

height, *n.* **1.** altitude, stature, elevation, tallness. **2.** hill, prominence, mountain. **3.** top, peak, pinnacle, apex, eminence, acme, summit, zenith, culmination.
Ant. depth, abyss.

heinous, *adj.* hateful, odious, reprehensible, grave, wicked, infamous, flagrant, flagitious, atrocious, villainous, nefarious.
Ant. good, beneficial.

hell, *n.* Gehenna, Tartarus, inferno, Abaddon, Avernus, Hades, Erebus, pandemonium, abyss, limbo.
Ant. heaven.

help, *v.* **1.** cooperate, aid, assist, encourage, befriend, support, second, uphold, back, abet, succor, save. **2.** further, facilitate, promote, ease, foster. **3.** relieve, ameliorate, alleviate, remedy, cure, heal, restore, improve, better. **4.** refrain from, avoid, forbear. —*n.* **5.** support, backing, aid, assistance, relief, succor. **6.** helper, handyman, assistant.
Ant. discourage, attack.

helper, *n.* aid, assistant, supporter, auxiliary, ally, colleague, partner.

helpful, *adj.* useful, convenient, beneficial, advantageous, profitable.

Ant. useless, inconvenient, disadvantageous, uncooperative.

herd, *n.* **1.** drove, flock, clutch, crowd. —*v.* **2.** flock, assemble, associate, keep company.

heritage, *n.* inheritance, estate, patrimony. *Ant.* posterity.

heroic, *adj.* intrepid, valiant, dauntless, gallant, valorous, brave, courageous, bold, daring, fearless; epic. *Ant.* cowardly, fearful.

heroism, *n.* intrepidity, valor, prowess, gallantry, bravery, courage, daring, fortitude, boldness. *Ant.* cowardice.

hesitate, *v.* **1.** waver, vacillate, falter. **2.** demur, delay, pause, wait. *Ant.* resolve, decide.

hesitation, *n.* **1.** hesitancy, indecision, vacillation, irresolution, delay, uncertainty, doubt. **2.** halting, stammering, faltering. *Ant.* resolution, certainty.

hew, *v.* **1.** cut, chop, hack. **2.** make, shape, fashion, form. **3.** sever, cut down, fell.

hide, *v.* **1.** conceal, secrete, screen, mask, cloak, veil, shroud, cover, disguise, withhold, suppress. —*n.* **2.** skin, pelt, rawhide. *Ant.* open, reveal.

hideous, *adj.* horrible, frightful, ugly, grisly, grim, revolting, repellent, repulsive, detestable, odious, monstrous, dreadful, appalling, terrifying, terrible, ghastly, macabre, shocking. *Ant.* beautiful, lovely, attractive.

high, *adj.* **1.** lofty, tall, elevated, towering, skyscraping. **2.** intensified, energetic, intense, strong. **3.** expensive, costly, dear, high-priced. **4.** exalted, elevated, eminent, prominent, preeminent, distinguished. **5.** shrill, sharp, acute, high-pitched, strident. **6.** chief, main, principal, head. **7.** consequential, important, grave, serious, capital, extreme. **8.** lofty, haughty, arrogant, snobbish, proud, lordly, supercilious. **9.** elated, merry, hilarious, happy. **10.** remote, primeval, early, antediluvian, prehistoric; northerly, arctic, southerly, polar. *Ant.* low.

hill, *n.* elevation, prominence, eminence, mound, monticule, knoll, hillock, foothill. *Ant.* valley, dale, glen, hollow, depth.

hinder, *v.* **1.** interrupt, check, retard, impede, encumber, delay, hamper, obstruct, trammel. **2.** block, thwart, prevent, obstruct. *Ant.* encourage, disencumber.

hindrance, *n.* **1.** impeding, stopping, stoppage, estoppage, preventing. **2.** impediment, deterrent, hitch, encumbrance, obstruction, check, restraint, hobble, obstacle. *Ant.* help, aid, support.

hint, *n.* **1.** suggestion, implication, intimation, allusion, insinuation, innuendo, memorandum, reminder, inkling. —*v.* **2.** imply, intimate, insinuate, suggest, mention.

hire, *v.* **1.** engage, employ; let, lease, rent, charter. **2.** bribe, reward. —*n.* **3.** rent, rental; pay, stipend, salary, wages, remuneration.

history, *n.* record, chronicle, account, annals, story, relation, narrative.

hit, *v.* **1.** strike. **2.** reach, attain, gain, win, accomplish, achieve. **3.** touch, suit, fit, befit, affect. **4.** find, come upon, meet with, discover, happen upon. **5.** collide, strike, clash. **6.** assail. —*n.* **6.** blow, stroke; success.

hitch, *v.* **1.** make fast, fasten, connect, hook, tether, attach, tie, unite, harness, yoke. —*n.* **2.** halt, obstruction, hindrance, catch, impediment.
Ant. loose, loosen, untie.

hoarse, *adj.* husky, throaty, guttural, gruff, harsh, grating, raucous, rough.

hoist, *v.* **1.** raise, elevate, lift, heave. —*n.* **2.** derrick, crane, elevator, lift.
Ant. lower.

hold, *v.* **1.** have, keep, retain, possess, occupy. **2.** bear, sustain, hold up, support, maintain, keep (up), continue, carry on. **3.** engage in, observe, celebrate, preside over, carry on, pursue. **4.** hinder, restrain, keep back, deactivate, confine, detain. **5.** occupy, possess, own. **6.** contain, admit. **7.** think, believe, embrace, espouse, entertain, have, regard, consider, esteem, judge, deem. **8.** continue, persist, last, endure, remain. **9.** adhere, cling, remain, stick. —*n.* **10.** grasp, grip. **11.** control, influence. **12.** prison, keep, tower, cell, dungeon, deep.

hole, *n.* **1.** aperture, opening, cavity, excavation, pit, hollow, concavity. **2.** burrow, lair, den, retreat, cave. **3.** hovel, den, cot.

holy, *adj.* **1.** blessed, sacred, consecrated, hallowed, dedicated. **2.** saintly, godly, divine, pious, devout, spiritual, pure.
Ant. unholy, desecrated, impious, piacular, sinful, impure, corrupt.

homage, *n.* **1.** respect, reverence, deference, obeisance, honor, tribute. **2.** fealty, allegiance, faithfulness, fidelity, loyalty, devotion. **3.** devotion, worship, adoration.
Ant. disrespect, irreverence, dishonor; faithlessness, disloyalty.

home, *n.* **1.** house, apartment, residence, household, abode, dwelling, domicile, habitation. **2.** refuge, retreat, institution, asylum. **3.** hearth, fireside, family; rightful place.

homely, *adj.* plain, simple, unpretentious, unattractive, coarse, inelegant, uncomely, ugly.
Ant. beautiful.

honest, *adj.* **1.** honorable, upright, fair, just, incorruptible, trusty, trustworthy, truthful, virtuous, moral. **2.** open, sincere, candid, straightforward, frank, unreserved, ingenuous. **3.** genuine, pure, unadulterated. **4.** chaste, virtuous, pure, virginal, decent.

Ant. dishonest; corrupt, disingenuous, untrustworthy, secretive; false, counterfeit; impure, venal, indecent.

honesty, *n.* **1.** uprightness, probity, integrity, justice, fairness, rectitude, equity, honor. **2.** truthfulness, sincerity, candor, frankness, truth, veracity.

Ant. dishonesty, inequity; deceit, insincerity.

honor, *n.* **1.** esteem, fame, glory, repute, reputation, credit. **2.** credit, distinction, dignity. **3.** respect, deference, homage, reverence, veneration, consideration, distinction. **4.** privilege, favor. **5.** character, principle, probity, uprightness, honesty, integrity, nobleness. **6.** purity, chastity, virginity. —*v.* **7.** revere, esteem, venerate, respect, reverence; adore, worship, hallow.

Ant. dishonor, disrepute, discredit; indignity; disfavor; indecency; execrate, abominate.

honorable, *adj.* **1.** upright, honest, noble, high-minded, just, fair, trusty, trustworthy, true, virtuous. **2.** dignified, distinguished, noble, illustrious, great. **3.** creditable, reputable, estimable, right, proper, equitable.

Ant. ignoble, untrustworthy, corrupt; undignified; disreputable.

hope, *n.* **1.** expectation, expectancy, longing, desire. **2.** confidence, trust, reliance, faith. —*v.* **3.** trust, expect.

Ant. hopelessness.

hopeful, *adj.* expectant, sanguine, optimistic, confident.

Ant. hopeless.

hopeless, *adj.* **1.** desperate, despairing, despondent, forlorn, disconsolate. **2.** irremediable, remediless, incurable.

Ant. hopeful.

horrible, *adj.* **1.** horrendous, terrible, horrid, dreadful, awful, appalling, frightful, hideous, grim, ghastly, shocking, revolting, repulsive, repellent, dire, formidable, horrifying, harrowing. **2.** unpleasant, deplorable, shocking, abominable, odious.

Ant. attractive, delightful, beautiful; pleasant.

horror, *n.* **1.** fear, abhorrence, terror, dread, dismay, consternation, panic, alarm. **2.** aversion, repugnance, loathing, antipathy, detestation, hatred, abomination.

Ant. calm, serenity; attraction, delight, love.

hospital, *n.* retreat, sanatorium, asylum, sanitarium, clinic.

hostile, *adj.* opposed, adverse, averse, unfriendly, inimical, antagonistic, contrary, warlike, oppugnant, repugnant.

Ant. friendly, amiable, amicable.

hostility, *n.* **1.** enmity, antagonism, animosity, animus, ill will, unfriendliness, opposition, hatred. **2.** (*plural*) war, warfare, fighting, conflict.

Ant. friendliness, good will, love; peace, truce.

hot, *adj.* **1.** heated, torrid, sultry, burning, fiery. **2.** pungent, piquant, sharp, acrid, spicy, peppery, biting, blistering. **3.** ardent, fervent, fervid, angry, furious, vehement, intense, excited, excitable, irascible, animated, violent, passionate, impetuous.
Ant. cold.

hotel, *n.* hostelry, hostel, inn, house, guest house, motel, tavern.

house, *n.* **1.** domicile, dwelling, residence, home, household. **2.** firm, company, partnership, business, establishment. —*v.* **3.** lodge, harbor, shelter, reside, dwell, lodge.

hubbub, *n.* noise, tumult, uproar, clamor, din, racket, disorder, confusion, disturbance, riot.
Ant. serenity, calm.

huge, *adj.* large, extensive, mammoth, vast, gigantic, colossal, stupendous, bulky, enormous, immense, tremendous, Cyclopean.
Ant. tiny, small, infinitesimal, microscopic.

humane, *adj.* **1.** merciful, kind, kindly, kindhearted, tender, human, benevolent, sympathetic, compassionate, gentle, accommodating, benignant, charitable. **2.** refining, polite, cultivating, elevating, humanizing, spiritual.
Ant. inhumane, cruel, ruthless, merciless; boorish, degrading.

humble, *adj.* **1.** low, lowly, unassuming, plain, common, poor, meek, modest, submissive, unpretending, unpretentious. **2.** respectful, polite, courteous, courtly. —*v.* **3.** lower, abase, debase, degrade, humiliate, reduce, mortify, shame, subdue, abash, crush, break.
Ant. haughty, immodest, snobbish, conceited, pretentious; impolite, discourteous; raise, elevate.

humbug, *n.* **1.** trick, hoax, fraud, imposture, deception, imposition. **2.** falseness, deception, sham, pretense, hypocrisy, charlatanism. **3.** cheat, impostor, swindler, charlatan, pretender, confidence man, deceiver, quack. —*v.* **4.** impose upon, delude, deceive, cheat, swindle, trick, fool, dupe.

humid, *adj.* damp, dank, wet, moist.
Ant. dry.

humiliate, *v.* mortify, degrade, debase, dishonor, disgrace, abash, shame, humble.
Ant. honor, elevate, exalt.

humiliation, *n.* mortification, shame, abasement, degradation, humbling, dishonoring.
Ant. honor, elevation.

humility, *n.* lowliness, meekness, humbleness, submissiveness.
Ant. haughtiness.

humor, *n.* **1.** wit, fun, facetiousness, pleasantry. **2.** disposition, tendency, temperament, mood; whim, caprice, fancy, vagary. —*v.* **3.** indulge, gratify.

humorous, *adj.* amusing, funny, jocose, jocular, droll,

comic, comical, witty, facetious, waggish, sportive, ludicrous, laughable.
Ant. serious, sad, melancholy.

hungry, *adj.* ravenous, famishing, famished, starved, starving.
Ant. sated.

hunt, *v.* **1.** chase, pursue, track. **2.** search for, seek, scour. —*n.* **3.** chase, pursuit, hunting; search.

hurry, *v.* **1.** rush, haste, hasten, be quick, move swiftly *or* rapidly *or* quickly. **2.** hasten, urge forward, accelerate, quicken, expedite, hustle, dispatch. —*n.* **3.** bustle, haste, dispatch, celerity, speed, quickness, alacrity, promptitude, expedition. **4.** bustle, ado, precipitation, flurry, flutter, confusion, perturbation.
Ant. delay, slow.

hurt, *v.* **1.** injure, harm, damage, mar, impair. **2.** pain, ache, grieve, afflict, wound. —*n.* **3.** injury, harm, damage, detriment, disadvantage; bruise, wound.

hut, *n.* cottage, cot, cabin, shed, hovel.

hybrid, *n.* half-breed, mongrel, mutt.

hypocrite, *n.* deceiver, pretender, dissembler, pharisee.

hypocritical, *adj.* sanctimonious, pharisaical, Pecksniffian; insincere, deceiving, dissembling, pretending, false, hollow, empty, deceptive, misleading, deceitful.
Ant. honest, direct, forthright, sincere.

I

icon, *n.* picture, image, symbol, idol, representation, sign.

idea, *n.* **1.** thought, conception, notion; impression, apprehension, fancy. **2.** opinion, view, belief, sentiment, judgment, supposition. **3.** intention, plan, object, objective, aim.

ideal, *n.* **1.** example, model, conception, epitome, standard. **2.** aim, object, intention, objective. —*adj.* **3.** perfect, consummate, complete. **4.** unreal, unpractical, impractical, imaginary, visionary, fanciful, fantastic, illusory, chimerical.

idiotic, *adj.* foolish, senseless, half-witted, stupid, fatuous, imbecilic.
Ant. intelligent, sensible.

idle, *adj.* **1.** unemployed, unoccupied, inactive. **2.** indolent, slothful, lazy, sluggish. **3.** worthless, unimportant, trivial, trifling, insignificant, useless, fruitless, vain, futile, ineffective, unavailing, ineffectual, abortive, baseless, groundless. **4.** frivolous, vain, wasteful. —*v.* **5.** waste, fritter away, idle away, loiter.
Ant. employed, occupied; active, energetic; worthy, important; thrifty.

idol, *n.* **1.** image, icon, symbol, statue, false god, pagan deity. **2.** favorite, fair-haired boy, darling, pet. **3.** figment, delusion, illusion.

if, *conj.* **1.** in case, provided, providing, granting, supposing, even though, though; whether, whether or not. —*n.* **2.** condition, supposition.

ignite, *v.* kindle, fire, set fire to, set on fire.
Ant. quench.

ignoble, *adj.* **1.** mean, base, ignominious, degraded, dishonorable, contemptible, vulgar, low, peasant. **2.** inferior, base, mean, insignificant. **3.** lowly, humble, obscure, plebeian, contemptible.
Ant. noble, honorable; superior, significant; haughty.

ignominious, *adj.* discreditable, humiliating, degrading, disgraceful, dishonorable, shameful, infamous, disreputable, opprobrious, despicable, scandalous, contemptible.
Ant. creditable, honorable, reputable.

ignominy, *n.* disgrace, dishonor, disrepute, contempt, discredit, shame, infamy, obloquy, opprobrium, scandal, odium, abasement.
Ant. credit, honor, repute, fame, distinction.

ignorant, *adj.* illiterate, unlettered, uneducated, unlearned, uninstructed, untutored, untaught, unenlightened, nescient.
Ant. literate, lettered, educated.

ignore, *v.* overlook, slight, disregard, neglect.
Ant. notice, note, regard, mark.

ill, *adj.* **1.** unwell, sick, indisposed, unhealthy, ailing, diseased, afflicted. **2.** evil, wicked, bad, wrong, iniquitous, naughty. **3.** objectionable, unsatisfactory, poor, faulty. **4.** hostile, unkindly, unkind, unfavorable, adverse. —*n.* **5.** evil, wickedness, depravity, badness. **6.** harm, injury, hurt, pain, affliction, misery, trouble, misfortune, calamity. **7.** disease, ailment, illness, affliction. —*adv.* **8.** illy, wickedly, badly. **9.** poorly, unsatisfactorily. **10.** unfavorably, unfortunately. **11.** faultily, improperly.
Ant. well, hale, healthy; good; satisfactory; favorably, properly.

illegal, *adj.* unauthorized, unlawful, illegitimate, illicit, unlicensed.
Ant. legal, licit, authorized.

ill-mannered, *adj.* impolite, uncivil, discourteous, uncourtly, rude, coarse, uncouth, unpolished, crude, rough, ill-bred.

ill-natured, *adj.* cross, cranky, petulant, testy, snappish, unkindly, unpleasant, sulky, ill-tempered, crabbed, morose, sullen, dour, gloomy, sour, crusty, perverse, acerb, bitter.
Ant. good-natured, kindly, pleasant, amiable, friendly.

illusion, *n.* delusion, hallucination, deception, fantasy, chimera.
Ant. fact, reality.

illustration, *n.* comparison, example, case, elucidation, explanation, explication.

image, *n.* **1.** icon, idol, representation, statue. **2.** reflection, likeness, effigy, figure, representation. **3.** idea, conception, notion, mental picture. **4.** form, appearance, semblance. **5.** counterpart, facsimile, copy. —*v.* **6.** imagine, conceive.
Ant. original.

imaginary, *adj.* fanciful, unreal, visionary, baseless, chimerical, shadowy, fancied, illusory, imagined.
Ant. real.

imagine, *v.* conceive, image, picture, conceive of, realize, think, believe, fancy, assume, suppose, guess, conjecture, hypothesize.

imbibe, *v.* drink, absorb, swallow, take in, receive.

imitate, *v.* follow, mimic, ape, mock, impersonate, copy, duplicate, reproduce, simulate, counterfeit.

immediate, *adj.* **1.** instant, without delay, present, instantaneous. **2.** present, next, near, close, proximate. **3.** direct, unmediated.
Ant. later.

immediately, *adv.* **1.** instantly, at once, without delay, presently, directly, instantly, instanter, instantaneously, forthwith. **2.** directly, closely, without intervention.
Ant. later, anon.

immense, *adj.* huge, great, vast, extensive.
Ant. small, tiny, submicroscopic.

immerse, *v.* **1.** plunge, dip, sink, immerge, duck, douse. **2.** embed, bury; involve, absorb, engage.
Ant. withdraw; disinter.

imminent, *adj.* **1.** impending, threatening, near, at hand. **2.** overhanging, leaning forward.
Ant. delayed, far off.

immoderate, *adj.* excessive, extreme, exorbitant, unreasonable, inordinate, extravagant, intemperate.
Ant. moderate, reasonable, temperate.

immoral, *adj.* abandoned, depraved, self-indulgent, dissipated, licentious, dissolute, profligate, unprincipled, vicious, sinful, corrupt, amoral, wicked, bad, wrong, evil.
Ant. moral, pious, good.

immunity, *n.* **1.** insusceptibility. **2.** exemption, franchise, privilege, license, charter, right, liberty, prerogative.
Ant. susceptibility; proneness.

impair, *v.* injure; worsen, diminish, deteriorate, lessen.
Ant. repair.

impart, *v.* **1.** communicate, disclose, divulge, reveal, make known, tell, relate. **2.** give, bestow, grant, cede, confer.
Ant. conceal, hide.

impartial, *adj.* unbiased, just, fair, unprejudiced, disinterested, equitable.
Ant. partial.

impatient, *adj.* **1.** uneasy, restless, unquiet. **2.** hasty,

impetuous, vehement, precipitate, sudden, curt, brusque, abrupt. **3.** irritable, testy, fretful, violent, hot.
Ant. patient, restful, quiet; gradual, slow; calm, unperturbed.

impecunious, *adj.* penniless, poor, destitute, poverty-stricken.
Ant. wealthy, rich.

impede, *v.* retard, slow, delay, hinder, hamper, prevent, obstruct, check, stop, block, thwart, interrupt, restrain.
Ant. aid, encourage.

impediment, *n.* bar, hindrance, obstacle, obstruction, encumbrance, check.
Ant. help, support, encouragement.

impel, *v.* compel, drive, urge, press on, incite, constrain, force, actuate.
Ant. restrain.

imperfect, *adj.* **1.** defective, faulty, incomplete. **2.** rudimentary, undeveloped, underdeveloped, incomplete; immature.

imperious, *adj.* **1.** domineering, overbearing, dictatorial, tyrannical, despotic, arrogant. **2.** urgent, imperative, necessary.
Ant. submissive; unnecessary.

impertinent, *adj.* **1.** intrusive, presumptuous, impudent, insolent, rude, fresh, bold, arrogant, insulting, officious, saucy, pert, brazen. **2.** irrelevant, inappropriate, incongruous, inapplicable. **3.** trivial, silly, absurd, ridiculous, inane.
Ant. polite, courteous; appropriate; important, serious.

impetuous, *adj.* impulsive, rash, precipitate, spontaneous, violent, hasty, furious, hot.
Ant. planned, careful.

implacable, *adj.* unappeased, unpacified, inexorable, inflexible, unbending, relentless, unappeasable, rancorous, merciless.
Ant. flexible, merciful.

implicate, *v.* involve, concern, entangle.
Ant. disentangle.

implore, *v.* call upon, supplicate, beseech, entreat, crave, beg, solicit.

impolite, *adj.* uncivil, rude, discourteous, disrespectful, insolent, unpolished, unrefined, boorish, ill-mannered, rough, savage.
Ant. polite.

importance, *n.* consequence, weight, moment, significance, import, momentousness, weightiness.
Ant. unimportance, insignificance.

impostor, *n.* pretender, deceiver, cheat, confidence man, con man, intruder, trickster, knave, hypocrite, charlatan, mountebank.

impregnable, *adj.* unassailable, invincible, invulnerable.
Ant. pregnable, vulnerable.

improper, *adj.* **1.** inapplicable, unsuited, unfit, inappropriate, unsuitable. **2.** indecent, unbecoming, unseemly, indecorous, unfitting. **3.** abnormal, irregular.
Ant. proper.

improve, *v.* **1.** ameliorate, better, amend, emend, correct, right, rectify. **2.** mend, gain, get better.
Ant. worsen, impair; fail, sink.

improvident, *adj.* **1.** incautious, unwary, thoughtless, careless, imprudent, heedless, without *or* lacking foresight. **2.** thriftless, shiftless, neglectful, wasteful, prodigal.
Ant. provident, cautious; thrifty.

improvised, *adj.* extemporaneous, impromptu, unpremeditated, unrehearsed, spontaneous.
Ant. premeditated.

impudence, *n.* impertinence, effrontery, insolence, rudeness, brass, brazenness, face, lip, boldness, presumption, presumptiveness, sauciness, pertness, flippancy; (*colloquial*) nerve.
Ant. politeness, courtesy.

impudent, *adj.* bold, brazen, brassy, presumptuous, insolent, impertinent, insulting, rude, presumptive, saucy, pert, flippant, fresh.
Ant. polite, courteous, well-behaved.

impulsive, *adj.* emotional, impetuous, rash, quick, hasty, unpremeditated.
Ant. cool, cold, unemotional, premeditated.

impunity, *n.* exemption, license, permission.
Ant. responsibility, blame, culpability.

impute, *v.* attribute, charge, ascribe, refer.

inability, *n.* incapability, incapacity, disqualification, impotence, incompetence.
Ant. ability.

inaccuracy, *n.* **1.** incorrectness, erroneousness, inexactness, inexactitude. **2.** error, blunder, mistake, slip.
Ant. accuracy.

inaccurate, *adj.* inexact, loose, general, unspecific; incorrect, wrong, erroneous, faulty, improper.
Ant. accurate.

inactive, *adj.* inert, dormant, unmoving, immobile, inoperative; indolent, lazy, sluggish, torpid, passive, idle, slothful, dilatory.
Ant. active.

inadequate, *adj.* inapt, incompetent, insufficient, incommensurate, defective, imperfect, incomplete.
Ant. adequate.

inadvertent, *adj.* heedless, inattentive, unintentional, thoughtless, careless, negligent.
Ant. intentional, purposive, purposeful.

inanimate, *adj.* **1.** lifeless, inorganic, vegetable, mineral, mechanical. **2.** spiritless, lifeless, sluggish, inert, spiritless; dead, defunct.
Ant. animate, alive; spirited.

inapt, *adj.* **1.** unsuited, unsuitable, inappropriate,

unfit, inapposite, not pertinent. **2.** incapable, clumsy, awkward, slow, dull.
Ant. apt, suitable, appropriate, fit; capable, efficient.
inborn, *adj.* innate, inbred, native, natural, congenital, inherent, instinctive, inherited.
Ant. acquired, learned, conditioned, environmental.
incapable, *adj.* unable, incompetent, inefficient, impotent, unqualified; incapacious.
Ant. capable, competent, efficient, potent, qualified.
incarcerate, *v.* imprison, commit, confine, jail; constrict, enclose, restrict.
Ant. liberate, free.
incense, *n.* **1.** perfume, aroma, scent, fragrance. —*v.* **2.** inflame, enrage, exasperate, provoke, irritate, goad, vex, excite.
incentive, *n.* motive, inducement, incitement, enticement, stimulus, spur, impulse, goad, encouragement, prod.
Ant. discouragement.
incessant, *adj.* uninterrupted, unceasing, ceaseless, continual, continuous, constant, unending, neverending, relentless, unrelenting, unremitting, perpetual, eternal, everlasting.
Ant. interrupted, spasmodic, sporadic; temporary.
incident, *n.* event, occurrence, happening, circumstance.
incidental, *adj.* fortuitous, chance, accidental, casual, contingent.
Ant. fundamental.
incisive, *adj.* **1.** penetrating, trenchant, biting, acute, sarcastic, sardonic, satirical, acid, severe, cruel. **2.** sharp, keen, acute.
Ant. superficial; dull.
incite, *v.* urge on, stimulate, encourage, back, prod, push, spur, goad, instigate, provoke, arouse, fire; induce.
Ant. discourage.
inclination, *n.* **1.** bent, leaning, tendency, set, propensity, liking, preference, predilection, predisposition, proclivity, bias, proneness, prejudice, penchant. **2.** slope, slant, leaning, inclining; verging, tending, tendency.
Ant. dislike, antipathy.
include, *v.* contain, embrace, comprise, comprehend, embody.
Ant. exclude, preclude.
income, *n.* return, returns, receipts, revenue, profits, salary, wages, pay, stipend, interest, annuity, gain, earnings.
Ant. expense, expenditure.
incommode, *v.* **1.** inconvenience, discomfort, disturb, annoy, vex, trouble, discommode. **2.** impede, hinder, interfere, delay.
Ant. comfort; encourage, aid, abet, support, expedite.
incompatible, *adj.* **1.** inconsistent, incongruous, unsuitable, unsuited, contradictory, irreconcilable. **2.**

discordant, contrary, opposed, difficult, contradictory, inharmonious.
Ant. compatible, consistent, appropriate; harmonious.

incompetent, *adj.* unqualified, unable, incapable, inadequate, unfit, insufficient.
Ant. competent, efficient, able, capable, adequate, fit.

incongruous, *adj.* **1.** unbecoming, inappropriate, incompatible, out of keeping, discrepant, absurd. **2.** inconsonant, inharmonious, discordant. **3.** inconsistent, incoherent, illogical, unfitting, contrary, contradictory.
Ant. congruous, becoming, appropriate, proper; harmonious; logical, consistent, coherent, sensible.

inconsistent, *adj.* incompatible, inharmonious, incongruous, unsuitable, irreconcilable, incoherent, discrepant, out of keeping, inappropriate.
Ant. consistent, coherent, harmonious, suitable.

inconstant, *adj.* changeable, fickle, inconsistent, variable, moody, capricious, vacillating, wavering, mercurial, volatile, unsettled, unstable, mutable, uncertain.
Ant. constant, steady, invariant, settled, staid.

incontrovertible, *adj.* undeniable, indisputable, incontestable, unquestionable.
Ant. deniable, controvertible, disputable, questionable.

inconvenient, *adj.* awkward, inopportune, disadvantageous, troublesome, annoying, vexatious, untimely, incommodious, discommodious.
Ant. convenient, opportune, advantageous.

incorrect, *adj.* **1.** wrong, not valid, untrue, false, erroneous, inexact, inaccurate. **2.** improper, faulty; indecent.
Ant. correct.

increase, *v.* **1.** augment, add to, enlarge, greaten; extend, prolong. **2.** grow, dilate, expand, enlarge, multiply. **—*n.*** **3.** growth, augmentation, enlargement, expansion, addition, extension.
Ant. decrease.

incredulous, *adj.* unbelieving, skeptical, doubtful, dubious.
Ant. credulous.

inculpate, *v.* charge, blame, accuse, incriminate, censure, impeach.
Ant. exonerate.

indecent, *adj.* offensive, distasteful, improper, unbecoming, unseemly, outrageous, vulgar, indelicate, coarse, rude, gross, immodest, unrefined, indecorous, obscene, filthy, lewd, licentious, lascivious, pornographic.
Ant. decent.

indefinite, *adj.* **1.** unlimited, unconfined, unrestrained, undefined, undetermined, indistinct, confused. **2.** vague, obscure, confusing, equivocal, dim, unspecific, doubtful, unsettled, uncertain.
Ant. definite.

independence, *n.* freedom, liberty.
Ant. dependence, reliance.

indifference, *n.* **1.** unconcern, listlessness, apathy, insensibility, coolness, insensitiveness, inattention. **2.** unimportance, triviality, insignificance. **3.** mediocrity, inferiority.
Ant. concern, warmth, sensibility; importance, significance, superiority.

indignation, *n.* consternation, resentment, exasperation, wrath, anger, ire, fury, rage, choler.
Ant. calm, serenity, composure.

indignity, *n.* injury, slight, contempt, humiliation, affront, insult, outrage, scorn, obloquy, contumely, reproach, abuse, opprobrium, dishonor, disrespect.
Ant. dignity; honor, respect.

indiscriminate, *adj.* **1.** miscellaneous, undiscriminating, undistinguishing. **2.** confused, undistinguishable, mixed, promiscuous.
Ant. discriminating; distinguishing.

indispensable, *adj.* necessary, requisite, essential, needed.
Ant. dispensable, disposable, unnecessary, nonessential.

indisposed, *adj.* **1.** sick, ill, unwell, ailing. **2.** disinclined, unwilling, reluctant, averse, loath.
Ant. well, healthy, hardy, hale; eager, willing.

indisputable, *adj.* incontrovertible, incontestable, unquestionable, undeniable, indubitable; evident, apparent, obvious, certain, sure.
Ant. questionable, dubitable, dubious; uncertain.

indolent, *adj.* idle, lazy, slothful, slow, inactive, sluggish, torpid, listless, inert.
Ant. energetic, active, industrious.

indomitable, *adj.* invincible, unconquerable, unyielding.
Ant. yielding, weak, feeble.

induce, *v.* **1.** persuade, influence, move, actuate, prompt, instigate, incite, urge, impel, spur, prevail upon. **2.** bring about, produce, cause, effect, bring on.
Ant. dissuade.

inducement, *n.* incentive, motive, cause, stimulus, spur, incitement.
Ant. discouragement.

indulge, *v.* yield to, satisfy, gratify, humor, pamper, give way to, favor; suffer, foster, permit, allow.
Ant. dissatisfy; disallow, forbid.

industrious, *adj.* busy, hard-working, diligent, assiduous, operose, sedulous, persistent, persevering.
Ant. lazy, indolent.

inebriate, *v.* **1.** intoxicate, make drunk; exhilarate. —*n.* **2.** drunkard.

ineffectual, *adj.* **1.** useless, unavailing, futile, nugatory, ineffective, fruitless, pointless, abortive, purposeless. **2.** powerless, impotent, feeble, weak.
Ant. effectual, efficacious, efficient.

inefficient, *adj.* incapable, ineffective, feeble, weak.

Ant. efficient, effectual, efficacious.
inept, *adj.* **1.** inapt, unfitted, unfitting, unsuitable, unsuited, inappropriate, out of place, anomalous. **2.** absurd, foolish, stupid, pointless, inane, ridiculous. *Ant.* fit, suitable, apt, appropriate.
inert, *adj.* inactive, immobile, unmoving, lifeless, passive, motionless.
Ant. active, kinetic.
inexorable, *adj.* unyielding, unalterable, inflexible, unbending, firm, solid, steadfast, severe; relentless, unrelenting, implacable, merciless, cruel, pitiless.
Ant. flexible, yielding; merciful, relenting.
inexpensive, *adj.* cheap, low-priced.
Ant. expensive.
inexperienced, *adj.* untrained, unskilled, raw, green, unknowledgeable, unpracticed, unschooled, untutored, uninformed, naive, uninitiated.
Ant. experienced, skilled, practiced.
infallible, *adj.* trustworthy, sure, certain, reliable, unfailing.
Ant. fallible, unreliable, uncertain.
infamous, *adj.* **1.** disreputable, ill-famed, notorious. **2.** disgraceful, scandalous, detestable, dishonorable, shameful, bad, nefarious, odious, wicked, outrageous, shocking, vile, base, ignominious, dark, heinous, villainous.
Ant. reputable, famed; honorable, good.
infamy, *n.* notoriety, disgrace, dishonor, discredit, shame, disrepute, obloquy, odium, opprobrium, scandal, debasement, abasement, ignominy.
Ant. honor, credit, repute.
infantile, *adj.* babyish, childish, puerile, immature, weak.
Ant. mature, adult.
infectious, *adj.* contagious, catching, communicable.
inflame, *v.* kindle, excite, rouse, arouse, incite, fire, stimulate.
Ant. discourage.
inflate, *v.* distend, swell, swell out, dilate, expand, puff up *or* out, bloat, blow up.
Ant. deflate.
inflexible, *adj.* rigid, unbending, undeviating, unyielding, rigorous, implacable, stern, relentless, unrelenting, inexorable, unremitting, immovable, resolute, steadfast, firm, stony, solid, persevering, stubborn, dogged, pig-headed, obstinate, refractory, willful, headstrong, intractable, obdurate, adamant.
Ant. flexible.
influence, *n.* **1.** sway, rule, authority, power, control, predominance, direction. —*v.* **2.** modify, affect, sway, impress, bias, direct, control. **3.** move, impel, actuate, activate, incite, rouse, arouse, instigate, induce, persuade.
inform, *v.* **1.** apprise, make known, advise, notify, tell, acquaint. **2.** animate, inspire, quicken, enliven, inspirit.

Ant. conceal, hide.

informal, *adj.* **1.** irregular, unusual, anomalous, unconventional, natural, easy, unceremonious. **2.** colloquial, flexible.

Ant. formal, regular, customary, conventional; inflexible.

information, *n.* knowledge, news, data, facts, circumstances, situation, intelligence, advice.

Ant. secret.

infringe, *v.* **1.** violate, transgress, breach, break, disobey. **2.** trespass, encroach; poach.

Ant. obey.

infuriate, *v.* enrage, anger, incense.

Ant. calm, pacify.

ingenious, *adj.* clever, skillful, adroit, bright, gifted, able, resourceful, inventive.

Ant. unskillful, maladroit.

ingenuous, *adj.* unreserved, unrestrained, frank, candid, free, open, guileless, artless, innocent, naive, straightforward, sincere, open-hearted.

Ant. reserved, restrained, secretive, sly, insincere.

ingredient, *n.* constituent, element, component.

Ant. whole.

inherent, *adj.* innate, inherited, native, natural, inborn, inbred, essential.

Ant. acquired.

inheritance, *n.* heritage, patrimony.

inhibit, *v.* **1.** restrain, hinder, arrest, check, repress, obstruct, stop; discourage. **2.** prohibit, forbid, interdict, prevent.

Ant. encourage, support, abet.

inimical, *adj.* **1.** adverse, unfavorable, harmful, noxious. **2.** unfriendly, hostile, antagonistic, contrary.

Ant. friendly, favorable.

initiate, *v.* **1.** begin, originate, set going, start, commence, introduce, inaugurate, open. **2.** teach, instruct, indoctrinate, train. *—adj.* **3.** initiated, begun, started. *—n.* **4.** new member, pledge, tyro, beginner, learner, amateur, freshman.

Ant. terminate, conclude, finish.

injure, *v.* **1.** damage, impair, harm, hurt, spoil, ruin, break, mar. **2.** wrong, maltreat, mistreat, abuse.

injurious, *adj.* **1.** harmful, hurtful, damaging, ruinous, detrimental, pernicious, deleterious, baneful, destructive, mischievous. **2.** unjust, wrongful, prejudicial, biased, inequitable, iniquitous. **3.** offensive, insulting, abusive, derogatory, defamatory, slanderous, libelous, contumelious, scornful, deprecatory.

Ant. beneficial; just, right; complimentary.

injury, *n.* **1.** harm, damage, ruin, detriment, wound, impairment, mischief. **2.** wrong, injustice.

inn, *n.* hotel, hostelry, hostel, tavern.

innocent, *adj.* **1.** pure, untainted, sinless, virtuous, virginal, blameless, faultless, impeccable, spotless,

immaculate. **2.** guiltless, blameless. **3.** upright, honest, forthright. **4.** naive, simple, unsophisticated, artless, guileless, ingenuous.
Ant. impure, tainted, sinful, piacular; guilty, culpable; dishonest; disingenuous, sophisticated, artful.

innumerable, *adj.* countless, numberless, many, numerous; infinite.

inquire, *v.* ask, question, query, investigate, examine.
Ant. answer, reply.

inquiry, *n.* **1.** investigation, examination, study, scrutiny, exploration, research. **2.** inquiring, questioning, interrogation; query, question.
Ant. answer, reply.

inquisitive, *adj.* inquiring, prying, curious, scrutinizing, questioning.

insane, *adj.* deranged, demented, lunatic, crazed, crazy, maniacal, *non compos mentis*, of unsound mind, mad; paranoiac, schizophrenic, delirious; foolish, senseless, stupid, thoughtless.
Ant. sane.

insanity, *n.* derangement, dementia, lunacy, madness, craziness, mania, aberration; dementia praecox, schizophrenia, paranoia.
Ant. sanity, probity.

inscrutable, *adj.* unpenetrable, mysterious, hidden, incomprehensible, undiscoverable, inexplicable, unexplainable, unfathomable.
Ant. penetrable, comprehensible, understandable.

insecure, *adj.* **1.** unsafe, exposed, unprotected. **2.** uncertain, unsure, risky.
Ant. secure, safe; certain, sure.

insensibility, *n.* **1.** unconsciousness. **2.** indifference, apathy, insusceptible.
Ant. consciousness; concern, sensibility.

inside, *prep.* **1.** within, inside of, in. —*n.* **2.** interior. **3.** (*plural*) innards, organs.
Ant. outside.

insidious, *adj.* **1.** corrupting, entrapping, beguiling, guileful. **2.** treacherous, stealthy, deceitful, artful, cunning, sly, wily, intriguing, subtle, crafty, tricky, arch, crooked, foxy.
Ant. upright, forthright; artless, ingenuous.

insinuate, *v.* **1.** hint, suggest, intimate. **2.** instill, infuse, introduce, inject, inculcate.

insolent, *adj.* bold, rude, disrespectful, impertinent, brazen, brassy, abusive, overbearing, contemptuous, insulting.
Ant. polite, courteous, retiring; complimentary.

inspection, *n.* examination, investigation, scrutiny.

instance, *n.* case, example, illustration, exemplification.

instant, *n.* moment, minute, second, twinkling, flash, jiffy, trice.

instantly, *adv.* immediately, at once, instanter, instantaneously, forthwith, in a flash, *or* trice, *or* jiffy.
Ant. later.

instruct, *v.* **1.** direct, command, order, prescribe. **2.** teach, train, educate, tutor, coach, drill, discipline, indoctrinate, school, inform, enlighten, apprise.
Ant. learn, study.

instruction, *n.* **1.** education, tutoring, coaching, training, drill, exercise, indoctrination, schooling, teaching. **2.** order, direction, mandate, command.

instructor, *n.* teacher, tutor, pedagogue, schoolmaster, preceptor.
Ant. student, pupil.

instrument, *n.* tool, implement, utensil.

insult, *v.* **1.** affront, offend, scorn, injure, slander, abuse. —*n.* **2.** affront, indignity, offense, contumely, scorn, outrage.
Ant. compliment, dignify; dignity.

insurrection, *n.* revolt, uprising, rebellion, mutiny, insurgency.

intact, *adj.* uninjured, unaltered, sound, whole, unimpaired, complete, undiminished, unbroken, entire.
Ant. impaired, unsound, incomplete.

integrity, *n.* **1.** uprightness, honesty, honor, rectitude, right, righteousness, probity, principle, virtue, goodness. **2.** wholeness, entirety, completeness.
Ant. dishonesty, disrepute; part.

intellect, *n.* mind, understanding, reason, sense, common sense, brains.
Ant. inanity.

intellectual, *adj.* **1.** mental; intelligent; high-brow. —*n.* **2.** (*colloquial*) high-brow, egghead, professor, brain, mental giant, longhair.
Ant. sensual, low-brow; dunderpate, fool.

intelligence, *n.* **1.** mind, understanding, discernment, reason, acumen, aptitude, penetration. **2.** knowledge, news, information, tidings.
Ant. stupidity.

intelligent, *adj.* **1.** understanding, intellectual, quick, bright. **2.** astute, clever, quick, alert, bright, apt, discerning, shrewd, smart.
Ant. stupid, unintelligent, slow; dull.

intend, *v.* have in mind, mean, design, propose, contemplate, plan, expect, meditate, project, aim for *or* at, purpose.

intensify, *v.* aggravate, deepen, quicken, strengthen; concentrate.
Ant. alleviate, lessen, weaken, dilute.

intent, *n.* **1.** intention, design, purpose, meaning, plan, plot, aim, end, object, mark. —*adj.* **2.** fixed, steadfast, bent, resolute, set, concentrated, unshakable, eager.
Ant. phlegmatic, undetermined, irresolute, apathetic.

intention, *n.* intent.

intentional, *adj.* deliberate, purposeful, premeditated, designed, planned, intended.
Ant. unintentional, purposeless, unpremeditated; involuntary.

interesting, *adj.* pleasing, attractive, gratifying, engaging, absorbing, exciting, fulfilling, entertaining. *Ant.* uninteresting, dull, prosaic.

interpret, *v.* **1.** explain, explicate, elucidate, shed *or* cast light on, define, translate, decipher, decode. **2.** explain, construe, understand.

interrupt, *v.* **1.** discontinue, suspend, intermit. **2.** stop, cease, break off, disturb, hinder, interfere with. *Ant.* continue.

intimate, *adj.* **1.** close, closely associated, familiar, dear, confidential. **2.** private, personal, privy, secret. **3.** detailed, deep, cogent, exacting, exact, precise. **4.** inmost, deep within; intrinsic, inner, deep-rooted, deep-seated. —*n.* **5.** friend, associate, confidant, crony, familiar. —*v.* **6.** hint, suggest, insinuate, allude to.
Ant. open, public, known, blatant; enemy, foe; announce, proclaim.

intimidate, *v.* overawe, cow, subdue, dismay, frighten, alarm; discourage, dissuade.
Ant. encourage, calm.

intolerable, *adj.* unbearable, unendurable, insufferable, insupportable.
Ant. tolerable, bearable, endurable.

intolerant, *adj.* bigoted, illiberal, narrow, proscriptive, prejudiced, biased, dictatorial, fascistic, totalitarian, fanatical.
Ant. tolerant, liberal, unprejudiced.

intractable, *adj.* stubborn, obstinate, unmanageable, perverse, fractious, refractory, headstrong, pigheaded, dogged, unbending, inflexible, obdurate, adamant, stony, willful, unyielding, contumacious, froward.
Ant. tractable, amiable, amenable, easy-going, flexible.

intrinsic, *adj.* essential, native, innate, inborn, inbred, natural, true, real, genuine.
Ant. extrinsic.

introduce, *v.* present, acquaint; lead, bring, conduct.

intrude, *v.* trespass, obtrude, encroach, violate, infringe.

inundate, *v.* flood, deluge, overflow, overspread, overwhelm, glut.

invaluable, *adj.* priceless, precious, valuable, intestimable.
Ant. worthless.

invariable, *adj.* unalterable, unchanging, uniform, constant, invariant, changeless, unvarying; unchangeable, immutable.
Ant. variable, changing, varying, mutable.

invective, *n.* **1.** denunciation, censure, reproach, abuse, contumely, scorn. **2.** accusation, vituperation, railing. —*adj.* **3.** abusive, censorious, denunciatory, vituperative, captious.
Ant. praise, honor; commendatory.

invent, *v.* **1.** devise, contrive, originate, discover.

2. produce, create, imagine, fancy, conceive, fabricate, concoct.

inventory, *n.* roll, list, roster, listing, record, account, catalogue, register.

invert, *v.* reverse, turn around *or* upside down.

investigation, *n.* examination, inspection, inquiry, scrutiny, research, exploration.

invigorate, *v.* animate, innerve, enliven, strengthen, fortify, energize, quicken, vitalize.
Ant. enervate, enfeeble, weaken, devitalize.

invincible, *adj.* unconquerable, unvanquishable, insuperable, insurmountable, impregnable, impenetrable, indomitable, persistent, unyielding, irrepressible.
Ant. conquerable, pregnable, penetrable.

invite, *v.* **1.** call, request, ask, bid, summon, solicit. **2.** attract, allure, lure, tempt, entice, draw.

involuntary, *adj.* **1.** unintentional, reluctant, accidental. **2.** automatic, reflex, unwilled, instinctive, uncontrolled.
Ant. voluntary, intentional.

involve, *v.* **1.** include, embrace, contain, comprehend, comprise, entail, imply. **2.** entangle, implicate, connect, tie, bind.
Ant. exclude, preclude.

iota, *n.* tittle, jot, bit, whit, particle, atom, grain, mite, scrap, scintilla, trace, glimmer, shadow, spark.

irascible, *adj.* testy, short-tempered, hot-tempered, quick-tempered, touchy, temperamental, irritable, waspish, snappish, petulant, peppery, choleric.
Ant. calm, even-tempered, temperate.

irate, *adj.* angry, enraged, furious, piqued, provoked, irritated.
Ant. pleased, calm.

irony, *n.* sarcasm, satire, mockery, derision.

irregular, *adj.* **1.** unsymmetrical, uneven. **2.** unmethodical, unsystematic, disorderly, capricious, erratic, eccentric, lawless, aberrant, devious, unconforming, nonconformist, unusual, abnormal, anomalous.
Ant. regular.

irritate, *v.* vex, annoy, chafe, fret, gall, nettle, ruffle, pique, incense, anger, ire, enrage, infuriate, exasperate, provoke.
Ant. please, delight.

isolation, *n.* solitude, loneliness; separation, disconnection, segregation, detachment.

issue, *n.* **1.** delivery, emission, sending, promulgation. **2.** copy, number, edition, printing. **3.** point, crux; problem, question. **4.** product, effect, result, consequence, event, outcome, upshot, denouement, conclusion, end, consummation. **5.** egress, outlet, vent, **6.** offspring, progeny, children. —*v.* **7.** put out, deliver, circulate, publish, distribute. **8.** send out, discharge, emit. **9.** come forth, emerge, flow out. **10.** come, proceed, emanate, flow, arise, spring, originate, ensue.

itinerant, *adj.* wandering, nomadic, unsettled, roving, roaming, traveling, journeying, itinerating.
Ant. stationary, fixed, settled.

J

jam, *v.* **1.** wedge, pack, crowd, ram, force, squeeze, bruise, crush. —*n.* **2.** preserve, conserve, marmalade.
jargon, *n.* **1.** gibberish, babble, gabble, twaddle, nonsense, balderdash, palaver, moonshine. **2.** language, cant, argot, patois, slang; lingua franca, pidgin English.
jealous, *adj.* **1.** envious, resentful; suspicious. **2.** solicitous, watchful, vigilant.
Ant. generous, open, trusting.
jeer, *v.* **1.** deride, scoff, gibe, mock, taunt, sneer at, ridicule, flout. —*n.* **2.** sneer, scoff, gibe, derision, ridicule, flout.
jeopardy, *n.* hazard, risk, danger, peril.
Ant. security.
jest, *n.* **1.** witticism, joke, pleasantry, mot, quip. **2.** raillery, banter; sport, fun, jape, gibe. —*v.* **3.** joke, trifle (with). **4.** deride, jeer, scoff, gibe.
job, *n.* position, situation, post, employment.
Ant. unemployment.
jocose, *adj.* joking, jesting, jovial, humorous, playful, facetious, waggish, witty, funny, comical, droll, sportive, merry.
Ant. serious, morose, melancholy,
jocular, *adj.* jocose.
jocund, *adj.* cheerful, merry, gay, blithe, happy, glad, joyous, joyful, frolicsome, frolicking, blithesome, jolly, playful, lively, debonair.
Ant. sad, cheerless, unhappy, miserable.
join, *v.* **1.** link, couple, fasten, attach, conjoin, combine, confederate, associate, consolidate, amalgamate, connect, unite, bring together. **2.** adjoin, abut, touch, be adjacent to.
Ant. separate, divide.
joke, *n.* witticism, jape, quip, jest, sally, trick, raillery, prank.
jolly, *adj.* gay, glad, happy, spirited, jovial, merry, sportive, playful, cheerful, convivial, festive, joyous, mirthful, jocund, frolicsome.
Ant. serious, morose, mirthless.
journey, *n.* **1.** excursion, trip, jaunt, tour, expedition, pilgrimage, travel. —*v.* **2.** travel, tour, peregrinate, roam, rove; go, proceed, fare.
jovial, *adj.* merry, jolly, convivial, gay, jocose, jocular, jocund, joyous, joyful, blithe, happy, glad, mirthful.
Ant. serious, mirthless, cheerless, unhappy.
joy, *n.* **1.** satisfaction, exultation, gladness, delight,

rapture. **2.** happiness, felicity, bliss, pleasure, ecstasy, transport.
Ant. dissatisfaction, misery; unhappiness.

joyful, *adj.* glad, delighted, joyous, happy, blithe, buoyant, elated, jubilant, gay, merry, jocund, blithesome, jolly, jovial.
Ant. sad, unhappy, melancholy, depressed.

joyless, *adj.* sad, cheerless, unhappy, gloomy, dismal, miserable.
Ant. joyous.

judge, *n.* **1.** justice, magistrate; arbiter, arbitrator, umpire, referee. **—***v.* **2.** try, pass sentence upon. **3.** estimate, consider, regard, esteem, appreciate, reckon, deem. **4.** decide, determine, conclude, form an opinion, pass judgment.

judgment, *n.* **1.** verdict, decree, decision, determination, conclusion, opinion, estimate. **2.** understanding, discrimination, discernment, perspicacity, sagacity, wisdom, intelligence, prudence, brains, taste, penetration, discretion, common sense.

judicial, *adj.* critical, discriminating, judicious, juridical, forensic.

judicious, *adj.* **1.** practical, expedient, discreet, prudent, politic. **2.** wise, sensible, well-advised, rational, reasonable, sober, sound, enlightened, sagacious, considered, common-sense.
Ant. impractical, indiscreet, imprudent; silly, nonsensical, unsound, unreasonable.

jumble, *v.* **1.** mix, confuse, mix up. **—***n.* **2.** medley, mixture, hodgepodge, hotchpotch, muddle, mess, farrago, chaos, disorder, confusion, gallimaufry, potpourri.
Ant. separate, isolate; order.

jump, *v.* **1.** spring, bound, skip, hop, leap, vault. **—***n.* **2.** leap, bound, spring, caper, vault, hop, skip.

junction, *n.* combination, union, joining, connection, linking, coupling; juncture; seam, welt, joint.

junket, *n.* excursion.

just, *adj.* **1.** upright, equitable, fair, impartial, evenhanded, right, lawful. **2.** true, correct, accurate, exact, proper, regular, normal. **3.** rightful, legitimate, lawful, legal; deserved, merited, appropriate, condign, suited, suitable, apt, due. **4.** righteous, blameless, honest, upright, pure, conscientious, good, uncorrupt, virtuous, honorable, straightforward.
Ant. unjust.

justify, *v.* vindicate, exonerate, exculpate, absolve, acquit, defend, warrant, excuse.
Ant. inculpate, convict, indict, accuse, condemn.

K

keen, *adj.* **1.** sharp, acute, honed, razor-sharp. **2.** sharp, cutting, biting, severe, bitter, poignant, caustic,

acrimonious. **3.** piercing, penetrating, discerning, astute, sagacious, sharp-witted, quick, shrewd, clever, keen-eyed, keen-sighted, clear-sighted, clear-headed. **4.** ardent, eager, zealous, earnest, fervid.
Ant. dull.

keep, *v.* **1.** maintain, reserve, preserve, retain, hold, withhold, have, continue. —*n.* **2.** subsistence, board and room. **3.** tower, dungeon, stronghold.
Ant. lose.

keeper, *n.* guard, warden, custodian, jailer, guardian.

keeping, *n.* **1.** congruity, harmony, conformity, consistency, agreement. **2.** custody, protection, care, charge, guardianship, trust.
Ant. incongruity, nonconformity, inconsistency.

kill, *v.* **1.** slaughter, slay, assassinate, massacre, butcher, execute; murder; hang, electrocute, behead, guillotine, strangle, garrote. **2.** extinguish, destroy, do away with.
Ant. create, originate.

kind, *adj.* **1.** gracious, kindhearted, kindly, good, mild, benign, bland; benevolent, benignant, beneficent, friendly, humane, generous, bounteous, accommodating; gentle, affectionate, loving, tender, compassionate, sympathetic, tender-hearted, soft-hearted, good-natured. —*n.* **2.** sort, nature, character, race, genus, species, breed, set, class.
Ant. unkind.

kindhearted, *adj.* kind.
Ant. hardhearted, cruel.

kindle, *v.* **1.** set fire to, ignite, inflame, fire, light. **2.** rouse, arouse, awaken, bestir, inflame, provoke, incite, stimulate, animate, foment.
Ant. extinguish, quench.

kindly, *adj.* **1.** benevolent, kind, good-natured, sympathetic, compassionate. **2.** gentle, mild, benign. **3.** pleasant, genial, benign. —*adv.* **4.** cordially, politely, heartily; favorably.
Ant. unkindly, malevolent, unsympathetic; cruel, harsh; unpleasant; unfavorable.

kindness, *n.* **1.** service, favor, good turn. **2.** benevolence, beneficence, humanity, benignity, generosity, philanthropy, charity, sympathy, compassion, tenderness, amiability.
Ant. unkindness, malevolence.

kingdom, *n.* monarchy, realm, sovereignty, dominion, empire, domain.

kingly, *adj.* kinglike, princely, regal, royal, imperial, sovereign, majestic, august, magnificent, grand, grandiose.
Ant. serflike, slavish, low, lowly.

kinship, *n.* relationship, affinity, connection, bearing.

knack, *n.* **1.** aptitude, aptness, facility, dexterity, skill, adroitness, dexterousness, skillfulness, expertness. **2.** habit, practice.

knave, *n.* rascal, rogue, scoundrel, blackguard, villain, scamp, scapegrace, swindler.

Ant. hero.

knot, *n.* **1.** group, company, cluster, clique, band, crew, gang, squad, crowd. **2.** lump, knob, quarl. **3.** difficulty, perplexity, puzzle, conundrum, rebus.

know, *v.* **1.** perceive, understand, apprehend, comprehend, discern. **2.** recognize. **3.** distinguish, discriminate.

knowledge, *n.* **1.** elightenment, erudition, wisdom, science, information, learning, scholarship, lore. **2.** understanding, discernment, perception, apprehension, comprehension, judgment.

L

labor, *n.* **1.** toil, work, exertion, drudgery. **2.** travail, childbirth, parturition, delivery. **3.** workingmen, working class; bourgeoisie. **—***v.* **4.** work, toil, strive, drudge. **5.** be burdened *or* troubled *or* distressed, suffer. **6.** overdo, elaborate.

Ant. idleness, indolence, sloth.

labored, *adj.* overdone, overworked, overwrought, elaborate, ornate, unnatural.

laborious, *adj.* **1.** toilsome, arduous, onerous, burdensome, difficult, tiresome, wearisome, fatiguing. **2.** diligent, hard-working, assiduous, industrious, sedulous, painstaking.

Ant. easy, simple.

lacerate, *v.* **1.** tear, mangle, maim, rend, claw. **2.** hurt, injure, harm, wound, damage.

lack, *n.* **1.** deficiency, need, want, dearth, scarcity, paucity, shortcoming, deficit, scantiness, insufficiency, defectiveness. **—***v.* **2.** want, need.

Ant. sufficiency, copiousness, abundance.

laconic, *adj.* brief, concise, succinct, sententious, pithy, concentrated, terse, compact.

Ant. voluble.

lag, *v.* **1.** fall behind *or* back, loiter, linger. **—***n.* **2.** retardation, slowing, slowdown.

Ant. speed, quicken, expedite; expedition.

lament, *v.* **1.** bewail, bemoan, deplore, grieve, weep, mourn *or* sorrow over *or* for. **—***n.* **2.** lamentation, moan, wail, wailing, moaning. **3.** dirge, elegy, monody, threnody.

Ant. rejoice.

lane, *n.* path, way, passage, track, channel, course, alley.

language, *n.* **1.** speech, communication, tongue. **2.** dialect, jargon, terminology, vernacular; lingo, lingua franca. **3.** speech, phraseology, jargon, style, expression, diction.

languid, *adj.* **1.** faint, weak, feeble, weary, exhausted, debilitated. **2.** indifferent, spiritless, listless, inactive, inert, sluggish, torpid, dull.

Ant. strong, distinct, sharp, tireless; active, energetic.

large, *adj.* **1.** big, huge, enormous, immense, gigantic, colossal, massive, vast, great, extensive, broad, sizeable, grand, spacious; pompous. **2.** multitudinous; abundant, copious, ample, liberal, plentiful.
Ant. small, tiny; scanty, sparse, scarce, rare.

last, *adj.* **1.** final, ultimate, latest, concluding, conclusive, utmost, extreme, terminal, hindmost. *—v.* **2.** go on, continue, endure, perpetuate, remain.
Ant. first; fail, die.

late, *adj.* **1.** tardy, slow, dilatory, delayed, belated. **2.** continued, lasting, protracted. **3.** recent, modern, advanced. **4.** former, recently deceased.
Ant. early, fast.

latent, *adj.* hidden, concealed, veiled; potential.
Ant. kinetic, open.

latitude, *n.* range, scope, extent, liberty, freedom, indulgence.

laud, *v.* praise, extol, applaud, celebrate, esteem, honor.
Ant. censure, condemn, criticize.

laugh, *v.* **1.** chortle, cackle, cachinnate, hawhaw, guffaw, roar; giggle, snicker, snigger, titter. *—n.* **2.** chuckle, grin, smile; laughter, cachinnation.
Ant. cry, mourn, wail.

laughable, *adj.* funny, amusing, humorous, droll, comical, ludicrous, farcical, ridiculous, risible.
Ant. sad, melancholy.

lavish, *adj.* **1.** unstinted, extravagant, excessive, prodigal, profuse, generous, openhanded; wasteful, improvident. *—v.* **2.** expend, bestow, endow; waste, dissipate, squander.
Ant. stingy, niggardly; provident; save.

lawful, *adj.* **1.** legal, legitimate, valid. **2.** licit, sanctioned, allowed.
Ant. illegal, illicit, illegitimate; forbidden.

lay, *v.* **1.** place, put, deposit, set, locate. **2.** allay, appease, calm, still, quiet, suppress. **3.** wager, bet, stake, risk. **4.** impute, ascribe, attribute, charge. **5.** burden, penalize, assess, impose. *—n.* **6.** position, lie, site. **7.** song, lyric, musical poem, poem, ode. *—adj.* **8.** unclerical, laic, laical. **9.** unprofessional, amateur.

lazy, *adj.* idle, indolent, slothful, slow-moving, sluggish, inert, inactive, torpid.
Ant. industrious, quick.

lead, *v.* **1.** conduct, go before, precede, guide, direct, escort. **2.** guide, influence, induce, persuade, convince, draw, entice, lure, allure, seduce, lead on. **3.** excel, outstrip, surpass. *—n.* **4.** precedence, advance, vanguard, head. **5.** weight, plumb.
Ant. follow.

leading, *n.* **1.** guidance, direction, lead. **2.** lead, spacing, space. *—adj.* **3.** chief, principal, most important, foremost, capital, ruling, governing.
Ant. deputy; secondary, following.

league, *n.* **1.** covenant, compact, alliance, confederation, combination, coalition, confederacy, union. —*v.* **2.** unite, combine, confederate.

lean, *v.* **1.** incline, tend toward, bend, slope. **2.** repose, rest, rely, depend, trust, confide. —*adj.* **3.** skinny, thin, gaunt, emaciated, lank, meager. **4.** sparse, barren, unfruitful, inadequate, deficient, jejune. —*n.* **5.** meat, essence.
Ant. fat, obese; fertile, fruitful, adequate; superfluity, excess.

leap, *v., n.* jump, bound, spring, vault, hop.

learn, *v.* ascertain, detect, discover, memorize, acquire, hear.

learning, *n.* erudition, lore, knowledge, scholarship, store of information.

leave, *v.* **1.** quit, vacate, abandon, forsake, desert, depart from, retire from, withdraw *or* escape from, relinquish, renounce. **2.** desist from, stop, forbear, cease, abandon, let alone. **3.** omit, forget, exclude. **4.** bequeath, will, devise, transmit. —*n.* **5.** permission, allowance, freedom, liberty, license.
Ant. arrive, gain.

legend, *n.* fable, myth, story, fiction.
Ant. fact, history.

legitimate, *adj.* **1.** legal, lawful, licit, sanctioned. **2.** normal, regular. **3.** reasonable, logical, sensible, common-sense, valid, warranted, called-for, correct, proper. —*v.* **4.** authorize, justify, legalize.
Ant. illegitimate; unreasonable, incorrect, improper.

leisurely, *adj.* deliberate, slow, premeditated, unhurried, easily.
Ant. unpremeditated, quick, hurried, hasty.

lengthen, *v.* extend, stretch, prolong, protract, attenuate, elongate, draw out, continue, increase.
Ant. shorten, abbreviate.

lenient, *adj.* mild, clement, merciful, easy, gentle, soothing, tender, forbearing, long-suffering.
Ant. harsh, cruel, brutal, merciless.

lessen, *v.* **1.** diminish, decrease, abate, dwindle, fade, shrink. **2.** diminish, decrease, depreciate, disparage, reduce, micrify, lower, degrade. **3.** decrease, diminish, abate, abridge, reduce.
Ant. increase; raise; lengthen, enlarge.

let, *v.* **1.** allow, permit, suffer, grant. **2.** disappoint, fail. **3.** lease, rent, sublet, hire.
Ant. prevent, disallow.

level, *adj.* **1.** even, flat, smooth, uniform, plain, flush. **2.** horizontal. **3.** equal, on a par, equivalent. **4.** even, equable, uniform. —*v.* **5.** even, equalize, smooth, flatten. **6.** raze, demolish, destroy. **7.** aim, direct, point.
Ant. uneven; vertical; unequal.

liable, *adj.* **1.** subject, exposed, likely, open. **2.** obliged, responsible, answerable, accountable.
Ant. protected, secure.

liberal, *adj.* **1.** progressive, reform. **2.** tolerant, unbigoted, broad-minded, unprejudiced, magnanimous,

generous, honorable. **3.** generous, bountiful, beneficent, free, charitable, openhanded, munificent; abundant, ample, bounteous, unstinting, lavish, plentiful.
Ant. illiberal; intolerant, prejudiced; stingy, parsimonious, niggardly.

liberate, *v.* set free, release, emancipate, free, disengage, unfetter, disenthrall, deliver, set loose, loose, let out, discharge.
Ant. imprison, incarcerate; enthrall, enslave.

libertine, *n.* **1.** rake, roué, debauchee, lecher, sensualist, profligate. —*adj.* **2.** amoral, licentious, lascivious, lewd, dissolute, depraved, corrupt, perverted, immoral, sensual.
Ant. prude.

liberty, *n.* freedom, liberation, independence; franchise, permission, leave, license, privilege, immunity.

licentious, *adj.* sensual, libertine, lewd, lascivious, libidinous, lustful, lecherous, lawless, immoral, wanton, concupiscent, loose, amoral, unchaste, impure.
Ant. prudish, moral; chaste, pure.

lie, *n.* **1.** falsehood, prevarication, mendacity, untruth, falsification, fib. **2.** place, position, location, lay, site. —*v.* **3.** falsify, prevaricate, fib. **4.** recline.
Ant. truth.

life, *n.* **1.** animation, vigor, vivacity, vitality, sprightliness, verve, effervescence, sparkle, spirit, activity, energy. **2.** biography, memoir. **3.** existence, being.

lifeless, *adj.* **1.** inanimate, inorganic, mineral. **2.** dead, defunct, extinct. **3.** dull, inactive, inert, passive, sluggish, torpid, spiritless.
Ant. alive, animate, live, organic; alive, extant; active, animated, spirited.

lift, *v.* raise, elevate, hold up, exalt, uplift.
Ant. lower.

light, *n.* **1.** illumination, radiance, daylight; dawn, sunrise, daybreak. **2.** aspect, viewpoint, point of view, angle, approach. —*adj.* **3.** pale, whitish, blanched. **4.** buoyant, lightsome, easy. **5.** shallow, humorous, slight, trivial, trifling, inconsiderable, unsubstantial, flimsy, insubstantial, gossamer, airy, flighty. **6.** airy, nimble, agile, alert. **7.** carefree, gay, cheery, cheerful, happy, light-hearted. **8.** frivolous, lightsome, light-headed, volatile. **9.** wanton. **10.** dizzy, delirious, light-headed, giddy. —*v.* **11.** alight, get *or* come down, descend, land, disembark. **12.** kindle, set fire to, ignite, set afire, fire.
Ant. darkness, sunset; swarthy; difficult; deep, considerable, substantial; cheerless, sad; serious; board, embark, mount; quench.

lighten, *v.* **1.** illuminate, brighten, shine, gleam illume. **2.** mitigate, disburden, unburden, ease. **3.** cheer, gladden.
Ant. darken, adumbrate; intensify, aggravate; sadden.

light-hearted, *adj.* carefree, cheerful, lightsome, gay,

cheery, joyous, joyful, blithe, glad, happy, merry, jovial, jocund.
Ant. heavy-hearted, cheerless, morose, sad, gloomy, melancholy.

likely, *adj.* apt, liable, probable, possible, suitable, appropriate.
Ant. unlikely.

liking, *n.* preference, inclination, favor, disposition, bent, bias, leaning, propensity, capacity, proclivity, proneness, predilection, predisposition, tendency; partiality, fondness, affection.
Ant. dislike, disfavor, disinclination.

limb, *n.* **1.** part, member, extremity; leg, arm, wing. **2.** branch, bough, offshoot.

limber, *adj.* pliant, flexible, supple, pliable, lithe.
Ant. rigid, unbending, unyielding.

limit, *n.* **1.** bound, extent, boundary, confine, frontier, termination. **2.** restraint, restriction, constraint, check, hindrance. —*v.* **3.** restrain, restrict, confine, check, hinder, bound, circumscribe, define.

limpid, *adj.* clear, transparent, pellucid, lucid, crystal-clear.
Ant. cloudy, dim, dull.

linger, *v.* remain, stay on, tarry, delay, dawdle, loiter.

link, *n.* **1.** bond, tie, connection, connective, copula, vinculum. —*v.* **2.** bond, join, unite, connect, league, conjoin, fasten, pin, bind, tie.
Ant. separation; separate, split, rive.

liquid, *n., adj.* fluid, liquor.
Ant. solid, gas.

lissome, *adj.* lithesome, lithe, limber, supple, agile, active, energetic.
Ant. inflexible, rigid, clumsy, awkward.

list, *n.* **1.** catalogue, inventory, roll, schedule, series, register. **2.** border, strip, selvage, band, edge. **3.** leaning, tilt, tilting, careening. —*v.* **4.** register, catalogue, enlist, enroll. **5.** border, edge. **6.** careen, incline, lean.

listen, *v.* hearken, hear, hark, attend, give ear, lend an ear.

listlessness, *n.* indifference, inattention, inattentiveness, heedlessness; thoughtlessness, carelessness.
Ant. concern, care, attention, attentiveness.

literature, *n.* belles-lettres, letters, humanities, writings.

litter, *n.* **1.** rubbish, shreds, fragments. **2.** untidiness, disorder, confusion. **3.** brood. **4.** stretcher. **5.** straw *or* hay bedding. —*v.* **6.** strew, scatter, derange, mess up, disarrange, disorder.

little, *adj.* **1.** small, diminutive, minute, tiny, infinitesimal, wee. **2.** short, brief. **3.** weak, feeble, slight, inconsiderable, trivial, paltry, insignificant, unimportant, petty, scanty. **4.** mean, narrow, illiberal, paltry, stingy, selfish, small, niggardly. —*adv.* **5.** slightly, barely, just.

Ant. large, immense, huge; important; liberal, generous.

livelihood, *n.* maintenance, living, sustenance, support, subsistence.

lively, *adj.* **1.** energetic, active, vigorous, brisk, peart, vivacious, alert, spry, nimble, agile, quick. **2.** animated, spirited, vivacious, sprightly, gay, blithe, blithesome, buoyant, gleeful. **3.** eventful, stirring, moving. **4.** strong, keen, distinct, vigorous, forceful, clear, piquant. **5.** striking, telling, effective. **6.** vivid, bright, brilliant, fresh, clear, glowing. **7.** sparkling, fresh.

Ant. inactive, torpid; leaden; uneventful; weak, dull, unclear; ineffective; dim; stale.

living, *adj.* **1.** alive, live, quick, existing; extant, surviving. **2.** active, lively, strong, vigorous, quickening. —*n.* **3.** livelihood, maintenance, sustenance, subsistence, support.

Ant. dead.

load, *n.* **1.** burden, onus, weight, encumbrance, incubus, pressure. —*v.* **2.** lade, weight, weigh down, burden, encumber, freight, oppress.

Ant. disburden, unload, lighten.

loath, *adj.* reluctant, averse, unwilling, disinclined, backward.

Ant. eager, anxious, willing.

loathe, *v.* abominate, detest, hate, abhor.

Ant. adore, love.

loathing, *n.* disgust, dislike, aversion, abhorrence, hatred, hate, antipathy; animus, animosity, hostility.

Ant. liking, love; friendship, regard.

loathsome, *adj.* disgusting, nauseating, sickening, repulsive, offensive, repellent, revolting, detestable, abhorrent, hateful, odious, abominable, execrable.

Ant. attractive, delightful, lovable.

locale, *n.* place, location, site, spot, locality.

lodge, *n.* **1.** shelter, habitation, cabin, hut, cottage, cot. **2.** club, association, society. —*v.* **3.** shelter, harbor, house, quarter. **4.** place, put, set, plant, infix, deposit, lay, settle.

lofty, *adj.* **1.** high, elevated, towering, tall. **2.** exalted, elevated, sublime. **3.** haughty, proud, arrogant, prideful.

Ant. lowly; debased; humble.

loiter, *v.* linger, dally, dawdle, idle, loaf, delay, tarry, lag.

lone, *adj.* **1.** alone, unaccompanied, solitary, lonely, secluded, apart, separate, separated; deserted, uninhabited, unoccupied, unpopulated, empty. **2.** isolated, solitary, sole, unique, lonely.

Ant. accompanied, together; inhabited, occupied.

lonely, *adj.* lone, solitary, lonesome, sequestered, remote, dreary.

Ant. crowded, populous.

lonesome, *adj.* lonely, alone, secluded; desolate, isolated.

long, *adj.* **1.** lengthy, extensive, drawn out, attenuated, protracted, stretched, prolonged, extended. **2.** overlong, long-winded, tedious, boring, wordy, prolix. —*v.* **3.** crave, desire, yearn for, pine for, hanker for *or* after.
Ant. short, abbreviated; interesting; forgo.

longing, *n.* craving, desire, hankering, yearning, aspiration.
Ant. disinterest, antipathy, apathy.

look, *v.* **1.** gaze, glance, watch. **2.** appear, seem. **3.** await, wait for, expect, anticipate. **4.** face, front. **5.** seek, search for. —*n.* **6.** gaze, glance. **7.** search, examination. **8.** appearance, aspect, mien, manner, air.

loose, *adj.* **1.** free, unfettered, unbound, untied, unrestrained, unrestricted, released, unattached, unfastened, unconfined. **2.** uncombined. **3.** lax, slack, careless, negligent, heedless. **4.** wanton, libertine, unchaste, immoral, dissolute, licentious. **5.** general, vague, indefinite, inexact, imprecise, ill-defined, indeterminate, indistinct. —*v.* **6.** loosen, free, set free, unfasten, undo, unlock, unbind, untie, unloose, release, liberate. **7.** relax, slacken, ease, loosen.
Ant. bound, fettered; combined; tight, taut; moral, chaste; definite, specific; bind, commit; tighten.

loot, *n.* **1.** spoils, plunder, booty. —*v.* **2.** plunder, rob, sack, rifle, despoil, ransack, pillage, rape.

loquacious, *adj.* talkative, garrulous, wordy, verbose, voluble.
Ant. taciturn, closemouthed.

lordly, *adj.* **1.** grand, magnificent, majestic, royal, regal, kingly, aristocratic, dignified, noble, lofty. **2.** haughty, arrogant, lofty, imperious, domineering, insolent, overbearing, despotic, dictatorial, tyrannical.
Ant. menial, servile; humble, obedient.

lore, *n.* **1.** learning, knowledge, erudition. **2.** wisdom, counsel, advice, teaching, doctrine, lesson.

loss, *n.* **1.** detriment, disadvantage, damage, injury, destruction. **2.** privation, deprivation.
Ant. gain.

lost, *adj.* **1.** forfeited, gone, missing, missed. **2.** bewildered, confused, perplexed, puzzled. **3.** wasted, misspent, squandered, dissipated. **4.** defeated, vanquished. **5.** destroyed, ruined. **6.** depraved, abandoned, dissolute, corrupt, reprobate, profligate, licentious, shameless. hardened, irredeemable, irreclaimable.
Ant. found; pure, honorable, chaste.

loud, *adj.* **1.** noisy, clamorous, resounding, deafening, stentorian, boisterous, tumultuous. **2.** gaudy, flashy, showy, obtrusive, vulgar, obvious, blatant, coarse, rude, crude, cheap.
Ant. soft, quiet; sedate, tasteful, artistic.

love, *n.* **1.** affection, predilection, liking, inclination, regard, friendliness, kindness, tenderness, fondness, devotion, warmth, attachment, passion, adoration.

—*v.* **2.** like, be fond of, have affection for, be enamored of, be in love with, adore, adulate, worship.
Ant. hatred, dislike; detest, abhor, abominate, hate.

lovely, *adj.* beautiful, charming, exquisite, enchanting, winning.
Ant. ugly, unattractive, homely.

low, *adj.* **1.** prostrate, dead, prone, supine. **2.** profound, deep. **3.** feeble, weak, exhausted, sinking, dying, expiring. **4.** depressed, dejected, dispirited, unhappy, sad, miserable. **5.** undignified, infra dig, lowly, dishonorable, disreputable, unbecoming, disgraceful. **6.** groveling, abject, sordid, mean, base, lowly, degraded, menial, servile, ignoble, vile. **7.** humble, lowly, meek, lowborn, poor, plain, plebeian, vulgar, base. **8.** coarse, vulgar, rude, crude. **9.** soft, subdued, gentle, quiet. —*adv.* **10.** cheaply, inexpensively. —*v.*, *n.* **11.** moo, bellow.
Ant. high, upright.

lowbred, *adj.* unrefined, vulgar, coarse, rude, lowborn.
Ant. refined, noble, highborn.

lower, *v.* **1.** reduce, decrease, diminish, lessen. **2.** soften, turn down, quiet down. **3.** degrade, humble, abase, humiliate, disgrace, debase. **4.** let down, drop, depress, take down, sink. **5.** darken, threaten, glower; frown, scowl.
Ant. raise, increase; elevate, honor; brighten.

loyal, *adj.* faithful, true, patriotic, devoted, constant.
Ant. faithless, disloyal, treacherous.

loyalty, *n.* faithfulness, allegiance, fealty, devotion, constancy, patriotism, fidelity.
Ant. faithlessness, disloyalty.

lubricous, *adj.* **1.** slippery, oily, smooth. **2.** unsteady, unstable, uncertain, shifty, wavering, undependable. **3.** lewd, lascivious, licentious, salacious, wanton, unchaste, incontinent, lecherous, perverse, perverted, immoral, vulgar, lustful, carnal, libidinous, dissolute, libertine, profligate, depraved, corrupt, loose, sensual, concupiscent, impure, pornographic, obscene, dirty, filthy, lubricious, lubrical.
Ant. dependable, sure, certain, reliable; prudish, chaste, moral.

lucid, *adj.* **1.** shining, bright, lucent, radiant, brilliant, resplendent, luminous. **2.** clear, transparent, pellucid, limpid, crystalline; luculent, intelligible, plain, unmistakable, obvious, distinct, evident, understandable; rational, sane, sober, sound, reasonable.
Ant. dull; unclear, dull; unreasonable.

lucky, *adj.* fortunate, fortuitous, happy, favored, blessed; auspicious, propitious, favorable, prosperous.
Ant. unfortunate, unlucky.

ludicrous, *adj.* laughable, ridiculous, amusing, comical, funny, droll, absurd, farcical.
Ant. miserable, serious, tragic.

lugubrious, *adj.* doleful, mournful, dismal, sorrowful, melancholy, gloomy, depressing.
Ant. cheerful, happy.

luminous, *adj.* **1.** bright, shining, lucid, lucent, radiant, brilliant, resplendent. **2.** lighted, lit, illuminated. **3.** brilliant, bright, intelligent, smart, clever, enlightening. **4.** clear, intelligible, understandable, perspicacious, perspicuous, plain, lucid.
Ant. dull; dark; stupid; unclear, unintelligible.

lure, *n.* **1.** enticement, decoy, attraction, allurement, temptation, bait; fly, minnow. **—*v.* 2.** allure, decoy, entice, draw, attract, tempt, seduce.

lurid, *adj.* **1.** vivid, glaring, sensational; shining, fiery, red, intense, fierce, terrible, unrestrained, passionate. **2.** wan, pale, pallid, ghastly, gloomy, murky, dismal, lowering.
Ant. mild, controlled; cheery.

lurk, *v.* skulk, sneak, prowl, slink, steal; lie in wait, lie in ambush, lie hidden *or* concealed.

luscious, *adj.* **1.** delicious, juicy, delectable, palatable, savory. **2.** sweet, cloying, saccharine, honeyed.
Ant. unpalatable, disgusting, nauseating; bitter, acrid, acid.

lush, *adj.* **1.** tender, juicy, succulent, luxuriant, fresh. **—*n.* 2.** (*slang*) drunk, toper, tippler, dipsomaniac, alcoholic, heavy drinker.
Ant. stale, moldy.

lust, *n.* **1.** desire, passion, appetite, craving, eagerness, cupidity. **2.** lechery, concupiscence, carnality, lubricity, salaciousness, licentiousness, wantonness, lasciviousness, libertinism, license. **—*v.* 3.** crave, desire, need, want, demand, hunger for.

luster, *n.* **1.** glitter, glisten, sheen, gloss. **2.** brilliance, brightness, radiance, luminosity, resplendence. **3.** excellence, merit, distinction, glory, honor, repute, renown, eminence, celebrity, dash, élan, éclat. **4.** chandelier, sconce, candelabrum.
Ant. dullness, tarnish; disrepute, dishonor.

lusty, *adj.* hearty, vigorous, strong, healthy, robust, sturdy, stout.
Ant. weak, frail, unhealthy.

luxurious, *adj.* **1.** splendid, rich, sumptuous, ornate, delicate, opulent, well-appointed. **2.** voluptuous, sensual, self-indulgent, epicurean.
Ant. poor, squalid.

M

macabre, *adj.* gruesome, horrible, grim, ghastly, morbid, weird.
Ant. beautiful, lovely, attractive, delightful.

Machiavellian, *adj.* crafty, deceitful, cunning, wily, astute, unscrupulous, clever, artful, designing, insidious, sly, shrewd, subtle, arch, crooked, tricky, intriguing, double-dealing, equivocal.

Ant. naive, ingenuous, honest.

mad, *adj.* **1.** insane, lunatic, deranged, raving, distracted, crazed, maniacal, crazy. **2.** furious, exasperated, angry, enraged, raging, incensed, provoked, wrathful, irate. **3.** violent, furious, stormy. **4.** excited, frantic, frenzied, wild, rabid. **5.** senseless, foolish, imprudent, impractical, ill-advised, excessive, reckless, unsound, unsafe, harmful, dangerous, perilous. **6.** infatuated, wild about, desirous.
Ant. sane; calm; serene; sensible, wise.

madden, *v.* infuriate, irritate, provoke, vex, annoy, enrage, anger, inflame, exasperate.
Ant. calm, mollify.

magic, *n.* enchantment, sorcery, necromancy, witchcraft, legerdemain, conjuring, sleight of hand.

magician, *n.* sorcerer, necromancer, witch doctor, enchanter, conjuror.

magnanimous, *adj.* **1.** big, large, generous, forgiving, unselfish, liberal, disinterested. **2.** noble, lofty, honorable, elevated, high-minded, exalted.
Ant. small, niggardly; base, vile.

magnificence, *n.* splendor, grandeur, impressiveness, sumptuousness, pomp, state, majesty, luxury, luxuriousness, éclat.
Ant. squalor, poverty.

magnificent, *adj.* **1.** splendid, fine, superb, august, stately, majestic, imposing, sumptuous, rich, lavish, luxurious, grand, gorgeous, beautiful, princely, impressive, dazzling, brilliant, radiant, excellent, exquisite, elegant, superior, extraordinary; showy, ostentatious. **2.** noble, sublime, dignified, great.
Ant. squalid, poor; base.

magnify, *v.* **1.** enlarge, augment, increase, add to, amplify. **2.** exaggerate, overstate.
Ant. decrease, micrify; understate.

maid, *n.* **1.** girl, maiden, demoiselle, lass, lassie, virgin. **2.** maidservant.

maim, *v.* mutilate, cripple, lacerate, mangle, injure, disable, wound, deface, mar, impair.

main, *adj.* **1.** chief, cardinal, prime, paramount, primary, principal, leading, capital. **2.** pure, sheer, utmost, direct. —*n.* **3.** pipe, duct, conduit, channel. **4.** force, power, strength, might, effort. **5.** point, idea, crux. **6.** ocean, sea, high seas.
Ant. secondary, unimportant; least; weakness.

maintain, *v.* **1.** keep, continue, preserve, retain, keep up, uphold, support. **2.** affirm, assert, aver, asseverate, state, hold, allege, declare. **3.** contend, hold, claim, defend, vindicate, justify. **4.** provide for, support, sustain, keep up.
Ant. discontinue.

maintenance, *n.* subsistence, support, livelihood, living, bread, victuals, food, provisions.
Ant. desuetude.

majestic, *adj.* regal, royal, princely, kingly, imperial,

noble, lofty, stately, grand, august, dignified, imposing, pompous, splendid, magnificent, sublime.
Ant. base, squalid.

major, *adj.* greater, larger, capital.
Ant. minor.

make, *v.* **1.** form, build, produce, fabricate, create, construct, manufacture, fashion, mold, shape. **2.** cause, render, constitute. **3.** transform, convert, change, turn, compose. **4.** give rise to, prompt, occasion. **5.** get, gain, acquire, obtain, secure, procure, earn, win. **6.** do, effect, bring about, perform, execute, accomplish, practice, act. **7.** estimate, reckon, judge, gauge. **8.** cause, induce, compel, force. —*n.* **9.** style, form, build, shape, brand, trade name, construction, structure, constitution. **10.** disposition, character, nature. **11.** quantity made, output, produce, production, product.
Ant. destroy.

maladroit, *adj.* **1.** unskillful, awkward, clumsy, bungling, inept. **2.** tactless, gauche.
Ant. adroit; tactful, subtle.

malady, *n.* disease, illness, sickness, affliction, disorder, complaint, ailment, indisposition.

malcontent, *adj.* dissatisfied, discontented, unsatisfied, unfulfilled.
Ant. satisfied, contented, content.

male, *adj.* masculine, manly, virile, paternal; staminate.
Ant. female.

malediction, *n.* curse, imprecation, denunciation, cursing, damning, damnation, execration; slander.
Ant. benediction, blessing.

malefactor, *n.* evil-doer, culprit, criminal, felon, outlaw, offender.
Ant. benefactor.

malevolence, *n.* ill will, rancor, malignity, resentment, malice, maliciousness, spite, spitefulness, grudge, hate, hatred, venom.
Ant. benevolence, good will.

malevolent, *adj.* malicious, malignant, resentful, spiteful, begrudging, hateful, venomous, vicious, hostile, ill-natured, evil-minded, rancorous, mischievous, envious.
Ant. benevolent, friendly, amiable.

malice, *n.* ill will, spite, spitefulness, animosity, animus, enmity, malevolence, grudge, venom, hate, hatred, bitterness, rancor.
Ant. good will, benevolence.

malicious, *adj.* malevolent.
Ant. benevolent.

malign, *v.* **1.** slander, libel, revile, abuse, calumniate, defame, disparage, vilify. —*adj.* **2.** evil, pernicious, baleful, injurious, unfavorable, baneful. **3.** malevolent.
Ant. compliment, praise; good, favorable; benevolent.

malignant, *adj.* **1.** malicious, spiteful, malevolent,

rancorous, bitter. **2.** dangerous, perilous, harmful, hurtful, virulent, pernicious, lethal, deadly.
Ant. benevolent; benign.

malignity, *n.* malevolence.
Ant. benignity.

maltreat, *v.* mistreat, abuse, injure, illtreat.
Ant. amuse, entertain.

mammoth, *adj.* huge, gigantic, immense, colossal.
Ant. tiny, microscopic.

manage, *v.* **1.** bring about, succeed, accomplish, arrange, contrive. **2.** conduct, handle, direct, govern, control, guide, regulate, engineer, rule, administer, supervise, superintend. **3.** handle, wield, manipulate, control. **4.** dominate, influence; train, educate, handle.
Ant. mismanage, bungle.

management, *n.* handling, direction, control, regulation, conduct, charge, administration, superintendence, care, guidance, disposal, treatment, oversight, surveillance.
Ant. mismanagement.

manager, *n.* administrator, executive, superintendent, supervisor, boss, director, overseer, governor.
Ant. employee.

mandate, *n.* command, order, fiat, decree, ukase, injunction, edict, ruling, commission, requirement, precept, requisite, prerequisite.

maneuver, *n.* **1.** procedure, move; scheme, plot, plan, design, stratagem, ruse, artifice, trick. —*v.* **2.** manipulate, handle, intrigue, trick, scheme, plot, plan, design, finesse.

manful, *adj.* manly.
Ant. feminine, cowardly.

mangle, *v.* cut, lacerate, crush, slash, disfigure, maim, ruin, spoil, mar, deface, mutilate, destroy.

mania, *n.* **1.** excitement, enthusiasm, craze, fad. **2.** insanity, madness, aberration, derangement, dementia, frenzy, lunacy.
Ant. phobia; rationality.

manifest, *adj.* **1.** evident, obvious, apparent, plain, clear, distinct, patent, open, palpable, visible, unmistakable, conspicuous. —*v.* **2.** show, display, reveal, disclose, open, exhibit, evince, evidence, demonstrate, declare, express, make known.
Ant. latent, hidden, inconspicuous; conceal.

manifold, *adj.* **1.** various, many, numerous, multitudinous. **2.** varied, various, divers, multifarious, multifaceted.
Ant. simple, singular.

manly, *adj.* **1.** manful, mannish, masculine, male, virile. **2.** strong, brave, honorable, courageous, bold, valiant, intrepid, undaunted.
Ant. feminine; weak, cowardly.

manner, *n.* **1.** mode, fashion, style, way, habit, custom, method, form. **2.** demeanor, department, air, bearing, behavior, carriage, mien, aspect, look appearance. **3.** kind, sort. **4.** nature, guise, character.

mannish, *adj.* manly.
Ant. feminine; cowardly, pusillanimous.

manufacture, *v.* assemble, fabricate, make, construct, build, compose.
Ant. destroy.

many, *adj.* numerous, multifarious, abundant, myriad, innumerable, manifold, divers, sundry, various, varied.
Ant. few.

map, *n.* chart, graph, plan, outline, diagram.

mar, *v.* damage, impair, ruin, spoil, injure, blot, deface, disfigure, deform, distort, maim.

maraud, *v.* raid, plunder, pillage, ravage, ransack.

margin, *n.* border, edge, rim, limit, confine, bound, marge, verge, brink.
Ant. center.

mariner, *n.* sailor, seaman, tar, seafarer, seafaring man.
Ant. landlubber.

mark, *n.* **1.** trace, impression, line, cut, dent, stain, bruise. **2.** badge, brand, sign. **3.** symbol, sign, token, inscription, indication. **4.** note, importance, distinction, eminence, consequence. **5.** trait, characteristic, stamp, print. **6.** aim, target, end, purpose, object, objective. *—v.* **7.** label, tag, mark up, mark down. **8.** indicate, designate, point out, brand, identify, imprint, impress, characterize. **9.** destine, single out. **10.** note, pay attention to, heed, notice, observe, regard, eye, spot.

marriage, *n.* **1.** wedding, nuptials; wedlock, matrimony. **2.** union, alliance, association, confederation.
Ant. divorce; separation.

marshal, *v.* arrange, array, order, rank, dispose; gather, convoke.
Ant. disorder; scatter.

marvelous, *adj.* **1.** wonderful, wondrous, extraordinary, amazing, astonishing, astounding, miraculous. **2.** improbable, incredible, unbelievable, surprising.
Ant. terrible, ordinary, commonplace; believable.

mask, *n.* **1.** face-covering, veil, false face. **2.** disguise, concealment, pretense, pretext, ruse, trick, subterfuge, evasion. **3.** masquerade, revel, *bal masqué, ballo di maschera,* mummery. *—v.* **4.** disguise, conceal, hide, veil, screen, cloak, shroud, cover.

mass, *n.* **1.** aggregate, aggregation, assemblage, heap, congeries, combination. **2.** collection, accumulation, conglomeration, pile, assemblage, quantity. **3.** main body, bulk, majority. **4.** size, bulk, massiveness, magnitude, dimension. **5.** (*plural*) proletariat, working class, common people, plebeians. *—v.* **6.** assemble; collect, gather, marshal, amass, convoke; heap *or* pile up, aggregate.

massacre, *n.* **1.** killing, slaughter, carnage, extermination, annihilation, butchery, murder, genocide. *—v.* **2.** kill, butcher, slaughter, murder, slay.

massive, *adj.* **1.** bulky, heavy, large, immense, huge, tremendous. **2.** solid, substantial, great, imposing, massy, ponderous.
Ant. diminutive; flimsy.

master, *n.* **1.** adept, expert. **2.** employer, boss. **3.** commander, chief, head, commander in chief, captain. *—adj.* **4.** chief, principal, head, leading, cardinal, primary, prime, main. **5.** dominating, predominant. **6.** skilled, adept, expert, skillful. *—v.* **7.** conquer, subdue, subject, subjugate, overcome, overpower. **8.** rule, direct, govern, manage, superintend, oversee.

matchless, *adj.* peerless, unrivaled, unequaled, inimitable, unparalleled, incomparable, unmatched, consummate, exquisite.
Ant. unimportant, unimpressive.

material, *n.* **1.** substance, matter, stuff. **2.** element, constituent. *—adj.* **3.** physical, corporeal. **4.** important, essential, vital, consequent, momentous.
Ant. spiritual; immaterial.

matter, *n.* substance, material, stuff. **2.** thing, affair, business, question, subject, topic. **3.** consequence, importance, essence, import, significance, moment. **4.** trouble, difficulty. **5.** ground, reason, cause. *—v.* **6.** signify, be of importance, count.
Ant. insignificance; ease.

mature, *adj.* **1.** ripe, aged, complete, grown, adult, full-grown, fully-developed, maturated. **2.** completed, perfected, elaborated, ready, prepared. *—v.* **3.** ripen, age, develop. **4.** perfect, complete.
Ant. immature, childish, adolescent.

maxim, *n.* proverb, aphorism, saying, adage, apothegm.

meager, *adj.* scanty, deficient, sparse, mean, insignificant; thin, lean, emaciated, spare, gaunt, skinny, lank.
Ant. abundant.

mean, *v.* **1.** intend, purpose, contemplate, destine, foreordain, predestinate, design. **2.** signify, indicate, denote, imply, express. *—adj.* **3.** inferior. **4.** common, humble, low, undignified, ignoble, plebeian, coarse, rude, vulgar. **5.** unimportant, unessential, nonessential, inconsequent, dispensable, insignificant, petty, paltry, little, poor, wretched, despicable, contemptible, low, base, vile, foul, disgusting, repulsive, repellent, depraved, immoral; small-minded. **6.** unimposing, shabby, sordid, unclean, unscrupulous, squalid, poor. **7.** penurious, parsimonious, illiberal, stingy, miserly, tight, niggardly, Scotch, selfish, narrow, mercenary. **8.** intermediate, middle, medium, average, moderate. *—n.* (*plural*) **9.** agency, instrumentality, method, approach, mode, way. **10.** resources, backing, support. **11.** (*sing.*) average, median, middle, mid-point, center. **12.** revenue, income, substance, wherewithal, property, wealth.
Ant. exalted, dignified; important, essential; imposing, splendid, rich, generous; superior; expense.

meander, *v.* **1.** wander, stroll; wind, turn. **—*n.* 2.** labyrinth, maze, intricacy.

meaning, *n.* **1.** tenor, gist, trend, idea, purport, significance, signification, sense, import, denotation, connotation, interpretation. **2.** intent, intention, aim, object, purpose, design. **—*adj.* 3.** expressive, significant, poignant, pointed, knowing, meaningful.
Ant. insignificant, meaningless.

measureless, *adj.* limitless, boundless, immeasurable, immense, vast, endless, infinite, unending.
Ant. limited, finite.

mechanic, *n.* repairman, workman, machinist; craftsman, artificer, artisan.

meddlesome, *adj.* prying, curious, interfering, intrusive, officious.

mediate, *v.* intercede, interpose, arbitrate, reconcile, settle.

medicine, *n.* medication, medicament, remedy, drug, physic.

mediocre, *adj.* indifferent, ordinary, common, commonplace, medium, average, middling, passable, mean.
Ant. superior.

meditate, *v.* **1.** contemplate, plan, reflect on, devise, scheme, plot, concoct, contrive, think over, dwell on. **2.** reflect, ruminate, contemplate, ponder, muse, cogitate, think, study.

meditative, *adj.* pensive, thoughtful, reflecting, contemplative; studious.
Ant. impetuous.

medium, *n.* **1.** mean, average, mean proportion, mean average. **2.** means, agency, instrumentality, instrument. **3.** environment, atmosphere, ether, air, temper, conditions, influences. **—*adj.* 4.** average, mean, middling; mediocre.

meek, *adj.* humble, patient, submissive, spiritless, tame, yielding, forbearing, docile, unassuming, mild, peaceful, pacific, calm, soft, gentle, modest.
Ant. forward, unyielding, immodest.

meet, *v.* **1.** join, connect, intersect, cross, converge, come together, unite. **2.** encounter, come upon, confront, face. **3.** encounter, oppose, conflict. **4.** settle, discharge, fulfill, satisfy, gratify, answer, comply with. **5.** gather, assemble, congregate, convene, collect, muster. **6.** concur, agree, see eye-to-eye, unite, conjoin. **—*n.* 7.** meeting, contest, competition, match. **—*adj.* 8.** suited, suitable, apt, fitting, proper, appropriate, fit, befitting, adapted.
Ant. diverge; dissatisfy; scatter; disagree, diverge; unsuited, unapt.

melancholy, *n.* **1.** gloom, depression, sadness, dejection, despondency, gloominess, blues, hypochondria. **2.** pensiveness, thoughtfulness, sobriety, seriousness. **—*adj.* 3.** sad, depressed, dejected, gloomy, despondent, blue, dispirited, sorrowful, unhappy, disconsolate inconsolable, miserable, dismal, doleful, lugubrious, moody, glum, down-in-the-mouth, downhearted, downcast, low-spirited. **4.** sober, serious, thoughtful, pensive.

Ant. cheer, happiness; cheerful, happy.

mellow, *adj.* **1.** ripe, full-flavored, soft, mature, well-matured. **2.** softened, toned down, improved. **3.** soft, rich, delicate, mellifluous, dulcet, melodious, tuneful, sweet, smooth. **4.** genial, jovial, good-humored, good-natured. **—*v.* 5.** soften, ripen, develop, mature, improve, perfect.

Ant. immature.

melody, *n.* tune, song, air, descant, theme.

melt, *v.* **1.** liquefy, fuse, dissolve, thaw. **2.** pass, dwindle, fade, fade out, blend. **3.** soften, gentle, mollify, relax.

Ant. freeze.

member, *n.* **1.** limb, leg, arm, wing, head, branch. **2.** constituent, element, part, portion.

menace, *n.* **1.** threat, minaciousness, minacity, threatening. **—*v.* 2.** threaten, intimidate.

mend, *v.* **1.** darn, patch, repair, renew, fix, restore, retouch. **2.** correct, rectify, make better, amend, emend, ameliorate, meliorate, improve, set right. **3.** heal, recover, amend, improve, become better. **—*n.* 4.** repair, improvement, amelioration, emendation, correction, restoration, rectification, amendment, renewal.

Ant. ruin, destroy; die, languish.

mendacious, *adj.* lying, untrue, false, untruthful, deceitful.

Ant. truthful, honest.

menial, *adj.* **1.** servile, mean, base, low. **—*n.* 2.** servant, domestic, attendant, footman, butler, valet, maid, maidservant, waiter; flunky, slave, underling, hireling, serf, minion, lackey.

Ant. noble, dignified; master.

mention, *v.* **1.** refer to, allude to, name, specify, speak of, make known, impart, disclose, divulge, communicate, declare, state, tell, aver. **—*n.* 2.** reference, indirect reference, allusion.

mercenary, *adj.* venal, grasping, sordid, acquisitive, avaricious, covetous, penurious, parsimonious, stingy, tight, miserly, mean, niggardly, selfish.

Ant. generous, unselfish.

merciful, *adj.* compassionate, kind, clement, lenient, forgiving, gracious, benignant, beneficent, generous, big, large; tender, humane, kindhearted, tender-hearted, soft-hearted, sympathetic.

Ant. merciless.

merciless, *adj.* pitiless, cruel, hard, hard-hearted, severe, relentless, unrelenting, fell, unsympathetic, uncompassionate, unfeeling, inexorable.

Ant. merciful.

mercurial, *adj.* **1.** sprightly, volatile, active, spirited, lively, nimble, energetic. **2.** flighty, fickle, changeable, volatile, inconstant, undecided.

Ant. inactive, dispirited, phlegmatic; constant, steady.

mercy, *n.* **1.** compassion, pity, benevolence, consideration, forgiveness, indulgence, clemency, leniency, forbearance, lenity, kindness, tenderness, mildness, gentleness. **2.** disposal, discretion, disposition.
Ant. cruelty, pitilessness, harshness.

mere, *adj.* bare, scant, simple, pure, sheer, unmixed, entire.
Ant. considerable.

meretricious, *adj.* tawdry, showy, gaudy, ornate, spurious, sham, false.
Ant. genuine, sincere.

merit, *n.* **1.** worth, excellence, value, desert, entitlement, due, credit. **—***v.* **2.** deserve, be worthy of, earn, be entitled to.

merriment, *n.* gaiety, mirth, hilarity, laughter, jollity, joviality, jocularity.
Ant. misery, melancholy.

merry, *adj.* jolly, gay, happy, jovial, joyful, joyous, mirthful, hilarious, gleeful, blithe, blithesome, frolicsome, cheery, cheerful, glad.
Ant. sad, unhappy.

mess, *n.* **1.** dirtiness, untidiness. **2.** confusion, muddle, medley, farrago, hodgepodge, hotchpotch, jumble, litter, mixture, miscellany, mélange, salmagundi. **3.** unpleasantness, difficulty, predicament, plight, muddle, pickle. **—***v.* **4.** muddle, confuse, mix, mix up.
Ant. tidiness; order, system; arrange.

metamorphosis, *n.* change, transformation, transmutation, mutation.
Ant. stasis.

mete, *v.* **1.** distribute, apportion, parcel out, dole, allot, deal, measure. **—***n.* **2.** limit, bound, boundary, term.

method, *n.* **1.** mode, procedure, way, means, manner, fashion, technique, process, course. **2.** order, system, arrangement, disposition, rule.

meticulous, *adj.* careful, finical, finicky, solicitous, exact, precise, demanding.
Ant. careless, inexact, imprecise.

mettle, *n.* **1.** disposition, temper, character, spirit. **2.** spirit, courage, valor, pluck, vigor, ardor, fire, nerve, fiber.
Ant. cowardice, pusillanimity.

middle, *adj.* **1.** central, equidistant, halfway, medial. **2.** intermediate, intervening. **—***n.* **3.** center, midpoint, midst.
Ant. end, final, initial.

midst, *n.* middle, center stage, arena, center, thick, heart, core.
Ant. rim, edge.

might, *n.* power, ability, force, main, puissance, strength, efficacy.
Ant. weakness, inability.

mighty, *adj.* **1.** powerful, strong, vigorous, robust,

sturdy, puissant, potent. **2.** sizable, huge, immense, enormous, vast, tremendous.
Ant. feeble, weak, impotent; small, negligible.

migrate, *v.* immigrate, emigrate, move, resettle.
Ant. remain, stay.

mild, *adj.* **1.** amiable, gentle, temperate, kind, compassionate, indulgent, clement, soft, pleasant. **2.** placid, peaceful, tranquil, pacific, calm. **3.** bland, emollient, mollifying, assuasive, soothing.
Ant. intemperate, unkind, unpleasant; stormy, turbulent; piquant, biting, bitter.

milieu, *n.* environment, medium, background, class, sphere, surroundings, element.

mind, *n.* **1.** intellect, intelligence, understanding, reason, sense. **2.** brain, brains. **3.** sanity, reason, mental balance. **4.** disposition, temper, inclination, bent, intention, leaning, proclivity, bias. **5.** opinion, sentiments, belief, contemplation, judgment, consideration. **6.** purpose, intention, intent, will, wish, liking, desire, wont. **7.** remembrance, recollection, recall, memory. **—***v.* **8.** pay attention, heed, obey, attend, attend to, mark, regard, notice, note. **9.** tend, take care of, watch, look after. **10.** be careful *or* cautious *or* wary. **11.** care, object.

mingle, *v.* **1.** mix, blend, unite, commingle, intermix, join, conjoin, combine, intermingle, concoct, compound. **2.** participate, associate.

minor, *adj.* **1.** lesser, smaller, inferior, secondary, subordinate, petty, inconsiderable, unimportant, small. **—***n.* **2.** child, adolescent.
Ant. major.

minute, *n.* **1.** moment, instant; jiffy, second. **2.** (*plural*) note, memorandum, record, proceedings. —*adj.* **3.** small, tiny, little, infinitesimal, minuscule, diminutive. **4.** detailed, exact, precise, critical.
Ant. tremendous, huge, large; general, inexact, rough.

miraculous, *adj.* **1.** marvelous, wonderful, wondrous, extraordinary, incredible. **2.** supernatural, preternatural.
Ant. prosaic, commonplace; natural.

mirth, *n.* rejoicing, joy, joyousness, gaiety, jollity, glee, merriment, joviality, laughter, hilarity.
Ant. sadness, misery.

misadventure, *n.* mischance, mishap, ill fortune, ill luck, misfortune; accident, disaster, calamity, catastrophe.
Ant. luck, fortune.

miscellaneous, *adj.* indiscriminate, promiscuous, mixed, heterogeneous, divers, diversified, varied, various, mingled, confused.
Ant. specific, special, discerning.

mischief, *n.* **1.** harm, trouble, injury, damage, hurt, detriment, disadvantage. **2.** evil, malice, malicious mischief, vandalism; misfortune, trouble.
Ant. good, advantage.

misconstrue, *v.* misinterpret, misread, misunderstand, misapprehend, misjudge, mistake.
Ant. construe, understand.

misdemeanor, *n.* misbehavior, misdeed, transgression, fault, misconduct; offense, trespass.
Ant. behavior.

miser, *n.* niggard, skinflint, tightwad, pinchpenny.
Ant. Maecenas.

miserable, *adj.* **1.** wretched, unhappy, uneasy, uncomfortable, distressed, disconsolate, doleful, forlorn, broken-hearted, heartbroken. **2.** poverty-stricken, poor, needy, destitute, penniless. **3.** contemptible, bad, wretched, mean, despicable, low, abject, worthless. **4.** deplorable, pitiable, lamentable, unfortunate, unlucky, ill-starred, star-crossed, luckless; calamitous, catastrophic.
Ant. happy; wealthy; good; fortunate, lucky.

miserly, *adj.* penurious, niggardly, cheap, stingy, parsimonious, tight-fisted, penny-pinching, close, mean.
Ant. generous, unselfish.

misery, *n.* **1.** wretchedness, distress, tribulation, woe, trial, suffering, agony, anguish, torture. **2.** grief, anguish, woe, unhappiness, sorrow, torment, desolation.
Ant. happiness, joy; delight.

misfortune, *n.* **1.** ill luck, bad luck, ill fortune. **2.** accident, disaster, calamity, catastrophe, reverse, affliction, mishap, mischance, adversity, distress, hardship, trouble, blow.
Ant. luck, fortune.

misgiving, *n.* apprehension, doubt, distrust, suspicion, mistrust, hesitation.
Ant. trust.

mislead, *v.* misguide, lead astray, misconduct, delude, deceive, misdirect.
Ant. lead, conduct.

misplace, *v.* **1.** displace, mislay, lose. **2.** misapply, misbestow.
Ant. find; apply, place.

misprint, *n.* typographical error, erratum, typo.

mist, *n.* **1.** cloud, fog, fogbank, haze, smog; soup. **2.** bewilderment, haze, perplexity, obscurity. **—*v.* 3.** fog, cloud over, drizzle, foggle.
Ant. clarity.

mistake, *n.* **1.** error, blunder, slip, inaccuracy, erratum, typo, misprint, fault, oversight. **2.** misapprehension, misconception, misunderstanding. **—*v.* 3.** misapprehend, misconceive, misunderstand, misjudge, err.
Ant. accuracy; understanding.

mistaken, *adj.* erroneous, wrong, incorrect, misconceived, inaccurate.
Ant. correct, accurate.

misunderstanding, *n.* **1.** mistake, misapprehension, error, misconception. **2.** disagreement, dissension, discord, difference, difficulty, quarrel.

Ant. understanding; agreement, concord.

mix, *v.* **1.** blend, combine, mingle, commingle, confuse, jumble, unite, compound, amalgamate, homogenize. **2.** consort, mingle, associate, join. —*n.* **3.** mixture, concoction.
Ant. separate; dissociate.

mixed, *adj.* mingled, commingled, joined; coeducational, coed.
Ant. separated.

mixture, *n.* **1.** blend, combination, compound. **2.** hodgepodge, hotchpotch, gallimaufry, conglomeration, jumble, medley, melange, olio, potpourri, miscellany, farrago, salmagundi; variety, diversity.
Ant. element, constituent.

moan, *n.* **1.** groan, wail, lament, lamentation; dirge, elegy, threnody, monody. —*v.* **2.** bemoan, bewail, grieve, lament, mourn, deplore.

mock, *v.* **1.** ridicule, deride, taunt, flout, give, tantalize, tease, jeer, chaff, scoff, banter, make sport of; mimic, ape, satirize, imitate. **2.** defy. **3.** deceive, delude, disappoint, cheat, dupe, fool, defeat, mislead. —*n.* **4.** mockery, derision, ridicule, banter, sport, sneer. —*adj.* **5.** feigned, pretended, counterfeit, sham, false, spurious, fake.
Ant. praise, honor.

mockery, *n.* **1.** ridicule, derision, scorn, contumely. **2.** imitation, show, mimicry. **3.** travesty, pretense, pretext, sham, satire.

mode, *n.* **1.** method, way, manner, style, fashion. **2.** form, variety, degree, modification, gradation.

model, *n.* **1.** standard, paragon, prototype, ideal, pattern, example, archetype, mold, original. **2.** representation, facsimile, copy, image, imitation. —*v.* **3.** form, plan, pattern, mold, shape, fashion, design.

moderate, *adj.* **1.** reasonable, temperate, judicious, just, fair, deliberate, mild, cool, steady, calm, peaceful. **2.** medium, average, usual. **3.** mediocre, fair. **4.** middle-of-the-road, conservative, temperate. —*n.* **5.** mugwump, middle-of-the-roader, conservative. —*v.* **6.** allay, meliorate, pacify, calm, assuage, sober, mitigate, soften, mollify, temper, qualify, appease, abate, lessen, diminish, reduce. **7.** preside, chair, arbitrate, referee, regulate, umpire.
Ant. immoderate; unusual; radical; disturb, increase, intensify.

modern, *adj.* recent, up-to-date, late, present, new, novel, fresh, neoteric.
Ant. old, archaic, ancient, obsolete.

modest, *adj.* **1.** moderate, humble, unpretentious, decent, becoming, proper. **2.** inextravagant, unostentatious, retiring, unassuming, unobtrusive. **3.** decent, demure, prudish, chaste, pure, virtuous.
Ant. immodest, immoderate, improper; extravagant.

modesty, *n.* **1.** unobtrusiveness. **2.** moderation, decency, propriety, simplicity, purity, chastity, prudery, prudishness.

Ant. indecency, licentiousness.

modify, *v.* **1.** change, alter, vary, qualify, temper, adjust, restrict, limit, shape, reform. **2.** reduce, qualify, moderate.

moil, *v.* **1.** work hard, toil, drudge, labor. **—*n.* 2.** toil, drudgery, labor. **3.** confusion, turmoil, trouble.
Ant. indolence, laziness.

moist, *adj.* damp, humid, dank, wet.
Ant. dry, arid.

molest, *v.* attack, assail; harass, harry, disturb, trouble, annoy, vex, plague, tease, pester, torment, torture, irritate, fret, hector, inconvenience, discommode, worry, bother.

moment, *n.* **1.** minute, instant, second, jiffy, trice, flash, twinkling. **2.** importance, consequence, significance, weight, gravity, import, consideration. **3.** momentum, force, power, impetus, drive.
Ant. insignificance; inertia.

momentous, *adj.* important, consequent, vital, weighty, serious.
Ant. unimportant, trivial, trifling.

monarchy, *n.* kingdom, realm, empire.
Ant. anarchy.

monetary, *adj.* pecuniary, financial; nummary, nummular.

money, *n.* **1.** coin, cash, currency, specie, change; coin of the realm. **2.** funds, capital, assets, property, wealth, riches. **3.** (*slang*) mazuma, long green, lettuce, dough.

mongrel, *n.* **1.** cross, hybrid, mutt, half-breed. **—*adj.* 2.** hybrid.
Ant. purebreed, thoroughbred.

monk, *n.* friar, brother; cenobite, eremite.

monotonous, *adj.* tedious, humdrum, tiresome, uniform, boring, dull, unvaried, unvarying.
Ant. interesting, amusing, diverting.

monster, *n.* **1.** brute, griffin, gargoyle, sphinx, centaur, hippogriff. **2.** mooncalf, monstrosity. **3.** fiend, brute, miscreant, wretch, villain, demon, devil. **—*adj.* 4.** huge, enormous, monstrous.

monstrous, *adj.* **1.** huge, great, large, tremendous, gigantic, monster, prodigious, enormous, immense, vast, stupendous, colossal. **2.** frightful, hideous, revolting, shocking, repulsive, horrible, atrocious, terrible, dreadful, horrendous.
Ant. small, tiny; delightful, attractive.

mood, *n.* **1.** disposition, frame of mind, humor, temper, vein. **2.** mode.

moody, *adj.* gloomy, sullen, ill-humored, perverse, sulky, waspish, snappish, pettish, testy, short-tempered, irritable, irascible, captious, peevish, fretful, spleeny, splenetic, spiteful, morose, intractable, stubborn.
Ant. amiable, temperate, tractable.

moot, *adj.* **1.** doubtful, debatable, disputable, dis-

puted, unsettled. —*v.* **2.** argue, debate, dispute, discuss.
Ant. indubitable, indisputable; agree, concur.

moral, *adj.* **1.** ethical, upright, honest, straightforward, righteous, open, just, good, virtuous, honorable. —*n.* **2.** (*plural*) ethics, integrity, standards, morality.
Ant. immoral, amoral.

morbid, *adj.* **1.** gloomy, sensitive, extreme. **2.** unwholesome, diseased, unhealthy, sick, sickly, tainted, corrupted, vitiated.
Ant. cheerful; wholesome, salubrious.

moreover, *adv.* besides, further, furthermore, and, also, too, likewise.

morning, *n.* morn, daybreak, sunrise, dawn.
Ant. evening.

morose, *adj.* sullen, gloomy, moody, sour, sulky, churlish, splenetic, surly, ill-humored, ill-natured, perverse.
Ant. cheerful, happy, good-natured.

mortal, *adj.* **1.** human. **2.** fatal, final, lethal, deadly. —*n.* **3.** human being, man.
Ant. immortal.

mortify, *v.* **1.** shame, humiliate, humble, abash, abase, subdue, restrain. **2.** gangrene, necrose.
Ant. honor.

mostly, *adv.* in the main, generally, chiefly, especially, particularly, for the most part, customarily.
Ant. seldom.

motion, *n.* **1.** movement, move, action. **2.** gait, deportment, bearing, air. **3.** gesture, movement, move. —*v.* **4.** move, gesture.
Ant. stasis.

motionless, *adj.* stable, fixed, unmoving, still, transfixed, quiescent, stationary.
Ant. mobile.

motive, *n.* motivation, inducement, incentive, incitement, stimulus, spur, influence, occasion, reason, ground, cause, purpose.

mount, *v.* **1.** go up, ascend, climb, scale, get up on. **2.** raise, put into position, fix on. **3.** prepare, produce, make ready, ready. —*n.* **4.** horse, steed, charger, palfrey. **5.** mountain, hill.
Ant. descend.

mountebank, *n.* quack, pitchman, charlatan, pretender, phony.

mourn, *v.* **1.** grieve, lament, bewail, bemoan, sorrow for. **2.** deplore.
Ant. laugh, rejoice.

move, *v.* **1.** stir, advance, budge, progress, make progress, proceed, move on, remove. **2.** turn, revolve, spin, gyrate, rotate, operate. **3.** act, bestir oneself, take action. **4.** stir, shake, agitate, excite, arouse, rouse; shift, transfer, propel. **5.** prompt, actuate, induce, influence, impel, activate, incite, rouse, instigate. **6.** affect, touch. **7.** propose, recommend, suggest, bring up *or* forward. —*n.* **8.** motion, movement, action.

movement, *n.* **1.** move, motion, change. **2.** motion, progress, activity, eventfulness. **3.** (*Music*) part, section, division; motion, rhythm, time, tempo.
Ant. inertia, stasis.

multitude, *n.* host, crowd, throng, mass, army, swarm, collection.

mumble, *v.* murmur, mutter, muffle.
Ant. articulate, enunciate, pronounce.

mundane, *adj.* worldly, earthly, terrestrial, terraqueous, secular, temporal.
Ant. unearthly, clerical.

munificent, *adj.* liberal, generous, bountiful, beneficent, bounteous.
Ant. stingy, penurious, mean, niggardly.

murder, *n.* **1.** killing, assassination, homicide, manslaughter. —*v.* **2.** kill, slay, assassinate, destroy, put an end to. **3.** spoil, mar, ruin, abuse.

murky, *adj.* dark, gloomy, cheerless, obscure, dim, cloudy, dusky, lowering, overcast, misty, hazy.
Ant. bright, light, clear.

murmur, *n.* **1.** grumble, susurration, susurrus, mumble, complaint, plaint, whimper, mutter. —*v.* **2.** mumble, mutter, whisper. **3.** complain, grumble, grouse.

muse, *v.* reflect, meditate, ponder, contemplate, think of *or* about, cogitate, deliberate, ruminate, think, brood; dream.

muster, *v.* **1.** assemble, gather, summon, convoke, collect, marshal, convene, congregate. —*n.* **2.** gathering, assembly, assemblage, collection, convention, congregation.
Ant. scatter, separate.

mutable, *adj.* **1.** changeable, alterable, variable. **2.** fickle, changing, inconstant, unstable, vacillating, unsettled, wavering, unsteady, flickering, varying, variable.
Ant. immutable, invariable; stable, settled, motionless.

mute, *adj.* silent, dumb, speechless, still.
Ant. loquacious, voluble, talkative.

mutilate, *v.* injure, disfigure, maim, damage, mar, cripple, mangle.

mutinous, *adj.* **1.** seditious, insurrectionary, revolutionary, insurgent. **2.** rebellious, refractory, insubordinate, unruly, contumacious, turbulent, riotous.
Ant. patriotic; obedient.

mutiny, *n.* **1.** revolt, rebellion, insurrection, revolution, uprising, sedition. —*v.* **2.** revolt, rebel, rise up.
Ant. obedience.

mutter, *v.* murmur.

mutual, *adj.* reciprocal, balanced, correlative, common, interchangeable.
Ant. single, singular.

mysterious, *adj.* secret, esoteric, occult, cryptic, in-

scrutable, mystical, obscure, puzzling, inexplicable, unexplainable, unintelligible, incomprehensible, enigmatic, impenetrable, recondite, hidden, concealed, dark, abstruse, cabalistic, unfathomable.
Ant. open.

myth, *n.* legend, story, fiction, fable, tradition, epic.

N

nag, *v.* **1.** torment, pester, harass, harry, hector, importune, irritate, annoy, vex. —*n.* **2.** shrew, virago, pest, termagant, maenad. **3.** horse, pony.

naive, *adj.* unsophisticated, ingenuous, simple, unaffected, natural, unsuspecting, artless, guileless, candid, open, plain.
Ant. sophisticated, disingenuous, artful, sly.

naked, *adj.* **1.** nude, bare, uncovered, undressed, unclothed. **2.** bare, stripped, destitute, desert, denuded. **3.** unsheathed, exposed, bare. **4.** unfurnished, bare. **5.** defenseless, unprotected, unguarded, exposed, unarmed, open. **6.** simple, plain, manifest, evident, undisguised, unadorned, mere, bare, sheer. **7.** plainspoken, blunt, direct, outspoken, unvarnished, uncolored, unexaggerated, plain.
Ant. covered, dressed; protected; ornate; exaggerated, embellished.

name, *n.* **1.** appellation, title, label, tag, designation, epithet. **2.** reputation, repute, character, credit. **3.** fame, repute, note, distinction, renown, eminence, honor, praise. —*v.* **4.** call, title, entitle, dub, denominate. **5.** specify, mention, indicate, designate, identify, nominate.

narrate, *v.* recount, relate, tell, retail, describe, detail, recite.

narrative, *n.* story, account, recital, history, chronicle, tale, description.

narrow-minded, *adj.* prejudiced, biased, bigoted, intolerant, illiberal, partial.
Ant. liberal, broad-minded, tolerant, unprejudiced.

nasty, *adj.* **1.** filthy, dirty, disgusting, unclean, foul, impure, loathsome, polluted, defiled. **2.** nauseous, nauseating, disgusting, sickening, offensive, repulsive, repellent, objectionable. **3.** obscene, smutty, pornographic, lewd, licentious, lascivious, indecent, ribald, gross, indelicate. **4.** vicious, spiteful, ugly, bad-tempered, disagreeable. **5.** unpleasant, inclement, stormy.
Ant. clean, pure, unpolluted; delightful; decent, honorable; amiable, agreeable; pleasant, fair.

nation, *n.* **1.** race, stock, ethnic group, population, people, tribe. **2.** state, country, commonwealth, kingdom, realm.

native, *adj.* **1.** inborn, inherent, inherited, natural, innate, inbred, congenital. **2.** indigenous, autochthonous, aboriginal, natural. **3.** unadorned, natural, real, genuine, original. **—*n.*** **4.** inhabitant, aborigine.
Ant. acquired; imported; decorated; foreigner, alien.

nature, *n.* **1.** character, quality, attributes, qualification. **2.** kind, sort, character, type, species, quality. **3.** universe, world, earth. **4.** reality, matter.

nauseate, *v.* **1.** sicken, revolt, disgust. **2.** loathe, abhor, abominate, detest, reject.
Ant. delight, enchant, attract; like, love, adore.

nauseous, *adj.* **1.** sickening, revolting, nasty, repellent, disgusting, loathsome, abhorrent, detestable, despicable, nauseating, offensive. **2.** ill, sick to one's stomach.
Ant. attractive, lovable; well.

near, *adj.* close, nigh, at within, at hand, nearby, adjacent, contiguous, touching, adjoining, bordering, abutting. **2.** imminent, impending, approaching, forthcoming, at hand. **3.** related, connected, intimate, familiar, allied, attached. **4.** faithful, close, accurate, literal. **5.** narrow, close, niggardly, parsimonious, stingy, miserly, tight, tight-fisted.
Ant. far; generous.

nearly, *adv.* **1.** almost, approximately, well-nigh. **2.** intimately, closely. **3.** parsimoniously, penuriously.

neat, *adj,* **1.** orderly, ordered, trim, tidy, spruce, smart, nice. **2.** clever, effective, adroit, finished, well-planned, dexterous, apt. **3.** unadulterated, undiluted, straight, unmixed, pure.
Ant. disorderly, sloppy; maladroit, ineffective; adulterated; impure.

nebulous, *adj.* **1.** hazy, vague, confused, indistinct. **2.** cloudy, cloudlike, nebular.
Ant. clear, fair, distinct.

necessary, *adj.* **1.** essential, indispensable, required, requisite, needed, needful, vital, unavoidable. **2.** involuntary. **—*n.*** **3.** requisite, prerequisite, requirement, necessity, *sine qua non*, essential.
Ant. unnecessary, dispensable; voluntary; nonessential.

necessity, *n.* **1.** needfulness, indispensability, need, indispensableness. **2.** requirement, requisite, demand, necessary, *sine qua non*, essential, prerequisite. **3.** compulsion, fate, destiny, kismet, karma, inevitability, inevitableness, unavoidability, unavoidableness, irresistibility. **4.** poverty, neediness, indigence, necessitousness, need, want.
Ant. dispensability; wealth.

necromancy, *n.* magic, enchantment, conjuration, sorcery, divination.

need, *n.* **1.** requirement, want, necessity, exigency, emergency, urgency. **2.** want, necessity, lack, demand. **3.** destitution, poverty, neediness, want,

deprivation, necessity, indigence, penury, distress, privation. —*v.* **4.** require, want, lack.
Ant. wealth, opulence.

nefarious, *adj.* wicked, depraved, iniquitous, evil, abominable, detestable, atrocious, execrable, flagitious, heinous, vile, horrible, dreadful, horrendous, infamous, villainous, base.
Ant. good, honest, honorable, exalted.

neglect, *v.* **1.** disregard, ignore, slight, overlook, omit, be remiss. —*n.* **2.** disregard, dereliction, negligence, remissness, carelessness, failure, omission, default, inattention, heedlessness.
Ant. regard, attend; regard, attention, care.

neglectful, *adj.* disregardful, remiss, careless, negligent, inattentive, indifferent, heedless, thoughtless.
Ant. regardful, careful, thoughtful.

negligence, *n.* neglect.
Ant. regard.

negligent, *adj.* neglectful.
Ant. regardful.

negotiate, *v.* **1.** arrange, arrange for, settle. **2.** circulate; sell, transfer, deliver, assign.

neophyte, *n.* **1.** convert, proselyte. **2.** beginner, tyro, amateur, greenhorn, novice, novitiate, pupil, student.
Ant. old hand, expert.

nerve, *n.* **1.** strength, vigor, energy, power, force, might. **2.** courage, firmness, steadfastness, intrepidity, fortitude, resolution, resoluteness, endurance. —*v.* **3.** strengthen, fortify, innervate, invigorate, steel, brace.
Ant. weakness, frailty, cowardice; weaken, enervate.

nerveless, *adj.* feeble, weak, enervated, flaccid, spiritless, flabby, cowardly, pusillanimous.
Ant. strong, brave, bold, fearless.

nervous, *adj.* excitable, uneasy, apprehensive, fearful, timid, timorous.
Ant. confident, bold, intrepid.

new, *adj.* **1.** recent, modern, up to date, late, neoteric, novel, fresh. **2.** further, additional, fresh. **3.** unaccustomed, unused, fresh. —*adv.* **4.** recently, lately; freshly, anew, newly, afresh.
Ant. old, stale.

nice, *adj.* **1.** pleasing, pleasant, agreeable, delightful, good. **2.** kind, amiable, pleasant, friendly. **3.** accurate, precise, skilled, delicate, fastidious, exact, exacting, critical, rigorous, strict, demanding, scrupulous. **4.** tactful, careful, delicate, discriminating, discerning, particular. **5.** minute, fine, subtle, refined. **6.** refined, well-mannered, well-spoken. **7.** suitable, proper, polite. **8.** neat, trim, fastidious, finical, finicky, dainty, squeamish, fussy.
Ant. unpleasant; unkind; inaccurate; tactless, careless; unrefined; improper, impolite; sloppy.

nickname, *n.* sobriquet.

niggardly, *adj.* stingy, parsimonious, penurious, miserly, mean, tight-fisted, close-fisted, small, avari-

cious, mercenary; illiberal, niggard, close, tight; scanty, poor, saving, chary, sparing.
Ant. generous, liberal.

nimble, *adj.* agile, quick, lively, active, brisk, spry, ready, alert, swift, light, awake, on the qui vive.
Ant. slow, clumsy, awkward.

noble, *adj.* **1.** high-born, aristocratic. **2.** high-minded, magnanimous, superior, elevated, exalted, worthy, lofty, honorable, great, large, generous. **3.** admirable, dignified, imposing, stately, magnificent, impressive, grand, lordly, splendid. **—*n.* 4.** nobleman, peer, aristocrat, lord, lady.
Ant. lowborn; base; undignified; serf, slave.

noise, *n.* **1.** clamor, din, hubbub, racket, clatter, rattle, blare, uproar, outcry, tumult, ado. **—*v.* 2.** spread, rumor, bruit about.
Ant. quiet, peace.

noiseless, *adj.* silent, quiet, still, inaudible, soundless.
Ant. noisy, clamorous, tumultuous.

noisome, *adj.* **1.** offensive, disgusting, fetid, putrid, foul, rotten. **2.** harmful, injurious, poisonous, noxious, nocuous, lethal, deadly, mephitic, miasmatic, miasmal, miasmic, pestilential, hurtful, pernicious, unhealthy, detrimental, deleterious, unwholesome, baneful, destructive.
Ant. delightful; pleasant, wholesome, healthful.

noisy, *adj.* loud, stentorian, clamorous, boisterous, tumultuous, riotous, vociferous, obstreperous, blustering, blatant, uproarious.
Ant. quiet, silent, peaceful.

nominal, *adj.* titular, so-called, formal.

nonchalant, *adj.* unconcerned, indifferent, cool, apathetic, unexcited, calm, casual.
Ant. concerned, excitable.

nondescript, *adj.* odd, peculiar, strange, unclassifiable, amorphous, indescribable.
Ant. regular, natural, ordinary.

nonesuch, *n.* paragon, ideal, model, pattern, nonpareil.

nonpareil, *adj.* **1.** peerless, unequaled, unparalleled. **—*n.* 2.** nonesuch.
Ant. average, common, ordinary.

nonplus, *v.* puzzle, confound, confuse, perplex, disconcert.

nonsense, *n.* twaddle, balderdash, senselessness, moonshine, absurdity, folly, trash.

notable, *adj.* **1.** noteworthy, noted, noticeable, remarkable, signal, distinguished, unusual, uncommon, extraordinary, great, conspicuous, memorable. **2.** prominent, important, eminent, distinguished, famed, famous, well-known, conspicuous, notorious. **3.** capable, thrifty, industrious, diligent, sedulous, assiduous, careful, clever, smart, alert, watchful. **—*n.* 4.** celebrity.
Ant. common, ordinary; unimportant, undistinguished; careless.

note, *n.* **1.** memorandum, record, minute. **2.** comment, remark, commentary, criticism, critique, assessment, annotation, footnote. **3.** IOU. **4.** eminence, distinction, repute, celebrity, fame, renown, reputation, name. **5.** notice, heed, observation; consideration, regard. *—v.* **6.** mark down, jot down, record, make a note of, register. **7.** mention, designate, refer to, indicate, denote. **8.** notice, see, perceive, spot, remark, observe, regard, look at.

noted, *adj.* famous, celebrated, distinguished, famed, notable, renowned, eminent, illustrious, well-known.
Ant. unknown, undistinguished; notorious, infamous.

notice, *n.* **1.** information, intelligence, advice, news, notification, mention, announcement. **2.** intimation, warning, premonition. **3.** sign, placard, poster, billboard, advertisement. **4.** observation, perception, attention, heed, note, cognizance. **5.** comment, mention, account, criticism, critique, review. *—v.* **6.** discern, perceive, see, become aware of, pay attention to, distinguish, discriminate, recognize, understand, regard, heed, note, observe, mark, remark.

notify, *v.* give notice to, inform, apprise, acquaint, make known to.

notion, *n.* **1.** conception, idea, concept. **2.** opinion, view, belief, sentiment, impression, judgment. **3.** whim, caprice, fancy, crotchet.

notwithstanding, *prep.* **1.** despite, in spite of. *—adv.* **2.** nevertheless, yet, however. *—conj.* **3.** although, though, however, yet, nevertheless.
Ant. on account of, because of.

nourish, *v.* **1.** nurture, nurse, sustain, support, tend, attend. **2.** foster, promote, promulgate, foment, succor, aid, help, encourage.
Ant. discourage; neglect.

novel, *n.* **1.** romance, fiction, tale, story. *—adj.* **2.** new, different.

noxious, *adj.* **1.** harmful, hurtful, unhealthy, unwholesome, injurious, mephitic, miasmatic, nocuous, noisome, detrimental, baneful, deleterious, pestilential, poisonous, destructive, deadly. **2.** corrupting, immoral, pernicious.
Ant. harmless, wholesome, beneficial; moral.

nucleus, *n.* center, kernel, core, heart.

nude, *adj.* uncovered, undressed, unclothed, undraped, naked, bare, exposed, denuded, stark naked, *au naturel*, in the altogether.
Ant. covered, dressed.

nugatory, *adj.* **1.** trifling, worthless, futile, vain, trivial. **2.** useless, ineffectual, inoperative.
Ant. important, vital; useful, effectual.

number, *n.* **1.** sum, total, count, aggregate, collection. **2.** numeral, digit, figure. **3.** issue, copy, edition. **4.** quantity, collection, company, multitude, horde, many. **5.** beat, rhythm. *—v.* **6.** count, enumerate, calculate, compute, reckon, numerate, tell; account; include, consist of.

numberless, *adj.* innumerable, numerous, myriad, countless, uncounted, untold, infinite.
Ant. finite.
numerous, *adj.* many, numberless.
Ant. few.
nurse, *v.* **1.** tend, take care of, attend. **2.** foster, cherish, succor, promote, foment, encourage, aid, abet, help. **3.** nourish, nurture, feed, rear, raise. **4.** suckle, feed, give suck to.
Ant. neglect.
nurture, *v.* nurse.
nutrition, *n.* food, nutriment, aliment, nourishment, sustenance, subsistence.
nymph, *n.* sylph, naiad, nereid, oceanid, oread, dryad, hamadryad.

O

oaf, *n.* **1.** simpleton, blockhead, dunce, dolt, fool, nincompoop, ninny. **2.** idiot, imbecile, moron. **3.** changeling.
Ant. genius.
oath, *n.* **1.** promise, vow, pledge, affirmation. **2.** profanity, curse, blasphemy, malediction, imprecation.
obdurate, *adj.* **1.** hard-hearted, hardened, hard, firm, obstinate, callous, stubborn, pig-headed, unyielding, unbending, inflexible, inexorable. **2.** impenitent, lost, unregenerate, reprobate, irreclaimable, shameless, graceless.
Ant. soft-hearted, soft, malleable; abashed, humble.
obedient, *adj.* submissive, compliant, docile, tractable, yielding, deferential, respectful, dutiful, subservient.
Ant. disobedient, recalcitrant, refractory.
obese, *adj.* fat, stout, plump, pudgy, corpulent, portly, gross.
Ant. thin, skinny, slender, slim.
obfuscate, *v.* **1.** confuse, stupefy, muddle, bewilder, perplex. **2.** darken, obscure, adumbrate, cloud.
Ant. clarify; brighten.
object, *n.* **1.** thing, reality, fact, manifestation, phenomenon. **2.** target, objective, goal, end, destination, aim. **3.** purpose, reason, basis, base, target, goal, end, motive, intent, intention. —*v.* **4.** protest, disapprove, be averse, refuse.
Ant. approve.
objective, *n.* **1.** end, termination, object, destination, aim, target, butt. —*adj.* **2.** unprejudiced, unbiased, impartial, fair, impersonal.
Ant. subjective, biased, personal.
obligation, *n.* **1.** requirement, duty, responsibility,

accountableness. **2.** agreement, contract, covenant, bond, stipulation.

oblige, *v.* **1.** require, constrain, compel, force, necessitate, bind, coerce. **2.** obligate, bind. **3.** favor, accommodate, serve, please, benefit.
Ant. disoblige, liberate, free; unfetter.

obliterate, *v.* destroy, erase, efface, do away with, expunge, rub out, cancel, dele, delete, blot out.
Ant. construct, create, originate; restore

oblivious, *adj.* heedless, disregardful, neglectful, careless, negligent
Ant. heedful, regardful, careful.

obloquy, *n.* **1.** discredit, disgrace. **2.** censure, blame, reproach, odium, calumny, contumely, scorn, defamation, aspersion, revilement.
Ant. credit; exoneration, favor.

obnoxious, *adj.* **1.** objectionable, offensive, odious, hateful. **2.** exposed, liable, subject, answerable.
Ant. delightful, favorable; franchised, licensed, irresponsible.

obscene, *adj.* immodest, indecent, lewd, pornographic, coarse, ribald, smutty, offensive, filthy, immoral, indelicate, impure, unchaste, gross, disgusting, lubricous.
Ant. modest, decent, moral, pure, chaste.

obscure, *adj.* **1.** unclear, uncertain, doubtful, dubious, ambiguous, mysterious. **2.** inconspicuous, unnoticeable, unnoticed, unknown, undistinguished, undistinguishable, unnoted. **3.** remote, retired, secluded. **4.** indistinct, blurred, blurry, imperfect, dim, veiled, **5.** dark, murky, dim, clouded, cloudy, gloomy, dusky. somber, shadowy, lurid, unilluminated.
Ant. clear, certain, unambiguous, conspicuous, noted; distinct; bright.

obsequious, *adj.* **1.** servile, compliant, deferential, cringing, slavish, mean, submissive **2.** deferential, fawning, sycophantic, flattering.
Ant. haughty, overbearing, domineering.

observant, *adj.* **1.** attentive, watchful, heedful, mindful, aware. **2.** perceptive, quick, alert. **3.** careful, obedient
Ant. inattentive, careless; dull; disobedient.

observation, *n.* **1.** noticing, perceiving, watching, regarding, attending **2.** notice, observance, attention. **3.** information, record, memorandum. **4.** remark, comment, aside, utterance.

observe, *v.* **1.** perceive, notice, see, discover, detect. **2.** regard, witness, mark, watch, note, view. **3.** remark, comment, mention; utter, say. **4.** obey, comply, conform, follow, fulfill. **5.** solemnize, celebrate, keep.
Ant. ignore.

obsession, *n.* domination.
Ant. submission.

obsolete, *adj.* antiquated, old-fashioned, ancient, old, archaic.

Ant. modern, new, up-to-date.

obstacle, *n.* obstruction, hindrance, impediment, interference, check, block, barrier.

Ant. aid, support; license, franchise, permission.

obstinate, *adj.* **1.** mulish, obdurate, unyielding, recusant, stubborn, perverse, unbending, contumacious, inflexible, wilfull, headstrong, refractory, firm, intractable, resolute, pertinacious, persistent, dogged. **2.** uncontrollable, wild.

Ant. submissive, flexible, tractable, irresolute; controlled, tame.

obstreperous, *adj.* unruly, uncontrolled, boisterous, noisy, clamorous, tumultuous, riotous, uproarious.

Ant. obedient, calm.

obstruct, *v.* block, stop, close, occlude, oppilate, choke, clog, bar, hinder, barricade, dam up, impede, prevent; retard, slow, check, arrest, interrupt.

Ant. encourage, help, support, further.

obstruction, *n.* **1.** obstacle, hindrance, barrier, occlusion, impediment, bar. **2.** stopping, estoppage.

Ant. encouragement, furtherance; continuation.

obtain, *v.* get, acquire, procure, secure, gain, achieve, earn, win, attain.

Ant. lose, forgo.

obviate, *v.* preclude, prevent, avert, anticipate.

Ant. include, foster.

obvious, *adj.* plain, manifest, evident, clear, open, apparent, patent, palpable, perceptible, distinct, unmistakable.

Ant. concealed, hidden, indistinct, imperceptible.

occasion, *n.* **1.** occurrence, event, time, incident. **2.** opportunity, chance, convenience, opening. **3.** ground, reason, cause, motive, inducement, influence. —*v.* **4.** bring about, cause, motivate, originate, create, move, give rise to, produce.

Ant. cease, stop.

occult, *adj.* **1.** mysterious, hidden, concealed, secret, undisclosed, unrevealed, unknown, mystical, recondite, cabalistic, veiled, shrouded. **2.** supernatural, metaphysical.

Ant. open, manifest, obvious; natural.

occupation, *n.* **1.** calling, trade, business, profession, metier, vocation, employment, pursuit, craft. **2.** possession, tenure, use, occupancy. **3.** seizure, invasion, capture.

occupy, *v.* **1.** take up, use, engage, employ, busy. **2.** possess, capture, seize, keep, take hold of.

occur, *v.* **1.** come to pass, take place, happen, befall. **2.** appear, be met with, be found, arise, offer, meet the eye.

occurrence, *n.* event, incident, circumstance, affair, proceeding, transaction.

odd, *adj.* **1.** different, extraordinary, unusual, strange, weird, peculiar, singular, unique, queer, quaint, eccentric, uncommon, rare, fantastic, bizarre, whimsical. **2.** out-of-the-way, secluded, retired. **3.** occasional,

casual. —*n.* **4.** (*plural*) bits, scraps, remnants, oddments.
Ant. ordinary, common, unexceptional, usual.

odious, *adj.* **1.** hateful, despicable, detestable, execrable, abominable, invidious. **2.** obnoxious, offensive, disgusting, loathsome, repellent, repulsive, forbidding.
Ant. attractive, lovable; inviting.

odium, *n.* **1.** hatred, detestation, abhorrence, dislike, antipathy. **2.** reproach, discredit, opprobrium, obloquy.
Ant. love.

odor, *n.* smell, aroma, fragrance, redolence, scent, perfume.

odoriferous, *adj.* odorous, fragrant, aromatic, perfumed, redolent.
Ant. noisome, noxious.

offend, *v.* **1.** irritate, annoy, vex, chafe, provoke, nettle, mortify, gall, fret, displease, affront, insult. **2.** sin, transgress, err, stumble.
Ant. please, delight, compliment.

offense, *n.* **1.** transgression, wrong, sin, trespass, misdemeanor, crime, fault, felony. **2.** displeasure, unpleasantness, umbrage, resentment, wrath, indignation, anger, ire. **3.** attack, assault, onset, aggression. **4.** besiegers, enemy, foe, attackers.
Ant. delight, pleasure; defense; allies, friends.

offensive, *adj.* **1.** displeasing, irritating, annoying, vexing, vexacious, unpleasant, impertinent, rude, insolent, hateful, detestable, opprobrious, insulting, abusive. **2.** disagreeable, distasteful, disgusting, repulsive, obnoxious, unpalatable, unpleasant, revolting, repellent, nauseating, nauseous, sickening, loathsome. **3.** repugnant, insulting, execrable, abominable, shocking, revolting. **4.** aggressive, assailant, invading, attacking.
Ant. pleasing, pleasant, polite, courteous; agreeable, tasteful, attractive; delightful; defensive.

offer, *v.* **1.** present, proffer, tender. **2.** propose, give, move, put forward, tender. **3.** volunteer, sacrifice, immolate, present. —*n.* **4.** proposal, proposition, overture; bid.
Ant. refuse; refusal, denial.

offhand, *adj.* **1.** cavalier, curt, brusque, short, abrupt. **2.** informal, unpremeditated, casual, extempore, impromptu, extemporaneous.
Ant. considered, premeditated, thoughtful.

office, *n.* **1.** staff, organization. **2.** position, post, station, berth, situation. **3.** duty, function, responsibility, charge, appointment, trust. **4.** service, task, work, duty.

officious, *adj.* forward, obtrusive, forceful, direct, interfering, meddlesome.
Ant. retiring, shy, backward.

often, *adv.* frequently, generally, usually, repeatedly, customarily.
Ant. seldom.

ointment, *n.* unguent, nard, salve, balm.

old, *adj.* **1.** aged, elderly. **2.** familiar, known. **3.** former, past, ancient, primeval, olden, primitive, antediluvian, antiquated, passé, antique, old-fashioned. **4.** deteriorated, dilapidated, worn, decayed. **5.** experienced, practiced, skilled, adroit. **6.** sedate, sensible, wise, intelligent, thoughtful.
Ant. new, modern; inexperienced, green; wild, senseless.

old-fashioned, *adj.* outmoded, obsolete, antique, passé, antiquated, old, ancient, archaic.
Ant. modern.

omen, *n.* sign, augury, foreboding, portent.

ominous, *adj.* **1.** portentous, inauspicious, threatening, unpropitious. **2.** significant, foreboding.
Ant. favorable, propitious; insignificant, meaningless.

omnipresent, *adj.* ubiquitous, present.
Ant. nowhere.

only, *adv.* **1.** alone, solely, exclusively. **2.** merely, but, just, no more than. **3.** singly, uniquely. **—*adj.* 4.** sole, single, unique, solitary, lone. **5.** distinct, exclusive, alone. **—*conj.* 6.** but, excepting *or* except that, however.

onus, *n.* burden, responsibility, load.
Ant. relief.

onward, *adv.* **1.** forward, ahead. **—*adj.* 2.** forward, advanced, improved; advancing.
Ant. backward; retreating, retrograde.

ooze, *v.* **1.** percolate, exude, seep, drip, drop. **—*n.* 2.** mire, slime, mud.
Ant. pour, flood.

opalescent, *adj.* iridescent, nacreous, polychromatic.

open, *adj.* **1.** unclosed, uncovered, unenclosed. **2.** accessible, available, public, unrestricted, free. **3.** unfilled, unoccupied. **4.** undecided, unsettled, undetermined, debatable, disputable. **5.** liable, subject to, unprotected, bare, undefended, exposed. **6.** mild, moderate. **7.** unreserved, candid, frank, ingenuous, artless, guileless, unconcealed, undisguised; sincere, honest, fair, aboveboard. **8.** perforated, porous, reticulated. **9.** expanded, patulous, extended, spread out, unclosed. **10.** generous, liberal, free, bounteous, bountiful, munificent, magnanimous, open-handed. **11.** obvious, evident, clear, apparent, plain. **—*v.* 12.** unclose. **13.** recall, revoke. **14.** uncover, lay bare, bare, expose, reveal, divulge, disclose. **15.** expand, extend, spread out. **16.** begin, start, commence, initiate.
Ant. closed; close.

opening, *n.* **1.** gap, hole, aperture, orifice, perforation; slit, slot, breach, rift, chasm, cleft, fissure, rent. **2.** beginning, start, commencement, initiation, dawn. **3.** vacancy, chance, opportunity.
Ant. closing.

operate, *v.* **1.** work, run, use, act. **2.** manage, carry

on, perform. **3.** bring about, effect, produce, occasion, cause.
Ant. fail.

operation, *n.* **1.** action, process, procedure, manipulation, performance, proceeding. **2.** efficacy, influence, virtue, effect, force, action. **3.** course, transaction, business, affair, maneuver.
Ant. failure.

operative, *n.* **1.** worker, workman, artisan, hand, laborer. **2.** detective, investigator, private eye, agent. —*adj.* **3.** operating, exerting, influencing, influential. **4.** effective, efficacious, efficient, effectual, serviceable.
Ant. inoperative; ineffectual, inefficient.

opiate, *n.* narcotic, drug, anodyne, sedative, sedation, soporific.
Ant. stimulant.

opinion, *n.* sentiment, view, conclusion, persuasion, belief, judgment, notion, conception, idea, impression, estimation.

opinionated, *adj.* obstinate, stubborn, conceited, dogmatic, prejudiced, biased, bigoted.
Ant. liberal, open-minded, unprejudiced.

opponent, *n.* adversary, antagonist, competitor, rival, contestant; enemy, foe.
Ant. ally, friend, associate.

opportune, *adj.* **1.** appropriate, favorable, suitable, apt, suited, fit, fitting, fitted, fortunate, propitious. **2.** convenient, timely, well-timed, lucky, felicitous, seasonable, timely.
Ant. inopportune, inappropriate; inconvenient.

opportunity, *n.* chance, occasion, time, opportune moment.

oppose, *v.* **1.** resist, combat, withstand, thwart, confront, contravene, interfere, oppugn. **2.** hinder, obstruct, prevent, check. **3.** offset, contrast. **4.** contradict, gainsay, deny, refuse.
Ant. support, aid, help.

opposite, *adj.* **1.** facing, fronting. **2.** contrary, reverse, incompatible, irreconcilable, inconsistent, unlike, differing, different. **3.** opposed, adverse, refractory, hostile, antagonistic, inimical.
Ant. compatible, consistent, like, same; friendly, amiable.

opposition, *n.* **1.** opposing, resisting, combating. **2.** antagonism, hostility, resistance, counteraction. **3.** competition, enemy, foe, adversary, antagonist. **4.** offset, antithesis, contrast. **5.** contrariety, inconsistency, incompatibility, difference.
Ant. help, support, furtherance; consistency, compatibility.

oppress, *v.* **1.** depress, weigh down, burden, load. **2.** maltreat, persecute, wrong. **3.** overwhelm, crush, overpower, subdue, suppress.
Ant. unburden, liberate, disencumber.

oppression, *n.* **1.** cruelty, injustice, tyranny, despot-

ism, persecution, severity. **2.** hardship, misery, suffering, calamity. **3.** depression, sadness, misery.
Ant. kindness, justice; happiness, joy.

opprobrious, *adj.* **1.** reproachful, infamous, abusive, scurrilous, vituperative, contemptuous, insolent, offensive, insulting, scandalous. **2.** disgraceful, shameful, infamous, dishonorable, disreputable, ignominious, hateful.
Ant. complimentary, praising, laudatory; honorable, reputable.

oppugn, *v.* criticize, argue *or* act against, dispute, doubt, question, oppose.
Ant. favor.

option, *n.* choice, election, selection, preference.

opulent, *adj.* **1.** wealthy, rich, affluent, moneyed, sumptuous, luxurious. **2.** abundant, copious, plentiful.
Ant. poor, squalid; scarce.

oracular, *adj.* **1.** prophetic, portentous, auspicious. **2.** authoritative, inspired, inspirational, dogmatic, sententious. **3.** ambiguous, obscure, equivocal, two-faced.

oral, *adj.* verbal, spoken, mouthed, uttered, said, vocal.
Ant. tacit, silent, taciturn.

oration, *n.* speech, address, lecture, discourse, declamation, harangue.

orb, *n.* sphere, globe, ball.
Ant. cube.

orbit, *n.* **1.** path, course. —*v.* **2.** circle, circumvent.

ordain, *v.* **1.** appoint, call, nominate, elect, select, destine. **2.** decree, order, enact, prescribe, determine. **3.** predestine, predetermine, destine, fate.

ordeal, *n.* trial, test, proof, assay.

order, *n.* **1.** direction, injunction, mandate, law, ukase, command, instruction, rule, canon, prescription. **2.** succession, sequence. **3.** method, arrangement, harmony, regularity, symmetry. **4.** disposition, array, arrangement. **5.** class, kind, sort, genus, sub-class; tribe, family. **6.** rank, status, grade, class, degree. **7.** fraternity, society, brotherhood, community. **8.** peace, calm, serenity. **9.** custom, usage. **10.** direction, commission. —*v.* **11.** direct, command, instruct, bid, require; ordain. **12.** regulate, conduct, manage, run, operate, adjust, arrange, systematize.

orderly, *adj.* **1.** regular, systematic, methodical. **2.** well-regulated, neat, trim, organized, well-organized. **3.** well-disciplined, well-trained, well-behaved.
Ant. irregular, unsystematic; sloppy, unregulated; undisciplined.

ordinary, *adj.* **1.** common, usual, customary, regular, normal, accustomed, habitual, frequent. **2.** inferior, second-rate, mean, mediocre, indifferent. **3.** plain, homely, common-looking, commonplace.
Ant. uncommon, extraordinary, unusual; superior; beautiful.

organic, *adj.* **1.** systematic, systematized, organized. **2.** constitutional, structural, inherent, fundamental, essential, vital, radical.
Ant. inorganic.
organize, *v.* **1.** coordinate, harmonize, unite, construct, form, dispose, constitute, make, shape, frame. **2.** systematize, order. **3.** combine, unionize.
Ant. destroy, ruin; disorder.
origin, *n.* **1.** source, rise, fountainhead, derivation, beginning, root, cradle, foundation, birthplace. **2.** parentage, birth, extraction, lineage, heritage, descent.
Ant. end; posterity.
original, *adj.* **1.** primary, primordial, primeval, primitive, aboriginal. **2.** new, fresh, novel, inventive, creative. **—***n.* **3.** archetype, pattern, prototype, model.
Ant. secondary; old, old-fashioned.
originate, *v.* **1.** arise, spring, rise, begin, emanate, flow, proceed. **2.** initiate, invent, discover, create, author.
Ant. terminate; follow.
ornament, *n.* **1.** accessory, detail, embellishment, adornment, decoration, ornamentation, design. **—***v.* **2.** decorate, adorn, embellish, beautify, trim, garnish, grace, bedeck.
Ant. essential, necessity.
ornate, *adj.* elaborate, adorned, embellished, showy, splendid, sumptuous, elegant, decorated, florid; flowery.
Ant. simple, plain.
oscillate, *v.* vibrate, vacillate, swing, fluctuate, vary.
ostensible, *adj.* apparent, professed, pretended, ostensive, specious, plausible.
Ant. concealed, hidden, implausible.
ostentation, *n.* pretension, pretentiousness, semblance, show, showiness, pretense, pretext, display, pageantry, pomp, pompousness, flourish.
ostracize, *v.* banish, exile, expatriate, disenfranchise, excommunicate.
Ant. accept.
outcome, *n.* end, result, consequence, issue.
outdo, *v.* surpass, excel, exceed, beat, outstrip, outdistance.
outgrowth, *n.* **1.** development, product, result. **2.** offshoot, excrescence.
outlaw, *n.* **1.** criminal, highwayman, holdup man, robber, thief, bandit, brigand. **—***v.* **2.** proscribe, prohibit.
outline, *n.* **1.** contour, silhouette. **2.** plan, draft, drawing, rough, sketch, cartoon. **—***v.* **3.** delineate, draft, draw.
outlive, *v.* survive, outlast.
outrage, *n.* **1.** violence, violation. **2.** affront, insult, offense, abuse, indignity. **—***v.* **3.** shock, abuse, maltreat, injure, offend. **4.** ravish, rape.

outspoken, *adj.* frank, open, unreserved, candid, free. *Ant.* reserved, taciturn.

outstanding, *adj.* **1.** prominent, eminent, conspicuous, striking. **2.** unsettled, unpaid, owing, due. *Ant.* inconspicuous; paid, settled.

overbearing, *adj.* domineering, dictatorial, haughty, arrogant, imperious, supercilious. *Ant.* humble, servile.

overcome, *v.* **1.** conquer, defeat, subdue, vanquish, rout, crush. **2.** surmount. **3.** overpower, overwhelm, discomfit.

overlook, *v.* **1.** slight, disregard, miss, neglect, ignore. **2.** excuse, forgive, pardon. **3.** oversee, superintend, supervise. **4.** bewitch. *Ant.* regard, attend.

overpower, *v.* overcome, overwhelm, vanquish, subjugate, subdue, conquer, overmaster, rout, crush, defeat, beat.

overrule, *v.* disallow, rescind, revoke, repeal, recall, repudiate, set aside, nullify, cancel, annul; prevail over, influence. *Ant.* allow, permit, approve.

oversee, *v.* supervise, direct, manage, superintend, survey, watch, overlook.

oversight, *n.* **1.** mistake, blunder, slip, error, erratum, omission, lapse, neglect, fault, inattention. **2.** management, direction, control, superintendence, supervision, charge, surveillance, care. *Ant.* attention.

overt, *adj.* open, plain, manifest, showing, apparent, public. *Ant.* private, concealed, clandestine, secret.

overthrow, *v.* **1.** cast down, overcome, defeat, vanquish, overwhelm, conquer, master, overpower, subjugate, crush. **2.** upset, overturn. **3.** knock down, demolish, destroy, raze, level. **4.** subvert, ruin, destroy. —*n.* **5.** deposition, fall, displacement. **6.** defeat, destruction, ruin, rout, dispersion, demolition. *Ant.* support.

overture, *n.* **1.** opening, proposal, proposition, offer. **2.** prelude, introduction; prologue. *Ant.* finale, termination, close, end, epilogue.

overturn, *v.* **1.** overthrow, destroy, vanquish, conquer, upset. **2.** upset, capsize, founder.

overwhelm, *v.* **1.** overpower, crush, overcome, subdue, defeat, vanquish. **2.** overload, overburden, cover, bury, sink, drown, inundate.

own, *v.* **1.** have, hold, possess. **2.** acknowledge, admit, allow, confess, concede, avow; recognize.

P

pace, *n.* **1.** step, rate; gait. **2.** step, walk, trot, jog, singlefoot, amble, rack, canter, gallop, run. **3.** dais, platform. —*v*. **4.** step, plod, trudge, walk, move, go.

pacific, *adj*. **1.** conciliatory, appeasing. **2.** peaceable, peaceful, calm, tranquil, at peace, quiet, unruffled, gentle.
Ant. hostile; agitated, perturbed.

pacify, *v*. **1.** quiet, calm, tranquilize, assuage, still, smooth, moderate, soften, ameliorate, mollify, meliorate, better, soothe. **2.** appease, conciliate.
Ant. agitate, perturb, aggravate, worsen; estrange.

pack, *n*. **1.** package, bundle, parcel, packet; knapsack. **2.** set, gang, group, band, company, crew, squad. —*v*. **3.** stow, compress, cram. **4.** load, burden, lade.

package, *n*. **1.** bundle, parcel, packet, pack, bale. **2.** case, crate, carton, box.

pact, *n*. agreement, compact, contract, deal, arrangement, treaty, bond, covenant, league, union, concordat, alliance, bargain.

pagan, *n*. **1.** heathen, idolater, gentile. —*adj*. **2.** heathen, heathenish, gentile, irreligious, idolatrous.
Ant. Christian, believer; pious, religious.

pageant, *n*. **1.** spectacle, extravaganza, show, masque. **2.** display, show, procession, parade.

pain, *n*. **1.** suffering, distress, torture, misery, anguish, agony, torment, throe, pang, ache, twinge, stitch. **2.** (*plural*) care, efforts, labor. —*v*. **3.** afflict, torture, torment, distress, hurt, harm, injure, trouble, grieve, aggrieve, disquiet, discommode, incommode, inconvenience, displease, worry, tease, irritate, vex, annoy.
Ant. joy, delight, pleasure; ease; please.

painful, *adj*. **1.** distressing, torturous, agonizing, tormenting, excruciating. **2.** laborious, difficult, arduous, severe.
Ant. pleasant, soothing; easy, simple.

painstaking, *adj*. careful, assiduous, diligent, sedulous, strenuous.
Ant. careless, frivolous.

pair, *n*. **1.** brace, couple, span, yoke, two, team. —*v*. **2.** match, mate, couple, marry, join.

palatable, *adj*. agreeable, savory, sapid, tasty, gustatory, luscious, delicious, delectable, flavorsome.
Ant. unpalatable, distasteful, tasteless, flavorless.

pale, *adj*. **1.** pallid, wan, white, ashy, ashen, colorless. **2.** dim, faint, feeble, obscure. —*v*. **3.** blanch, etiolate, whiten. —*n*. **4.** picket, stake. **5.** enclosure, fence, barrier, paling, limits, bounds, confines.
Ant. ruddy, hale, hearty; robust; blacken, soil.

palpable, *adj*. **1.** obvious, evident, manifest, plain, unmistakable. **2.** tangible, material, real, corporeal.
Ant. obscure, unclear; intangible, spiritual.

palpitate, *v*. pulsate, throb, flutter, beat.

paltry, *adj*. trifling, petty, minor, trashy, mean, worthless, contemptible, insignificant, unimportant, trivial, inconsiderable, slight.
Ant. important, major, significant, considerable, essential.

pamper, *v.* indulge, gratify, humor, coddle, baby, cater to, spoil.
Ant. discipline.

pandemic, *adj.* general, prevalent, universal, epidemic.
Ant. isolated, unique, singular.

panegyric, *n.* eulogy, encomium, tribute; commendation, praise.
Ant. condemnation, invective.

panic, *n.* **1.** terror, fright, alarm. —*v.* **2.** terrorize, frighten.
Ant. security; soothe, calm.

pant, *v.* **1.** gasp, breathe heavily, puff, blow. **2.** long, yearn, thirst, hunger, desire. **3.** throb, pulsate, palpitate. —*n.* **4.** puff, gasp, heave; throb.

paragon, *n.* model, ideal, pattern, nonesuch, masterpiece.

parallel, *adj.* **1.** corresponding, similar, analogous, like, resembling, correspondent. **2.** tonic, harmonic. —*n.* **3.** match, counterpart. **4.** correspondence, analogy, similarity, resemblance, likeness. —*v.* **5.** match, resemble. **6.** equal, be equivalent to.
Ant. unique, unlike, singular, unusual; dissimilarity; differ.

paralyze, *v.* stun, shock, benumb, unnerve, deaden.

paramount, *adj.* superior, preeminent, chief, principal.
Ant. base, inferior, unimportant.

paraphernalia, *n.* belongings, effects; equipment, apparatus, appointments, appurtenances, accouterments, trappings, rig, equipage.

paraphrase, *n.* **1.** rendering, version, translation. —*v.* **2.** restate, render, translate; explain, explicate, interpret.

parasite, *n.* yes-man, sycophant, leech, hanger-on, blood-sucker, toady, flatterer, flunky.

parcel, *n.* **1.** package, bundle, pack, packet. **2.** quantity, lot, group, batch, collection. **3.** lot, plot, tract, acreage, portion, land. —*v.* **4.** divide, distribute, mete out, apportion, deal out, allot.

pardon, *n.* **1.** indulgence, allowance, excuse, forgiveness; remission, amnesty, absolution. —*v.* **2.** forgive, absolve, remit, condone, excuse, overlook; acquit, clear, release.
Ant. censure, blame.

pare, *v.* **1.** peel; clip, cut, shave. **2.** diminish, lessen, clip, reduce.
Ant. increase.

parentage, *n.* birth, descent, lineage, ancestry, origin, extraction, pedigree, family, stock.

parity, *n.* equality; equivalence, correspondence, similarity, analogy, parallelism, likeness; sameness.
Ant. inequality, dissimilarity, difference.

parley, *n.* **1.** conference, discussion, talk, conversation, discourse. —*v.* **2.** confer, discuss, speak, converse, talk, discourse.

parody, *n.* travesty, burlesque, imitation, caricature.

parry, *v.* **1.** ward off, avert, avoid, evade, elude; prevent, obviate, preclude. —*n.* **2.** prevention; avoidance, evasion.
Ant. encourage, further.

parsimonious, *adj.* sparing, frugal, stingy, tight, tight-fisted, close, niggardly, miserly, illiberal, mean, close-fisted, grasping, avaricious, penurious, covetous.
Ant. generous, openhanded, unsparing.

parsimony, *n.* economy, frugality, niggardliness, stinginess, miserliness, sparingness, closeness, illiberality, close-fistedness, tight-fistedness, cupidity, meanness.
Ant. generosity, liberality.

part, *n.* **1.** portion, division, piece, fragment, fraction, section, constituent, component, ingredient, element, member, organ. **2.** allotment, share, apportionment, portion, lot, dividend, concern, participation, interest, stock. **3.** (*usually plural*) region, quarter, district, section. **4.** duty, function, role, office, responsibility, charge. —*v.* **5.** divide, break, cleave, separate, sever, sunder, disunite, dissociate, dissever, disconnect, disjoin, detach. **6.** share, allot, portion, parcel out, apportion, distribute, deal out, mete out. **7.** depart, leave, go, quit; pass on *or* away, die.
Ant. all, none, nothing, everything.

partake, *v.* participate, share.

partial, *adj.* **1.** incomplete, unfinished, imperfect, limited. **2.** constituent, component. **3.** biased, prejudiced, one-sided, unfair, unjust, influenced.
Ant. complete, perfect; unbiased, unprejudiced, liberal, just, fair.

partiality, *n.* **1.** bias, favor, prejudice, one-sidedness, injustice, unfairness, favoritism. **2.** fondness, liking, preference, bent, leaning, tendency, predilection, inclination.
Ant. justice, fairness; dislike, disfavor.

participate, *v.* share, partake.

particle, *n.* **1.** mite, whit, jot, iota, tittle, bit, mote, grain, ace, scrap, speck. **2.** molecule, atom, meson, deuteron, electron, positron, neutron, neutrino.

particular, *adj.* **1.** special, specific, especial. **2.** one, individual, single, separate, distinct, discrete. **3.** noteworthy, marked, unusual, notable, extraordinary; peculiar, singular, strange, odd, uncommon. **4.** exceptional, especial, characteristic, distinctive. **5.** certain, personal, special. **6.** detailed, descriptive, minute, circumstantial, critical, scrupulous, strict, careful, exact, precise. **7.** critical, finical, finicky, discriminating, dainty, nice, fastidious, scrupulous. —*n.* **8.** point, detail, circumstance, item, feature, particularity.
Ant. general, over-all; common, ordinary; inexact, imprecise; undiscriminating, indiscriminate.

particularly, *adv.* **1.** exceptionally, especially, specially. **2.** specially, especially, individually, characteristically, uniquely, separately, discretely, unusually,

specifically, singly. **3.** in detail, minutely, exactly, precisely, strictly.
Ant. generally; commonly, usually, customarily.

partisan, *n.* **1.** adherent, supporter, follower, disciple. —*adj.* **2.** biased, partial.
Ant. leader; unbiased, impartial.

partition, *n.* division, distribution, portion, share, allotment, apportionment. **2.** separation, division. **3.** part, section, division, segment, piece. **4.** barrier, wall, dividing wall, screen. —*v.* **5.** divide, separate, apportion, portion, parcel out, deal out, mete out, share.
Ant. unity; unite, blend.

partner, *n.* **1.** sharer, partaker, associate, accessory, accomplice, participant, colleague. **2.** husband, wife, spouse.

party, *n.* **1.** group, gathering, assembly, assemblage, company. **2.** body, faction, circle, coterie, clique, set, combination, ring, league, alliance. **3.** attachment, devotion, partisanship.

parvenu, *n.* upstart, snob, Johnny-come-lately, climber.

pass, *v.* **1.** go, move, proceed. **2.** disregard, pass over, skim over, skim, ignore. **3.** transcend, exceed, surpass, excel. **4.** spend; circulate. **5.** convey, transfer, transmit, send, deliver. **6.** sanction, approve, okay, enact. **7.** express, pronounce, utter, deliver. **8.** leave, go away, depart. **9.** end, terminate, expire, cease. **10.** go on, happen, take place, occur. **11.** vanish, fade, die, disappear. —*n.* **12.** notch, defile, ravine, gorge, gulch, canyon, channel. **13.** permission, license, ticket, passport, visa. **14.** thrust, lunge. **15.** stage, state, juncture, situation, condition.
Ant. attend, regard, note, notice; disapprove; arrive, come; initiate, begin, start; appear.

passage, *n.* **1.** paragraph, verse, line, section, clause, text, passus. **2.** way, route, avenue, channel, road, path, byway, lane, street, thoroughfare. **3.** movement, transit, transition, passing. **4.** voyage, trip, tour, excursion, journey. **5.** progress, course. **6.** passing, enactment. **7.** exchange, altercation, dispute, encounter, combat, skirmish, conflict, affair. **8.** transference, transmission. —*v.* **9.** cross, pass, voyage.

passion, *n.* **1.** feeling, emotion, zeal, ardor, fervor, transport, rapture, excitement, impulse; hope, fear, joy, grief, anger, love, desire. **2.** love, desire, attachment, affection, fondness, warmth. **3.** anger, ire, resentment, fury, wrath, rage, vehemence, indignation.
Ant. coolness, apathy.

passionate, *adj.* **1.** impassioned, emotional, ardent, vehement, excited, excitable, impulsive, fervent, fervid, zealous, warm, enthusiastic, earnest, glowing, burning, fiery; animated, impetuous, violent. **2.**

quick-tempered, irascible, short-tempered, testy, touchy, choleric, hasty, hot-headed, fiery.
Ant. dispassionate, cool, cold; calm, collected.

passive, *adj.* **1.** inactive, quiescent, inert, receptive, prone. **2.** suffering, receiving, submitting, submissive, patient, unresisting.
Ant. active, energetic; hostile, resisting.

password, *n.* watchword, shibboleth, countersign.

pastime, *n.* diversion, amusement, sport, entertainment, recreation.

patch, *v.* mend, repair, restore, fix, correct, emend; settle, smooth.
Ant. break, crack, ruin, spoil.

patent, *n.* **1.** invention. —*adj.* **2.** patented, trademarked, copyrighted. **3.** open, manifest, evident, plain, clear, apparent, obvious, palpable, unmistakable, conspicuous, unconcealed.
Ant. concealed, hidden, unclear, dim.

path, *n.* way, walk, lane, trail, footpath, pathway, route, course, track, passage, road, avenue.

pathetic, *adj.* **1.** pitiable, touching, moving, affecting, tender, plaintive. **2.** emotional, pathetical.
Ant. cruel, ruthless; unemotional, apathetical.

patience, *n.* **1.** calmness, composure, endurance, fortitude, stoicism, stability, courage, self-possession, inner strength, submissiveness, submission, sufferance, resignation. **2.** perseverance, diligence, assiduity, sedulousness, indefatigability, indefatigableness, persistence.
Ant. hostility; weakness, frailty; fatigue.

patient, *n.* **1.** invalid. —*adj.* **2.** persevering, diligent, persistent, sedulous, assiduous, indefatigable, untiring. **3.** long-suffering, submissive, resigned, passive, unrepining, calm. **4.** quiet, calm, serene, unruffled, unexcited, self-possessed, stoical, composed. **5.** susceptible.
Ant. hostile, agitated; excited, perturbed; unsusceptible, impervious.

patron, *n.* **1.** customer, client. **2.** protector, supporter, advocate, defender.
Ant. critic.

pattern, *n.* **1.** decoration, design, figure. **2.** style, type, kind, sort. **3.** original, model, paragon, example, exemplar, guide, archetype, prototype. **4.** sample, example, specimen; illustration. —*v.* **5.** model, imitate, copy, follow.

paucity, *n.* smallness, fewness, sparseness, scarcity, poverty.
Ant. abundance.

pause, *n.* **1.** rest, wait, hesitation, suspension, lacuna, hiatus, interruption, delay, intermission, break; stop, halt, cessation, stoppage. —*v.* **2.** hesitate, waver, deliberate, wait, rest, interrupt, tarry, delay. **3.** cease, stop, arrest, halt, desist, forbear.
Ant. continuity, continuousness.

pay, *v.* **1.** settle, liquidate, discharge. **2.** satisfy,

compensate, reimburse, remunerate, recompense; reward; indemnify. **3.** yield, be profitable to, repay, requite. **4.** punish, repay, retaliate, requite, revenge. **5.** make amends, suffer, be punished, make compensation. —*n.* **6.** payment, wages, salary, income, stipend, remuneration, emolument, fee, allowance. **7.** requital, reward, punishment, just deserts. —*adj.* **8.** profitable, interest-bearing, gold-bearing, precious, valuable.
Ant. dissatisfy; unprofitable.

payment, *n.* pay.

peace, *n.* **1.** agreement, treaty, armistice, truce, pact, accord, entente, entente cordiale, amity, harmony, concord. **2.** order, security. **3.** calm, quiet, tranquillity, peacefulness, calmness.
Ant. insecurity; agitation, disturbance.

peaceable, *adj.* pacific, peaceful, amicable, friendly, amiable, mild, gentle; calm, tranquil, serene, quiet.
Ant. hostile, unfriendly; noisy.

peaceful, *adj.* tranquil, placid, serene, unruffled, calm, complacent; composed, dignified, gracious, mellow; unexcited, unagitated, pacific.
Ant. perturbed, disturbed.

peak, *n.* point, top, crest, summit, arete, acme, pinnacle.
Ant. base, bottom, abyss.

peccadillo, *n.* petty sin *or* offense, slight crime, trifling fault; shortcoming, weakness.

peculiar, *adj.* **1.** strange, odd, queer, eccentric, bizarre, uncommon, unusual, extraordinary, singular, exceptional. **2.** distinguished, distinctive. **3.** characteristic, appropriate, proper, individual, particular, select, especial, special, specific, unique, exclusive.
Ant. usual, common, ordinary; general, unspecific.

peculiarity, *n.* **1.** idiosyncrasy, characteristic, odd trait. **2.** singularity, oddity, rarity, eccentricity. **3.** distinction, feature, characteristic.

pecuniary, *adj.* monetary, financial, nummular.

pedestrian, *n.* **1.** walker, stroller. —*adj.* **2.** on foot, walking, afoot. **3.** commonplace, prosaic, dull.
Ant. interesting, fascinating, engaging.

pedigree, *n.* genealogy, descent, family tree, family, heritage, ancestry, lineage, line, race, derivation; patrimony.

peek, *v.* peep, peer, pry.

peel, *v.* **1.** strip, skin, decorticate, pare, flay. —*n.* **2.** skin, rind, bark.
Ant. cover, plate.

peer, *n.* **1.** equal, compeer, match. **2.** nobleman, lord; duke, count, marquis, earl, viscount, baron.

peerless, *adj.* matchless, unequaled, unsurpassed, unique, superlative, unmatched.

peevish, *adj.* cross, querulous, fretful, vexatious, vexed, captious, discontented, petulant, testy, irritable, crusty, snappish, waspish, acrimonious, sple-

netic, short-tempered, ill-tempered, ill-natured, unpleasant, disagreeable, nasty.
Ant. good-natured, friendly, pleasant, amiable, agreeable.

pejorative, *adj.* depreciative, deprecatory, disparaging, opprobrious.
Ant. favorable, complimentary.

pellucid, *adj.* translucent; limpid, clear, crystalline, crystal-clear, transparent.
Ant. dull, opaque.

pelt, *v.* **1.** strike (*with missiles*), beat, belabor, batter. —*n.* **2.** blow, stroke. **3.** skin, hide, peltry.

penetrate, *v.* **1.** pierce, bore, probe, enter; permeate, sink in. **2.** affect *or* impress deeply, touch. **3.** understand, discern, comprehend, fathom.

penetrating, *adj.* **1.** piercing, sharp, acute, subtle. **2.** acute, discerning, critical, keen, shrewd, sharp, sharp-witted, intelligent, wise, sagacious.
Ant. blunt; uncritical, silly, stupid, undiscriminating.

penitent, *adj.* sorry, contrite, repentant, atoning, amending, remorseful.

penniless, *adj.* poor, indigent, poverty-stricken, destitute, needy, necessitous, impecunious.
Ant. rich, wealthy.

pensive, *adj.* serious, sober, thoughtful, meditative, reflective, dreamy, wistful; contemplative, thinking.
Ant. frivolous, silly, unthinking, thoughtless, vapid.

pent-up, *adj.* confined, restrained; frustrated.

penurious, *adj.* mean, parsimonious, stingy, tight, tight-fisted, close-fisted, close, miserly, niggardly, mercenary.
Ant. generous.

penury, *n.* poverty, destitution, indigence, need, want.
Ant. wealth, opulence, abundance.

people, *n.* **1.** community, tribe, race, nation, clan, family. **2.** persons, human beings, humans, men, man; folks. **3.** populace, commonalty, public. —*v.* **4.** populate; stock.

peppery, *adj.* **1.** pungent, hot, spicy. **2.** sharp, stinging, biting. **3.** irascible, irritable, hot-tempered, short-tempered, hot-headed, touchy, testy, petulant, snarling, snappish, waspish, churlish, choleric.
Ant. mild, tasteless; insipid; calm, amiable, friendly, good-natured.

perceive, *v.* **1.** see, discern, notice, note, discover, observe, descry, espy, distinguish. **2.** apprehend, understand, see, discern, appreciate.
Ant. ignore.

perceptible, *adj.* cognizable, appreciable, understandable, discernible, apparent, perceivable.
Ant. undiscernible, concealed.

perception, *n.* **1.** cognition, recognition, perceiving, apprehension, understanding, discernment. **2.** percept.
Ant. misapprehension, misunderstanding.

perdition, *n.* ruin, damnation, destruction, downfall, hell.
Ant. blessedness, sanctity.

peremptory, *adj.* **1.** imperative, undeniable, irrefutable; categorical, positive, absolute. **2.** dictatorial, imperious, dogmatic, arbitrary, authoritative.
Ant. refutable, indefinite, uncertain, unsure; obedient; lenient.

perennial, *adj.* lasting, enduring, perpetual, perdurable, everlasting, permanent, imperishable, undying, deathless, eternal, immortal; constant, incessant, continual, uninterrupted, unceasing.
Ant. evanescent, temporary, flimsy, mortal; inconstant; sporadic.

perfect, *adj.* **1.** complete, finished, completed, full, consummate. **2.** faultless, spotless, unblemished, excellent, exquisite. **3.** skilled, adept, adroit, expert, accomplished. **4.** typical, exact; thorough, sound, unqualified, pure, unmixed, unadulterated. **—***v.* **5.** complete, finish, bring to perfection, consummate, accomplish.
Ant. incomplete, unfinished; imperfect; maladroit; mixed, impure.

perfidious, *adj.* faithless, treacherous, false, disloyal, dishonest; unfaithful, traitorous, deceitful, venal, untrustworthy.
Ant. faithful, honest, loyal, trustworthy.

perfidy, *n.* treachery, faithlessness, traitorousness, treason, disloyalty.
Ant. allegiance, faithfulness, faith, loyalty.

perform, *v.* **1.** carry out, execute, do, discharge, transact. **2.** fulfill, accomplish, achieve, effect.
Ant. fail.

perfume, *n.* **1.** essence, attar, scent, toilet water; incense. **2.** redolence, scent, odor, smell, aroma, fragrance.
Ant. stench, stink, noxiousness.

perfunctory, *adj.* mechanical, indifferent, careless, superficial, negligent, slovenly, heedless, reckless, uninterested, thoughtless.
Ant. careful, diligent, thoughtful.

peril, *n.* **1.** risk, jeopardy, danger, hazard. **—***v.* **2.** imperil, endanger, risk.
Ant. safety, security.

period, *n.* **1.** interval, age, era, epoch, term, time. **2.** course, cycle.

periphery, *n.* **1.** boundary, circumference, perimeter. **2.** surface, outside.
Ant. center; meat.

perish, *v.* **1.** die, pass away, pass on, expire, decease. **2.** decay, wither, shrivel, rot, molder, disappear, vanish.
Ant. appear.

perky, *adj.* jaunty, pert, brisk.
Ant. flaccid; retiring.

permanent, *adj.* lasting, unchanging, unchanged,

unaltered, stable, immutable, invariant, invariable, constant; enduring, durable, abiding, perpetual, everlasting, remaining, perdurable.
Ant. unstable, temporary, variable, inconstant; temporal.

permeate, *v.* pass through, penetrate, pervade, diffuse through, osmose, saturate, sink in.

permission, *n.* liberty, license, enfranchisement, franchise, leave, permit, liberty, freedom, allowance, consent.
Ant. refusal.

permit, *v.* **1.** allow, let, tolerate, agree to, endure, suffer. —*n.* **2.** license, franchise, permission.
Ant. refuse, disallow.

pernicious, *adj.* **1.** ruinous, harmful, hurtful, detrimental, deleterious, injurious, destructive, damaging, baneful, noxious. **2.** deadly, fatal, lethal. **3.** evil, wicked, malevolent, malicious, bad.
Ant. beneficial, salubrious, healthful; good.

perpendicular, *adj.* vertical, upright, standing.
Ant. horizontal, parallel.

perpetual, *adj.* everlasting, permanent, continuing, continuous, enduring, constant, eternal, ceaseless, unceasing, incessant, unending, endless, uninterrupted, interminable, infinite.
Ant. temporary, finite, impermanent; discontinuous.

perplex, *v.* **1.** confuse, puzzle, bewilder, mystify, confound. **2.** complicate, confuse, tangle, snarl, entangle, involve, encumber. **3.** hamper, discourage, vex, annoy, bother, trouble, harass, disturb.
Ant. clarify; disencumber; encourage, calm.

persecute, *v.* **1.** oppress, harass, badger, molest, vex, afflict. **2.** punish, discriminate against; torture, torment. **3.** importune, annoy, tease, bother, pester, harass, harry.

perseverance, *n.* persistence, tenacity, pertinacity, resolution, doggedness, determination, steadfastness, indefatigability.
Ant. irresolution.

persevere, *v.* persist, continue, keep on, last, stick it out, hold on.
Ant. fail, cease, desist.

persist, *v.* **1.** persevere, continue, last, endure, remain. **2.** insist.
Ant. stop, discontinue.

persistent, *adj.* **1.** persisting, persevering, enduring, indefatigable, pertinacious, tenacious, stubborn, pigheaded, immovable, steadfast. **2.** continued, continual, continuous, repeated, constant, steady.
Ant. amenable, obedient; inconstant, sporadic.

person, *n.* **1.** human being, human, man, somebody, individual, personage, one. **2.** character, part, role.

personality, *n.* character; personal identity.

perspicacious, *adj.* keen, perceptive, discerning, acute, penetrating, sharp-witted, clear-sighted.

Ant. dull, stupid, dim-witted.

perspicacity, *n.* perception, discernment, penetration, shrewdness, acuity, astuteness, insight, sharpness, acumen.

Ant. dullness, stupidity.

perspicuity, *n.* clearness, clarity, lucidity, transparency, plainness, distinctness, explicitness, intelligibility.

Ant. dimness, opacity.

perspicuous, *adj.* clear, lucid, intelligible, plain, distinct, explicit, transparent, unequivocal.

Ant. opaque, unintelligible, indistinct, unclear, confused, clouded.

persuade, *v.* **1.** prevail on, induce, urge, influence, actuate, move, entice, impel. **2.** win over, convince, satisfy.

Ant. dissuade, discourage.

pert, *adj.* bold, forward, impertinent, saucy, presumptuous, impudent, flippant.

Ant. retiring, shy, bashful; polite, courteous.

pertinacious, *adj.* tenacious, persevering, persistent, dogged.

Ant. relenting, flexible.

pertinacity, *n.* perseverance, persistence, tenacity, tenaciousness, inflexibility, firmness, steadfastness, determination, resolution.

Ant. flexibility.

pertinent, *adj.* pertaining, relating, relevant, apt, appropriate, apposite, fit, fitting, fitted, suited, suitable, applicable, proper.

Ant. irrelevant, inappropriate, unsuited, unsuitable, improper.

perturb, *v.* **1.** disturb, disquiet, agitate, stir up, trouble. **2.** disturb, derange, disorder, confuse, addle, muddle.

Ant. pacify, calm, tranquilize; clarify.

pervade, *v.* permeate, diffuse, fill; penetrate, pass through.

perverse, *adj.* **1.** contrary, contumacious, disobedient, wayward, cantankerous. **2.** willful, persistent, obstinate, stubborn, headstrong, pig-headed, dogged, intractable, unyielding. **3.** wicked, evil, bad, sinful, piacular, perverted, distorted.

Ant. amiable, obedient; amenable, tractable; good.

perverted, *adj.* wicked, misguided, misapplied, distorted.

Ant. straight, good, sensible.

pessimistic, *adj.* cynical, gloomy, dark, foreboding.

Ant. optimistic, rosy, bright.

pest, *n.* **1.** nuisance, annoyance. **2.** pestilence, plague, scourge, bane; epidemic, pandemic.

pester, *v.* harass, annoy, vex, torment, torture, molest, harry, hector, tease, trouble, plague, nettle, disturb, provoke, bother, worry, gall, badger, irritate, chafe.

Ant. please, delight, entertain, divert.

pet, *n.* **1.** favorite, darling; lap-dog. **2.** peevishness, cantankerousness, moodiness. —*v.* **3.** fondle, indulge, baby, caress. **4.** sulk, be peevish.

petition, *n.* **1.** request, supplication, suit, prayer, entreaty, solicitation, appeal, application. —*v.* **2.** entreat, supplicate, beg, pray, appeal, solicit, sue.

petty, *adj.* **1.** unimportant, trifling, paltry, nugatory, trivial, lesser, little, small, insignificant, negligible, inconsiderable, slight, diminutive. **2.** narrow, narrow-minded, small. **3.** mean, ungenerous, stingy, miserly. *Ant.* important, considerable, significant; broad-minded; generous.

petulance, *n.* petulancy, irritability, peevishness, fretfulness, pettishness, testiness, waspishness. *Ant.* calm, tranquillity.

petulant, *adj.* irritable, peevish, fretful, vexatious, waspish, snappish, testy, short-tempered, hot-headed, hot-tempered, peppery, pettish, touchy, irascible, cross, snarling, captious, acrimonious. *Ant.* even-tempered, temperate, pleasant.

phantasm, *n.* apparition, specter, phantom, vision, illusion, ghost. *Ant.* reality.

phantom, *n.* **1.** phantasm. —*adj.* **2.** unreal, illusive, spectral, illusory, phantasmal; imaginary, hallucinatory. *Ant.* real, flesh-and-blood, material.

phenomenon, *n.* **1.** fact, occurrence, event, incident, circumstance. **2.** prodigy, marvel, wonder, miracle.

philander, *v.* flirt, coquet, trifle, dally.

phlegm, *n.* **1.** mucus. **2.** sluggishness, stoicism, apathy, indifference. **3.** coolness, calm, self-posesssion, coldness, impassivity, impassiveness. *Ant.* concern; interest, warmth.

phobia, *n.* dread, fear; aversion, hatred. *Ant.* like, attraction, love.

phraseology, *n.* diction, expression, style, language.

physical, *adj.* **1.** bodily, corporeal, corporal, mortal; tangible, sensible. **2.** material, real, natural. *Ant.* mental, spiritual; unnatural, unreal.

pick, *v.* **1.** choose, select, cull. **2.** criticize, find fault with. **3.** steal, rob, pilfer. **4.** pierce, indent, dig into, break up, peck. **5.** pluck, gather, reap, collect, get, acquire. —*n.* **6.** pickax. **7.** choice, selection, choicest part, best. **8.** plectrum.

picture, *n.* **1.** painting, drawing, photograph, representation. **2.** image, representation, similitude, semblance, likeness. **3.** description, account, representation. **4.** motion picture, movie, screen play, photoplay, film. —*v.* **5.** imagine; depict, describe, delineate, paint, draw, represent.

picturesque, *adj.* **1.** striking, interesting, colorful, scenic, beautiful. **2.** graphic, vivid, impressive; intense, lively. *Ant.* uninteresting, dull.

piece, *n.* **1.** portion, quantity, segment, section, scrap, shred, fragment, part. **2.** thing, example, instance,

specimen. **3.** short story, story, article, essay, composition, paper, theme, novella; poem, ode, sonnet; play. —*v.* **4.** mend, patch. **5.** complete, enlarge, extend, augment, add to.
Ant. all, everything; none, nothing.

pierce, *v.* **1.** penetrate, enter, run through *or* into, perforate, stab, puncture, bore, drill. **2.** affect, touch, move, rouse, strike, thrill, excite.

piety, *n.* **1.** reverence, regard, respect. **2.** godliness, devoutness, devotion, sanctity, grace, holiness.
Ant. irreverence, disrespect.

pile, *n.* **1.** assemblage, collection, mass, heap, accumulation. **2.** pyre, burning ghat. **3.** building, edifice, structure. **4.** pier, post. **5.** hair, down; wool, fur, pelage; nap. —*v.* **6.** heap up, accumulate, assemble, amass, collect.

pilgrim, *n.* **1.** palmer, crusader. **2.** wayfarer, sojourner, traveler, wanderer.

pilgrimage, *n.* journey, trip, excursion, tour, expedition.

pillage, *v.* **1.** rob, plunder, rape, despoil, sack, spoil. —*n.* **2.** booty, plunder, spoils. **3.** rapine, depredation, devastation, spoliation.

pillar, *n.* shaft, column, stele, lally-column, support, pier, prop.

pillow, *n.* cushion, pad, bolster.

pin, *n.* **1.** peg, fastening, bolt. **2.** brooch. —*v.* **3.** fasten, fix.

pinnacle, *n.* peak, eminence, culmination, tower, summit, apex, acme, zenith.
Ant. base.

pious, *adj.* **1.** devout, reverent, godly, religious, holy. **2.** sacred.
Ant. impious, irreligious, unholy; unsacred, defiled.

piquant, *adj.* **1.** pungent, sharp, flavorsome, tart, spicy. **2.** stimulating, interesting, attractive, sparkling. **3.** smart, racy, sharp, clever.
Ant. insipid; uninteresting, unattractive; dull.

pique, *v.* **1.** offend, nettle, sting, irritate, chafe, vex; affront, wound, displease. **2.** interest, stimulate, excite, incite, stir, spur, prick, goad.
Ant. please, delight; compliment.

pirate, *n.* plunderer, filibuster, freebooter, picaroon, buccaneer, corsair.

pit, *n.* **1.** hole, cavity, burrow, hollow. **2.** excavation, well, pitfall, trap. **3.** hollow, depression, dent, indentation. **4.** stone, pip, seed, core.

piteous, *adj.* pathetic, pitiable, deplorable, wretched, miserable; affecting, distressing, moving, pitiful, lamentable, woeful, sorrowful, sad, mournful, morose, doleful.
Ant. good, fine, pleasant, delightful.

pitiful, *adj.* **1.** pitiable, pathetic, piteous. **2.** contemptible, deplorable, mean, low, base, vile, despicable.
Ant. superior, delightful, lovable.

pitiless, *adj.* merciless, cruel, mean, unmerciful, ruthless, implacable, relentless, inexorable, hard-hearted. *Ant.* merciful, soft-hearted, kind, kindly.

pity, *n.* **1.** sympathy, compassion, commiseration, condolence, mercy. —*v.* **2.** commiserate, be *or* feel sorry for, sympathize with, feel for. *Ant.* apathy, cruelty, ruthlessness.

placate, *v.* appease, satisfy, conciliate. *Ant.* dissatisfy, displease.

place, *n.* **1.** space, plot, spot, location, locale, locality, site. **2.** position, situation, circumstances. **3.** job, post, office, function, duty, charge, responsibility, employment, rank. **4.** region, area, section, sector. **5.** residence, dwelling, house, home, domicile, abode. **6.** stead, lien. **7.** opportunity, occasion, reason, ground, cause. —*v.* **8.** position, range, order, dispose, arrange, situate, put, set, locate, station, deposit, lay, seat, fix, establish. **9.** appoint, hire, induct. **10.** identify, connect. *Ant.* misplace, displace; forget.

placid, *adj.* calm, peaceful, unruffled, tranquil, serene, quiet, undisturbed. *Ant.* turbulent, tumultuous, perturbed.

plague, *n.* **1.** epidemic, pestilence, disease, Black Death, Great Plague, Oriental Plague. **2.** affliction, calamity, evil, curse. **3.** trouble, vexation, annoyance, nuisance, torment. —*v.* **4.** trouble, torment, torture, molest, bother, incommode, discommode. **5.** vex, harry, hector, harass, fret, worry, pester, badger, annoy, tease, irritate, disturb.

plain, *adj.* **1.** clear, distinct, lucid, unambiguous, unequivocal, intelligible, understandable, perspicuous, evident, manifest, obvious, unmistakable, patent, apparent. **2.** downright, sheer, direct, transparent. **3.** unambiguous, candid, outspoken, blunt, direct, frank, guileless, artless, ingenuous, open, unreserved, honest, sincere, open-hearted. **4.** homely, unpretentious, homey, simple, unadorned, frugal. **5.** ugly, homely, unattractive. **6.** ordinary, common, commonplace, unostentatious. **7.** flat, level, plane, smooth, even. —*n.* **8.** mesa, plateau, savanna, prairie, pampas. *Ant.* unclear, ambiguous, unintelligible; artful, sly, cunning, deceptive, insincere; beautiful, attractive; uncommon, extraordinary.

plaintive, *adj.* sorrowful, melancholy, mournful, sad, wistful; discontented. *Ant.* happy, pleasant.

plan, *n.* **1.** scheme, plot, complot, procedure, project, formula, method, system, design, contrivance. **2.** drawing, sketch, floorplan, draft, map, chart, diagram, representation. —*v.* **3.** arrange, scheme, plot, design, devise, contrive, invent, concoct, hatch.

platform, *n.* **1.** stage, dais, rostrum, pulpit; landing. **2.** principles, beliefs, tenets.

plausible, *adj.* **1.** specious, deceptive, deceiving, deceitful, hypocritical. **2.** fair-spoken, glib, convincing. *Ant.* implausible.

play, *n.* **1.** drama, piece, show; comedy, tragedy, melodrama, farce. **2.** amusement, recreation, game, sport, diversion, pastime. **3.** fun, jest, trifling, frolic. **4.** action, activity, movement, exercise, operation, motion. **5.** freedom, liberty, scope, elbow-room. —*v.* **6.** act, perform, enact, characterize, impersonate, personate. **7.** compete, contend with *or* against, engage. **8.** use, employ. **9.** stake, bet, wager. **10.** represent, imitate, emulate, mimic. **11.** do, perform, bring about, execute. **12.** toy, trifle, sport, dally, caper, romp, disport, frolic, gambol, skip, revel, frisk. *Ant.* work.

plead, *v.* **1.** entreat, appeal, beg, supplicate. **2.** argue, persuade, reason. **3.** allege, cite, make a plea, apologize, answer, make excuse.

pleasant, *adj.* **1.** pleasing, agreeable, enjoyable, pleasurable, acceptable, welcome, gratifying. **2.** delightful, congenial, polite, courteous, friendly, personable, amiable. **3.** fair, sunny. **4.** gay, sprightly, merry, cheery, cheerful, lively, sportive, vivacious. **5.** jocular, facetious, playful, humorous, witty, amusing, clever, jocose.
Ant. unpleasant, displeasing.

pleasing, *adj.* agreeable, pleasant, acceptable, pleasurable, charming, delightful, interesting, engaging. *Ant.* disagreeable, unpleasant, unacceptable.

pleasure, *n.* **1.** happiness, gladness, delectation, enjoyment, delight, joy, well-being, satisfaction, gratification. **2.** luxury, sensuality, voluptuousness. **3.** will, desire, choice, preference, purpose, wish, mind, inclination, predilection.
Ant. displeasure, unhappiness; disinclination.

plentiful, *adj.* bountiful, ample, plenteous, copious, abundant, full, rich, fertile, fruitful, bounteous, productive, exuberant, luxuriant.
Ant. sparse, scanty, barren, fruitless.

plenty, *n.* fullness, abundance, copiousness, plenteousness, plentifulness, profusion, luxuriance, exuberance, affluence, overflow, extravagance, prodigality; superabundance, overfullness, plethora.
Ant. paucity, scarcity.

pliant, *adj.* pliable, supple, flexible, flexile, lithe, limber; compliant, easily influenced, yielding, adaptable, manageable, tractable, ductile, facile, docile.
Ant. inflexible; unyielding, rigid, intractable.

plight, *n.* **1.** condition, state, situation, predicament, category, case, dilemma. —*v.* **2.** propose, pledge, hypothecate.

plod, *v.* **1.** walk heavily, pace, trudge. **2.** toil, moil, labor, drudge, sweat.

plot, *n.* **1.** plan, scheme, complot, intrigue, conspiracy, cabal, stratagem, machination. **2.** story, theme, thread, story line. —*v.* **3.** devise, contrive, concoct, brew, hatch, frame. **4.** conspire, scheme, contrive.

pluck, *v.* **1.** pull, jerk, yank, snatch, tug, tear, rip. —*n.* **2.** courage, resolution, spirit, bravery, boldness, determination, mettle, nerve.

plump, *adj.* **1.** fleshy, fat, chubby, stout, portly, corpulent, obese, round. **2.** direct, downright, blunt, unqualified, unreserved, complete, full. —*v.* **3.** gain weight; fatten. **4.** drop, sink, fall. —*n.* **5.** fall, drop. —*adv.* **6.** directly, bluntly, suddenly, abruptly.
Ant. thin, slender, skinny; subtle.

plunder, *v.* **1.** rob, despoil, fleece, pillage, ravage, rape, sack, devastate, strip, lay waste. —*n.* **2.** pillage, rapine, spoliation, robbery, theft, plundering. **3.** loot, booty, spoils.

plunge, *v.* **1.** immerse, submerge, dip. **2.** dive; rush, hasten; descend, drop, hurtle over. —*n.* **3.** leap, dive, rush, dash, dip.

poetry, *n.* verse, meter, rhythm, poesy, numbers.

poignant, *adj.* **1.** distressing, heartfelt, serious, intense, severe, bitter, sincere. **2.** keen, strong, biting, mordant, caustic, acid, pointed. **3.** pungent, piquant, sharp, biting, acrid, stinging.
Ant. superfluous, trivial; mild.

pointed, *adj.* **1.** sharp, piercing, penetrating, epigrammatic, stinging, piquant, biting, mordant, sarcastic, caustic, severe, keen. **2.** directed, aimed, explicit, marked, personal. **3.** marked, emphasized, accented, accentuated.
Ant. blunt, dull, mild.

poise, *n.* **1.** balance, equilibrium, equipoise, counterpoise. **2.** composure, self-possession, steadiness, stability, self-control, control. **3.** suspense, indecision. **4.** carriage, mien, demeanor, savoir-faire, breeding, behavior. —*v.* **5.** balance, equilibrate.
Ant. instability, unsteadiness; decision.

poison, *n.* **1.** toxin, venom, virus. —*v.* **2.** envenom, infect. **3.** corrupt, ruin, vitiate, contaminate, pollute, taint, canker.

policy, *n.* **1.** course (*of action*), expediency, tactic, approach, procedure, rule, management, administration, handling. **2.** prudence, wisdom, sagacity, shrewdness, acumen, astuteness, discretion, skill, art, cunning, stratagem.
Ant. ingenuousness, naiveté.

polish, *v.* **1.** brighten, smooth, burnish, shine. **2.** finish, refine, civilize, make elegant. —*n.* **3.** smoothness, gloss, shine, sheen, luster, brightness, brilliance. **4.** refinement, elegance, poise, grace.
Ant. dull.

polished, *adj.* **1.** smooth, glossy, burnished, shining, shiny, shined, lustrous, brilliant. **2.** refined, cultured, finished, elegant, polite, poised. **3.** flawless, excellent, perfect.
Ant. dull, dim; unrefined, impolite; inelegant; imperfect.

polite, *adj.* well-mannered, courteous, civil, well-bred,

gracious, genteel, urbane, polished, poised, courtly, cultivated, refined, finished, elegant.
Ant. impolite, rude, discourteous, uncivil.

politic, *adj.* **1.** sagacious, prudent, wise, tactful, diplomatic, discreet, judicious, provident, astute, wary, prudential. **2.** shrewd, artful, sly, cunning, underhanded, tricky, foxy, clever, subtle, Machiavellian, wily, intriguing, scheming, crafty, unscrupulous, strategic. **3.** expedient, judicious, political.
Ant. imprudent, indiscreet, improvident; artless, ingenuous, direct, open, honest.

pollute, *v.* **1.** befoul, dirty, defile, soil, taint, tarnish, stain, contaminate, vitiate, corrupt, debase, deprave. **2.** desecrate, profane, blaspheme, violate, dishonor, defile.
Ant. purify; honor, revere, respect.

ponder, *v.* consider, meditate, reflect, cogitate, deliberate, ruminate, muse, think, study; weigh, contemplate, examine.
Ant. forget, ignore.

ponderous, *adj.* **1.** heavy, massive, weighty, bulky. **2.** important, momentous, weighty.
Ant. light, weightless; unimportant.

poor, *adj.* **1.** needy, indigent, necessitous, straitened, destitute, penniless, poverty-stricken, impecunious, impoverished, reduced, hard up, distressed. **2.** deficient, insufficient, meager, lacking, incomplete. **3.** faulty, inferior, unsatisfactory, substandard, shabby, jerry-built, seedy, worthless, valueless. **4.** sterile, barren, unfertile, fruitless, unproductive. **5.** lean, emaciated, thin, skinny, meager, hungry, underfed, lank, gaunt, shrunk. **6.** cowardly, abject, mean, base. **7.** scanty, paltry, meager, insufficient, inadequate. **8.** humble, unpretentious. **9.** unfortunate, hapless, unlucky, star-crossed, doomed, luckless, miserable, unhappy, pitiable, piteous.
Ant. rich, wealthy; sufficient, adequate, complete; superior; fertile; well-fed; bold, brave; bold, pretentious; fortunate, lucky.

popular, *adj.* **1.** favorite, approved, accepted, received, liked. **2.** common, prevailing, current, general, prevalent, in vogue, faddish.
Ant. unpopular; uncommon, rare, unusual.

port, *n.* harbor, haven, refuge, anchorage.

portent, *n.* indication, omen, augury, sign, warning, presage.

portion, *n.* **1.** part, section, segment, piece, bit, scrap, morsel, fragment. **2.** share, allotment, quota, dole, dividend, division, apportionment, lot. **3.** serving. **4.** dowry, dot. —*v.* **5.** divide, distribute, allot, apportion, deal or parcel out. **6.** endow.
Ant. all, everything; none, nothing.

portray, *v.* picture, delineate, limn, depict, paint, represent, sketch.

pose, *v.* **1.** sit, model; attitudinize. **2.** state, assert, propound. —*n.* **3.** attitude, posture, position; affectation.

position, *n.* **1.** station, place, locality, spot, location, site, locale, situation, post. **2.** situation, condition, state, circumstances. **3.** status, standing, rank, place. **4.** post, job, situation, place, employment. **5.** placement, disposition, array, arrangement. **6.** posture, attitude, pose. **7.** proposition, thesis, contention, principle, dictum, predication, assertion, doctrine. —*v.* **8.** put, place, situate. **9.** locate, fix, discover.

positive, *adj.* **1.** explicit, express, sure, certain, definite, precise, clear, unequivocal, categorical, unmistakable, direct. **2.** arbitrary, enacted, decided, determined, decisive, unconditional. **3.** incontrovertible, substantial, indisputable, indubitable. **4.** stated, expressed, emphatic. **5.** confident, self-confident, self-assured, assured, convinced, unquestioning, over-confident, stubborn, peremptory, obstinate, dogmatic, overbearing. **6.** absolute. **7.** practical.
Ant. unsure, indefinite, unclear, equivocal; conditional; doubtful; tacit; tractable, self-effacing; relative; impractical, unpractical.

possess, *v.* **1.** have, hold, own. **2.** occupy, hold, have, control. **3.** impart, inform, familiarize, acquaint, make known.
Ant. lose.

possession, *n.* **1.** custody, occupation, tenure. **2.** ownership.
Ant. loss.

possible, *adj.* feasible, practicable, likely, potential.
Ant. impossible, impractical, unlikely.

post, *n.* **1.** column, pillar, pole, support, upright. **2.** position, office, assignment, appointment. **3.** station, round, beat, position. —*v.* **4.** announce, advertise, publicize. **5.** station, place, set.

postpone, *v.* **1.** put off, defer, delay, procrastinate, adjourn. **2.** subordinate.

posture, *n.* **1.** position, pose, attitude. **2.** position, condition, state.

potent, *adj.* **1.** powerful, mighty, strong, puissant. **2.** cogent, influential, efficacious.
Ant. weak, impotent, powerless, feeble, frail; ineffectual.

potential, *adj.* **1.** possible. **2.** capable, able, latent. —*n.* **3.** possibility, potentiality.
Ant. kinetic, impossible; incapable, unable; impossibility.

pound, *v.* **1.** strike, beat, thrash. **2.** crush, bray, pulverize, powder, triturate, comminute. **3.** impound, imprison, pen, jail, shut up, confine, coop up. —*n.* **4.** *pound avoirdupois, pound troy, pound sterling, pound Scots.* **5.** enclosure, pen, confine, trap.

poverty, *n.* **1.** destitution, need, lack, want, privation, necessitousness, necessity, neediness, indigence, penury, distress. **2.** deficiency, sterility, barrenness,

unfruitfulness. **3.** scantiness, jejuneness, sparingness, meagerness.
Ant. wealth; abundance, fertility, fruitfulness.

power, *n.* **1.** ability, capability, capacity, faculty, competence, competency, might, strength, puissance. **2.** strength, might, force, energy. **3.** control, command, dominion, authority, sway, rule, ascendancy, influence, sovereignty, suzerainty, prerogative.
Ant. inability, incapacity, incompetence.

powerful, *adj.* **1.** mighty, potent, forceful, strong. **2.** cogent, influential, forcible, convincing, effective, efficacious, effectual.
Ant. weak, frail, feeble; ineffective, ineffectual.

practicable, *adj.* possible, feasible, workable, performable, doable, achievable, attainable.
Ant. unpracticable, impossible, unattainable.

practical, *adj.* **1.** sensible, businesslike, pragmatic, efficient. **2.** judicious, discreet, sensible, discriminating, balanced, reasoned, sound, shrewd.
Ant. impractical, inefficient; indiscreet, unsound.

practice, *n.* **1.** custom, habit, wont. **2.** exercise, drill, experience, application, study. **3.** performance, operation, action, process. **4.** plotting, intriguing, trickery, chicanery; plot, intrigue, stratagem, ruse, maneuver. —*v.* **5.** carry out, perform, do, drill, exercise. **6.** follow, observe.
Ant. inexperience.

praise, *n.* **1.** praising, commendation, acclamation, plaudit, compliment, laudation, approval, approbation, applause, kudos. **2.** encomium, eulogy, panegyric. —*v.* **3.** laud, approve, commend, admire, extol, celebrate, eulogize, panegyrize. **4.** glorify, magnify, exalt, worship, bless, adore, honor.
Ant. condemnation, disapprobation, disapproval, criticism.

pray, *v.* importune, entreat, supplicate, beg, beseech, implore, sue, petition, invoke.

precarious, *adj.* **1.** uncertain, unstable, unsure, insecure, dependent, unsteady. **2.** doubtful, dubious, unreliable, undependable, risky, perilous, hazardous, dangerous. **3.** groundless, unfounded, baseless.
Ant. certain, stable, sure, secure, independent; reliable, dependable; well-founded.

precaution, *n.* foresight, prudence, providence, wariness, forethought.

precious, *adj.* **1.** valuable, costly, dear, invaluable, priceless. **2.** dear, beloved, darling, cherished. **3.** choice, fine, delicate, select, pretty. **4.** arrant, gross, egregious.
Ant. inexpensive, cheap; worthless; ugly, unattractive.

precipitate, *v.* **1.** hasten, accelerate, hurry, speed up, expedite, speed, rush, quicken, advance, dispatch. **2.** cast down, hurl *or* fling down, plunge. —*adj.* **3.** headlong, hasty, rash, reckless, indiscreet. **4.** sudden, abrupt, violent.

Ant. slow, retard; considered.

precipitous, *adj.* steep, abrupt, sheer, perpendicular.
Ant. gradual, sloping.

precise, *adj.* **1.** definite, exact, defined, fixed, correct, strict, explicit, accurate. **2.** rigid, particular, puritanical, demanding, crucial.
Ant. indefinite, incorrect, inexact, lenient; flexible, tractable.

predatory, *adj.* predacious, plundering, ravaging, pillaging, rapacious, voracious.

predicament, *n.* dilemma, plight, quandary; situation, state, condition, position, case.

predict, *v.* foretell, prophesy, foresee, forecast, presage, augur, prognosticate, foretoken, portend, divine.

prediction, *n.* prophecy, forecast, augury, prognostication, foretoken, portent, divination, soothsaying, presage.

predilection, *n.* prepossession, favoring, partiality, predisposition, disposition, inclination, bent, preference, leaning, bias, prejudice.
Ant. disfavor, disinclination, dislike.

predominant, *adj.* ascendant, prevailing, prevalent, dominant, in sway, sovereign.
Ant. rare, retrograde.

predominate, *v.* preponderate, prevail, outweigh, overrule, surpass, dominate.

preeminent, *adj.* eminent, surpassing, dominant, superior, over, above, distinguished, excellent, peerless, unequalled, paramount, consummate, predominant, supreme.
Ant. undistinguished, inferior.

preface, *n.* introduction, foreword, preamble, prologue, proem, prelude, preliminary, prolegomena.
Ant. appendix, epilogue.

prefer, *v.* **1.** like better, favor, choose, elect, select, pick out, pick, single out, fix upon, fancy. **2.** put forward, advance, present, offer, proffer, tender, promote.
Ant. exclude, dislike; retract, withdraw.

preference, *n.* choice, selection, pick, predilection.
Ant. exclusion.

prejudice, *n.* **1.** preconception, bias, partiality, prejudgment, predilection, predisposition, disposition. **—***v.* **2.** bias, influence, warp, twist.
Ant. judgment, decision.

preliminary, *adj.* **1.** preceding, introductory, preparatory, prefatory, precursive, prior. **—***n.* **2.** introduction, prelude, preface, prolegomena, preparation.
Ant. resulting, concluding; conclusion, end, appendix, epilogue.

premeditate, *v.* consider, plan, deliberate, precontrive, predetermine, prearrange, predesign.

premium, *n.* **1.** prize, door prize, bounty. **2.** bonus, gift, reward, recompense.
Ant. punishment.

preoccupied, *adj.* absorbed, engrossed, meditating,

meditative, pondering, musing, concentrating, inattentive, in a brown study.
Ant. unthinking, thoughtless, frivolous.

prepare, *v.* **1.** contrive, devise, plan, plan for, anticipate, get *or* make ready, provide, arrange, order. **2.** manufacture, make, compound, fix, compose.
Ant. destroy, ruin.

preposterous, *adj.* absurd, senseless, foolish, inane, asinine, unreasonable, ridiculous, excessive, extravagant, irrational.
Ant. rational, reasonable, sensible.

prerogative, *n.* right, privilege, precedence, license, franchise, immunity, freedom, liberty.

presage, *n.* **1.** presentiment, foreboding, foreshadowing, indication, premonition, foreknowledge. **2.** portent, omen, sign, token, augury, warning, signal, prognostic. **3.** forecast, prediction. **—*v.*** **4.** portend, foreshadow, forecast, predict.

prescribe, *v.* lay down, predetermine, appoint, ordain, enjoin, direct, dictate, decree, establish, hand down, institute.

presence, *n.* **1.** attendance, company. **2.** nearness, vicinity, neighborhood, proximity, vicinage, closeness. **3.** personality; bearing, carriage, mien, aspect, impression, appearance.
Ant. absence.

present, *adj.* **1.** current, existing, extant; here, at hand, near, nearby. **—*n.*** **2.** now. **3.** gift, donation, bonus, benefaction, largess, grant, gratuity, boon, tip. **—*v.*** **4.** give, endow, bestow, grant, confer, donate. **5.** afford, furnish, yield, offer, proffer. **6.** show, exhibit; introduce. **7.** represent, personate, act, enact, imitate, impersonate. **8.** point, level, aim, direct.
Ant. absent; then; receive.

presently, *adv.* anon, at once, immediately, directly, right away, without delay, shortly, forthwith, soon.
Ant. later.

preserve, *v.* **1.** keep, conserve. **2.** guard, safeguard, shelter, shield, protect, defend, save. **3.** keep up, maintain, continue, uphold, sustain. **4.** retain, keep.
Ant. forgo; lose.

prestige, *n.* reputation, influence, weight, importance, distinction.
Ant. disrepute, notoriety.

presume, *v.* **1.** assume, presuppose, suppose, take for granted, believe. **2.** venture, undertake.

presumptuous, *adj.* bold, impertinent, forward, arrogant, insolent, audacious, rude, fresh.
Ant. modest, polite.

pretend, *v.* **1.** feign, affect, put on, assume, falsify, simulate, fake, sham, counterfeit. **2.** allege, profess; lie. **3.** make believe.

pretense, *n.* **1.** pretending, feigning, shamming, make-believe; subterfuge, fabrication, pretext, excuse. **2.**

show, cover, cover-up, semblance, dissembling, mask, cloak, veil; pretension.

preternatural, *adj.* abnormal, unusual, peculiar, odd, strange, extraordinary, irregular, unnatural, anomalous; supernatural.
Ant. usual, common, regular, natural.

pretty, *adj.* **1.** fair, attractive, comely, pleasing, beautiful. **2.** fine, pleasant, excellent, splendid. —*adv.* **3.** moderately, fairly, somewhat, to some extent. **4.** very, quite.
Ant. ugly; unpleasant; completely.

prevail, *v.* **1.** predominate, preponderate. **2.** win, succeed.
Ant. lose.

prevailing, *adj.* **1.** prevalent, predominant, preponderating, dominant, preponderant. **2.** current, general, common. **3.** superior, influential, effectual, effective, efficacious, successful.
Ant. rare, uncommon; inferior, ineffectual, ineffective, unsuccessful.

prevalent, *adj.* widespread, current, common, prevailing, extensive, predominant, predominating, accepted, used, general.
Ant. rare, unusual, uncommon.

prevaricate, *v.* equivocate, quibble, cavil, shift; fib, lie.

prevent, *v.* hinder, stop, obstruct, hamper, impede, forestall, thwart, intercept, preclude, obviate, interrupt.
Ant. encourage, aid, help, abet, support, continue.

previous, *adj.* prior, earlier, former, preceding, foregoing.
Ant. later, following.

price, *n.* charge, cost, expense, outlay, expenditure.

pride, *n.* **1.** conceit, self-esteem, vanity, arrogance, vainglory, self-importance. **2.** insolence, haughtiness, snobbishness, superciliousness, hauteur, presumption.
Ant. modesty; humility.

prim, *adj.* stiff, starched, formal, strait-laced, precise, proper, puritanical, rigid, blue, priggish; prunes and prisms.
Ant. flexible, informal; lewd, licentious, profligate.

primary, *adj.* **1.** first, highest, chief, principal, main. **2.** first, earliest, primitive, original, primeval, aboriginal. **3.** elementary, beginning, opening, fundamental, basic, ordinate. **4.** direct, immediate.
Ant. last, final, ultimate; secondary; indirect.

prime, *adj.* primary.
Ant. last.

primeval, *adj.* prime, primary, primordial, primitive, original, primigenial, pristine.

primitive, *adj.* **1.** prehistoric, primal, primeval, prime, primary, primordial, original, aboriginal, pristine, prehistoric, first, antediluvian. **2.** uncivilized, uncultured, simple, unsophisticated, quaint.
Ant. secondary; civilized, sophisticated, cultured.

principal, *adj.* **1.** first, highest, prime, paramount, capital, chief, foremost, main, leading, cardinal, preeminent. **—*n.* 2.** chief, head, leader, chieftain. **3.** headmaster, dean, master.
Ant. ancillary, secondary.

principally, *adv.* especially, chiefly, mainly, primarily, firstly, particularly.
Ant. lastly.

principle, *n.* **1.** canon, rule, standard, test, parameter. **2.** theorem, axiom, postulate, maxim, law, proposition. **3.** doctrine, tenet, belief, opinion. **4.** integrity, honesty, probity, righteousness, uprightness, rectitude, virtue incorruptibility, goodness, trustworthiness, honor.

private, *adj.* **1.** individual, personal, singular, especial, special, particular, peculiar. **2.** confidential, secret, top secret, "eyes only." **3.** alone, secluded, cloistered, sequestered, solitary, retired.
Ant. public, general; known; open.

privation, *n.* hardship, deprivation, loss; destitution, want, need, necessity, distress, lack.
Ant. ease, wealth.

privilege, *n.* right, immunity, leave, prerogative, advantage, license, freedom, liberty, permission, franchise.

prize, *n.* **1.** reward, premium. **—*v.* 2.** value, esteem, appraise.

probe, *v.* examine, explore, question, investigate, scrutinize, search, sift, prove, test.
Ant. overlook, ignore.

probity, *n.* honesty, uprightness, rectitude, integrity.
Ant. dishonesty.

problem, *n.* question, doubt, uncertainty, puzzle, riddle, enigma.
Ant. certainty, certitude, surety.

procedure, *n.* **1.** proceeding, conduct, management, operation, course, process. **2.** act, deed, transaction, maneuver, goings-on.

proceed, *v.* **1.** advance, go on, progress, move on, continue, pass on. **2.** go *or* come forth, issue, emanate, spring, arise, result, ensue, originate.
Ant. retreat.

process, *n.* course, procedure, operation, proceeding.

proclaim, *v.* announce, declare, advertise, promulgate, publish.

proclivity, *n.* inclination, tendency, bent, leaning, propensity, predisposition, disposition, proneness, favor, bias, prejudice.
Ant. dislike, aversion.

procrastinate, *v.* delay, postpone, put off, defer, adjourn, prolong.
Ant. speed, expedite.

procure, *v.* **1.** acquire, gain, get, secure, win, obtain. **2.** bring about, effect, cause, contrive. **3.** pander, bawd, pimp.
Ant. lose.

prod, *v.* poke, jab; goad, rouse, incite.

prodigal, *adj.* **1.** reckless, profligate, extravagant, lavish, wasteful, profuse. **2.** abundant, profuse, plenteous, copious, plentiful, bounteous, bountiful. **—***n.* **3.** spendthrift, waster, wastrel, squanderer, carouser, playboy.

Ant. cautious, provident, thrifty; scarce, scanty.

prodigious, *adj.* **1.** enormous, immense, huge, gigantic, tremendous, monstrous. **2.** wonderful, marvelous, amazing, stupendous, astonishing, astounding, extraordinary, miraculous, wondrous, uncommon, unusual, strange. **3.** abnormal, monstrous, anomalous.

Ant. small, tiny, infinitesimal; negligible, common; normal, usual.

produce, *v.* **1.** give rise to, cause, generate, occasion, originate, create, effect, make, manufacture, bring about. **2.** bear, bring forth, yield, furnish, supply, afford, give. **3.** exhibit, show, demonstrate, bring forward. **—***n.* **4.** yield, product, crops, fruits, production.

Ant. destroy, ruin; subdue, squelch; hide, conceal.

productive, *adj.* generative, creative; prolific, fertile, fruitful.

Ant. barren, sterile, unproductive.

profane, *adj.* **1.** irreverent, irreligious, blasphemous, sacrilegious, piacular, wicked, impious, ungodly, godless, unredeemed, unredeemable. **2.** unconsecrated, secular, temporal. **3.** unholy, heathen, pagan, unhallowed, impure, polluted. **4.** common, low, mean, base, vulgar. **—***v.* **5.** debase, misuse, defile, desecrate, violate, pollute.

Ant. sacred, repentant; spiritual; pure, hallowed, holy; elevated, exalted.

profession, *n.* **1.** vocation, calling, occupation, business, employment. **2.** professing, avowal, declaration, asseveration, assertion.

proffer, *v.* offer, tender, volunteer, propose, suggest, hint.

Ant. refuse.

proficient, *adj.* skilled, adept, skillful, competent, practiced, experienced, qualified, trained, conversant, accomplished, finished, able, apt.

Ant. unskilled, maladroit, awkward, clumsy, untrained, unable, inept.

profit, *n.* **1.** gain, return. **2.** returns, proceeds, revenue, dividend. **3.** advantage, benefit, gain, good, welfare, improvement, advancement. **—***v.* **4.** gain, improve, advance, better.

Ant. loss; lose.

profound, *adj.* deep, intense, extreme, penetrating, sagacious; abstruse.

Ant. shallow, superficial.

profuse, *adj.* extravagant, abundant, lavish, prodigal, wasteful, profligate, improvident.

Ant. scarce, scanty, thrifty.

profusion, *n.* **1.** abundance, plenty, copiousness, bounty, prodigality, profligacy. **2.** lavishness, luxury, extravagance, prodigality, profligacy, excess, waste. *Ant.* scarcity, need, want; penury, niggardliness.

progress, *n.* **1.** proceeding, advancement, advance, progression. **2.** growth, development, improvement, increase, betterment. *—v.* **3.** advance, proceed; develop, improve, grow, increase.
Ant. retrogression; recession; recede, decrease, diminish.

prohibit, *v.* **1.** forbid, interdict, disallow. **2.** prevent, hinder, preclude, obstruct.
Ant. allow, permit; encourage, foster, further.

prohibition, *n.* interdiction, prevention, embargo, ban, restriction.
Ant. permission.

project, *n.* **1.** plan, scheme, design, proposal. **2.** activity, lesson, homework. *—v.* **3.** propose, contemplate, plan, contrive, scheme, plot, devise, concoct, brew, frame. **4.** throw, cast, toss. **5.** extend, protrude, obtrude, bulge, jut out, stick out.

prolific, *adj.* **1.** fruitful, fertile, productive, teeming. **2.** abundant.
Ant. fruitless, unfruitful, barren, sterile; scarce.

prolong, *v.* lengthen, extend, protract.
Ant. abbreviate, shorten, curtail.

prominent, *adj.* **1.** conspicuous, noticeable, outstanding, manifest, principal, chief, important, main. **2.** projecting, jutting out, protuberant, embossed. **3.** important, leading, well-known, eminent, celebrated, famed, famous, distinguished.
Ant. inconspicuous, unimportant; recessed; negligible, unknown.

promiscuous, *adj.* **1.** miscellaneous, hodgepodge, hotchpotch, indiscriminate, confused, mixed, intermixed, intermingled, mingled, jumbled, garbled. **2.** nonselective, indiscriminate, careless.
Ant. special, discriminate, pure, unmixed; selective, careful, select.

promise, *n.* **1.** word, pledge, assurance. *—v.* **2.** pledge, covenant, agree, engage.

promote, *v.* **1.** further, advance, encourage, forward, assist, aid, help, support. **2.** elevate, raise, exalt.
Ant. discourage, obstruct; lower, debase.

prone, *adj.* **1.** inclined, disposed, liable, tending, bent. **2.** prostrate, recumbent.
Ant. averse; upright.

proof, *n.* **1.** evidence, testimony, certification, confirmation, demonstration. **2.** test, trial, examination, essay. **3.** impression. *—adj.* **4.** impenetrable, impervious, invulnerable, steadfast, firm.

propensity, *n.* inclination, bent, leaning, tendency, disposition, bias.
Ant. disinclination, aversion, distaste.

proper, *adj.* **1.** appropriate, fit, suitable, suited, adapted, convenient, fitting, befitting, correct, right,

becoming, meet. **2.** correct, decorous, decent, respectable, polite, well-mannered. **3.** special, specific, individual, peculiar. **4.** strict, accurate, precise, exact, just, formal, correct.
Ant. improper.

property, *n.* **1.** possession, possessions, goods, effects, chattels, estate, belongings. **2.** land, real estate, acreage. **3.** ownership, right. **4.** attribute, quality, characteristic, feature.

prophesy, *v.* foretell, predict, augur, prognosticate, divine.

propitiate, *v.* appease, conciliate, pacify.
Ant. anger, arouse.

proportion, *n.* **1.** relation, arrangement; comparison, analogy. **2.** size, extent, dimensions. **3.** portion, part, piece, share. **4.** symmetry, harmony, agreement, balance, distribution, arrangement. —*v.* **5.** adjust, regulate, redistribute, arrange, balance, harmonize.
Ant. disproportion.

proposal, *n.* plan, scheme, offer, recommendation, suggestion, design, overture, approach, proposition.

propose, *v.* **1.** offer, proffer, tender, suggest, recommend, present. **2.** nominate, name. **3.** plan, intend, design, mean, purpose. **4.** state, present, propound, pose, posit.
Ant. refuse.

proposition, *n.* proposal.

propriety, *n.* **1.** decorum, etiquette, protocol, good behavior, decency, modesty. **2.** suitability, appropriateness, aptness, fitness, suitableness, seemliness. **3.** rightness, justness, correctness, accuracy.
Ant. impropriety, immodesty, indecency; unseemliness, ineptitude; inaccuracy.

prosaic, *adj.* prosy, commonplace, dull, matter-of-fact, unimaginative, vapid, humdrum, tedious, tiresome, wearisome, uninteresting.
Ant. interesting, fascinating, beguiling.

prospect, *n.* **1.** anticipation, expectation, expectance, contemplation. **2.** view, scene, outlook, survey, vista, perspective. —*v.* **3.** search, explore.

prosper, *v.* succeed, thrive, flourish.
Ant. fail, die.

prosperous, *adj.* **1.** fortunate, successful, flourishing, thriving. **2.** wealthy, rich, well-to-do, well-off. **3.** favorable, propitious, fortunate, lucky, auspicious, golden, bright.
Ant. unfortunate, unsuccessful; poor, impoverished; unfavorable.

prostitute, *n.* **1.** harlot, whore, strumpet, call-girl, trollop, quean, street-walker, courtesan. —*v.* **2.** misapply, misuse, abuse.

protect, *v.* defend, guard, shield, cover, screen, shelter, save, harbor, house, secure.
Ant. attack, assail.

protection, *n.* **1.** preservation, guard, defense, shelter,

screen, cover, security, refuge, safety. **2.** shield, aegis, bulwark. **3.** treaty, safe-conduct, passport, visa, pass, permit. **4.** aegis, patronage, sponsorship.
Ant. attack.

protest, *n.* **1.** objection, disapproval, protestation. —*v.* **2.** remonstrate, complain, object. **3.** declare, affirm, assert, asseverate, avow, aver, testify, attest.
Ant. approval; approve.

prototype, *n.* model, pattern, example, exemplar, original, archetype.

protract, *v.* draw out, lengthen, extend, prolong, continue.
Ant. curtail, abbreviate, discontinue.

proud, *adj.* **1.** contented, self-satisfied, egotistical, vain, conceited. **2.** arrogant, over-weening, haughty, overbearing, self-important, over-confident, disdainful, supercilious, snooty, imperious, presumptuous. **3.** honorable, creditable. **4.** stately, majestic, magnificent, noble, imposing, splendid.
Ant. discontented, dissatisfied; humble, self-effacing; dishonorable; ignoble, base.

prove, *v.* **1.** demonstrate, show, confirm, manifest, establish, evince, evidence, substantiate, verify, justify, ascertain, determine. **2.** try, test, examine, assay.
Ant. disprove.

proverb, *n.* maxim, saying, adage, epigram, precept, truth, saw, aphorism, by-word, apothegm.

provide, *v.* **1.** furnish, supply, afford, yield, produce, contribute, give. **2.** prepare, get ready, procure, provide for, make provision for.
Ant. deprive.

provided, *conj.* on the condition *or* supposition that, if, in case, granted.
Ant. lest.

provision, *n.* **1.** stipulation, condition, if, proviso. **2.** catering, purveying, supplying. **3.** (*plural*) food, supplies, stores, provender, stock.

provoke, *v.* **1.** anger, enrage, exasperate, irk, vex, irritate, incense, annoy, chafe, aggravate, exacerbate, infuriate, ire, nettle, affront. **2.** stir up, arouse, call forth, incite, stimulate, excite, fire, rouse, inflame, animate, inspirit, instigate. **3.** give rise to, induce, bring about.
Ant. assuage, calm, propitiate.

prowl, *v.* lurk, rove, roam, wander; prey, plunder, pillage, steal.

prudence, *n.* **1.** calculation, foresight, forethought, judgment, discretion, common sense, circumspection, caution, wisdom. **2.** providence, care, economy, frugality, carefulness.
Ant. carelessness, imprudence, incaution.

prudent, *adj.* **1.** wise, judicious, cautious, discreet, tactful, sensible, sagacious, circumspect, careful, wary, provident. **2.** provident, frugal, sparing, economical, thrifty, saving, careful.

Ant. imprudent, indiscreet, tactless, careless; improvident, prodigal.
prudish, *adj.* modest, proper, demure, pure, coy, reserved.
Ant. immodest, indecent.
prying, *adj.* curious, inquisitive, peeping, peering, peeking; nosy.
Ant. blasé, unconcerned, uninterested.
pseudo, *adj.* sham, counterfeit, false, spurious, pretended, fake.
Ant. genuine, real.
publish, *v.* **1.** issue, distribute. **2.** announce, proclaim, promulgate, declare, disclose, divulge, reveal, impart, advertise, publicize.
Ant. conceal, hide.
puerile, *adj.* **1.** boyish, juvenile, childish, youthful. **2.** childish, immature, foolish, irrational, trivial, nugatory, silly, ridiculous, idle.
Ant. manly; mature, rational.
pulsate, *v.* beat, palpitate, pulse, throb; vibrate, quiver.
punctilious, *adj.* strict, exact, precise, demanding, scrupulous, nice, careful, conscientious.
Ant. inexact, careless.
pungent, *adj.* **1.** biting, acrid, hot, peppery, piquant, sharp. **2.** poignant, distressing, painful. **3.** caustic, biting, sarcastic, sardonic, mordant, penetrating, piercing, trenchant, cutting, severe, acrimonious, bitter, waspish. **4.** stimulating, acute, keen, sharp.
Ant. mild, bland; painless; dull.
punish, *v.* **1.** correct, discipline, penalize, reprove. **2.** castigate, scold, berate, chastise, chasten, flog, whip, lash, scourge.
Ant. praise, laud; forgive.
pupil, *n.* disciple, scholar, student, learner, tyro, greenhorn, neophyte, novice, beginner.
Ant. teacher, expert.
purblind, *adj.* blind, sightless, dim-sighted, myopic, short-sighted, near-sighted.
Ant. sighted, clear-sighted, presbyopic.
purchase, *v.* **1.** buy, acquire, get, obtain, procure. **2.** haul, draw, raise. —*n.* **3.** buying, acquisition. **4.** bargain. **5.** tackle, lever, winch, capstan.
Ant. sell, lose; lower; sale.
pure, *adj.* **1.** unmixed, unadulterated, uncontaminated, unalloyed, clean, unsullied, untainted, unstained, undefiled, spotless, untarnished, immaculate, unpolluted, uncorrupted. **2.** unmodified, simple, homogeneous, genuine, faultless, perfect. **3.** thoroughbred, purebred, pedigreed. **4.** utter, sheer, unqualified, absolute. **5.** innocent, chaste, undefiled, unsullied, modest, virtuous. **6.** guiltless, innocent, true, guileless, honest, upright.
Ant. impure.
purge, *v.* purify, cleanse, clear, clean, clarify.
Ant. pollute.

purport, *v.* **1.** profess, claim, mean, intend, signify. **2.** express, imply. **—***n.* **3.** tenor, import, meaning, intention, claim, design, significance, signification, implication, drift, suggestion, gist, spirit.
Ant. understand, see; infer; insignificance, meaninglessness.

purpose, *n.* **1.** object, intent, intention, determination, aim, end, design, view. **2.** result, effect, advantage, consequence. **—***v.* **3.** propose, design, intend, mean, contemplate, plan.
Ant. purposelessness.

push, *v.* **1.** shove, shoulder, thrust, drive, move, slide. **2.** press, urge, persuade, drive, impel. **—***n.* attack, effort, onset.

put, *v.* **1.** place, lay, set, deposit. **2.** set, levy, impose, inflict. **3.** render, translate. **4.** express, state, utter.

puzzle, *n.* **1.** riddle, enigma, problem, poser, maze, question. **—***v.* **2.** bewilder, perplex, confound, mystify, confuse.

pygmy, *n.* dwarf, midget, Lilliputian, runt.
Ant. giant, colossus.

Q

quaint, *adj.* **1.** strange, odd, curious, unusual, extraordinary, unique, uncommon. **2.** picturesque, charming, old-fashioned, antiquated, antique, archaic.
Ant. common, usual, ordinary; modern, new-fangled.

quake, *v.* **1.** shake, shudder, tremble, shiver, quaver, quiver. **—***n.* **2.** temblor, earthquake.

qualify, *v.* **1.** fit, suit, adapt, prepare, equip. **2.** characterize, call, name, designate, label, signify. **3.** modify, limit, mitigate, restrain, narrow, restrict. **4.** moderate, mitigate, meliorate, soften, mollify, soothe, ease, assuage, temper, reduce, diminish.

quality, *n.* **1.** characteristic, attribute, property, character, feature, trait. **2.** nature, grade, kind, sort, description, status, rank, condition. **3.** excellence, superiority, standing. **4.** accomplishment, deed, feat, attainment. **5.** distinction, class.
Ant. inferiority, baseness; failure.

qualm, *n.* uneasiness, compunction, scruple, twinge, remorse, misgiving.
Ant. ease, comfort, security.

quandary, *n.* dilemma, predicament, strait, uncertainty, doubt.
Ant. certainty, assurance.

quarrel, *n.* **1.** dispute, altercation, disagreement, argument, contention, controversy, dissension, feud, breach, break, rupture, difference, spat, tiff, fight, misunderstanding, wrangle, brawl, tumult. **—***v.* **2.** squabble, fall out, disagree with, differ, disagree, bicker, dispute, argue, wrangle, spar, brawl, clash, jar, fight.

queer, *adj.* strange, unconventional, odd, singular, curious, fantastic, uncommon, weird, peculiar, extraordinary, eccentric, freakish.
Ant. conventional, ordinary, common.

quell, *v.* **1.** suppress, stifle, extinguish, put an end to, crush, quash, subdue, overpower, overcome. **2.** vanquish, put down, defeat, conquer. **3.** quiet, allay, calm, pacify, compose, lull, hush.
Ant. encourage, foster; defend, lose; agitate, disturb, perturb.

querulous, *adj.* complaining, petulant, peevish, snappish, abrupt, waspish, testy; caviling, carping, discontented, fault-finding.
Ant. calm, equable; pleased, contented.

question, *n.* **1.** inquiry, query, interrogation. **2.** dispute, controversy. —*v.* **3.** interrogate; ask, inquire, query, examine. **4.** doubt. **5.** dispute, challenge.
Ant. answer, reply; agree, concur.

questionable, *adj.* doubtful, uncertain, dubitable, dubious, debatable, disputable, controvertible.
Ant. certain, sure, positive.

quibble, *n.* **1.** evasion, prevarication, equivocation, sophism, shift, subterfuge, cavil. —*v.* **2.** evade, prevaricate, equivocate, cavil, shuffle, trifle.

quick, *adj.* **1.** prompt, immediate, rapid, fast, swift, speedy, instantaneous, fleet, hasty, hurried, expeditious. **2.** impatient, hasty, abrupt, curt, short, precipitate, sharp, unceremonious; testy, waspish, snappish, irritable, peppery, irascible, petulant, touchy. **3.** lively, keen, acute, sensitive, alert, sharp, shrewd, intelligent, discerning. **4.** vigorous, energetic, active, nimble, animated, agile, lively, alert, brisk.
Ant. slow; patient, deliberate; calm; dull, stupid; lethargic, lazy.

quiet, *n.* **1.** tranquillity, rest, repose, calm, stillness, quietude, serenity, peace, calmness, silence. **2.** peace. —*adj.* **3.** peaceable, peaceful, pacific, calm, tranquil, serene, silent. **4.** motionless, still, unmoving, unmoved. **5.** inconspicuous, subdued; repressed, restrained, unobtrusive. —*v.* **6.** still, hush, silence. **7.** tranquilize, pacify, calm, compose, lull, soothe.
Ant. disturbance, perturbation; war; warlike, noisy, clamorous; conspicuous, obvious, blatant; disturb, perturb.

quit, *v.* **1.** stop, cease, discontinue, desist. **2.** depart from, leave, go, withdraw *or* retire from. **3.** give up, let go, relinquish, release, resign, surrender. —*adj.* **4.** released, free, clear, liberated, rid, absolved, acquitted, discharged.
Ant. start; initiate, originate; continue; arrive, enter; chained, confined.

quiver, *v.* **1.** shake, tremble, vibrate, quake, shudder, shiver. —*n.* **2.** tremble, tremor, shudder, shiver, trembling, shake. **3.** arrow-case.

quixotic, *adj.* visionary, impracticable, romantic, imaginary, wild.
Ant. realistic, practicable, practical.

R

race, *n.* **1.** competition, contest. **2.** course, stream. **3.** nation, people, clan, family, tribe, generation, stock, line, lineage, breed, kin, kindred, progeny, descendants, offspring, children. **4.** man, mankind. —*v.* **5.** run, speed, hurry, hasten, hie.
rack, *n.* **1.** frame, framework, crib. **2.** torment, anguish, torture, pain, agony. —*v.* **3.** torture, distress, torment, agonize, excruciate. **4.** strain, force, wrest, stretch.
racket, *n.* **1.** din, uproar, noise, clamor, fuss, tumult, hubbub, outcry, disturbance. **2.** excitement, gaiety, dissipation.
Ant. quiet, tranquillity, peace.
racy, *adj.* **1.** vigorous, lively, animated, spirited. **2.** sprightly, piquant, pungent, strong, flavorful. **3.** suggestive, risqué.
Ant. dispirited, dejected; mild, bland.
radiant, *adj.* shining, bright, brilliant, beaming, effulgent, resplendent, sparkling, splendid, glittering.
Ant. dull.
radical, *adj.* **1.** fundamental, basic, original, constitutional, essential, innate, ingrained. **2.** thoroughgoing, extreme, complete, unqualified, thorough, fanatical, excessive, immoderate, extravagant, violent. —*n.* **3.** extremist.
Ant. superfluous; incomplete, moderate.
radioactive, *adj.* hot, dirty.
Ant. clean.
rage, *n.* **1.** anger, ire, fury, frenzy, passion, vehemence, wrath, madness, raving. **2.** fury, violence, turbulence, tumultuousness, storm. **3.** ardor, fervor, enthusiasm, eagerness, desire, vehemence. **4.** mode, fashion, fad, craze, vogue. —*v.* **5.** rave, fume, storm, chafe, fret.
Ant. calm, equanimity.
ragged, *adj.* **1.** tattered, torn, shredded, rent. **2.** shabby, poor, mean.
Ant. neat, whole.
raid, *n.* **1.** onset, attack, seizure. **2.** invasion, inroad, incursion.
Ant. defense.
raise, *v.* **1.** lift, lift up, elevate, heave, hoist, loft. **2.** rouse, arouse, awake, awaken, call forth, evoke, stir up, excite. **3.** build, erect, construct, rear, set up. **4.** cause, promote, cultivate, grow, propagate. **5.** originate, engender, give rise to, bring up *or* about,

produce, effect, cause. **6.** invigorate, animate, inspirit, heighten, intensify. **7.** advance, elevate, promote, exalt. **8.** gather, collect, assemble, bring together. **9.** increase, intensify, heighten, aggravate, amplify, augment, enhance, enlarge. —*n.* **10.** increase, rise.

Ant. lower; pacify; destroy, raze; kill; weaken, dispirit; debase, dishonor; scatter, disperse, broadcast; decrease.

ramble, *v.* **1.** stroll, amble, walk, wander, saunter, stray, roam, rove, range, straggle. —*n.* **2.** walk, stroll, amble, excursion, tour.

rambling, *adj.* wandering, aimless, irregular, straggling, straying, discursive.

Ant. direct, pointed.

rampart, *n.* fortification, breastwork, bulwark, barricade, stronghold, security, guard, defense.

ramshackle, *adj.* shaky, rickety, flimsy, dilapidated.

Ant. luxurious, sumptuous.

rancor, *n.* resentment, bitterness, ill will, hatred, malice, spite, venom, malevolence, animosity, enmity.

Ant. amiability, good will, benevolence.

random, *adj.* haphazard, chance, fortuitous, casual, stray, aimless.

Ant. specific, particular.

range, *n.* **1.** extent, limits, scope, sweep, latitude, reach, compass. **2.** rank, class, order, kind, sort. **3.** row, line, series, tier, file. **4.** area, trace, region. —*v.* **5.** align, rank, classify, class, order, arrange, array, dispose. **6.** vary, course. **7.** extend, stretch out, run, go, lie. **8.** roam, rove, wander, stroll, straggle. **9.** extend, be found, occupy, lie, run.

rank, *n.* **1.** position, standing, station, order, class, level, division. **2.** row, line, tier, series, range. **3.** distinction, eminence, dignity. **4.** membership, body, rank and file. **5.** order, arrangement, array, alignment. —*v.* **6.** arrange, line up, align, array, range. **7.** classify, dispose, sort, class, arrange. —*adj.* **8.** tall, vigorous, luxuriant, abundant, over-abundant, exuberant. **9.** strong, gamy, pungent, offensive, noxious, fetid, rancid, putrid. **10.** utter, absolute, complete, entire, sheer, gross, extravagant, excessive. **11.** offensive, disgusting, repulsive, repellent, miasmatic, mephitic. **12.** coarse, indecent, foul, gross.

ransom, *n.* **1.** redemption, deliverance, liberation, release. —*v.* **2.** redeem, release, restore, deliver, deliver up.

rapacious, *adj.* greedy, predatory, extortionate, ravenous, voracious, avaricious, grasping; predacious, raptorial, preying.

Ant. generous, yielding; parasitic.

rapid, *adj.* speedy, fast, quick, swift, fleet.

Ant. slow.

rapidity, *n.* swiftness, speed, fleetness, quickness, haste, velocity, alacrity, celerity.

Ant. sloth, lethargy.

rapture, *n.* ecstasy, joy, delight, transport, bliss, beatitude, exultation.
Ant. misery, disgust, revulsion.

rare, *adj.* **1.** scarce, uncommon, exceptional, unusual, sparse, infrequent, extraordinary, singular. **2.** excellent, admirable, fine, choice, exquisite, incomparable, inimitable. **3.** underdone.
Ant. common, usual, frequent, ordinary; base, inferior; medium, well done.

rascal, *n.* **1.** rapscallion, knave, rogue, scamp, villain, scoundrel, miscreant, scapegrace. —*adj.* **2.** knavish, roguish, miscreant, dishonest, base, paltry, mean, low, rascally.

rash, *adj.* **1.** hasty, impetuous, reckless, headlong, precipitate, impulsive, thoughtless, heedless, indiscreet, incautious, unwary, foolhardy, audacious. —*n.* **2.** eruption, efflorescence, eczema, dermatitis, breaking out, exanthema.
Ant. thoughtful, considered, discreet, cautious.

ratify, *v.* confirm, corroborate, consent to, agree to, approve, sanction, substantiate, validate, establish.
Ant. refute, veto, disapprove.

ration, *n.* **1.** allowance, portion, food. —*v.* **2.** apportion, distribute, mete, dole, deal, parcel out. **3.** put on rations, restrict to rations.

rational, *adj.* **1.** reasonable, sensible. **2.** intelligent, wise; judicious, discreet, sagacious, enlightened. **3.** sane, lucid, sound, sober.
Ant. irrational, unreasonable; unintelligent, stupid, unwise, indiscreet; unsound, dim.

ravage, *n.* **1.** devastation, destruction, ruin, waste, desolation, damage, havoc, despoilment, plunder, pillage. —*v.* **2.** damage, mar, ruin, devastate, destroy, lay waste, despoil, plunder, pillage, sack.
Ant. construction, creation; build; repair.

ravening, *adj.* ravenous.

ravenous, *adj.* ravening, voracious, greedy, starved, hungry, famished, insatiable, gluttonous, devouring; rapacious, raptorial, predacious, predatory.
Ant. sated, satisfied.

raw, *adj.* **1.** unprepared, unfinished, unrefined, unmade, crude, rude, rough, makeshift. **2.** uncooked. **3.** ignorant, inexperienced, untrained, undisciplined, green, unskilled, untried, unpracticed. **4.** frank, candid, bold, exposed. **5.** damp, chilly, cold, wet, windy.
Ant. prepared, finished, refined, done, polished; cooked, done; intelligent, disciplined, skilled; secretive; dry, warm, arid.

reach, *v.* **1.** get to, attain, arrive at, come to. **2.** touch, seize. **3.** stretch, extend. —*n.* **4.** extent, distance, range, compass, area, sphere, influence, stretch, scope, grasp.
Ant. fail.

reactionary, *n., adj.* conservative.
Ant. radical.

readily, *adv.* promptly, quickly, easily; willingly, cheerfully.
Ant. slowly, lethargically; reluctantly.

ready, *adj.* **1.** prepared, set, fitted, fit. **2.** equipped, geared, completed, adjusted, arranged. **3.** willing, agreeable, cheerful, disposed, inclined. **4.** prompt, quick, alert, acute, sharp, keen, adroit, facile, clever, skillful, nimble. —*v.* **5.** make ready, prepare.
Ant. unprepared, unfit; unwilling, indisposed, disinclined; slow, deliberate, unskillful.

real, *adj.* true, actual, faithful, factual, authentic, genuine; sincere, unfeigned.
Ant. false, fake, counterfeit, fraudulent; insincere.

realize, *v.* **1.** grasp, understand, comprehend, conceive. **2.** imagine. **3.** accomplish, effect, effectuate, perform.
Ant. misunderstand; begin.

realm, *n.* **1.** kingdom. **2.** sovereignty, sphere, domain, province, department.

rear, *n.* **1.** back, background. —*v.* **2.** bring up, nurture, raise, nurse. **3.** raise, elevate, lift, loft, lift up, hold up. **4.** build, put up, erect, construct. **5.** rise; buck.
Ant. front; face.

reason, *n.* **1.** ground, cause, motive, purpose, end, design, *raison d'être*, objective, aim, object. **2.** justification, explanation, excuse, rationale, ratiocination, rationalization. **3.** judgment, common sense, understanding, intellect, intelligence, mind. **4.** sanity. —*v.* **5.** argue, ratiocinate, justify; rationalize. **6.** conclude, infer. **7.** bring, persuade, convince, influence.

reasonable, *adj.* **1.** rational, logical, sensible, intelligent, wise, judicious, right, fair, equitable. **2.** moderate, tolerable. **3.** sane, rational, sober, sound.
Ant. unreasonable, illogical, irrational; immoderate, intolerable; unsound, insane.

reassure, *v.* encourage, hearten, embolden, bolster, comfort, inspirit.
Ant. disconcert, unnerve, dishearten, discourage.

rebel, *n.* **1.** insurgent, insurrectionist, mutineer, traitor. —*adj.* **2.** insurgent, mutinous, rebellious, insubordinate. —*v.* **3.** revolt.
Ant. patriot; loyal, obedient.

rebellion, *n.* resistance, defiance, insurrection, mutiny, sedition, revolution, revolt; insubordination, disobedience, contumacy.

rebellious, *adj.* defiant, insubordinate, mutious, rebel, seditious, insurgent, refractory, disobedient, contumacious.
Ant. subordinate, obedient, patriotic.

rebuke, *v.* **1.** reprove, reprimand, censure, upbraid, chide, reproach, reprehend, admonish, scold, remonstrate with. —*n.* **2.** reproof, reprimand, censure, reproach, reprehension, chiding, scolding, remonstration, expostulation.
Ant. praise.

recalcitrant, *adj.* resistant, resistive, disobedient, uncompliant, refractory, rebellious, contumacious, opposing.
Ant. obedient, compliant.

recall, *v.* **1.** recollect, remember. **2.** call back, revoke, rescind, retract, withdraw, recant, repeal, annul, countermand, nullify. —*n.* **3.** memory, recollection. **4.** revocation, retraction, repeal, withdrawal, recantation, nullification; impeachment.
Ant. forget; enforce; ratify; sanction.

recapitulate, *v.* review, summarize, repeat, reiterate.

recent, *adj.* late, modern, up-to-date, fresh, new, novel.
Ant. early, old, ancient.

reciprocal, *adj.* **1.** mutual, correlative, interchangeable. —*n.* **2.** equivalent, counterpart, complement.
Ant. unequal.

recital, *n.* account, narrative, description, relation, history, story.

recite, *v.* **1.** repeat, relate, narrate, recount, describe. **2.** enumerate, count, number, detail, recapitulate.

reckless, *adj.* careless, rash, heedless, incautious, negligent, thoughtless, imprudent, improvident, remiss, inattentive, indifferent, regardless, unconcerned.
Ant. careful, heedful, cautious, thoughtful, provident.

reckon, *v.* **1.** count, compute, calculate, enumerate. **2.** esteem, consider, regard, account, deem, estimate, judge, evaluate.

reclaim, *v.* recover, bring *or* get back, regain, restore.

recoil, *v.* **1.** draw *or* shrink back, falter, flinch, quail. **2.** rebound, spring *or* fly back, react, reverberate.
Ant. advance.

recollect, *v.* recall, remember.
Ant. forget.

recommend, *v.* **1.** commend, approve, condone. **2.** advise, counsel.
Ant. condemn, disapprove.

recompense, *v.* **1.** repay, remunerate, reward, requite, compensate for. —*n.* **2.** compensation, payment, reward, requital, remuneration, repayment, amends, indemnification, satisfaction, retribution.

reconcile, *v.* **1.** content, win over, convince, persuade. **2.** pacify, conciliate, placate, propitiate, appease. **3.** compose settle, adjust, make up, harmonize, make compatible *or* consistent.
Ant. dissuade; anger, arouse, disturb.

recondite, *adj.* **1.** abstruse, profound, deep. **2.** obscure, dim, mysterious, hidden, occult, dark, secret, concealed.
Ant. clear, obvious, patent.

record, *v.* **1.** set down, enter, register, enroll. —*n.* **2.** account, chronicle, history, note, register, memorandum.

recount, *v.* relate, narrate, tell, recite, describe, enumerate.

recover, *v.* **1.** regain, get again, reclaim, retrieve, restore. **2.** heal, mend, recuperate, rally.

recreant, *adj.* **1.** cowardly, craven, dastardly, base, pusillanimous, faint-hearted, yellow. **2.** unfaithful, disloyal, false, faithless, untrue, treacherous, apostate. —*n.* **3.** coward, craven, dastard. **4.** apostate, traitor, renegade.
Ant. bold, brave; faithful, loyal, true; hero; patriot.

rectify, *v.* **1.** set right, correct, remedy, mend, emend, amend, improve, better, ameliorate. **2.** adjust, regulate, put right, straighten.
Ant. worsen, ruin.

redeem, *v.* **1.** buy *or* pay off, ransom, recover, buy back, repurchase. **2.** ransom, free, liberate, rescue, save. **3.** discharge, fulfill, perform.

redress, *n.* **1.** reparation, restitution, amends, indemnification, compensation, satisfaction, indemnity, restoration, remedy, relief, atonement, *Wiedergutmachung.* —*v.* **2.** remedy, repair, correct, amend, mend, emend, right, rectify, adjust, relieve, ease.
Ant. blame, punishment; damage.

reduce, *v.* **1.** diminish, decrease, shorten, abridge, curtail, retrench, abate, lessen, attenuate, contract. **2.** subdue, suppress, subject, subjugate, conquer, vanquish, overcome, overpower, overthrow, depose. **3.** debase, depress, lower, degrade. **4.** control, adjust, correct.
Ant. increase; defend; honor, exalt, elevate.

refer, *v.* **1.** direct, commit, deliver, consign. **2.** assign, attribute, ascribe, impute. **3.** relate, apply, obtain, pertain, belong, respect. **4.** advert, allude, hint at.

referee, *n.* **1.** arbitrator, umpire, judge, arbiter. —*v.* **2.** judge, arbitrate, umpire.

reference, *n.* **1.** direction, allusion, referral, mention, citation. **2.** witness. **3.** testimonial, endorsement. **4.** relation, regard, respect, concern.

refined, *adj.* **1.** cultivated, polished, genteel, elegant, polite, courteous, courtly, civilized, well-bred. **2.** purified, clarified, distilled, strained. **3.** subtle. **4.** minute, precise, exact, exquisite.
Ant. unrefined, inelegant, impolite, discourteous; polluted, contaminated; obvious, direct, candid; general, inexact.

reflect, *v.* **1.** mirror, cast *or* throw back, rebound. **2.** reproduce, show, manifest, espouse. **3.** meditate, think, ponder, ruminate, cogitate, muse, deliberate, study, contemplate, consider.

reflection, *n.* **1.** image, representation, counterpart. **2.** consideration, deliberation, cogitation, rumination, meditation, study, contemplation, thinking, musing. **3.** imputation, aspersion, reproach, censure.
Ant. original; thoughtlessness; praise.

reflective, *adj.* pensive, meditative, contemplative, thoughtful, pondering, deliberating, reflecting, reasoning, cogitating.
Ant. thoughtless, inconsiderate, unthinking.

reform, *n.* **1.** improvement, amendment, correction, reformation, betterment, amelioration. —*v.* **2.** better,

rectify, correct, amend, emend, ameliorate, mend, improve, repair, restore.
Ant. deterioration; worsen, deteriorate.

reformation, *n.* improvement, betterment, correction, reform, amendment.

refractory, *adj.* stubborn, unmanageable, obstinate, perverse, mulish, headstrong, pigheaded, contumacious, intractable, disobedient, recalcitrant, cantankerous, ungovernable, unruly.
Ant. obedient, tractable.

refrain, *v.* **1.** restrain, cease, abstain, desist, curb oneself, hold oneself back, withhold. —*n.* **2.** chorus, verse, theme, burden.
Ant. continue, persist.

refresh, *v.* **1.** reinvigorate, revive, stimulate, freshen, cheer, enliven, reanimate. **2.** restore, repair, renovate, renew, retouch.
Ant. dispirit, discourage.

refuge, *n.* **1.** shelter, protection, security, safety. **2.** asylum, retreat, sanctuary, hiding-place, haven, harbor, stonghold, cloister.

refurbish, *v.* renovate, refurnish, redecorate, brighten.

refuse, *v.* **1.** decline, reject, spurn, turn down, deny, rebuff, repudiate. —*n.* **2.** rubbish, trash, waste, garbage; slag, lees, dregs, scum, sediment, marc, scoria, dross.
Ant. allow, permit, sanction, approve.

refute, *v.* disprove, rebut, confute.
Ant. agree, concur.

regain, *v.* recover, recapture, repossess, retrieve, get back.
Ant. lose, miss.

regal, *adj.* royal, kingly; stately, princely, splendid.
Ant. servile.

regard, *v.* **1.** look upon, think of, consider, esteem, account, judge, deem, hold, suppose, estimate. **2.** respect, esteem, honor, revere, reverence, value. **3.** look at, observe, notice, note, see, remark, mark. **4.** relate to, concern, refer to, respect. —*n.* **5.** reference, relation. **6.** point, particular, detail, matter, consideration. **7.** thought, concern, attention. **8.** look, gaze, view. **9.** respect, deference, concern, esteem, estimation, consideration, reverence. **10.** liking, affection, interest, love.
Ant. disregard; disrespect, dishonor; inattention; dislike.

regardless, *adj.* inattentive, negligent, neglectful, indifferent, heedless, disregarding, ignoring, unmindful, unconcerned.
Ant. attentive, mindful.

region, *n.* part, area, division, district, section, portion, quarter, territory, locale, site, sphere, vicinity, vicinage, space, tract.

register, *n.* **1.** record, catalogue, account book, ledger, archive. **2.** roll, roster, catalogue, list, record, chronicle, schedule, annals. **3.** registry, entry, registration, enrollment. —*v.* **4.** enrol, list, record, catalogue, chronicle, enter. **5.** demonstrate, show, evince.

regret, *v.* **1.** deplore, lament, feel sorry about, grieve at, bemoan, bewail, rue, mourn for, repent. —*n.* **2.** sorrow, lamentation, grief. **3.** remorse, penitence, contrition, repentance, compunction.
Ant. rejoice; joy; unregeneracy.

regular, *adj.* **1.** usual, normal, customary. **2.** conforming, symmetrical, uniform, even, systematic, formal, fixed, orderly, invariant, unvarying, methodical, constant. **3.** recurrent, periodic, habitual, established, fixed. **4.** (*colloquial*) out-and-out, thorough, complete, unregenerate, perfect.
Ant. irregular.

regulate, *v.* control, direct, manage, rule, order, adjust, arrange, set, systematize, dispose, conduct, guide.

regulation, *n.* **1.** rule, order, direction, law, precept. **2.** direction, control, management, arrangement, ordering, disposition, disposal, adjustment.
Ant. misdirection, mismanagement.

rehearse, *v.* **1.** recite, act, practice, drill, train, repeat. **2.** relate, enumerate, recount, delineate, describe, portray, narrate, recapitulate.
Ant. extemporize.

reign, *n.* **1.** rule, sway, dominion, sovereignty, suzerainty, power, influence. —*v.* **2.** rule, govern, prevail, predominate, hold sway, influence.
Ant. obey.

reiterate, *v.* repeat.

reject, *v.* **1.** refuse, repudiate, decline, deny, rebuff, repel, renounce. **2.** discard, throw away, exclude, eliminate; jettison. —*n.* **3.** second.
Ant. accept.

rejoinder, *n.* answer, reply, riposte, response, replication, surrejoinder.

relate, *v.* **1.** tell, recite, narrate, recount, rehearse, report, describe, delineate, detail, repeat. **2.** associate, connect, ally.
Ant. dissociate, disconnect, separate, alienate.

relation, *n.* **1.** connection, relationship, association, alliance, dependence. **2.** reference, regard, respect. **3.** narration, recitation, recital, description, rehearsal, relating, telling. **4.** narrative, account, recital, report, story, chronicle, tale, history.
Ant. independence.

relationship, *n.* **1.** relation, connection, association. **2.** kinship, affinity, family tie, consanguinity.
Ant. dissociation.

relax, *v.* **1.** loosen, slacken. **2.** diminish, mitigate, weaken, lessen, reduce, remit, abate, debilitate, enfeeble, enervate. **3.** ease, unbend, relent, soften.
Ant. tighten; intensify, increase; harden.

release, *v.* **1.** free, liberate, set free, loose, unloose, unfasten, set at liberty, discharge, deliver, dismiss.

2. disengage, loose, extricate. **3.** proclaim, publish, announce. —*n.* **4.** liberation, deliverance, emancipation, discharge, freedom.
Ant. fasten, fetter, imprison; engage, involve; hide, conceal; incarceration, imprisonment.

relentless, *adj.* unrelenting, inflexible, rigid, stern, severe, unbending, unforgiving, unappeasable, implacable, merciless, ruthless, unmerciful, pitiless, unpitying, hard, obdurate, adamant, unyielding, remorseless, inexorable.
Ant. relenting, flexible, soft, pliant, merciful, remorseful.

relevant, *adj.* pertinent, applicable, germane, apposite, appropriate, suitable, fitting, apt, proper, suited.
Ant. irrelevant.

reliable, *adj.* trustworthy, trusty, dependable, infallible, unfailing.
Ant. unreliable, untrustworthy, undependable.

relief, *n.* **1.** deliverance, alleviation, ease, assuagement, mitigation, comfort. **2.** help, assistance, aid, succor, redress, remedy. **3.** release, replacement.
Ant. intensity, intensification.

relieve, *v.* **1.** ease, alleviate, assuage, mitigate, allay, lighten, comfort, soothe, lessen, abate, diminish. **2.** unburden, disburden, ease. **3.** aid, help, assist, succor, remedy, support, sustain.
Ant. intensify, increase; burden.

religious, *adj.* **1.** pious, holy, devout, faithful, reverent, godly. **2.** conscientious, scrupulous, exacting, punctilious, strict, rigid, demanding. —*n.* **3.** monk, friar, nun.
Ant. irreligious, impious, unfaithful, irreverent; flexible, lenient.

relinquish, *v.* renounce, surrender, give up, resign, yield, cede, waive, forswear, forgo, abdicate, leave, forsake, desert, renounce, quit, abandon, let go, resign.
Ant. demand, require.

relish, *n.* **1.** liking, taste, enjoyment, appreciation, gusto, zest, inclination, bent, partiality, predilection, preference. **2.** condiment, appetizer. **3.** taste, flavor, savor. —*v.* **4.** like, enjoy, appreciate, prefer.
Ant. distaste, disfavor.

reluctant, *adj.* unwilling, disinclined, hesitant, loath, averse, indisposed.
Ant. willing, agreeable, amenable, unhesitating.

remain, *v.* **1.** continue, stay, last, abide, endure. **2.** wait, tarry, delay, stay, rest. —*n.* (*plural*) **3.** remnant, scrap, remainder, refuse, leavings, crumbs, orts, residue, relics. **4.** corpse, dead body, cadaver.
Ant. leave, depart.

remainder, *n.* residuum, remnant, excess, residue, rest, balance, surplus.
Ant. insufficiency, inadequacy.

remark, *v.* **1.** say, observe, note, perceive, heed, regard, notice. **2.** comment, say, state. —*n.* **3.** notice,

regard, observation, heed, attention, consideration. **4.** comment, utterance, note, observation, declaration, assertion, asseveration, statement.
Ant. disregard, ignore; inattention.

remarkable, *adj.* notable, conspicuous, unusual, extraordinary, noteworthy, striking, wonderful, uncommon, strange, rare, distinguished, prominent, singular.
Ant. common, usual, ordinary.

remedy, *n.* **1.** cure, relief, medicine, treatment, restorative, specific, medicament, medication, ointment, nard, balm. **2.** antidote, corrective, antitoxin, counteractive. **—***v.* **3.** cure, heal, put *or* set right, restore, recondition, repair, redress. **4.** counteract, remove, correct, right.
Ant. disease, illness, sickness; sicken, worsen.

remember, *v.* **1.** recall, recollect. **2.** retain, memorize, keep *or* bear in mind.
Ant. forget.

remembrance, *n.* **1.** recollection, reminiscence; memory. **2.** keepsake, memento, souvenir, remembrancer, trophy, token, memorial.

remiss, *adj.* **1.** negligent, careless, thoughtless, lax, neglectful; inattentive, heedless. **2.** languid, sluggish, dilatory, slothful, slow, tardy, lax.
Ant. careful, thoughtful, attentive; energetic, quick.

remission, *n.* **1.** pardon, forgiveness, absolution, indulgence, exoneration, discharge. **2.** abatement, diminution, lessening, relaxation, moderation, mitigation. **3.** release, relinquishment. **4.** decrease, subsidence, respite, stoppage, pause, interruption, relief, hiatus, suspense, suspension, abatement.
Ant. blame, censure, conviction; increase, intensification; increase.

remissness, *n.* slackness, neglect, dilatoriness, languor, languidness.
Ant. responsibility.

remit, *v.* **1.** transmit, send, forward. **2.** pardon, release, forgive, excuse, overlook, absolve. **3.** slacken, abate, diminish, relax. **4.** return, give back, restore, replace. **5.** put off, postpone.
Ant. retain, keep, hold; condemn; increase.

remnant, *n.* **1.** remainder, remains, residue, residuum, rest. **2.** trace, vestige.

remorse, *n.* regret, compunction, penitence, contrition.
Ant. conviction, assertion, assertiveness.

remorseful, *adj.* regretful, penitent, contrite, repentant.
Ant. responsible, courageous, impenitent.

remorseless, *adj.* relentless, pitiless, uncompassionate, unrelenting, merciless, unmerciful, ruthless, cruel, savage, implacable, inexorable.
Ant. merciful, relenting.

remote, *adj.* **1.** distant, far apart, far off, removed, alien, foreign, unrelated, unconnected. **2.** slight, faint, inconsiderable. **3.** separated, abstracted.

Ant. close, near, connected, related; considerable, substantial.

remove, *v.* **1.** replace, displace, dislodge, transfer, transport, carry. **2.** take, withdraw, separate, extract, eliminate. **3.** kill, assassinate, do away with, destroy, murder.
Ant. leave.

rend, *v.* tear apart, aplit, divide, rip, rive, sunder, sever, cleave, chop, fracture, tear, dissever, crack, snap, lacerate, rupture.

render, *v.* **1.** make, cause to be, cause to become. **2.** do, perform. **3.** furnish, supply, give, contribute, afford. **4.** exhibit, show, demonstrate. **5.** present, give, assign. **6.** deliver. **7.** translate, interpret. **8.** give back, restore, return. **9.** give up, surrender, cede, yield.

renew, *v.* **1.** restore, replenish, restock. **2.** re-create, rejuvenate, regenerate, restore, reinstate, renovate, repair, mend. **3.** revive, reestablish.

renounce, *v.* **1.** give up, put aside, forsake, forgo, relinquish, abandon, forswear, leave, quit, resign, abdicate. **2.** repudiate, disown, disclaim, reject, disavow, deny, recant.
Ant. claim, accept, desire.

renovate, *v.* renew.

renown, *n.* repute, fame, celebrity, glory, distinction, note, eminence, reputation, name, honor.
Ant. disrepute, infamy.

rent, *n.* **1.** rental, return, payment. **2.** tear, split, fissure, slit, crack, crevice, cleft, rift, gap, opening, rip, rupture, breach, break, fracture, laceration. **3.** schism, separation, disunion, breach. **—*v.* 4.** lease, let, hire.

repair, *v.* **1.** restore, mend, remodel, renew, renovate, patch, amend, fix. **2.** make good, make up for, remedy, retrieve. **3.** make amends for, atone for, redress.
Ant. break, destroy, ruin.

reparation, *n.* **1.** (*usually plural*) amends, indemnification, atonement, restitution, satisfaction, compensation, *Wiedergutmachung.* **2.** restoration, repair, renewal, renovation.
Ant. destruction.

repay, *v.* pay back, return, reimburse, indemnify, refund.

repeat, *v.* **1.** reiterate, recapitulate, iterate, recite, rehearse, relate. **2.** reproduce, echo, re-echo, re-do. **—*n.* 3.** repetition, iteration.

repel, *v.* **1.** repulse, parry, ward off. **2.** resist, withstand, rebuff, oppose, confront. **3.** reject, decline, refuse, discourage.
Ant. attract; approve, accept.

repent, *v.* regret, atone.

repentance, *n.* compunction, contrition; contriteness, penitence, remorse, sorrow, regret.
Ant. impenitence.

replace, *v.* **1.** supersede, supplant, substitute, succeed. **2.** restore, return, make good, refund, repay; replenish.

reply, *v.* **1.** answer, respond, echo, rejoin. —*n.* **2.** answer, rejoinder, riposte, replication, surrejoinder, response.

represent, *v.* **1.** designate, stand for, denote, symbolize, exemplify, image, depict, express, portray, personate, delineate, figure, present. **2.** set forth, describe, state.

repress, *v.* **1.** check, suppress, keep down, subdue, put down, quell, quash, reduce, crush. **2.** check, restrain, curb, bridle, control.
Ant. foster, support, help, aid.

reprisal, *n.* **1.** retaliation, revenge, vengeance, redress. **2.** vendetta.

reproach, *v.* **1.** chide, abuse, reprimand, condemn, criticize, rebuke, scold, reprove, call to account, censure, blame, find fault with, shame, abash, discredit, reprehend, upbraid. —*n.* **2.** blame, censure, upbraiding, reproof, abuse, vilification, discredit, reprehension, rebuke, criticism, remonstrance, condemnation, expostulation, disapproval, disapprobation. **3.** disgrace, dishonor, shame, disrepute, odium, scandal, obloquy, opprobrium, ignominy, indignity, infamy, insult, scorn, offense.
Ant. praise, honor.

reproduce, *v.* **1.** copy, duplicate, repeat, imitate, represent. **2.** generate, propagate, beget.
Ant. initiate, originate.

reprove, *v.* rebuke, blame, censure, reproach, reprimand, upbraid, chide, lecture, reprehend, admonish, remonstrate *or* expostulate with.
Ant. praise; exonerate.

repudiate, *v.* **1.** reject, disclaim, disavow, disown, discard, renounce. **2.** condemn, disapprove.
Ant. accept; approve, commend.

repugnance, *n.* **1.** objection, distaste, aversion, dislike, reluctance, hatred, hostility, antipathy. **2.** contradictoriness, inconsistency, contrariety, unsuitableness, irreconcilableness, incompatibility.
Ant. attractiveness, attraction, liking, sympathy; consistency, compatibility.

repugnant, *adj.* **1.** distasteful, objectionable, offensive. **2.** opposing, objecting, protesting, averse, unfavorable, antagonistic, inimical, adverse, contrary, hostile, opposed.
Ant. attractive, tasteful; favorable, amiable.

reputation, *n.* **1.** estimation, regard, repute, standing, position, name, character. **2.** credit, esteem, honor, fame, celebrity, distinction, renown.
Ant. disrepute; dishonor, infamy.

repute, *n.* **1.** estimation, reputation. **2.** name, distinction, credit, honor. —*v.* **3.** consider, esteem, account, regard, hold, deem, reckon.
Ant. disrepute; dishonor; condemn, scorn.

request, *n.* **1.** solicitation, petition, suit, entreaty, supplication, prayer. **2.** demand. —*v.* **3.** ask for, sue, petition, entreat, beg, supplicate, solicit, beseech, require.

require, *v.* **1.** need, demand, request, order, enjoin, direct, ask. **2.** obligate, necessitate, want, need, call for.
Ant. forgo.

requirement, *n.* **1.** requisite, need, claim, requisition, prerequisite, demand. **2.** mandate, order, command, directive, injunction, ukase, charge, claim, precept.

requisite, *adj.* **1.** required, necessary, essential, indispensable, needed, needful. —*n.* **2.** necessity, requirement.
Ant. dispensable, unnecessary; luxury, superfluity.

requite, *v.* **1.** repay, remunerate, reimburse, recompense, pay, satisfy, compensate. **2.** retaliate, avenge, revenge, punish.
Ant. dissatisfy; forgive.

rescue, *v.* **1.** save, deliver, liberate, set free, release, redeem, ransom, extricate; recover, preserve. —*n.* **2.** liberation, release, redemption, ransom, recovery, deliverance.
Ant. incarceration, imprisonment.

research, *n.* **1.** inquiry, investigation, examination, scrutiny, study. —*v.* **2.** investigate, study, inquire, examine, scrutinize.

resemblance, *n.* **1.** similarity, likeness, analogy, semblance, similitude. **2.** appearance, representation, semblance, image.
Ant. dissimilarity; misrepresentation.

reserve, *v.* **1.** keep back, save, retain, husband, keep, hold, store up. **2.** set apart, set aside, bank. —*n.* **3.** reservation, qualification, exception. **4.** store, stock, supply. **5.** self-restraint, restraint, reticence, silence, taciturnity, constraint, coldness, coolness, retention.
Ant. splurge, squander, waste; prodigality; warmth, enthusiasm.

reside, *v.* **1.** dwell, abide, live, sojourn, stay, lodge, inhabit, remain. **2.** abide, lie, be present, habituate, inhere, exist.

residence, *n.* **1.** dwelling, house, home, habitation, domicile, mansion, manse. **2.** habitancy, stay, abode, sojourn, inhabitancy.

residue, *n.* remainder, rest, remains, residuum; surplus.

resign, *v.* **1.** give up, submit, yield, cede, surrender, abdicate, relinquish, forgo, abandon, forsake, quit, leave. **2.** renounce, withdraw.

resignation, *n.* **1.** abdication, abandonment, surrender, relinquishment. **2.** submission, meekness, patience, acquiescence, endurance, compliance, forbearance, sufferance.
Ant. application; boldness, recalcitrance.

resilient, *adj.* rebounding, elastic, recoiling; buoyant, cheerful.

Ant. rigid, inflexible, inelastic.

resist, *v.* **1.** withstand, strive against, oppose, impugn, confront, assail, attack, counteract, rebuff. **2.** refrain *or* abstain from.

Ant. defend; continue.

resolute, *adj.* resolved, firm, steadfast, determined, set, opinionated, purposeful, earnest, sincere, fixed, unflinching, unwavering, inflexible, hardy, unshaken, bold, undaunted, pertinacious.

Ant. weak, feeble, frail, flexible, lenient.

resolve, *v.* **1.** fix *or* settle on, determine, decide, confirm, establish. **2.** break up, disintegrate, separate, analyze, reduce. **3.** convert, transform, reduce, change. **4.** explain, explicate, solve. **5.** clear, dispel, scatter, disperse. **—*n.* 6.** resolution, determination, decision, purpose, intention.

Ant. unite, amalgamate; consolidate; indecision.

respect, *n.* **1.** particular, detail, point, regard, feature, matter. **2.** relation, reference, connection, regard. **3.** esteem, deference, regard, estimation, veneration, reverence, homage, honor, admiration, approbation, approval, affection, feeling. **4.** discrimination, bias, partiality, prejudice, preference, inclination. **—*v.* 5.** honor, revere, reverence, esteem, venerate, regard, consider, defer to, admire, adulate, adore, love. **6.** regard, heed, attend, notice, consider. **7.** regard, relate to, refer to.

Ant. disregard.

respectable, *adj.* **1.** estimable, worthy, honorable. **2.** proper, decent, honest, respected, reputable. **3.** fair, fairly good, moderate, middling, passable, tolerable. **4.** considerable, large, moderate.

Ant. unworthy, dishonorable; improper; poor, intolerable; small, insignificant.

respectful, *adj.* courteous, polite, well-mannered, well-bred, courtly, decorous, civil, deferential.

Ant. disrespectful, discourteous, impolite.

respite, *n.* **1.** relief, delay, hiatus, cessation, postponement, interval, rest, recess. **2.** stay, reprieve, suspension. **—*v.* 3.** relieve, delay, alleviate, postpone, put off, suspend.

Ant. intensity, perseverance.

response, *n.* answer, reply, rejoinder, replication.

responsible, *adj.* **1.** accountable, answerable, liable. **2.** chargeable, blamable, censurable. **3.** capable, able, reliable, solvent, trustworthy, trusty, dutiful, honest.

Ant. irresponsible; innocent; incapable, unable, unreliable.

restful, *adj.* calm, tranquil, peaceful, undisturbed, serene, pacific.

Ant. perturbed, disturbed, agitated.

restitution, *n.* reparation, redress, indemnification, restoration, recompense, amends, compensation, remuneration, requital, satisfaction, repayment, *Wiedergutmachung.*

restive, *adj.* **1.** uneasy, restless, nervous, impatient, ill at ease, recalcitrant, unquiet. **2.** refractory, disobedient, obstinate, mulish, stubborn, pigheaded.
Ant. restful, patient, quiet, serene; obedient.

restore, *v.* **1.** reestablish, replace, reinstate, renew. **2.** renew, renovate, repair, mend. **3.** return, give back. **4.** reproduce, reconstruct, rebuild.
Ant. disestablish, destroy; break, ruin; accept, receive; raze.

restrain, *v.* **1.** check, keep down, repress, curb, bridle, suppress, hold, keep, constrain. **2.** restrict, circumscribe, confine, hinder, abridge, narrow.
Ant. unbridle; broaden, widen.

restrict, *v.* confine, limit, restrain, abridge, curb, circumscribe, bound.
Ant. free, broaden, disencumber.

result, *n.* **1.** outcome, consequence, effect, conclusion, issue, event, end, termination, product, fruit. **—***v.* **2.** spring, arise, proceed, follow, flow, come, issue, ensue, rise, originate. **3.** terminate, end, resolve, eventuate.
Ant. cause.

retain, *v.* **1.** keep, hold, withhold, preserve, detain, reserve. **2.** remember, recall. **3.** hire, engage, employ.
Ant. loose, lose; forget; disengage, fire.

retaliate, *v.* avenge, requite, return, repay, revenge.
Ant. forgive, pardon.

retard, *v.* slow, delay, hinder, impede, decelerate, clog, obstruct, check.
Ant. speed, expedite, accelerate.

reticent, *adj.* taciturn, silent, reserved, quiet, uncommunicative.
Ant. voluble, communicative.

retire, *v.* withdraw, leave, depart, go away, retreat, retrograde, retrocede, fall back, recede; retract.
Ant. advance, attack.

retired, *adj.* withdrawn, secluded, sequestered, cloistered, isolated, enisled, removed, apart, solitary, abstracted.
Ant. advanced.

retort, *v.* **1.** reply, respond, return, answer, retaliate, rejoin. **—***n.* **2.** reply, response, answer, riposte, rejoinder, surrejoinder, replication; repartee.

retreat, *n.* **1.** departure, withdrawal, retirement, seclusion, privacy, solitude. **2.** shelter, refuge, asylum. **—***v.* **3.** retire, retrocede, retrograde, withdraw, leave, depart, draw back. **4.** recede, slope backward.
Ant. advance.

retribution, *n.* requital, revenge, vengeance, retaliation, repayment, reward, recompense, compensation.
Ant. forgiveness, pardon.

retrieve, *v.* **1.** recover, regain, restore. **2.** make good, repair, make amends for. **3.** rescue, save.

reveal, *v.* **1.** make known, communicate, disclose,

divulge, unveil, uncover, discover, publish, impart, tell, announce, proclaim. —*n.* **2.** revealing; revelation, disclosure.
Ant. conceal, hide, veil, cover; secretiveness.

revenge, *n.* **1.** vengeance, retaliation, requital, reprisal, retribution. **2.** vindictiveness, revengefulness, vengefulness. —*v.* **3.** avenge, retaliate, requite, vindicate.
Ant. forgiveness, pardon.

revengeful, *adj.* vindictive, spiteful, malevolent, resentful, malicious, malignant, implacable.
Ant. forgiving, benevolent.

reverence, *n.* **1.** worship, veneration, respect, homage, awe. **2.** bow, curtsy, obeisance. —*v.* **3.** venerate, revere, honor, adore, adulate.
Ant. disrespect; despise.

reverse, *adj.* **1.** opposite, contrary, converse. —*n.* **2.** opposite, contrary, converse, counterpart. **3.** back, rear, hind. **4.** check, misfortune, defeat, mishap, misadventure, affliction. —*v.* **5.** transpose, invert. **6.** alter, change. **7.** revoke, annul, repeal, veto, rescind, overthrow, countermand.
Ant. same.

review, *n.* **1.** critique, criticism, judgment, survey. **2.** rereading, study, reconsideration, reexamination. **3.** inspection, examination, investigation. —*v.* **4.** survey, inspect, criticize.

revive, *v.* **1.** reactivate, revitalize, reanimate, resuscitate, revivify, reinvigorate, reinspirit. **2.** bring back, quicken, renew, refresh, rouse. **3.** recover, recall, reawake.
Ant. kill; languish, die.

revoke, *v.* take back, withdraw, annul, cancel, reverse, rescind, repeal, retract.
Ant. advance, suggest.

revolt, *v.* **1.** rebel, mutiny, rise. **2.** disgust, repel, shock, nauseate, sicken. —*n.* **3.** insurrection, rebellion, mutiny, revolution, uprising, overthrow, sedition. **4.** aversion, disgust, loathing.
Ant. attract, delight.

revolution, *n.* **1.** overthrow, change, revolt, rebellion, mutiny. **2.** cycle, rotation, circuit, turn, round.

revolve, *v.* **1.** rotate, spin, circulate, turn, roll. **2.** orbit, circle. **3.** consider, think about, ruminate upon, ponder, reflect upon, brood over, study.

reward, *n.* **1.** recompense, prize, desert, compensation, pay, remuneration, requital, merit. **2.** bounty, premium, bonus. —*v.* **3.** recompense, requite, compensate, pay, remunerate.

ribald, *adj.* scurrilous, offensive, coarse, mocking, abusive, wanton, irreverent, loose, indecent, low, base, mean, vile, obscene, gross, filthy, dirty, vulgar.
Ant. pure, inoffensive, refined, polished, elegant.

rich, *adj.* **1.** well-to-do, wealthy, moneyed, opulent, affluent. **2.** abounding, abundant, bounteous, bountiful, fertile, plenteous, plentiful copious, ample, luxuriant, productive, fruitful, prolific. **3.** valuable,

valued, precious, costly, estimable, sumptuous. **4.** dear, expensive, high-priced, elegant. **5.** deep, strong, vivid, bright, gay. **6.** full, mellow, pear-shaped, harmonious, sweet. **7.** fragrant, aromatic.
Ant. poor, impoverished; scarce, barren, sterile; cheap; weak; dull; flat; noisome.

riddle, *n.* **1.** conundrum, puzzle, enigma, poser, question, problem. **2.** sieve, colander, strainer. —*v.* **3.** perforate, pierce, puncture.

ridicule, *n.* **1.** derision, mockery, gibes, jeers, taunts, raillery, satire, burlesque, sarcasm, sneer, banter, wit, irony. —*v.* **2.** deride, banter, rally, chaff, twit, mock, taunt, make fun of, sneer at, burlesque, satirize, rail at, lampoon, jeer *or* scoff at.
Ant. praise, honor; respect.

ridiculous, *adj.* absurd, preposterous, laughable, nonsensical, funny, ludicrous, droll, comical, farcical.
Ant. sensible.

rife, *adj.* **1.** common, prevalent, widespread, prevailing. **2.** current. **3.** abundant, plentiful, numerous, plenteous, abounding, multitudinous.
Ant. rare, unusual; scarce, scanty.

right, *adj.* **1.** just, good, equitable, fair, upright, honest, lawful. **2.** correct, proper, suitable, fit, appropriate, convenient, becoming, *de rigueur*, befitting, seemly, *comme il faut*. **3.** correct, true, accurate. **4.** sound, sane, normal. **5.** healthy. **6.** principal, front, upper, obverse. **7.** genuine, legitimate, rightful. **8.** straight, true, direct. —*n.* **9.** claim, title, due, ownership. **10.** virtue, justice, fairness, integrity, equity, equitableness, uprightness, rectitude, goodness, lawfulness. —*adv.* **11.** straight, directly. **12.** quite, completely. **13.** immediately. **14.** precisely, exactly, just, truly, actually. **15.** uprightly, righteously, rightfully, lawfully, rightly, justly, fairly, equitably. **16.** properly, fittingly, appropriately, fitly, suitably. **17.** advantageously, favorably, well.
Ant. wrong.

righteous, *adj.* moral, upright, justifiable, virtuous, good, honest, fair, right, equitable.
Ant. immoral, bad, dishonest, unfair.

rigid, *adj.* **1.** stiff, unyielding, unbending, firm, hard, inflexible. **2.** unmoving, immovable, static, stationary. **3.** inflexible, strict, severe, stern, rigorous, austere, unbending, harsh, stringent, inelastic.
Ant. flexible, soft; compliant, elastic, lenient.

rigorous, *adj.* **1.** rigid, severe, harsh, stern, austere, strict, hard, inflexible, stiff, unyielding, stringent. **2.** exact, demanding, finical, accurate. **3.** inclement, bitter, severe, sharp.
Ant. flexible, soft; inaccurate; fair, mild, bland.

rim, *n.* **1.** edge, border, lip, margin, brim, boundary, verge, skirt, confine. —*v.* **2.** edge, border, bound, margin, confine.
Ant. center, inside.

ring, *n.* **1.** circlet, loop, hoop; annulus. **2.** arena, rink, circle. **3.** competition, contest. **4.** clique, coterie, set, combination, confederacy, league; gang, mob, syndicate. —*v.* **5.** surround, encircle, circle. **6.** peal, resonate, vibrate, reverberate, resound, re-echo; tinkle, jingle, jangle. **7.** announce, proclaim, usher in *or* out, summon, call, signal.

riot, *n.* **1.** outbreak, disorder, brawl, uproar, tumult, disturbance, commotion, fray, melee, altercation. **2.** disorder, confusion. **3.** revelry, festivity. —*v.* **4.** create disorder, disturb the peace, create a disturbance, brawl, fight. **5.** carouse, revel.

rip, *v.* **1.** cut, tear, tear apart, slash, slit, rend. —*n.* **2.** rent, tear, laceration, cut.

ripe, *adj.* **1.** mature, mellow, grown, aged. **2.** ruddy, full, complete, consummate, perfect, finished. **3.** developed, ready, prepared, set.
Ant. immature; imperfect, unfinished; undeveloped, unprepared.

ripple, *v.* **1.** wave, undulate, ruffle, purl. **2.** agitate, curl, dimple. —*n.* **3.** wavelet, wave, ruffling, undulation.

rise, *v.* **1.** get up, arise, stand, stand up. **2.** revolt, rebel, oppose, resist. **3.** spring up, grow. **4.** come into existence, appear, come forth. **5.** occur, happen. **6.** originate, issue, arise, come up, be derived, proceed. **7.** move upward, ascend, mount, arise. **8.** succeed, be promoted, advance. **9.** swell, puff up, enlarge, increase. **10.** adjourn, close. —*n.* **11.** rising, ascent, mounting. **12.** advance, elevation, promotion. **13.** increase, augmentation, enlargement, swelling. **14.** source, origin, beginning.
Ant. sink; support; die; fail; decrease, deflate; open; end.

risk, *n.* **1.** hazard, chance, dangerous chance, venture, peril, jeopardy, exposure. —*v.* **2.** hazard, take a chance, endanger, imperil; jeopardize. **3.** venture upon, dare.

rite, *n.* ceremony, procedure, practice, observance, form, usage.

ritual, *n.* **1.** ceremony, rite. —*adj.* **2.** ceremonial, formal, sacramental.
Ant. unceremonious, informal.

rival, *n.* **1.** competitor, contestant, emulator, antagonist, opponent. —*adj.* **2.** competing, competitive, opposed, emulating, opposing. —*v.* **3.** compete *or* contend with, oppose. **4.** match, equal, emulate.
Ant. ally, friend; associate with.

roam, *v.* walk, go, travel, ramble, wander, peregrinate, rove, stray, stroll, range; prowl.

roar, *v.* **1.** cry, bellow, bawl, shout, yell, vociferate. **2.** laugh. **3.** resound, boom, thunder, peal.

rob, *v.* **1.** rifle, sack, steal, deprive, plunder, pillage, pilfer, pinch, shoplift. **2.** defraud, cheat, deprive, rook.

robber, *n.* thief, highwayman, footpad, second-story man, kleptomaniac, shoplifter, pilferer, brigand, bandit, marauder, freebooter, pirate, picaroon, filibuster.

robust, *adj.* **1.** sturdy, healthy, strong, hardy, vigorous, stalwart, hale, lusty, powerful, firm, sound, athletic, brawny, muscular, sinewy. **2.** rough, rude, coarse, boisterous, rambunctious, wild.
Ant. weak, feeble, unhealthy; refined, cultivated.

rogue, *n.* rascal, scamp, rapscallion, knave, mischief-maker, villain, scoundrel, scapegrace, trickster, swindler, cheat, mountebank, quack, sharper.

roll, *v.* **1.** turn, revolve, rotate, wheel, gyrate, spin, whirl, bowl. **2.** wave, undulate. **3.** sway, rock, swing, list, tilt. **4.** wrap, enfold, envelop, cover. —*n.* **5.** scroll, document. **6.** register, list, inventory, catalogue, roster. **7.** cylinder, roller, spindle.

roly-poly, *adj.* fat, plump, rotund, five-by-five, pudgy.
Ant. scrawny, gaunt, skinny.

romance, *n.* **1.** novel, *roman,* tale, story, fiction. **2.** fancy, extravagance, exaggeration; falsehood, fable, fiction, lie. **3.** love affair, amour.

romantic, *adj.* **1.** fanciful, unpractical, quixotic, extravagant, exaggerated, wild, imaginative, unrealistic, fantastic. **2.** improbable, imaginary, fantastic, chimerical, fictitious, fabulous, unreal. **3.** picturesque.
Ant. practical, realistic; probable.

rook, *n.* **1.** crow, raven. **2.** castle. **3.** sharper, cardsharp, cheat, swindler. —*v.* **4.** cheat, swindle, rob, fleece, defraud. **5.** castle.

rosy, *adj.* **1.** pink, reddish, roseate. **2.** red, rubicund, flushed, blooming, ruddy, healthy. **3.** bright, promising, cheerful, optimistic.
Ant. dark, dim, cheerless, pessimistic.

rot, *v.* **1.** decompose, decay, mold, molder, putrefy, spoil, corrupt. **2.** corrupt, degenerate. —*n.* **3.** decay, putrefaction, decomposition, corruption, mold.
Ant. purify.

rotate, *v.* turn, spin, revolve, wheel, whirl.

rotten, *adj.* **1.** decomposed, decayed, putrefied, putrescent, putrid, tainted, foul, miasmatic, noxious, ill-smelling, fetid, rank. **2.** corrupt, offensive, amoral, immoral. **3.** contemptible, disgusting, unwholesome, treacherous, dishonest, deceitful, corrupt. **4.** soft, yielding, friable; unsound, defective.
Ant. pure; moral; wholesome, honest; hard, inflexible; sound.

roué, *n.* debauchee, rake, profligate.

rough, *adj.* **1.** uneven, bumpy, irregular, rugged, jagged, scabrous, craggy. **2.** shaggy, coarse, hairy, bristly, hirsute. **3.** violent, disorderly, wild, boisterous, turbulent, riotous; sharp, severe, harsh. **4.** disturbed, stormy, agitated, tempestuous, inclement. **5.** harsh, grating, jarring, noisy, cacophonous, inharmonious, discordant, flat, raucous. **6.** uncultured, indelicate, unrefined, impolite, uncivil, unpolished, rude, inconvenient, uncomfortable, crude, coarse.

7. plain, imperfect, unpolished, uncorrected, unfinished. **8.** vague, inexact, incomplete. **9.** crude, unwrought, undressed, unpolished, unprepared, unset, uncut.
Ant. even, regular; bald, hairless, smooth; orderly; fair; harmonious; cultured, refined; finished, polished; precise, exact; dressed, polished.

round, *adj.* **1.** circular, disklike. **2.** ringshaped, hooplike, annular. **3.** curved, arched. **4.** cylindrical. **5.** spherical, globular, rotund, orbed. **6.** full, complete, entire, whole, unbroken. **7.** full, sonorous. **8.** vigorous, brisk, smart, quick. **9.** plain, honest, straightforward, candid, outspoken, frank, open, upright, fair. **10.** unmodified, positive, unqualified. —*n.* **11.** circle, ring, curve. **12.** cylinder, rung. **13.** course, cycle, revolution, period, series, succession.
Ant. angular, square, rectangular, polygonal.

rouse, *v.* **1.** stir, excite, animate, kindle, fire, inflame, stimulate, awaken, provoke. **2.** anger, provoke, incite, ire.
Ant. calm; pacify.

rove, *v.* roam, wander, range, ramble, stroll, amble, stray.

royal, *adj.* regal, majestic, kingly, imperial, princely.
Ant. servile.

rude, *adj.* **1.** discourteous, unmannerly, ill-mannered, impolite, unrefined, uncivil, coarse, curt, brusque, saucy, pert, impertinent, impudent, fresh. **2.** unlearned, untutored, uneducated, untaught, ignorant, uncultured, unrefined, untrained, uncivilized, coarse, uncouth, vulgar, boorish. **3.** rough, harsh, ungentle, coarse, rugged, crude. **4.** unwrought, raw, crude, rough, shapeless, amorphous. **5.** inartistic, inelegant, primitive, rustic, artless, simple, unadorned, unpolished, undecorated. **6.** violent, tempestuous, stormy, fierce, tumultuous, turbulent. **7.** robust, sturdy, vigorous.
Ant. courteous, mannerly; learned; gentle; artistic, elegant; calm.

rudimentary, *adj.* **1.** rudimental, elementary, fundamental, primary, initial. **2.** undeveloped, embryonic, elementary, imperfect. **3.** vestigial, abortive.
Ant. advanced; mature, perfect; complete.

ruffle, *v.* **1.** disarrange, rearrange, disorder, rumple, wrinkle, damage, derange. **2.** disturb, discompose, irritate, vex, annoy, upset, agitate, trouble, torment, plague, harry, harass, worry, molest. —*n.* **3.** disturbance, perturbation, annoyance, vexation, confusion, commotion, flurry, tumult, bustle, agitation. **4.** frill, trimming; ruff. **5.** drumbeat.
Ant. arrange, order; compose; composure, peace.

rugged, *adj.* **1.** broken, uneven, rocky, hilly, craggy, irregular. **2.** wrinkled, furrowed. **3.** rough, harsh, stern, severe, hard, stormy, austere. **4.** severe, hard, trying, difficult. **5.** tempestuous, stormy, rough. **6.**

harsh, grating, inharmonious, cacophonous, scabrous. **7.** rude, uncultivated, unrefined, unpolished, crude. **8.** homely, plain, ugly.
Ant. even, smooth, regular; easy, flexible; fair; harmonious; cultivated, refined; pretty, lovely, beautiful.

ruin, *n.* **1.** decay, dilapidation, ruination, perdition, destruction, havoc, damage, disintegration, devastation, spoliation. **2.** downfall, destruction, decay, fall, overthrow, defeat, undoing, subversion, wreck. —*v.* **3.** spoil, demolish, destroy, damage, reduce to ruin.
Ant. construction; creation; create, build.

rule, *n.* **1.** principle, regulation, standard, law, canon, ruling, guide, precept, order, ukase. **2.** control, government, dominion, command, domination, mastery, sway, authority, direction. —*v.* **3.** administer, command, govern, manage, control, handle, lead, direct, guide, conduct. **4.** decree, decide, deem, judge, settle, establish, order, demand.

ruminate, *v.* **1.** chew cud. **2.** ponder, muse, think, meditate, reflect.

rumor, *n.* story, talk, gossip, hearsay, bruit, news, report.

run, *v.* **1.** race, hasten, hurry, hie, scud, speed, scamper. **2.** flow, pour, stream; go, move, proceed. **3.** melt, fuse, liquefy. **4.** leak, overflow, flood, spread. **5.** creep, trail, climb. **6.** operate, continue. **7.** extend, stretch, reach, spread. **8.** contend, compete, challenge. **9.** pursue, hunt, chase. **10.** convey, transport, ferry, carry. **11.** pierce, stab, thrust, force, drive. **12.** operate, carry on, conduct, manage. **13.** melt, fuse, smelt, liquefy. —*n.* **14.** period, spell, interval. **15.** series, set, course, passage, motion, extent, progress. **16.** stream, rivulet, rill, runnel, brook, channel, burn. **17.** ordinary, standard, average, regular. **18.** way, track. **19.** herd, school, pack, bevy, covey, brood, flock, gaggle, pride; group, company, crowd.

rupture, *n.* **1.** breaking, bursting; breach, fracture, break, split, burst, disruption. **2.** hernia. —*v.* **3.** break, fracture, split, burst, disrupt, separate.
Ant. seam, union; unite, organize.

rural, *adj.* rustic, unsophisticated, rugged, rough; crude, boorish.
Ant. urban.

rush, *v.* **1.** dash, hasten, run. **2.** attack, overcome. —*n.* **3.** busyness, haste, hurry. **4.** straw, reeds, fiber.
Ant. sloth, lethargy.

rustic, *adj.* rural.
Ant. urban.

ruthless, *adj.* pitiless, merciless, unpitying, unmerciful, cruel, hard, harsh, severe, hard-hearted, uncompassionate, unrelenting, adamant, relentless, inexorable, fell, truculent, inhuman, ferocious, savage, barbarous.
Ant. merciful, compassionate, humane.

S

Sabbath, *n.* Lord's day, Sunday, day of rest.
sack, *n.* **1.** bag, pouch. **2.** pillaging, looting, plundering, pillage, destruction, devastation, desolation, spoliation, ruin, ruination, waste, ravage, rapine. *—v.* **3.** pillage, loot, rob, spoil, despoil, ruin, lay waste, plunder, devastate, demolish, destroy, ravage, rape.
sacred, *adj.* **1.** consecrated, holy, sainted, venerable, hallowed, divine, worshipful. **2.** dedicated, consecrated, revered. **3.** secure, protected, sacrosanct, immune, inviolate, inviolable.
Ant. blasphemous.
sad, *adj.* **1.** sorrowful, mournful, unhappy, despondent, disconsolate, depressed, dejected, melancholy, discouraged, gloomy, downcast, downhearted. **2.** somber, dark, dull. **3.** grievous, deplorable, disastrous, dire, calamitous.
Ant. happy.
safe, *adj.* **1.** secure, protected, sound, guarded. **2.** dependable, trustworthy, sure, reliable. **3.** cautious, wary, careful. *—n.* **4.** repository, strongbox, coffer, chest, safe deposit box.
Ant. unsafe.
saga, *n.* edda, epic, tale, tradition, legend, history.
sagacious, *adj.* wise, sage, shrewd, discerning, clever, intelligent, judicious, rational, acute, sharp, keen, perspicacious, sharp-witted.
Ant. unwise, irrational.
sage, *n.* **1.** wise man, philosopher. *—adj.* **2.** prudent, sagacious.
Ant. dolt; imprudent.
sailor, *n.* mariner, salt, tar, seaman, seafarer, seafaring man.
Ant. landlubber.
sake, *n.* **1.** cause, account, interest, score, regard, consideration, respect, reason. **2.** purpose, end, reason.
salacious, *adj.* lusty, lecherous, rakish, lewd, carnal, wanton, lascivious, libidinous, concupiscent; obscene, pornographic, prurient.
Ant. modest, prudish.
salient, *adj.* prominent, conspicuous, important, remarkable, striking.
Ant. inconspicuous; unimportant.
salutary, *adj.* healthy, health-giving, salubrious, wholesome.
Ant. unwholesome.
same, *adj.* **1.** identical; similar, like, corresponding, interchangeable, equal. **2.** agreeing; unchanging.
Ant. different; disagreeing.
sameness, *n.* identity, uniformity, monotony.
Ant. difference.

sample, *n.* specimen, example, illustration, pattern model.

sanction, *n.* **1.** authority, permission, countenance, support, ratification, solemnification, authorization. **—***v.* **2.** authorize, countenance, approve, confirm, ratify, support, allow, bind.
Ant. disapproval; disallow, disapprove.

sanctuary, *n.* church, temple, shrine, altar, sanctum, adytum.

sanguinary, *adj.* bloody, murderous, bloodthirsty, cruel, savage, fell, ruthless, truculent, pitiless, unmerciful, merciless.
Ant. merciful, kind.

sanguine, *adj.* cheerful, hopeful, confident, enthusiastic, buoyant, animated, lively, spirited.
Ant. morose, dispirited.

sanitary, *adj.* hygienic, unpolluted, clean, germfree; healthy, salutary.
Ant. polluted; unhealthy, unwholesome.

sapient, *adj.* wise, sage, sagacious.
Ant. stupid, dull, unwise.

sarcasm, *n.* irony, derision, bitterness, ridicule; taunt, gibe, jeer.

sarcastic, *adj.* cynical, biting, cutting, mordant, bitter, derisive, ironical, sardonic, satirical.

sardonic, *adj.* sarcastic, bitter, ironical, sneering, malignant, malicious.

satanic, *adj.* evil, wicked, diabolical, devilish, infernal, hellish, malicious, fiendish.
Ant. godly, angelic, benevolent.

satiate, *v.* cloy, glut, stuff, gorge, sate, surfeit; gall, disgust, weary.

satire, *n.* irony, sarcasm, ridicule, lampoon, pasquinade, burlesque, exposure, denunciation.

satirical, *adj.* cynical, sarcastic, sardonic, ironical, taunting, biting, keen, sharp, cutting, severe, mordant, mordacious, bitter, acid.

satisfaction, *n.* **1.** gratification, enjoyment, pleasure, contentment, ease, comfort. **2.** reparation, restitution, amends, expiation, atonement, compensation, indemnification, remuneration, recompense, requital, *Wiedergutmachung.* **3.** payment, discharge, repayment.
Ant. dissatisfaction, displeasure, discomfort.

satisfy, *v.* **1.** gratify, meet, appease, pacify, content, please. **2.** fulfill, fill, satiate, sate, suffice, surfeit. **3.** assure, convince, persuade.
Ant. dissatisfy, displease.

saturate, *v.* soak, impregnate, imbue, wet, ret, drench.
Ant. ted, dry.

saunter, *v.* stroll, walk, ramble, amble.

savage, *adj.* **1.** wild, rugged, uncultivated, sylvan, rough. **2.** barbarous, uncivilized, rude, unpolished, wild. **3.** fierce, ferocious, wild, untamed, feral, ravenous. **4.** enraged, furious, angry, irate, infuriated. **5.** cruel, brutal, beastly; inhuman, fell, merciless,

unmerciful, pitiless, ruthless, bloodthirsty, truculent, sanguinary.
Ant. cultivated, cultured; tame; calm; merciful.

save, *v.* **1.** rescue, salvage, preserve. **2.** safeguard, keep. **3.** set apart, reserve, lay by, economize, hoard, store up, husband. —*prep., conj.* **4.** except, but.

savor, *n.* **1.** taste, flavor, relish; odor, scent, fragrance. —*v.* **2.** flavor, season, spice.

say, *v.* **1.** utter, pronounce, speak, remark, affirm, allege. **2.** express, state, word, declare, tell, argue. **3.** recite, repeat, iterate, reiterate, rehearse. **4.** report, allege, maintain, hold.

scale, *n.* **1.** plate, lamina, flake, peel. **2.** coating, crust, incrustation. **3.** pan, dish. **4.** (*plural*) balance. **5.** steps, degrees, series, gradation, progression. —*v.* **6.** skip, play at ducks and drakes. **7.** weigh, balance. **8.** climb, ascend, mount. **9.** progress, gradate.

scandal, *n.* **1.** disgrace, damage, discredit, dishonor, offense, shame, disrepute, opprobrium, odium, ignominy. **2.** defamation, gossip, slander, character assassination, aspersion, detraction, calumny, obloquy.
Ant. honor, repute; praise, kudos.

scanty, *adj.* meager, sparse, insufficient, inadequate, deficient, thin, spare, small, paltry, poor, stinted, gaunt, lean.
Ant. abundant, adequate.

scarce, *adj.* rare, insufficient, deficient; uncommon, infrequent.
Ant. abundant, sufficient.

scarcely, *adv.* hardly, barely, not quite, scantly.
Ant. definitely, full.

scare, *v.* **1.** terrify, alarm, startle, frighten, shock, intimidate. —*n.* **2.** fright, terror, alarm, panic.

scatter, *v.* **1.** sprinkle, broadcast, strew. **2.** dispel, disperse, dissipate, separate, drive away.
Ant. gather.

scene, *n.* **1.** arena, stage, theater. **2.** view, picture, prospect, landscape. **3.** incident, episode, situation. **4.** exhibition, demonstration, spectacle, show, display.

scent, *n.* **1.** odor, aroma, fragrance, smell, savor, redolence, perfume. **2.** track, trail, spoor. —*v.* **3.** detect, perceive, smell.

schedule, *n.* **1.** roll, catalogue, table, list, inventory, register. **2.** timetable. —*v.* **3.** enter, register, list, enroll, tabulate, classify.

scheme, *n.* **1.** plan, design, program, project, system. **2.** plot, intrigue, stratagem, cabal, conspiracy, contrivance, machination. **3.** system, pattern, diagram, schema, arrangement. —*v.* **4.** plan, plot, contrive, project, devise, design.

scholar, *n.* **1.** savant, wise man, sage. **2.** student, pupil, disciple, learner.
Ant. teacher.

scholarship, *n.* learning, knowledge, erudition, wisdom.

Ant. stupidity.

scoff, *n., v.* mock, scorn, jeer, gibe, sneer, taunt, ridicule.
Ant. envy, praise, exalt.

scold, *v.* **1.** chide, reprove, reproach, rate, berate, censure, rail at, reprimand, blame, rebuke. —*n*. **2.** nag, shrew, virago, termagant, maenad, bacchante.
Ant. praise, honor.

scope, *n.* range, extent, space, opportunity, margin, room, latitude, liberty; tract, area, length.

scorch, *v.* **1.** burn, singe, char, blister, parch, shrivel. **2.** criticize, excoriate, condemn.
Ant. praise, laud.

score, *n.* **1.** record, account, reckoning. **2.** notch, scratch, stroke, line, mark. **3.** twenty. **4.** account, reason, ground, consideration, motive, purpose. —*v.* **5.** record, reckon, tabulate, count. **6.** notch, mark, scratch, cut. **7.** gain, win.

scorn, *n.* **1.** contempt, disdain, contumely. **2.** mockery, derision, scoff, sneer. —*v.* **3.** disdain, contemn, despise, detest.
Ant. affection, pleasure.

scoundrel, *n.* villain, knave, rogue, poltroon, scamp, cad, rascal, rapscallion, miscreant, trickster, sharper, cheat, mountebank, wretch.
Ant. hero, protagonist.

scourge, *n.* **1.** whip, lash, strap, thong. **2.** flogging, punishment. **3.** affliction, calamity, plague, bane, pest, nuisance. —*v.* **4.** lash, whip. **5.** punish, chastise, chasten, correct, castigate, afflict, torment.

scrap, *n.* **1.** fragment, piece, portion; morsel, crumb, bit, bite. —*adj.* **2.** fragmentary, piecemeal; waste. —*v.* **3.** break up, demolish. **4.** throw away, discard.
Ant. whole.

scream, *v.* **1.** shriek, screech, cry, screak. —*n.* **2.** outcry, cry, shriek, screech, screak.

screen, *n.* **1.** partition, shelter, cover, protection, guard, shield, defense. **2.** sieve, riddle, grating. —*v.* **3.** shelter, protect, veil, defend, shield, conceal, hide, cover, cloak, mask, shroud. **4.** sift.

scruple, *n.* **1.** hesitation, reluctance, conscience, restraint, compunction, qualm. —*v.* **2.** hesitate, waver, doubt.

scrupulous, *adj.* **1.** conscientious, reluctant, hesitant, cautious, wary, careful, circumspect. **2.** punctilious, minute, careful, exacting, exact, precise, demanding, rigorous.
Ant. unscrupulous; careless.

scrutinize, *v.* examine, investigate, dissect, study, sift.
Ant. neglect, overlook.

scrutiny, *n.* examination, investigation, dissection, study, inquiry, inspection, inquisition, search.

scurrilous, *adj.* **1.** gross, indecent, abusive, opprobrious, vituperative, reproachful, insolent, insulting, offensive, ribald. **2.** coarse, jocular, derisive, vulgar, obscene.

Ant. decent, polite; proper.

scurvy, *adj.* low, mean, base, contemptible, vile, despicable, worthless.

Ant. honorable, dignified, noble.

sear, *v.* **1.** burn, char, singe, scorch. **2.** brand, cauterize. **3.** dry up, wither. **4.** harden, callus.

search, *v.* **1.** look for, seek, explore, investigate, examine, scrutinize, inspect. **2.** probe; pierce, penetrate. —*n.* **3.** exploration, examination, investigation, inspection, scrutiny, searching, inquiry, inquisition, pursuit, quest.

seasonable, *adj.* suitable, timely, opportune, fit, convenient, appropriate.

Ant. unseasonable, unsuitable, untimely, inopportune.

seat, *n.* **1.** chair, bench, banquette, easy chair, throne, stool. **2.** bottom, base, fundament. **3.** site, situation, location, locality, locale.

secede, *v.* abdicate, withdraw, retire, separate, resign.

Ant. join.

secluded, *adj.* withdrawn, isolated, retired, sequestered, private.

Ant. public.

secret, *adj.* **1.** clandestine, hidden, concealed, covert, private, privy, unrevealed, mysterious, unknown, cabalistic, cryptic. **2.** reticent, close-mouthed, secretive. **3.** retired, secluded, private. **4.** occult, obscure, mysterious, latent, abstruse, recondite. —*n.* **5.** mystery.

Ant. open, manifest, obvious, apparent.

secrete, *v.* hide, conceal, cover, shroud, disguise.

Ant. open, manifest.

secure, *adj.* **1.** safe, protected. **2.** fixed, stable, fast, fastened. **3.** sure, certain, confident, assured. —*v.* **4.** obtain, procure, get, acquire, gain. **5.** protect, guard, safeguard. **6.** make certain, certain, ensure, assure, guarantee. **7.** make firm, fasten.

Ant. insecure; unstable; unsure; lose; unloose, loosen.

sedate, *adj.* calm, quiet, composed, sober, undisturbed, unexcited, staid, cool, collected, serene, placid, tranquil, unruffled, unperturbed, imperturbable, serious, settled, demure, grave, thoughtful, contemplative.

Ant. disturbed, perturbed, excited, nervous.

sediment, *n.* lees, dregs, grounds, precipitate.

sedition, *n.* treason, mutiny, rebellion, revolt, revolution, riot, insurrection, uprising.

Ant. allegiance, patriotism.

seduce, *v.* tempt, lead astray, corrupt, entice, beguile, inveigle, decoy, allure, lure, deceive.

Ant. repel, disgust.

seductive, *adj.* tempting, captivating, alluring, enticing, attractive, beguiling; deceptive.

Ant. repulsive, repellent, abhorrent.

see, *v.* **1.** perceive, look at, spy, espy, notice, discern, observe, distinguish, behold, regard. **2.** view, visit, watch. **3.** perceive, discern, penetrate, understand, comprehend, remark. **4.** learn, ascertain, find out, determine. **5.** experience, live through, know, feel, meet with, suffer, undergo. **6.** receive, entertain, visit with. **7.** attend, escort, accompany. **8.** consider, think, deliberate. —*n.* **9.** diocese, bishopric.

seedy, *adj.* shabby, worn, old.
Ant. neat, tidy, trim, modern, new.

seek, *v.* **1.** search for, look for. **2.** pursue, follow, solicit, go after. **3.** ask for, request, inquire after.

seem, *v.* appear, look; pretend, assume.

seemly, *adj.* fitting, becoming, suited, well-suited, suitable, appropriate, proper, befitting, meet; decent, decorous, right.
Ant. unseemly.

seep, *v.* ooze, osmose.
Ant. pour.

seethe, *v.* **1.** soak, steep, ret, saturate. **2.** boil; surge, foam, froth.

segregate, *v.* isolate, separate, set apart, dissociate.
Ant. unite, associate, blend; desegregate.

seize, *v.* **1.** grasp, grab, clutch. **2.** capture, take into custody, arrest, apprehend, catch, take.
Ant. loose.

seldom, *adv.* rarely, infrequently, not often.
Ant. often, frequently.

select, *v.* **1.** choose, prefer, pick, pick out. —*adj.* **2.** selected, chosen, preferred, choice, special, picked, valuable, excellent. **3.** careful, fastidious, exclusive, selective.

self-evident, *adj.* evident, obvious, axiomatic, self-explanatory, clear.
Ant. mysterious.

self-governed, *adj.* self-governing, autonomous, independent.
Ant. dependent.

selfish, *adj.* self-interested, self-seeking, egoistic, illiberal, parsimonious, stingy, mean.
Ant. unselfish.

self-satisfied, *adj.* self-complacent, complacent, smug, satisfied.
Ant. dissatisfied.

sell, *v.* trade, barter, vend, exchange, deal in.
Ant. buy.

semblance, *n.* **1.** appearance, aspect, form, show, exterior, mien, bearing, air. **2.** likeness, similarity, resemblance.
Ant. dissimilarity, difference.

send, *v.* **1.** transmit, dispatch, forward, convey. **2.** impel, throw, cast, hurl, toss, propel, fling, project.
Ant. receive.

sensation, *n.* **1.** sense, feeling, perception. **2.** excitement, stimulation, animation; agitation, commotion, perturbation.

sensational, *adj.* startling, thrilling, exciting, stimulating.
Ant. prosaic, dull.

sense, *n.* **1.** feeling, perception, sensation. **2.** awareness, recognition, realization, apprehension, appreciation, understanding, consciousness. **3.** perception, estimation, appreciation, discernment. **4.** meaning, signification, significance, import, interpretation, denotation, connotation. **5.** opinion, judgment, feeling, idea, notion, sentiment. —*v.* **6.** perceive, become aware of, discern, appreciate, recognize.

senseless, *adj.* **1.** insensate, unconscious, insensible, inert, knocked out, cold. **2.** unperceiving, undiscerning, unappreciative, unfeeling, apathetic, uninterested. **3.** stupid, foolish, silly, idiotic, inane, simple, weak-minded, witless; nonsensical, meaningless, asinine.
Ant. sensitive; intelligent.

sensibility, *n.* **1.** responsiveness, alertness, awareness, susceptibility, impressibility. **2.** quickness, keenness, acuteness, sensitivity, sensitiveness. **3.** consciousness, appreciation, understanding, rapport. **4.** delicacy, sensitiveness, perceptiveness.
Ant. insensibility; dullness; boorishness.

sensible, *adj.* **1.** judicious, intelligent, sagacious, sage, wise, rational, sound, sober, reasonable. **2.** cognizant, aware, conscious, understanding, observant. **3.** appreciable, considerable. **4.** perceptible, discernible, indentifiable.
Ant. insensible, irrational, unsound; unaware; trifling.

sensitive, *adj.* **1.** impressionable, susceptible, easily affected. **2.** sensate. **3.** delicate.
Ant. insensitive; hard, obdurate, indelicate.

sensitivity, *n.* sensibility.

sensual, *adj.* **1.** voluptuous, sensuous, luxurious. **2.** lewd, unchaste, gross, licentious, lascivious, dissolute.
Ant. modest, prudish.

sensuous, *adj.* sentient, feeling, sensible.
Ant. insensible.

sententious, *adj.* **1.** pithy, concise, laconic, epigrammatic, terse, succinct, didactic. **2.** judicial, magisterial.
Ant. prosaic, prosy, long-drawn.

sentiment, *n.* **1.** attitude, disposition, opinion, feeling, judgment, thought. **2.** emotion, sentimentality, sensitiveness, sensibility, tenderness.
Ant. coolness.

sentimentality, *n.* sentiment.

separate, *v.* **1.** keep apart, divide, part, put apart, disjoin, disconnect, dissever, sever, disunite, sunder, disengage, dissociate, split, break up. **2.** withdraw, cleave. —*adj.* **3.** separated, disjoined, disunited, unattached, apart, divided, severed, detached, distinct, discrete, dissociated; apart, withdrawn, sequestered, alone, isolated. **4.** independent, individual, particular.
Ant. unite, connect; together, indistinct, conglomerate; dependent, general.

sepulcher, *n.* **1.** tomb, grave, burial vault, ossuary. —*v.* **2.** bury, entomb, inter.

Ant. cradle, womb; unearth, disinter.

sequence, *n.* **1.** following, succession, order, arrangement, series. **2.** outcome, sequel, consequence, result.

seraglio, *n.* harem.

serene, *adj.* **1.** calm, peaceful, tranquil, unruffled, undisturbed, imperturbable, unperturbed, placid, composed, sedate, staid, collected, cool. **2.** fair, clear, unclouded, bright.
Ant. active, disturbed, upset; clouded, inclement.

serenity, *n.* calmness, composure, tranquillity, peacefulness, calm, sereneness, peace.
Ant. perturbation, disturbance.

serf, *n.* slave, esne, ryot, bondman, villein, thrall.
Ant. master.

series, *n.* sequence, succession, set, line; order, arrangement.

serious, *adj.* **1.** thoughtful, grave, solemn, sober, sedate, staid, earnest. **2.** weighty, important, momentous, grave, critical.
Ant. jocular; trivial.

servant, *n.* domestic, maid-servant, servant-girl, employee, maid, menial, servitor, attendant, retainer, butler, footman.
Ant. master.

serve, *v.* **1.** wait on, attend. **2.** assist, help, aid, succor. **3.** function, answer, do, suffice. **4.** promote, contribute, forward, advance, assist. **5.** provide, cater, satisfy, purvey.

servile, *adj.* submissive, obsequious, menial, slavish, cringing, low, fawning, abject, mean, base, sycophantic, groveling.
Ant. aggressive, overbearing, dignified.

servitude, *n.* slavery, bondage, serfdom, thralldom.

set, *v.* **1.** put, place, position, pose, locate, situate, post, appoint, station, plant. **2.** value, price, rate, prize, evaluate, estimate. **3.** fix, appoint, ordain, settle, establish, determine. **4.** prescribe, assign, predetermine. **5.** adjust, arrange, order, dispose, place, regulate. **6.** frame, mount. **7.** calibrate, regulate. **8.** decline, sink, wane, go down. **9.** solidify, congeal, harden. —*n.* **10.** assortment, outfit, collection, series. **11.** group, clique, coterie, company, circle, class, sect. **12.** direction, bent, inclination, disposition, attitude. **13.** bearing, carriage, mien, posture, appearance, aspect. **14.** stage, scene, scenery, decoration, setting. —*adj.* **15.** fixed, prefixed, predetermined. **16.** prescribed, foreordained. **17.** customary, usual. **18.** fixed, rigid, immovable. **19.** resolved, determined, habitual, stubborn, fixed, obstinate, stiff, unyielding.

settle, *v.* **1.** fix, agree upon, set, establish. **2.** pay, discharge, repay, liquidate. **3.** locate in, people, colonize. **4.** quiet, tranquilize, calm, compose, still, pacify. **5.** stabilize, establish, confirm. **6.** decide, arrange, agree, adjust. **7.** calm down, rest. **8.** sink down, decline, subside, sink, fall.

sever, *v.* separate, divide, put *or* cut apart, part, cut, cleave, sunder, break off, disunite, disjoin, detach, disconnect.
Ant. unite.

severe, *adj.* **1.** harsh, extreme, trenchant, biting, acerb, bitter, caustic, satirical, keen, stinging, mordant, mordacious, sharp, cutting. **2.** serious, grave, stern, austere, rigid, rigorous, strict, strait-laced, relentless, hard, unrelenting, inexorable, abrupt, peremptory, curt, short. **3.** rigid, restrained, plain, simple, unadorned, unornamented, chaste. **4.** uncomfortable, distressing, unpleasant, acute, afflictive, violent, intense. **5.** rigid, exact, critical, demanding, accurate, methodical, systematic, exacting.
Ant. mild; gradual; flexible; comfortable; inaccurate.

shack, *n.* cottage, cot, hut, cabin, cote.
Ant. palace.

shackle, *n.* **1.** fetter, chain, anklet, handcuff, manacle, gyve, hobble. **2.** impediment, obstacle, obstruction, encumbrance. **—***v.* **3.** confine, restrain, restrict, fetter, chain, handcuff, hobble. **4.** restrict, trammel, impede, slow, stultify, dull.
Ant. liberate, free.

shade, *n.* **1.** darkness, shadow, obscurity, gloom, gloominess, dusk, umbrage. **2.** specter, ghost, apparition, spirit, phantom. **3.** variation, amount, degree, hair, trace, hint, suggestion. **4.** veil, curtain, screen. **—***v.* **5.** obscure, dim, darken, cloud, blur, obfuscate. **6.** screen, hide, protect, conceal, cover, shelter.
Ant. light.

shake, *v.* **1.** sway, vibrate, oscillate, quiver, waver, tremble, agitate, shudder, shiver, totter. **2.** brandish, flourish. **3.** agitate, disturb, move, intimidate, frighten, daunt. **4.** unsettle, weaken, enfeeble. **—***n.* **5.** tremor, blow, disturbance, shock.

sham, *n.* **1.** imitation, pretense. **—***adj.* **2.** pretended, counterfeit, false, spurious, mock. **—***v.* **3.** pretend; imitate, deceive, feign, defraud, impose.
Ant. genuine.

shame, *n.* **1.** humiliation, mortification, abashment, chagrin. **2.** disgrace, derision, ignominy, dishonor, reproach, obloquy, opprobrium, odium, infamy, contempt. **3.** scandal. **—***v.* **4.** abash, humiliate, mortify, humble, confuse, disconcert. **5.** disgrace, reproach, dishonor, scandalize, debase, tarnish, stain, taint, sully, soil.
Ant. honor.

shameful, *adj.* disgraceful, scandalous, mortifying, humiliating, dishonorable, ignominious, disreputable, outrageous, infamous, vile, base, low.
Ant. honorable.

shameless, *adj.* **1.** immodest, audacious, unblushing, brazen, indecent, impudent, bold, insolent, indelicate, unabashed, unashamed. **2.** corrupt, sinful, unprincipled, depraved, profligate, piacular, dissolute, repro-

bate, vicious, hard, hardened, stony, obdurate, adamant, incorrigible, lost.
Ant. modest, proper; principled, flexible.

shanty, *n.* cottage, shack, cot, hut, hovel, cabin, house.
Ant. castle, palace.

shape, *n.* **1.** outline, silhouette, form, figure, appearance, aspect. **2.** phantom, specter, manifestation. **3.** guise, disguise. **4.** arrangement, order, pattern. **5.** condition, situation, order. **6.** mold, cast, pattern, form. **—***v.* **7.** form, fashion, mold, model. **8.** word, express, term. **9.** adjust, adapt, regulate, frame.

share, *n.* **1.** portion, part, allotment, contribution, quota, lot, proportion. **2.** dividend, stock. **—***v.* **3.** divide, apportion, allot, portion, parcel out, deal out, dole, mete out. **4.** partake, participate.

sharp, *adj.* **1.** keen, acute, trenchant. **2.** pointed, peaked. **3.** abrupt, sudden. **4.** distinct, marked, clear. **5.** pungent, biting, acrid, spicy, burning, hot, mordacious, bitter, piquant, sour. **6.** shrill, piercing, loud, high. **7.** cold, piercing, freezing, nipping, biting. **8.** painful, distressing, intense, severe, sore, excruciating, agonizing. **9.** harsh, merciless, unmerciful, severe, acute, cutting, caustic, acid, sarcastic, sardonic, acrimonious, pointed, biting, poignant. **10.** fierce, violent, intense. **11.** keen, eager, hungry. **12.** quick, brisk. **13.** vigilant, alert, awake, on the qui vive, attentive. **14.** acute, shrewd, astute, clever, penetrating, discerning, perspicacious, ingenious, discriminating, ready, smart, cunning, intelligent, bright, quick, sensitive, alert, observant, incisive, vigorous, understanding, active, reasoning. **15.** dishonest, shady, unlawful, deceitful, cheating.
Ant. dull; blunt; unclear; mild; soft; warm; merciful.

shatter, *v.* break, crush, shiver, split, crack; explode.

sheer, *adj.* **1.** transparent, diaphanous, thin, clear. **2.** unmixed, mere, simple, pure, downright, unadulterated, unqualified, utter. **3.** steep, precipitous, abrupt, perpendicular. **—***adv.* **4.** clear, quite, completely, totally, entirely. **—***n.* **5.** chiffon, voile. **—***v.* **6.** swerve, deviate, turn aside.
Ant. opaque; gradual.

shelter, *n.* **1.** protection, refuge, retreat, asylum, cover, screen, sanctuary, shield, haven, harbor. **—***v.* **2.** protect, guard, cover, safeguard, shield, hide, shroud, house, harbor, defend.
Ant. open.

shimmer, *v., n.* glisten, shine, gleam, glimmer.

shine, *v.* **1.** beam, glare, gleam, glisten, glimmer, shimmer, sparkle, glow, radiation. **—***n.* **2.** radiance, light. **3.** polish, luster, gloss.

shining, *adj.* **1.** radiant, gleaming, bright, brilliant, resplendent, glistening, effulgent, lustrous. **2.** conspicuous, fine, outstanding, distinguished, eminent, prime, splendid, choice, excellent, select.

shipment, *n.* freight, consignment, cargo, lading.

shiver, *v., n.* tremble, quake, shudder, shake.

shock, *n.* **1.** blow, impact, collision, encounter, concussion, clash. **2.** disturbance, commotion, agitation. —*v.* **3.** startle, stagger, surprise, stun, astound, paralyze, stupefy, bewilder, dumfound. **4.** horrify, disgust, outrage, nauseate, offend, sicken, revolt. **5.** collide, strike, meet.

shore, *n.* **1.** beach, coast, bank, seashore, riverbank, margin, strand. **2.** support, prop, brace, buttress, stay, post, beam, strut.

short, *adj.* **1.** brief; low. **2.** concise, brief, terse, succinct, laconic, condensed, curt, sententious. **3.** abrupt, curt, sharp, petulant, short-tempered, testy, uncivil, rude. **4.** scanty, poor, insufficient, deficient, inadequate, wanting, lacking. **5.** substandard, inferior, unacceptable, below. **6.** friable, brittle, crumbly. **7.** brachycephalic. —*adv.* **8.** suddenly, abruptly, without notice *or* warning. **9.** briefly, curtly.
Ant. long.

shorten, *v.* **1.** curtail, abbreviate, abridge, condense, lessen, limit, restrict, reduce. **2.** take in, reduce, diminish, lessen, contract.
Ant. lengthen.

short-sighted, *adj.* **1.** myopic, near-sighted. **2.** indiscreet, unthinking, thoughtless, imprudent, inconsiderate, tactless.
Ant. presbyopic, far-sighted; discreet, thoughtful, prudent.

shout, *v.* cry out, hoot, exclaim, vociferate.
Ant. whisper.

shove, *v.* **1.** push, propel. **2.** jostle.

show, *v.* **1.** exhibit, display, demonstrate. **2.** point out, indicate. **3.** guide, accompany, lead, usher, conduct. **4.** interpret, make clear *or* known, clarify, elucidate, explain, discover, reveal, disclose, divulge, publish, proclaim. **5.** prove, demonstrate, evidence. **6.** allege, assert, asseverate; plead. **7.** accord, grant, bestow, confer. **8.** look, appear, seem. —*n.* **9.** display, ostentation, pomp, exhibition, flourish, dash, pageantry, ceremony. **10.** showing, spectacle, appearance. **11.** deception, pretense, pretext, simulation, illusion. **12.** trace, indication. **13.** sight, spectacle, exhibition.
Ant. hide, conceal.

showy, *adj.* ostentatious, gaudy, flashy, garish, loud.
Ant. humble, quiet.

shrew, *n.* termagant, virago, hussy, nag, scold, bacchante, maenad.

shrewd, *adj.* astute, sharp, acute, quick, discerning, discriminating, perceptive, perspicuous, perspicacious, keen, intelligent, penetrating, ingenious, sagacious.
Ant. dull, stupid.

shriek, *n., v.* cry, scream, screech, yell.

shrink, *v.* **1.** retreat, withdraw, avoid, recoil, flinch,

retire. **2.** contract, wither, shrivel, lessen, diminish, decrease, dwindle, wane, peter out.
Ant. advance; inflate, dilate, increase.
shrivel, *v.* wither, wrinkle, decrease, contract, shrink.
Ant. blossom.
shroud, *n.* **1.** winding-sheet. **2.** covering, garment. —*v.* **3.** cover, hide, conceal, screen, veil, obscure.
shudder, *v., n.* tremble, shiver, quiver, shake.
shun, *v.* elude, avoid, evade, eschew.
Ant. seek.
shut, *v.* **1.** close; slam. **2.** confine, enclose, jail, imprison. **3.** bar, exclude, prohibit, preclude. —*adj.* **4.** closed, fastened.
Ant. open.
shy, *adj.* **1.** bashful, diffident, retiring, timid, coy. **2.** suspicious, distrustful, wary, heedful, cautious, careful, chary, reluctant. **3.** short. —*v.* **4.** recoil, draw back, shrink. **5.** throw, toss, hurl, pitch, cast, fling.
Ant. forward; trusting; incautious, careless; advance.
sick, *adj.* **1.** ill, unwell, ailing, infirm, indisposed. **2.** (*British*) nauseous, vomiting, nauseated. **3.** pale, wan, white, sickly. **4.** impaired, unsound, out of order.
Ant. well, hale, healthy.
sickly, *adj.* **1.** unhealthy, ailing, sick, unwell, puny, weak, frail, feeble, infirm, weakly. **2.** weak, mawkish, sentimental, faint.
Ant. strong, healthy.
siege, *n.* blockade, besieging, attack.
sign, *n.* **1.** token, indication, trace, vestige, hint, suggestion. **2.** mark, symbol; abbreviation. **3.** omen, presage, portent, augury, foreboding. —*v.* **4.** signify, betoken, indicate, mean, signal. **5.** affix a signature to.
significance, *n.* **1.** importance, consequence, moment, weight. **2.** import, meaning, sense, purport. **3.** meaningfulness, expressiveness.
Ant. triviality.
significant, *adj.* **1.** important, consequential, momentous, weighty, critical, crucial, vital. **2.** meaningful, expressive, signifying, indicative *or* suggestive of.
Ant. insignificant.
signify, *v.* **1.** signal, make known, express, indicate, communicate. **2.** mean, portend, represent, denote, indicate, betoken, purport, imply.
silent, *adj.* **1.** quiet, still, noiseless, soundless. **2.** speechless, dumb, mute; close-mouthed, taciturn, tacit. **3.** inactive, dormant, quiescent.
Ant. noisy, clamorous; voluble, talkative; active, kinetic.
silly, *adj.* **1.** foolish, stupid, dull-witted, dim-witted, witless, senseless. **2.** absurd, ridiculous, inane, asinine, frivolous, nonsensical, preposterous, idiotic.
Ant. sensible.
similar, *adj.* like, resembling.

Ant. unlike, dissimilar, different.

similarity, *n.* likeness, resemblance, similitude, correspondence, parallelism.
Ant. difference.

simmer, *v.* seethe, bubble, boil.

simple, *adj.* **1.** clear, intelligible, understandable, unmistakable, lucid. **2.** plain, unadorned, natural, unaffected, unembellished, neat. **3.** unaffected, unassuming, homely, unpretentious. **4.** mere, bare, elementary, simplex, uncomplicated. **5.** sincere, innocent, artless, naive, guileless, ingenuous, unsophisticated. **6.** humble, lowly. **7.** unimportant, insignificant, trifling, trivial, nonessential, unnecessary, immaterial, inconsequential. **8.** common, ordinary, usual, customary. **9.** unlearned, ignorant, uneducated, untutored, stupid, dense, silly, foolish, credulous, shallow.
Ant. complicated, complex.

sin, *n.* **1.** transgression, trespass, violation, crime offense, wrong, wickedness. —*v.* **2.** transgress, trespass, do wrong, offend.

since, *adv.* **1.** subsequently. **2.** ago, before now —*conj.* **3.** because, inasmuch as.

sincere, *adj.* candid, honest, open, earnest, guileless artless, plain, simple; genuine, true, unaffected, real, unfeigned.
Ant. insincere.

sincerity, *n.* honesty, candor, frankness, probity, genuineness, artlessness, ingenuousness, guilelessness.
Ant. insincerity.

sinful, *adj.* wicked, iniquitous, depraved, evil, immoral, amoral, bad, mischievous, piacular.

singe, *v.* char, burn, scorch.

single, *adj.* **1.** separate, only, individual, sole, distinct, particular. **2.** alone, solitary, isolated. **3.** unmarried, unwed, spinsterish, old-maid. **4.** sincere, honest, whole-hearted, concentrated, unbiased. **5.** simple, unmixed, pure, uncompounded, unadulterated. —*v.* **6.** pick, choose, select, single out. —*n.* **7.** one, individual, singleton.
Ant. conglomerate; married, wed; insincere, biased; adulterated, mixed.

singular, *adj.* **1.** extraordinary, remarkable, unusual uncommon, rare, strange, peculiar. **2.** strange, odd bizarre, fantastic, peculiar, unusual, eccentric, queer curious, unaccountable, exceptional, unparalleled unprecedented. **3.** unique. **4.** separate, individual single.
Ant. plural; common.

sinister, *adj.* **1.** threatening, portending, portentous ominous, inauspicious, unlucky, unfavorable, unfortunate, disastrous. **2.** bad, evil, base, wicked, sinful, piacular, depraved, corrupt, perverse, dishonest, crooked.
Ant. benign, favorable, fortunate; good, honest.

sinuous, *adj.* **1.** winding, sinuate, curved, crooked, serpentine. **2.** indirect, devious, roundabout.
Ant. straight; direct.

sip, *v.* **1.** drink; absorb; extract. **2.** savor, taste. —*n.* **3.** drink. **4.** taste, savor, sapor.

siren, *n.* seductress, temptress, Circe, vampire, vamp, mermaid.

sirocco, *n.* simoom, cyclone, windstorm, dust storm.

sit, *v.* **1.** be seated, roost, perch. **2.** be situated, dwell, settle, lie, rest, remain, abide, repose, stay. **3.** meet, convene.
Ant. stand, lie.

situation, *n.* **1.** location, position, site, place, locality, locale, spot. **2.** condition, case, plight, state, circumstances, predicament. **3.** position, post, job.

size, *n.* **1.** dimensions, proportions, magnitude, extent; volume, bulk, mass. **2.** amount, extent, range. **3.** glue, glaze, coating. —*v.* **4.** sort, catalogue; dimension, measure.

skeptic, *n.* **1.** disbeliever, agnostic, atheist, doubter, cynic, infidel, heathen, nullifidian. —*adj.* **2.** skeptical, cynical.
Ant. believer, theist.

skeptical, *adj.* skeptic, doubtful, dubious, incredulous, unbelieving.
Ant. confident.

sketch, *n.* **1.** drawing, outline, draft, design, delineation. **2.** skit, play, act, routine, stint. —*v.* **3.** depict, draw, outline, design, rough out, delineate, portray, represent.

sketchy, *adj.* hasty, imperfect, slight, superficial.
Ant. careful, perfect.

skilled, *adj.* skillful.
Ant. unskilled.

skillful, *adj.* skilled, expert, ready, adroit, deft, adept, proficient, dexterous, competent, qualified, practiced, accomplished, apt, clever, ingenious, intelligent, learned, knowledgeable.
Ant. unskillful, inexpert, maladroit, unqualified.

skin, *n.* **1.** hide, pelt, fur. **2.** integument, covering, peel, rind, hull, shell, husk, crust, coating, outside, film, membrane. —*v.* **3.** flay, peel, pare, strip, husk, excoriate.

skip, *v.* **1.** spring, jump, gambol, leap, bound, caper, hop. **2.** disregard, skip over, skim over. **3.** ricochet, rebound, bounce. —*n.* **4.** leap, jump, spring, bound, caper, hop.

skirmish, *n.* encounter, battle, fight, conflict, combat, brush.

skulk, *v.* **1.** lurk, slink, sneak, hide, lie in wait. **2.** shirk, malinger.

slack, *adj.* **1.** loose, relaxed. **2.** indolent, negligent, lazy, remiss, weak. **3.** slow, sluggish, dilatory, tardy, late, lingering. **4.** dull, inactive, blunted, idle, quiet. —*n.* **5.** decrease, slowing, loosening, relaxation, indolence, negligence, laziness, remissness, weakness. —*v.*

6. shirk, neglect, skulk, malinger. 7. relax, abate, reduce, slacken, moderate, mitigate.
Ant. tight, tense, taut.

slacken, *v.* 1. deactivate, relax, slack, abate. 2. loosen, relax, relieve, abate, mitigate, remit, lessen, diminish. 3. fail, neglect, defer. 4. restrain, check, curb, bridle, repress, subdue, control.
Ant. tighten; increase.

slang, *n.* argot, jargon, patois, dialect, cant, colloquialism.

slant, *v.* 1. slope, lean, incline. —*n.* 2. incline, inclination, pitch, slope, obliquity, obliqueness. 3. bent, leaning, prejudice, bias, inclination.

slash, *v.* 1. cut, lash, slit, slice. 2. cut, reduce, alter, abridge, abbreviate. —*n.* 3. stroke, cut, wound, gash, slit.

slaughter, *n.* 1. killing, butchering. 2. massacre, carnage, homicide, murder, butchery, slaying, killing, bloodshed, genocide. —*v.* 3. butcher, massacre, murder, slay, kill, wipe out, devastate, decimate.

slave, *n.* bond servant, esne, thrall, ryot, villein, serf, drudge, vassal, bondman.
Ant. master.

slavery, *n.* 1. bondage, servitude, subjection, thralldom, captivity, enthrallment. 2. toil, drudgery, moil, labor.

slavish, *adj.* 1. submissive, abject, servile, groveling, menial, drudging. 2. base, mean, ignoble, low, obsequious, fawning, sycophantic, sneaking, cringing. 3. imitative, emulative.
Ant. independent; elevated, exalted.

slay, *v.* 1. murder, kill, slaughter, massacre, butcher, assassinate. 2. destroy, extinguish, annihilate, ruin.

sleep, *v.* 1. rest, repose, slumber, nap, drowse, doze. —*n.* 2. dormancy, inactivity, slumber, rest, repose, nap.

slender, *adj.* 1. slight, slim, thin, spare, narrow. 2. small, trivial, few, meager, trifling, insignificant, inadequate, insufficient. 3. thin, weak, fragile, feeble, fine, delicate, flimsy, frangible, breakable.
Ant. large, fat, obese, corpulent.

slide, *v.* slip, slither, glide.

slight, *adj.* 1. small, insignificant, superficial, shallow, trivial, trifling, nugatory, paltry, unimportant. 2. slender, slim. 3. frail, flimsy, weak, feeble, delicate, fragile. 4. unsubstantial, inconsiderable. —*v.* 5. ignore, disregard, neglect, disdain, overlook, scorn. —*n.* 6. neglect, disregard, disdain, indifference, scorn, contumely, contempt, inattention. 7. affront, insult, disrespect.
Ant. considerable; compliment.

slim, *adj.* 1. slender, thin, slight. 2. small, poor, insignificant, trifling, trivial, nugatory, unimportant, paltry, inconsiderable, scanty, weak, unsubstantial.
Ant. fat; important.

slip, *v.* 1. slide, slither, glide. 2. be mistaken, err, blunder, mistake. —*n.* **3.** mistake, error, blunder, fault, oversight; faux pas, indiscretion, backsliding. **4.** scion, cutting, strip.

slope, *v., n.* slant, incline.

slothful, *adj.* idle, sluggardly, indolent, lazy, sluggish, inactive, inert, torpid, slack, supine.
Ant. industrious, active, energetic.

slovenly, *adj.* untidy, careless, loose, disorderly, slipshod.
Ant. careful, tidy, neat.

slow, *adj.* **1.** deliberate, gradual, moderate, leisurely, unhurried. **2.** sluggish, sluggardly, dilatory, indolent, lazy, slothful. **3.** dull, dense, stupid. **4.** slack. **5.** dragging, late, tardy, behindhand. **6.** tedious, humdrum, dull, boring. —*v.* **7.** retard, hinder, impede, obstruct.
Ant. fast; advance.

sluggish, *adj.* inactive, slow, lazy, slothful, indolent, dull, inert, dronish, phlegmatic.
Ant. quick, active, energetic.

slumber, *v., n.* sleep.

slur, *v.* **1.** slight, disregard, pass over, ignore, overlook. **2.** calumniate, disparage, slander, depreciate, asperse. —*n.* **3.** slight, innuendo, insult, affront. **4.** blot, stain, stigma, brand, mark, disgrace.
Ant. compliment.

sly, *adj.* **1.** cunning, wily, artful, subtle, foxy, crafty. **2.** stealthy, surreptitious, furtive, insidious, secret, underhanded, clandestine. **3.** mischievous, roguish, shrewd, astute, cautious.
Ant. direct, obvious.

small, *adj.* **1.** little, tiny, diminutive. **2.** slender, thin, slight, narrow. **3.** unimportant, trivial, minor, secondary, trifling, nugatory, inconsequential, petty, paltry, insignificant. **4.** humble, modest, unpretentious. **5.** mean-spirited, mean, stingy, ungenerous, parsimonious, niggardly, selfish, tight, illiberal, narrow. **6.** ashamed, mortified, abashed. **7.** weak, feeble, faint, diluted. **8.** gentle, soft, low.
Ant. large.

smart, *v.* **1.** pain, hurt, sting. **2.** wound, insult, affront. —*adj.* **3.** sharp, keen, stinging, poignant, penetrating, painful, severe. **4.** brisk, vigorous, active, energetic, effective, lively, quick. **5.** quick, prompt, nimble, agile, alert, active. **6.** intelligent, bright, sharp, clever, expert, adroit. **7.** shrewd, cunning, adept, quick. **8.** neat, trim, dashing, spruce, pretentious, showy. **9.** elegant, chic, fashionable, voguish, à la mode.
Ant. pleasure; dull, stupid.

smash, *v.* **1.** break, shatter, crush, crash. **2.** defeat, overthrow, destroy. **3.** ruin, bankrupt. —*n.* **4.** smashing, shattering, crash. **5.** collision, destruction, ruin; collapse.

smirch, *v.* **1.** besmirch, discolor, soil, smear, smudge, smut, smutch, dirty. **2.** sully, tarnish, disgrace, taint,

blot, smear. —*n.* **3.** smear, mark, smudge, smut, smutch, dirt. **4.** stain, blot, taint.
Ant. clean; honor.

smooth, *adj.* **1.** level, even, plain, flat. **2.** bald, hairless, glossy, polished, sleek. **3.** flat, unruffled, calm, undisturbed. **4.** regular, even, easy, fluent. **5.** unruffled, undisturbed, calm, peaceful, tranquil, equable, pacific, peaceable. **6.** elegant, polished, flowing, glib, voluble, soft-spoken, suave, unctuous, oily, bland. **7.** pleasant, agreeable, polite, courtly, courteous. —*v.* **8.** plane, stroke, scrape, level, press, flatten, iron, roll. **9.** polish, refine. **10.** tranquilize, calm, soothe, assuage, mollify, better. **11.** gloss over, palliate, soften, soothe.
Ant. rough, uneven, irregular.

smug, *adj.* **1.** complacent, self-satisfied, self-complacent, satisfied, conceited, self-sufficient, self-confident, self-important, egoistic, self-opinionated, self-reliant. **2.** trim, spruce, neat, smooth, sleek.
Ant. dissatisfied.

snare, *n.* **1.** trap, noose, net, seine. —*v.* **2.** trap, entrap, entangle, catch.

snarl, *v.* **1.** growl, grumble, complain, murmur. **2.** entangle, tangle, mat, complicate, confuse, ravel, involve, knot. —*n.* **3.** growl, grumble. **4.** tangle, entanglement, complication, knot, confusion, involvement, intricacy, difficulty.

sneak, *v.* **1.** slink, lurk, skulk, steal. —*n.* **2.** sneaker, lurker.

sneer, *v.* **1.** scorn, jeer, gibe, scoff, disdain, deride, ridicule, criticize, contemn. —*n.* **2.** scoff, gibe, jeer, derision, disdain.

sneeze, *v.* sternutate.

snide, *adj.* derogatory, nasty, insinuating, vicious, slanderous, libelous.
Ant. complimentary, favorable.

snub, *v.* **1.** disdain, contemn, mortify, humiliate, abash, humble, slight, discomfit. **2.** check, rebuke, stop, reprove, reprimand. —*n.* **3.** rebuke, slight, affront, insult.
Ant. accept.

soak, *v.* **1.** steep, drench, wet, sop, saturate. **2.** permeate, osmose, penetrate.
Ant. dry.

soar, *v.* **1.** fly, glide. **2.** tower, rise, ascend, mount.

sober, *adj.* **1.** unintoxicated; temperate, abstinent, abstemious. **2.** serious, grave, solemn, quiet, sedate, subdued, staid. **3.** calm, serene, tranquil, peaceful, cool, moderate, composed, unexcited, unimpassioned, unruffled, collected, dispassionate, unconcerned, reasonable, rational, controlled, sane, sound. **4.** somber, dull, neutral, dark.
Ant. drunk; wild; immoderate.

sociable, *adj.* social.
Ant. unfriendly.

social, *adj.* friendly, sociable, amiable, companionable, genial, affable, familiar.
Ant. unfriendly.

society, *n.* **1.** organization, association, circle, fellowship, club, fraternity, brotherhood, company, partnership, corporation. **2.** community. **3.** companionship, company, fellowship, sodality.

soft, *adj.* **1.** yielding, pliable, plastic, moldable, malleable, impressible. **2.** smooth, agreeable, delicate. **3.** gentle, low, subdued, melodious, mellifluous, dulcet, sweet, pleasing, pleasant, flowing. **4.** gentle, mild, balmy, genial. **5.** gentle, mild, lenient, compassionate, tender, bland, sympathetic. **6.** smooth, soothing, ingratiating, mollifying. **7.** impressionable, yielding, affected, compliant, flexible, irresolute, submissive, undecided, weak, delicate, sensitive. **8.** sentimental, weak, feeble, poor, wishy-washy.
Ant. hard, inflexible, unyielding.

soften, *v.* **1.** melt, tenderize. **2.** appease, assuage, mollify, moderate, mitigate, modify, soothe, alleviate, calm, quell, still, quiet, ease, allay, abate, qualify, temper, blunt, dull.
Ant. harden.

soi-disant, *adj.* self-styled, so-called, pretended.
Ant. genuine, real.

solace, *n.* **1.** comfort, alleviation, cheer, consolation, relief. **—***v.* **2.** comfort, console, cheer, soothe. **3.** relieve, alleviate, soothe, mitigate, assuage, allay, soften.

sole, *adj.* only, single, solitary, alone, individual, unattended, unique.

solemn, *adj.* **1.** grave, sober, mirthless, unsmiling, serious. **2.** impressive, awe-inspiring, august, imposing, venerable, grand, majestic, stately. **3.** earnest, serious. **4.** formal, dignified, serious, ceremonious, ritual, ceremonial. **5.** religious, reverential, devotional, sacred, ritual.
Ant. obstreperous; jovial; unimpressive; insincere; informal.

solicit, *v.* **1.** seek, entreat, ask for, request, apply for, beseech, pray, beg, importune, urge, implore, crave, supplicate, sue, petition, appeal to. **2.** influence, incite, activate, urge, impel, excite, arouse, awaken, stimulate.

solicitous, *adj.* **1.** anxious, concerned, apprehensive, uneasy, troubled, disturbed, restless, restive, worried. **2.** desirous, anxious to please. **3.** eager. **4.** careful, particular.
Ant. unconcerned, undisturbed; careless.

solid, *adj.* **1.** three-dimensional, cubic. **2.** dense, compact, firm, hard. **3.** unbroken, continuous, undivided, whole, entire, uniform. **4.** firm, cohesive, compact. **5.** dense, thick, heavy, substantial, sound, stable, stout. **6.** real, genuine, complete, sound, good. **7.** sober-minded, sober, sensible. **8.** thorough, vigorous, strong, solid, big, great, stout. **9.** united, con-

solidated, unanimous. **10.** successful, solvent, wealthy, rich, reliable, honorable, established, well-established, sound, trustworthy, honest, safe.
Ant. flat, two-dimensional; loose; divided; sparse; counterfeit; weak; separate; unsuccessful.

solitary, *adj.* **1.** unattended, alone, lone, lonely. **2.** isolated, retired, lonely, deserted, unfrequented, remote, secluded. —*n.* **3.** hermit, eremite, recluse.

solitude, *n.* **1.** seclusion, isolation, remoteness, loneliness, retirement, privacy. **2.** desert, waste, wilderness.

somber, *adj.* **1.** gloomy, dark, shadowy, dim, unlighted, dusky, murky, cloudy, dull, sunless, dismal. **2.** depressing, dismal, lugubrious, mournful, doleful, funereal, melancholy.
Ant. cheerful.

some, *adj.* **1.** any, one, anyone, unspecified. **2.** certain, specific, special, particular.
Ant. none.

soothe, *v.* **1.** tranquilize, calm, relieve, comfort, refresh. **2.** allay, mitigate, assuage, alleviate, appease, mollify, soften, lull, balm.
Ant. upset, disturb.

sophisticated, *adj.* **1.** artificial, changed, mundane, worldly. **2.** deceptive, misleading.
Ant. unsophisticated.

sorcery, *n.* magic, witchery, enchantment, witchcraft, spell, necromancy, divination, charm.

sordid, *adj.* **1.** dirty, filthy, soiled, unclean, foul, squalid. **2.** mean, ignoble, amoral, degraded, depraved, low, base. **3.** selfish, self-seeking, mercenary, avaricious, stingy, tight, close, close-fisted, parsimonious, penurious, miserly, niggardly.
Ant. clean; honorable; generous.

sore, *adj.* **1.** painful, sensitive, tender, irritated. **2.** grieved, distressed, aggrieved, sorrowful, hurt, pained, depressed, vexed. **3.** grievous, distressing, painful, depressing, severe, sharp, afflictive. —*n.* **4.** infection, abscess, wound, ulcer, pustule, boil, cancer, canker.
Ant. tough.

sorrow, *n.* **1.** distress, anxiety, anguish, grief, sadness, woe, suffering, misery, wretchedness, regret. **2.** affliction, adversity, trouble, misfortune. —*v.* **3.** grieve, mourn, bemoan, bewail, lament.
Ant. joy, gladness, delight.

sorrowful, *adj.* **1.** grieved, sad, unhappy, melancholy, depressed, dejected, aggrieved, afflicted, mournful, plaintive, grievous, lamentable. **2.** distressing, dismal, dreary, doleful, sorry, lugubrious, piteous.
Ant. happy.

sorry, *adj.* **1.** regretful, sorrowing, sympathetic, pitying. **2.** pitiable, miserable, deplorable. **3.** sorrowful, grieved, sad, unhappy, melancholy, depressed. **4.** grievous, melancholy, dismal, mournful, painful. **5.** wretched, poor, mean, pitiful, base, low, vile,

abject, contemptible, bad, despicable, paltry, worthless, shabby.
Ant. happy.

sort, *n.* **1.** kind, species, phylum, genera, variety, class, group, family, description, order, race, rank, character, nature, type. **2.** character, quality, nature. **3.** example, pattern, sample, exemplar. **4.** manner, fashion, way, method, means, style. —*v.* **5.** arrange, order, classify, class, separate, divide, assort, distribute. **6.** assign, join, unite.

sound, *n.* **1.** noise, tone. **2.** strait, channel. —*v.* **3.** resound, echo. **4.** utter, pronounce, express. **5.** plumb, probe; dive, plunge. **6.** examine, inspect, investigate, fathom, ascertain, determine. —*adj.* **7.** uninjured, unharmed, unbroken, whole, entire, complete, unimpaired, healthy, hale, hearty, robust, hardy, vigorous. **8.** solvent, secure, well-established. **9.** reliable, trustworthy, honest, honorable. **10.** true, truthful, just, fair, judicious, reasonable, rational, sane, sensible, wholesome. **11.** enduring, substantial. **12.** correct, orthodox, right, proper. **13.** upright, honest, good, honorable, loyal, true, virtuous. **14.** unbroken, deep, profound, fast, undisturbed. **15.** vigorous, hearty, thorough, complete.
Ant. unsound.

soupçon, *n.* hint, trace, suggestion, suspicion, flavor, taste, sip.
Ant. plethora.

sour, *adj.* **1.** acid, tart. **2.** fermented. **3.** distasteful, disagreeable, unpleasant, bitter. **4.** harsh, ill-tempered, bad-tempered, austere, severe, morose, peevish, testy, short-tempered, hot-tempered, touchy, acrimonious, cross, petulant, crabbed, snappish, waspish, uncivil, rude, crude, rough.
Ant. sweet.

sovereign, *n.* **1.** monarch, king, queen, emperor, empress, prince, lord, ruler, potentate. **2.** senate, government. —*adj.* **3.** regal, royal, majestic, princely, imperial, monarchical, kingly. **4.** supreme, chief, paramount, principal, predominant. **5.** utmost, extreme, greatest. **6.** potent, effective, efficacious, effectual.

spacious, *adj.* **1.** ample, large, capacious, roomy, wide. **2.** extensive, vast, huge, extended, tremendous, trackless.
Ant. small, cramped, crowded.

span, *n.* **1.** distance, amount, piece, length, extent; nine inches. **2.** extension, reach, extent, stretch. **3.** period, spell. **4.** pair, team, yoke, couple, brace. —*v.* **5.** measure; extend over, reach, pass over, stretch across, cross, compass.

spare, *v.* **1.** forbear, omit, refrain from, withhold, keep from. **2.** save, lay away *or* aside, reserve, set aside *or* apart. —*adj.* **3.** reserved, extra, reserve. **4.** restricted, meager, frugal, sparing, scanty, parsimonious. **5.** lean, thin, slender, slight, gaunt, lank, skinny, raw-boned, emaciated. **6.** economical, temperate, careful.

sparkle, *v.* **1.** glisten, glitter, shine, twinkle, gleam, coruscate, scintillate. **2.** effervesce, bubble. —*n.* **3.** luster, spark, scintillation, glister, glitter, twinkle, twinkling, coruscation. **4.** brilliance, liveliness, vivacity, spirit, glow, piquancy.

sparse, *adj.* **1.** thin, scattered, here and there. **2.** scanty, meager, spare, restricted.
Ant. abundant.

speak, *v.* utter, talk, voice, converse, communicate, disclose, reveal, pronounce, say, articulate, significate.

special, *adj.* **1.** distinct, distinguished, different, particular, especial, peculiar, singular, specific, plain, unambiguous, certain, individual, single, unusual, uncommon. **2.** extraordinary, exceptional.
Ant. unparticular, common; ordinary.

specific, *adj.* special.
Ant. unspecific, nonspecific.

specimen, *n.* type, example, sample, model, pattern.

specious, *adj.* plausible, ostensible, feasible; deceptive, false, misleading.
Ant. implausible; genuine.

specter, *n.* ghost, phantom, spirit, apparition, shade, shadow.
Ant. reality.

speculation, *n.* **1.** contemplation, consideration. **2.** conclusion, supposition, conjecture, surmise, view, hypothesis, theory.

speech, *n.* **1.** utterance, remark, observation, declaration, assertion, asseveration, averral, comment, mention, talk. **2.** talk, oration, address, discourse, harangue. **3.** language, words, lingo, tongue, dialect, patois. **4.** parlance, conversation, parley, communication.

speechless, *adj.* **1.** dumb, dumfounded, shocked, mute. **2.** silent, dumb, mute.
Ant. loquacious, voluble, talkative.

speed, *n.* **1.** rapidity, alacrity, celerity, quickness, fleetness, velocity, swiftness, dispatch, expedition, haste, hurry. —*v.* **2.** promote, advance, further, forward, expedite, favor. **3.** direct, guide. **4.** accelerate.
Ant. sloth.

spend, *v.* **1.** disburse, expend, pay out, dispose of, squander, throw out, waste, lavish, dissipate. **2.** exhaust, use up, consume. **3.** employ, use, apply, devote.
Ant. earn.

sphere, *n.* **1.** ball, orb, globe. **2.** shell, ball. **3.** planet, star. **4.** environment, orbit, area, place, province, circle, compass, coterie, set, realm, domain, quarter. **5.** stratum, walk of life, rank.
Ant. cube.

spin, *v.* **1.** draw out, twist, wind. **2.** twirl, whirl, turn, rotate, gyrate. **3.** produce, fabricate, evolve, develop.

4. tell, narrate, relate. **5.** draw out, extend, protract, prolong, lengthen. —*n.* **6.** run, ride, drive.

spineless, *adj.* limp, weak, feeble, irresolute, undetermined, thewless.
Ant. strong.

spirit, *n.* **1.** animation, vitality, soul, essence, life, mind, consciousness. **2.** goblin, sprite, elf, fairy, hobgoblin; angel, genius, demon, *prāna*. **3.** ghost, specter, apparition, phantom, shade, shadow. **4.** God, The Holy Ghost, The Holy Spirit, The Comforter, The Spirit of God. **5.** mettle, vigor, liveliness, enthusiasm, energy, zeal, zealousness, ardor, fire, vivacity, enterprise, resourcefulness. **6.** temper, disposition, attitude, mood, humor, sorts, frame of mind. **7.** character, nature, drift, tenor, gist, sense, complexion, quintessence, essence. **8.** meaning, intent, intention, significance, purport. —*v.* **9.** inspirit, vitalize, animate, instill, encourage, excite.

spirited, *adj.* excited, animated, vivacious, ardent, active, agog, energetic, lively, vigorous, courageous, mettlesome, bold.
Ant. dispirited, inactive, indolent.

spite, *n.* **1.** ill will, malevolence, maliciousness, malice, rancor, gall, malignity, venom, spleen. **2.** grudge, hate, pique, hatred. —*v.* **3.** annoy, thwart, injure, hurt, harm.

spiteful, *adj.* malicious, venomous, malevolent, revengeful, vindictive, mean, cruel, hateful, rancorous.
Ant. benevolent, friendly.

splendid, *adj.* **1.** gorgeous, magnificent, sumptuous, luxurious, superb, dazzling, imposing. **2.** grand, beautiful, impressive. **3.** glorious, renowned, famed, famous, illustrious, eminent, conspicuous, distinguished, remarkable, celebrated, brilliant, noble. **4.** fine, striking, admirable.
Ant. sordid, squalid; ignoble.

splendor, *n.* **1.** magnificence, brilliance, grandeur, pomp, show, display, dash, élan, éclat. **2.** distinction, glory, brilliance, fame, eminence, renown, celebrity. **3.** brightness, brilliance, light, luster, dazzle, refulgence.
Ant. squalor.

splenetic, *adj.* spleenish, spleeny, irritable, peevish, spiteful, vexatious, irascible, testy, fretful, touchy, edgy, petulant, snappish, waspish, cross, choleric.
Ant. moderate, temperate.

spoil, *v.* **1.** damage, impair, ruin, wreck, disfigure, destroy, demolish, mar, harm. **2.** corrupt, vitiate. **3.** plunder, pillage, rob, rape, despoil, ravage, waste. —*n.* **4.** (*often plural*) booty, plunder, loot, pillage.

spontaneous, *adj.* unpremeditated, natural, unconstrained, voluntary, gratuitous, free, unselfish.
Ant. premeditated.

sporadic, *adj.* scattered, occasional, isolated, unconnected, separate.
Ant. continuous.

sport, *n.* **1.** pastime, game, athletics, amusement, diversion, fun, entertainment, frolic, recreation, play. **2.** derision, jesting, ridicule, mockery. **3.** laughingstock. **4.** toy, plaything. —*v.* **5.** play, frolic, gambol, romp, caper, skip. **6.** trifle, deal lightly, discount. **7.** ridicule, make fun.

sportive, *adj.* **1.** playful, frolicsome, jesting, jocose, merry, jocular, gay, sprightly, frisky. **2.** joking, prankish, facetious.
Ant. sober, serious.

spot, *n.* **1.** mark, stain, blot, speck. **2.** blemish, flaw, stain, taint, stigma. **3.** place, locality, locale, site, situation. —*v.* **4.** stain, mark, blot, speckle. **5.** sully, blemish, stain, taint, stigmatize, soil, tarnish.

spout, *v.* **1.** spurt, squirt, flow, stream, pour. —*n.* **2.** pipe, tube, nozzle, nose.

sprain, *v.* strain, overstrain, wrench, injure, twist.

spread, *v.* **1.** unroll, unfold, open, expand, stretch out, draw out. **2.** extend, stretch, expand, dilate. **3.** display, set forth. **4.** dispose, distribute, scatter, disperse, ted. **5.** overlay, cover, coat. **6.** emit, scatter, diffuse, radiate. **7.** shed, scatter, diffuse, disseminate, broadcast, publish, circulate, divulge, promulgate, propagate, disperse. —*n.* **8.** expansion, extension, diffusion. **9.** extent, reach, compass; stretch, expanse. **10.** bedspread, cloth, cover, tablecloth. **11.** preserve, jam, jelly, peanut butter.

spring, *v.* **1.** leap, jump, bound, hop, vault. **2.** recoil, fly back, rebound. **3.** shoot, dart, fly. **4.** arise, start, originate, rise, issue, emanate, flow. **5.** grow, develop, increase, wax, thrive. **6.** emerge, emanate, issue, flow, proceed. **7.** bend, warp. **8.** explode. **9.** split, crack. —*n.* **10.** leap, jump, hop, bound, vault. **11.** elasticity, springiness, resiliency, buoyancy, vigor. **12.** split, crack, fissure; bend, warp. **13.** source, origin, mouth, fountainhead, head. —*adj.* **14.** vernal, springtime.

sprinkle, *v.* **1.** scatter, strew, spread, disperse, fling, distribute, rain. **2.** diversify, intersperse.

spry, *adj.* active, nimble, agile, brisk, lively, energetic, animated, quick, smart, alert, ready, prompt.
Ant. inactive.

spur, *n.* **1.** goad, prick, rowel. **2.** whip, goad, incitement, stimulus, incentive, inducement, provocation, impulse, instigation. —*v.* **3.** urge, goad, prick, whip, incite, provoke, stimulate, induce, instigate.
Ant. discourage.

spurious, *adj.* **1.** counterfeit, sham, false, pretended, unauthentic, bogus, phony, mock, feigned; meretricious, deceitful, fictitious. **2.** illegitimate, bastard.
Ant. genuine.

spurn, *v.* **1.** reject, disdain, scorn, despise, refuse, contemn. —*n.* **2.** rejection, disdain, scorn, contumely, contempt.
Ant. accept.

spurt, *v.* **1.** gush, spout, flow, issue, stream, jet, well, spring. —*n.* **2.** outburst, jet, spout.
Ant. drip, ooze.

squalid, *adj.* **1.** foul, repulsive, unclean, dirty, filthy, nasty. **2.** wretched, miserable, degraded.
Ant. splendid.

squalor, *n.* squalidness, filth, misery, foulness.
Ant. splendor.

squander, *v.* spend, waste, dissipate, throw away, lavish, misuse, expend.
Ant. save.

squeamish, *adj.* **1.** modest, prudish; blue. **2.** moral, particular, scrupulous, fastidious, finical, finicky, dainty, delicate, hypercritical, nice.
Ant. bold.

stab, *v.* **1.** pierce, wound, gore, spear, penetrate, pin, transfix. **2.** thrust, plunge. —*n.* **3.** thrust, blow, wound.

stability, *n.* firmness, continuance, permanence, constancy, steadiness, steadfastness, strength, immovability, fixedness.
Ant. instability.

stable, *n.* **1.** barn, mews. —*adj.* **2.** firm, steady, rigid, fixed, strong, sturdy, established, immovable, permanent, invariable, unvarying, steadfast, unchangeable, unchanging. **3.** enduring, permanent, constant, perdurable, lasting, abiding, secure, fast, perpetual, eternal, everlasting. **4.** unwavering, steadfast, stanch constant, reliable, steady, solid.
Ant. unstable.

stagger, *v.* **1.** sway, reel, totter, waver, falter, vacillate. **2.** hesitate, doubt. **3.** shock, astound, astonish, confound, amaze, nonplus, dumfound, surprise. **4.** alternate, zigzag, rearrange, reorder, overlap.

staid, *adj.* sedate, settled, sober, serious, proper, decorous, correct, quiet, composed, serene, calm, solemn, grave.
Ant. wild, indecorous.

stain, *n.* **1.** discoloration, spot, blemish, mark, imperfection, blot. **2.** stigma, disgrace, dishonor, taint, blot, tarnish. **3.** dye, reagent, tint. —*v.* **4.** discolor, taint, spot, streak, soil, dirty, blemish, blot. **5.** blemish, sully, spot, taint, soil, tarnish, disgrace, dishonor, stigmatize, corrupt, debase, defile, contaminate, pollute. **6.** tint, dye, tinge, color.

stake, *n.* **1.** stick, post, pale, picket, pike. **2.** wager, bet. **3.** (*often plural*) prize, winnings, purse. **4.** risk, jeopardy, hazard. —*v.* **5.** risk, hazard, jeopardize, wager, venture, bet, imperil.

stale, *adj.* **1.** vapid, flat, dry, hardened, hard, tasteless, sour, insipid. **2.** uninteresting, hackneyed, trite, stereotyped, old hat, old, common, commonplace.
Ant. fresh, modern.

stalemate, *n.* impasse, deadlock, standstill.

stalwart, *adj.* **1.** strong, stout, well-developed, robust, sturdy, brawny, sinewy, muscular, athletic, strapping,

vigorous. **2.** strong, brave, valiant, bold, valorous, intrepid, daring, fearless, firm, resolute, indomitable, gallant. **3.** firm, steadfast, resolute, uncompromising, redoubtable, formidable.
Ant. weak, feeble; fearful; infirm, unsteady.

stamina, *n.* strength, vigor, resistance, power, health, robustness.
Ant. weakness.

stammer, *v.* stutter, pause, hesitate, falter.

stamp, *v.* **1.** strike, beat, trample, crush, pound. **2.** eliminate, abolish, squash, quash, eradicate. **3.** impress, mark, label, brand, imprint. **4.** characterize, distinguish, reveal. —*n.* **5.** die, block, cut, engraving, brand, branding iron. **6.** impression, design, pattern, brand, mark, print, seal. **7.** character, kind, type, sort, description, cut, style, cast, mold, fashion, form, make.

stanch, *v.* **1.** stop, clot. —*adj.* **2.** firm, steadfast, stable, steady, constant, resolute, true, faithful, principled, loyal, substantial, strong, sound, stout. **3.** watertight, waterproof.
Ant. unsteady, disloyal.

stand, *v.* **1.** halt, stop, pause. **2.** remain, continue, persist, stay, abide, be firm *or* resolute *or* steadfast *or* steady. **3.** set, erect, place, put, fix. **4.** face, meet, encounter, resist, oppose. **5.** endure, undergo, submit to, bear, sustain, weather, outlast. **6.** tolerate, abide, stomach, endure, suffer, bear, admit, allow. —*n.* **7.** halt, stop, rest, stay. **8.** position, effort, determination, attitude. **9.** station, post, place, position, spot. **10.** platform, dais, grandstand. **11.** stall, booth, table, case, counter. **12.** copse, grove, forest, wood; growth, crop.

standard, *n.* **1.** criterion, measure, gauge, test, model, example, exemplar, sample, basis, pattern, guide, rule. **2.** grade, level. **3.** emblem, flag, symbol, ensign, banner, pennant, pennon, streamer. **3.** upright, support; bar, rod, timber. —*adj.* **5.** basic, exemplary, guiding, sample, typical.

standing, *n.* **1.** position, status, rank, credit, reputation, condition. **2.** existence, continuation, duration, residence, membership, experience. **3.** station, booth. —*adj.* **4.** still, stationary, stagnant, unmoving, motionless. **5.** continuing, continuous, unceasing, constant, permanent, unchanging, steady, lasting, durable. **6.** idle, out of use, unused. **7.** operative, in force, effective, in effect, established, settled.

stanza, *n.* quatrain, stave, poem, staff.

stare, *v., n.* gaze.

stark, *adj.* **1.** sheer, utter, downright, arrant, simple, mere, pure, absolute, entire, unmistakable. **2.** stiff, rigid. **3.** harsh, grim, desolate, dreary, drear. —*adv.* **4.** utterly, absolutely, completely, quite, irrevocably.
Ant. vague.

start, *v.* **1.** begin, set out *or* forth, commence, depart. **2.** issue, come up, come, arise. **3.** jump, jerk, twitch,

spring. **4.** set up, begin, establish, found, institute, initiate. —*n.* **5.** beginning, outset, initiation, commencement, onset. **6.** impulse, signal, go-ahead, starting gun. **7.** jerk, spasm, fit, twitch, jump. **8.** headstart, lead. **9.** chance, opportunity.
Ant. end, terminate.

startle, *v.* **1.** disturb, shock, agitate, surprise, alarm, amaze, astound, astonish, scare, frighten. —*n.* **2.** shock, surprise, alarm.
Ant. calm.

state, *n.* **1.** condition, case, circumstances, predicament, pass, plight, situation, status, surroundings, environment, rank, position, standing, stage. **2.** constitution, structure, form, phase. **3.** estate, station, rank, position, standing. **4.** dignity, pomp, display, grandeur, glory, magnificence. **5.** sovereign government, government, federation, commonwealth, community, teritorry. —*adj.* **6.** public, national, governmental, federal. **7.** ceremonial, ceremonious, pompous, stately, imposing, sumptuous, dignified. —*v.* **8.** declare, aver, assert, asseverate, set forth, express, affirm, specify. **9.** say. **10.** fix, settle, determine, authorize.

stately, *adj.* imposing, grand, dignified, majestic, elegant, magnificent, state.
Ant. base, mean, vile.

statement, *n.* declaration, communication, report, announcement, proclamation.

station, *n.* **1.** position, post, place, situation, location. **2.** depot, terminal, way-station, whistle-stop. **3.** standing, rank, dignity. **4.** position, office, rank, calling, occupation, metier, trade, business, employment, office, appointment. —*v.* **5.** assign, place, post, position, locate, establish, set, fix.

status, *n.* **1.** condition, state. **2.** condition, position, standing, rank.

stay, *v.* **1.** remain, dwell, reside, abide, sojourn, tarry, rest, lodge. **2.** continue, remain. **3.** stop, halt. **4.** pause, wait, delay, linger. **5.** hold back, detain, restrain, obstruct, arrest, check, hinder, delay, hold, curb, prevent. **6.** suspend, delay, adjourn. **7.** suppress, quell. **8.** appease, satisfy, curb, allay. **9.** wait out. **10.** support, prop, brace, buttress. **11.** rest, rely *or* depend on, confide *or* trust in, lean on. **12.** sustain, bolster, strengthen, uphold. —*n.* **13.** stop, halt, pause, delay, standstill; interruption, break, hiatus, lacuna. **14.** sojourn, rest, repose. **15.** prop, brace, support; crutch. **16.** rope, guy, guy wire.
Ant. leave.

steadfast, *adj.* **1.** fixed, directed, fast, firm, established, stable. **2.** stanch, steady, sure, dependable, reliable, resolute, constant, strong, firm, loyal, regular, purposeful, faithful, unwavering.
Ant. unsteady; weak; sporadic, unfaithful.

steady, *adj.* **1.** firm, fixed, steadfast, stable, balanced, even, regular. **2.** undeviating, invariable, unvarying,

regular, constant, unchanging, uninterrupted, uniform, unremitting, continuous. **3.** habitual, regular, constant, unchangeable. **4.** firm, unwavering, steadfast. **5.** settled, staid, sedate, sober. —*v.* **6.** stabilize.
Ant. unsteady.

steal, *v.* **1.** take, pilfer, purloin, filch, embezzle, peculate, swindle. **2.** win, gain, draw, lure, allure.
Ant. provide.

stealthy, *adj.* furtive, surreptitious, secret, clandestine, sly.
Ant. obvious, open, manifest.

stem, *n.* **1.** axis, stalk, trunk, petiole, peduncle, pedicel. **2.** stock, family, descent, pedigree, ancestry, lineage, race. —*v.* **3.** rise, arise, originate. **4.** stop, check, dam up, obstruct, hinder, stay. **5.** tamp, plug, tighten. **6.** progress against, oppose, breast, make headway against, withstand.

stereotyped, *adj.* fixed, settled, conventional, hackneyed, overused, commonplace, trite, banal, dull, ordinary, lifeless, uninteresting, stale, boring, worn, pointless, insipid, inane.
Ant. rare, uncommon, unusual; interesting, fresh, sensible.

sterile, *adj.* **1.** uncontaminated, unpolluted, uncorrupted, antiseptic. **2.** barren, unproductive, fruitless, infecund.
Ant. fertile.

stern, *adj.* **1.** firm, strict, adamant, unrelenting, uncomprising, severe, harsh, hard, inflexible, forbidding, unsympathetic, rough, cruel, unfeeling. **2.** rigorous, austere, steadfast, rigid.
Ant. lenient, flexible.

stew, *v.* **1.** simmer, boil, seethe. —*n.* **2.** ragout.

stick, *n.* **1.** branch, shoot, switch. **2.** rod, wand, baton. **3.** club, cudgel; bat. **4.** thrust, stab. **5.** stoppage, standstill, delay, pause, hiatus, lacuna, interruption. —*v.* **6.** pierce, puncture, stab, penetrate, spear, transfix, pin, gore. **7.** impale. **8.** fasten, attach, glue, cement, paste. **9.** adhere, cohere, cling, cleave, hold. **10.** remain, stay, persist, abide. **11.** hesitate, scruple, stickle, waver, doubt.

stiff, *adj.* **1.** rigid, firm, solid, inflexible, unbendable, rigid, unbending, unyielding. **2.** violent, strong, steady, unremitting, fresh. **3.** firm, purposive, unrelenting, unyielding, resolved, obstinate, stubborn, pertinacious. **4.** graceless, awkward, clumsy, inelegant, crude, harsh, abrupt. **5.** formal, ceremonious, punctilious, constrained, starched, prim, priggish. **6.** laborious, difficult. **7.** severe, rigorous, straitlaced, austere, strict, dogmatic, uncompromising, positive, absolute, inexorable. **8.** great, high. **9.** taut, tight, tense. **10.** dense, compact, tenacious. —*n.* **11.** prude, prig.
Ant. flexible.

stifle, *v.* **1.** smother, suffocate, strangle, garrote, choke. **2.** keep back, repress, check, stop, suppress. **3.**

crush, stop, obviate, prevent, preclude, put down, destroy, suppress.
Ant. encourage, further, foster.

stigma, *n.* **1.** mark, stain, reproach, taint, blot, spot, tarnish, disgrace, infamy, disrepute. **2.** brand.

still, *adj.* **1.** in place, at rest, motionless, stationary, unmoving, inert, quiescent. **2.** soundless, quiet, hushed, noiseless, silent, mute. **3.** tranquil, calm, peaceful, peaceable, pacific, placid, serene. **—***conj.* **4.** but, nevertheless, and yet. **—***v.* **5.** silence, hush, quiet, mute, stifle, muffle, smother. **6.** calm, appease, allay, soothe, compose, pacify, smooth, tranquilize. **—***n.* **7.** stillness, quiet, hush, calm. **8.** distillery.
Ant. mobile, moving; noisy, clamorous; noise.

stimulate, *v.* **1.** rouse, arouse, activate, incite, animate, excite, urge, provoke, instigate, goad, spur, prod, prick, inflame, fire. **2.** invigorate.
Ant. discourage.

stimulus, *n.* incentive, incitement, enticement, stimulation, motive, provocation; stimulant.
Ant. discouragement; wet blanket; soporific.

stingy, *adj.* niggardly, penurious, parsimonious, miserly, mean, close, tight, avaricious.
Ant. generous.

stint, *v.* **1.** limit, restrict, confine, restrain; pinch, straiten. **—***n.* **2.** limit, limitation, restriction, restraint, constraint. **3.** share, rate, allotment, portion.
Ant. liberate, free.

stir, *v.* **1.** move, agitate, disturb. **2.** shake. **3.** incite, instigate, prompt, rouse, foment, arouse, provoke, stimulate, animate, urge, goad, spur. **4.** affect, excite, move. **—***n.* **5.** movement, bustle, ado, agitation, commotion, disorder, uproar, tumult. **6.** impulse, sensation, feeling, emotion.

stock, *n.* **1.** store, goods, inventory, supplies, supply, provision, reserve, hoard. **2.** livestock, cattle, horses, sheep. **3.** trunk, stem. **4.** race, lineage, family, descent, pedigree, ancestry, line, parentage, house, tribe. **5.** handle, haft. **6.** pillory. **—***adj.* **7.** staple, standard, standing, customary, permanent. **8.** common, commonplace, ordinary, usual. **—***v.* **9.** supply, store, fill.

stoical, *adj.* stoic, impassive, calm, austere, apathetic, imperturbable, cool, indifferent.
Ant. sympathetic, warm.

stony, *adj.* **1.** rocky, pebbly, gritty. **2.** unfeeling, merciless, obdurate, adamant, inflexible, stiff, hard, flinty, pitiless, unbending. **3.** motionless, rigid, stock-still.

stoop, *v.* **1.** bend, lean, bow, crouch. **2.** descend, condescend, deign, lower oneself. **3.** stoop down, descend. **—***n.* **4.** descent, indignity, condescension, humiliation.

stop, *v.* **1.** cease, leave off, discontinue, desist *or* refrain from. **2.** interrupt, arrest, check, halt, restrain, intermit, terminate, end. **3.** cut off, intercept, withhold, thwart, interrupt, obstruct, impede, hinder, prevent, preclude, delay, restrain, repress, suppress. **4.** block, obstruct, close, seal off, blockade. **5.** cease, pause, quit. —*n.* **6.** halt, cessation, arrest, end, termination, check. **7.** stay, sojourn, stopover. **8.** station, depot, terminal. **9.** block, obstruction, obstacle, hindrance, impediment; plug, stopper, cork. **10.** check, control, governor.

Ant. start.

storm, *n.* **1.** gale, hurricane, tempest, tornado, cyclone, sirocco, simoom, dust storm, squall, northeaster, wind, rainstorm, bise, whirlwind, hailstorm, snowstorm, blizzard, thunderstorm. **2.** assault, siege, attack. **3.** violence, commotion, disturbance, strife. **4.** outburst, outbreak. —*v.* **5.** blow; rain, snow, hail, thunder and lightning. **6.** rage, rant, fume, complain. **7.** rush, attack, assault, besiege.

story, *n.* **1.** narrative, tale, legend, fable, romance, anecdote, record, history, chronicle. **2.** plot, theme, incident. **3.** narration, recital, rehearsal, relation. **4.** report, account, description, statement, allegation. **5.** floor, level.

stout, *adj.* **1.** bulky, thick-set, fat, corpulent, plump, portly, fleshy. **2.** bold, hardy, dauntless, brave, valiant, gallant, intrepid, fearless, indomitable, courageous. **3.** firm, stubborn, obstinate, contumacious, resolute. **4.** strong, stalwart, sturdy, sinewy, athletic, brawny, vigorous, able-bodied. **5.** thick, heavy.

Ant. slim, slender, thin; fearful; weak; light.

straight, *adj.* **1.** direct, right. **2.** candid, frank, open, honest, direct. **3.** honorable, honest, virtuous, upright, erect, just, fair, equitable, straightforward. **4.** right, correct. **5.** unmodified, unaltered, unchanged.

Ant. devious, crooked.

straightforward, *adj.* **1.** direct, straight, undeviating, unwavering, unswerving. **2.** honest, truthful, honorable, just, fair.

Ant. devious; dishonest.

strain, *v.* **1.** stretch, tighten, tauten. **2.** exert. **3.** sprain, impair, injure, weaken, wrench, twist, tear, overexert. **4.** filter, sift, sieve, filtrate, purify, percolate, seep through. **5.** clasp, hug, embrace, press. **6.** filter, percolate, ooze, seep. —*n.* **7.** force, pressure, effort, exertion. **8.** sprain, injury, wrench. **9.** family, stock, descent, race, pedigree, lineage, ancestry, extraction. **10.** character, tendency, trait. **11.** streak, trace, hint, suggestion.

strait, *n.* difficulty, distress, need, emergency, exigency, crisis, pinch, dilemma, predicament, plight.

Ant. ease.

strange, *adj.* **1.** unusual, extraordinary, curious, bizarre, odd, queer, singular, peculiar, unfamiliar, inexplicable, unexplained, irregular, unconventional, rare, mysterious, mystifying, eccentric, abnormal, anomalous, exceptional. **2.** alien, foreign, exotic,

outlandish, unfamiliar. **3.** unacquainted, unaccustomed, unused, unfamiliar, unknown, inexperienced. **4.** distant, reserved, aloof, supercilious, superior.
Ant. usual, commonplace.

stranger, *n.* alien, foreigner, outsider.
Ant. friend, relative, ally.

strangle, *v.* garrote; choke, stifle, suffocate, smother, throttle.

stratagem, *n.* plan, scheme, trick, ruse, deception, artifice, wile, intrigue, device, maneuver, contrivance, machination.

strategy, *n.* tactics, generalship; skillful management.

stream, *n.* **1.** current, rivulet, rill, streamlet, run, runnel, river. **2.** flow, course, tide. **3.** flow, succession, torrent, rush. *—v.* **4.** pour, flow, run, issue, emit.

street, *n.* way, road, roadway, avenue, boulevard, concourse, highway; path, footpath, alley, alleyway.

strength, *n.* **1.** power, force, vigor, health, might, potency, energy, capacity. **2.** firmness, courage, fortitude, resolution. **3.** effectiveness, efficacy, potency, cogency, soundness, validity. **4.** intensity, brightness, loudness, vividness, pungency. **5.** support, stay, prop, brace.
Ant. weakness.

strenuous, *adj.* vigorous, energetic, active, animated, spirited, eager, zealous, ardent, resolute, determined, forceful, earnest.
Ant. easy.

stress, *v.* **1.** emphasize, accent. **2.** strain. *—n.* **3.** importance, significance, emphasis, weight, accent, force.
Ant. unstress, de-emphasize, ease, underplay.

stretch, *v.* **1.** draw out, extend, lengthen, elongate. **2.** hold out, reach forth, reach, extend, stretch forth. **3.** spread. **4.** tighten, tauten, strain. **5.** lengthen, widen, distend, dilate, enlarge, broaden. **6.** strain, exaggerate. **7.** recline, lie down. *—n.* **8.** length, distance, tract, expanse, extent, extension, range, reach, compass.
Ant. curtail, abbreviate.

strew, *v.* scatter, sprinkle, overspread, broadcast.
Ant. gather, reap.

strict, *adj.* **1.** rigid, rigorous, stringent, inflexible, stiff, severe, unbending, unyielding, exacting, demanding, stern, narrow, illiberal, uncompromising, harsh, austere, strait-laced. **2.** exact, precise, accurate, scrupulous, particular. **3.** close, careful, minute, critical. **4.** absolute, perfect, complete.
Ant. flexible.

strife, *n.* **1.** conflict, discord, variance, difference, disagreement, contrariety, opposition. **2.** quarrel, struggle, clash, fight, conflict.
Ant. peace.

strike, *v.* **1.** thrust, hit, smite, knock, beat, pound, slap, cuff, buffet. **2.** catch, arrest, impress. **3.** come across, meet with, meet, encounter. **4.** affect, overwhelm, impress.

stringent, *adj.* **1.** strict. **2.** narrow, binding, restrictive. **3.** urgent, compelling, constraining. **4.** convincing, forceful, powerful, effective, forcible, persuasive.
Ant. flexible, mollifying, emollient; ineffective.

strip, *v.* **1.** uncover, peel, decorticate, denude. **2.** remove. **3.** withhold, deprive, divest, dispossess, dismantle. **4.** rob, plunder, despoil, pillage, sack, devastate, spoil, desolate, lay waste. **—***n.* **5.** band, ribbon.
Ant. cover.

strive, *v.* **1.** endeavor, try, exert oneself, essay, struggle, toil. **2.** contend, compete, fight, struggle.

stroke, *n.* **1.** striking, blow, hitting, beating, beat, knock, rap, tap, pat, thump. **2.** throb, pulsation, beat; rhythm. **3.** apoplexy, paralysis, shock, attack. **4.** feat, achievement, accomplishment. **—***v.* **5.** caress, rub gently, massage.

stroll, *v.* **1.** ramble, saunter, meander. **2.** wander, roam, rove, stray. **—***n.* **3.** ramble, saunter, promenade, walk.

strong, *adj.* **1.** powerful, vigorous, hale, hearty, healthy, robust, mighty, sturdy, brawny, athletic, sinewy, hardy, muscular, stout, stalwart, Herculean. **2.** powerful, able, competent, potent, capable, puissant, efficient. **3.** firm, courageous, valiant, brave, valorous, bold, intrepid, fearless. **4.** influential, resourceful, persuasive, cogent, impressive. **5.** clear, firm, loud. **6.** well-supplied, rich, substantial. **7.** cogent, forceful, forcible, effective, efficacious, conclusive, potent, powerful. **8.** resistive, resistant, solid, firm, secure, compact, impregnable, impenetrable. **9.** firm, unfaltering, tenacious, unwavering, resolute, solid, tough, stanch, stout. **10.** intoxicating, alcoholic, potent. **11.** intense, brilliant, glaring, vivid, dazzling. **12.** distinct, marked, sharp, stark, contrasty. **13.** strenuous, energetic, forceful, vigorous, zealous, eager, earnest, ardent. **14.** hearty, fervent, fervid, thoroughgoing, vehement, stubborn. **15.** pungent, racy, olent, aromatic, odoriferous; sharp, piquant, spicy, hot, biting. **16.** smelly, rank.
Ant. weak.

structure, *n.* **1.** construction, organization, system, arrangement, form, configuration, shape. **2.** building, edifice, bridge, dam, framework. **3.** composition, arrangement.

struggle, *v.* **1.** contend, strive, oppose, contest, fight, conflict. **—***n.* **2.** brush, clash, encounter, skirmish, fight, battle, conflict, strife. **3.** effort, strive, endeavor, exertion, labor, pains.

strut, *v.* **1.** swagger, parade. **—***n.* **2.** brace, support, prop, stretcher.

stubborn, *adj.* **1.** obstinate, perverse, contrary, dogged, persistent, intractable, refractory, inflexible,

unyielding, unbending, rigid, stiff, contumacious, headstrong, pig-headed, obdurate. **2.** fixed, set, opinionated, resolute, persevering. **3.** hard, tough, stiff, strong, stony.
Ant. tractable, flexible; irresolute.

student, *n.* pupil, scholar; observer.
Ant. teacher.

studied, *adj.* deliberate, premeditated, predetermined, willful, considered, elaborate.
Ant. unpremeditated.

study, *n.* **1.** attention, application, investigation, inquiry, research, reading, reflection, meditation, cogitation, thought, consideration, contemplation. **2.** field, area, subject. **3.** zealousness, endeavor, effort, assiduity, sedulousness, assiduousness. **4.** thought, reverie, abstraction. **5.** library, den. —*v.* **6.** read, investigate, practice. **7.** think, reflect, consider, ponder, weigh, estimate, examine, contemplate, scrutinize, turn over.

stuff, *n.* **1.** material, substance, matter. **2.** character, qualities, capabilities. **3.** rubbish, trash, waste, nonsense, twaddle, balderdash, inanity, absurdity. —*v.* **4.** fill, cram, pack, crowd, press, stow. **5.** stop up, choke, plug, obstruct.

stun, *v.* **1.** knock out, shock, dizzy. **2.** astound, stupefy, daze, astonish, amaze, overcome, bewilder, overwhelm, confound.

stupid, *adj.* **1.** dull, vapid, pointless, prosaic, tedious, uninteresting, boring, insipid, flat, humdrum, tiresome, heavy. **2.** foolish, inane, asinine, senseless, simple, half-witted, witless, obtuse, stolid, dumb.
Ant. bright, intelligent, clever, shrewd.

sturdy, *adj.* **1.** well-built, strong, robust, stalwart, hardy, muscular, brawny, sinewy, stout, powerful. **2.** firm, stout, indomitable, unbeatable, unconquerable, persevering, resolute, vigorous, determined.
Ant. weak.

style, *n.* **1.** kind, sort, type, form, appearance, character. **2.** mode, manner, method, approach, system. **3.** fashion, elegance, smartness, chic, élan, éclat. **4.** touch, characteristic, mark. **5.** stylus. **6.** etching, point *or* needle, graver. **7.** gnomon. —*v.* **8.** call, denominate, name, designate, address, entitle, title, christen, dub, characterize, term.

suave, *adj.* smooth, agreeable, polite, bland, urbane, sophisticated, worldly, mundane.
Ant. boorish.

subdue, *v.* **1.** conquer, defeat, suppress, subjugate, vanquish, overcome, overpower, subject. **2.** repress, reduce, overcome. **3.** tame, break, discipline, domesticate. **4.** tone down, soften, mollify.

subject, *n.* **1.** theme, topic, conception, point, thesis, object, subject matter. **2.** ground, motive, reason, rationale, cause. **3.** minion, dependent, subordinate. —*adj.* **4.** subordinate, subjacent, subservient, subjected, inferior. **5.** obedient, submissive. **6.** open, exposed, prone, liable. **7.** dependent, conditional, contingent. —*v.* **8.** dominate, control, influence. **9.** make liable, lay open, expose.

subjective, *adj.* **1.** mental, unreal, imaginary, illusory, fancied, imagined. **2.** personal, individual. **3.** introspective, contemplative, introversive. **4.** substantial, essential, inherent.
Ant. objective.

submerge, *v.* submerse, dip, sink, plunge, immerse.

submissive, *adj.* **1.** unresisting, humble, obedient, tractable, compliant, pliant, yielding, amenable, agreeable. **2.** passive, resigned, patient, docile, tame, long-suffering, subdued.

submit, *v.* yield, surrender, bow, comply, obey, agree, resign.
Ant. fight.

subordinate, *adj.* **1.** lower, inferior. **2.** secondary, unimportant, ancillary. **3.** subservient; dependent. —*n.* **4.** inferior, subject. —*v.* **5.** lower, subject, reduce.
Ant. superior; primary.

subside, *v.* **1.** sink, lower, decline, precipitate, descend, settle. **2.** quiet, abate, decrease, diminish, lessen, wane, ebb.
Ant. rise; increase.

subsidiary, *adj.* supplementary, auxiliary, tributary, subordinate, secondary, ancillary.
Ant. primary, principal.

subsidy, *n.* aid, grant, subvention, support, tribute.

substance, *n.* **1.** matter, material, stuff. **2.** essence, subject matter, theme, subject. **3.** meaning, gist, significance, import, pith, essence.

substantial, *adj.* **1.** real, actual, material, corporeal. **2.** ample, considerable, sizable. **3.** solid, stout, firm, strong, resolute, stable, sound. **4.** wealthy, influential, responsible. **5.** worthy, valuable. **6.** material, essential, important.
Ant. insubstantial, immaterial; trivial; unstable, unsound; poor; unworthy; unimportant.

subtract, *v.* withdraw, take away, deduct, diminish, detract, lessen, lower.
Ant. add.

subvention, *n.* subsidy.

succeed, *v.* **1.** flourish, prosper, thrive, go well, make a hit, go swimmingly, prevail. **2.** follow, replace.
Ant. fail; precede.

succession, *n.* **1.** order, sequence, course, series. **2.** descent, transmission, lineage, race.

successive, *adj.* consecutive, following, sequential, ordered.

succor, *n.* **1.** help, relief, aid, support, assistance. —*v.* **2.** aid, assist, relieve, help, support.

sudden, *adj.* unexpected, abrupt, unlooked for, unforeseen, quick, unanticipated.
Ant. deliberate, premeditated, foreseen.

suffer, *v.* undergo, experience, sustain, bear, tolerate, allow, permit, stomach, stand, meet with, feel.

sufficient, *adj.* enough, adequate, ample, satisfactory, competent.
Ant. insufficient.
suggest, *v.* propose, recommend, indicate, hint, insinuate, intimate, prompt, advise.
suggestive, *adj.* expressive.
sulky, *adj.* sullen, ill-humored, resentful, aloof, moody, surly, morose, cross, splenetic, churlish.
Ant. temperate, good-natured.
sullen, *adj.* **1.** silent, reserved, sulky, morose, moody. **2.** ill-humored, sour, vexatious, splenetic, bad-tempered. **3.** gloomy, dismal, cheerless, clouded, overcast, somber, mournful, dark. **4.** slow, sluggish, dull, stagnant.
Ant. cheerful.
sully, *v.* **1.** soil, stain, tarnish, taint, blemish, disgrace, dishonor. **2.** dirty, contaminate, corrupt, pollute.
Ant. honor.
summary, *n.* **1.** digest, extract, abstract, brief, synopsis, compendium, epitome, essence, outline, précis, abridgment. *—adj.* **2.** brief, comprehensive, concise, short, condensed, compact, succinct, pithy. **3.** curt, terse, peremptory, laconic.
summit, *n.* top, peak, apex, pinnacle, acme, vertex, culmination, zenith.
Ant. base, bottom.
summon, *v.* **1.** call, invite, bid; convene, convoke. **2.** call forth, rouse, arouse, activate, incite.
superannuated, *adj.* old, aged, decrepit, obsolete, antiquated, antique, anile, senile, passé.
Ant. young, youthful, new, voguish.
superb, *adj.* stately, majestic, grand, magnificent, admirable, fine, excellent, exquisite, elegant, splendid, sumptuous, rich, luxurious, gorgeous.
Ant. inferior.
supercilious, *adj.* haughty, disdainful, contemptuous, arrogant, scornful, contumelious.
Ant. humble.
superficial, *adj.* shallow, external, outward, exterior, slight.
Ant. basic, profound.
superfluous, *adj.* unnecessary, extra, needless, *de trop*, redundant, excessive, superabundant.
Ant. essential.
superintend, *v.* oversee, supervise, manage, direct, control, conduct, run.
supernatural, *adj.* **1.** unnatural, superhuman, miraculous, preternatural. **2.** extraordinary, abnormal.
supersede, *v.* **1.** replace, displace, supplant, succeed, remove. **2.** void, overrule, annul, neutralize, revoke, rescind.
supplant, *v.* displace, supersede, replace, succeed, remove.
supple, *adj.* **1.** flexible, pliant, pliable, lithe, limber, lissome, elastic. **2.** compliant, yielding, agreeable,

submissive. **3.** obsequious, servile, sycophantic, groveling, slavish, cringing, fawning.
Ant. rigid, inflexible.

supplement, *n.* **1.** reinforcement, extension, addition, complement, addendum, appendix, epilogue, postscript. **—***v.* **2.** complete, add to, complement.

supplicate, *v.* pray, entreat, petition, appeal to, beg, implore, crave, importune, sue, solicit, beseech.
Ant. order, command.

supply, *v.* **1.** furnish, provide, replenish, stock, fill. **2.** make up, make up for, satisfy, fulfill. **3.** fill, substitute for, occupy. **—***n.* **4.** stock, store, inventory, hoard, reserve.

support, *v.* **1.** bear, hold up, sustain, uphold. **2.** undergo, endure, suffer, submit to, tolerate, bear, stand, stomach, go through, put up with. **3.** sustain, keep up, maintain, provide for, nourish, nurture. **4.** back, uphold, second, further, advocate, endorse, forward, defend. **5.** aid, countenance, maintain, help, assist, advocate, succor, abet, relieve, patronize. **6.** corroborate, confirm. **—***n.* **7.** maintenance, sustenance, living, livelihood, subsistence, keep. **8.** help, aid, succor, assistance, relieve. **9.** prop, brace, stay.
Ant. fail.

suppose, *v.* **1.** assume, presume, infer, presuppose, take for granted. **2.** believe, think, consider, judge, deem, conclude.

sure, *adj.* **1.** undoubted, indubitable, indisputable. **2.** confident, certain, positive, assured, convinced. **3.** reliable, certain, trusty, trustworthy, honest, infallible, unfailing. **4.** firm, stable, solid, safe, secure, steady. **5.** unerring, accurate, precise, certain, infallible. **6.** inevitable, unavoidable, destined.
Ant. unsure, uncertain.

surfeit, *n.* **1.** excess, superabundance, superfluity. **2.** disgust, satiety, nausea. **—***v.* **3.** supply, satiate, fill, stuff, gorge, overfeed.
Ant. insufficiency.

surmise, *v.* **1.** think, infer, conjecture, guess, imagine, suppose, suspect. **—***n.* **2.** conjecture, idea, thought, possibility, likelihood.

surpass, *v.* exceed, excel, transcend, outdo, beat, outstrip.

surplus, *n.* remainder, excess, surfeit, superabundance, residue.
Ant. insufficiency, inadequacy.

surprise, *v.* **1.** astonish, amaze, astound, take unawares, startle, disconcert, bewilder, confuse. **—***n.* **2.** assault, attack. **3.** amazement, astonishment, wonder.

surrender, *v.* **1.** yield, give *or* deliver up, cede. **2.** give up, abandon, relinquish, renounce, resign, waive, forgo. **3.** submit, yield, capitulate, give up. **—***n.* **4.** resignation, capitulation, relinquishment.

surreptitious, *adj.* secret, unauthorized, stealthy, clandestine, subreptitious.

Ant. open.

surveillance, *n.* watch, care, control, management, supervision, superintendence.

survey, *v.* **1.** view, scan, observe, watch, inspect, examine, scrutinize. **—***n.* **2.** examination, inspection. **3.** poll.

survive, *v.* continue, persist, live, remain, succeed, outlive.
Ant. languish, die, fail.

susceptibility, *n.* sensibility, sensitivity, sensitiveness, susceptiveness, susceptibleness, impressibility.
Ant. insusceptibility.

suspect, *v.* **1.** distrust, mistrust, doubt. **2.** imagine, believe, surmise, consider, suppose, guess, conjecture. **—***n.* **3.** defendant. **—***adj.* **4.** suspected, suspicious.
Ant. trust.

suspend, *v.* **1.** hang, attach. **2.** defer, postpone, delay, withhold. **3.** stop, cease, desist, hold up, hold off, discontinue, intermit, interrupt, arrest, debar.

suspense, *n.* **1.** uncertainty, doubt, unsureness, incertitude, indetermination. **2.** indecision, vacillation, hesitation, hesitancy, wavering, irresolution, scruple, misgiving. **3.** suspension, intermission, pause, interruption, cessation, stop, remission, surcease, relief, respite, stay, rest, quiescence.
Ant. certainty; decision.

suspicion, *n.* **1.** doubt, mistrust, misgiving, distrust. **2.** imagination, notion, idea, supposition, conjecture, guess. **3.** trace, hint, suggestion.
Ant. trust.

sustain, *v.* **1.** hold *or* bear up, bear, carry, support, uphold. **2.** undergo, support, suffer, endure, bear. **3.** maintain, support, subsist, nourish, nurture. **4.** purvey, supply, cater, furnish, support, aid, countenance, help. **5.** uphold, confirm, establish, approve. **6.** confirm, ratify, corroborate, justify.
Ant. fail; disapprove.

swagger, *v.* **1.** strut, parade. **2.** boast, brag, bluster, blow. **—***n.* **3.** boasting, bragging, arrogance, affectation, braggadocio.

swallow, *v.* **1.** eat, gorge, gulp, engorge, imbibe, drink. **2.** consume, assimilate, absorb, engulf, devour. **3.** accept, receive. **—***n.* **4.** mouthful, gulp, draught, drink.

swap, *v., n.* trade, barter, exchange.

swarm, *n.* **1.** horde, bevy, crowd, multitude, throng, mass, host, flock, shoal. **—***v.* **2.** crowd, throng. **3.** abound, teem.

swarthy, *adj.* dark, dusky, brown, dark-skinned, tawny, swart.
Ant. pale.

sway, *v.* **1.** swing, wave, brandish. **2.** incline, lean, bend, tend. **3.** fluctuate, vacillate. **4.** rule, reign, govern, prevail. **5.** direct, dominate, control, influence. **—***n.* **6.** rule, dominion, control, power, sovereignty, government, authority, mastery, predominance, ascendency. **7.** influence, power, authority, bias.

swear, *v.* **1.** declare, affirm, avow, depose, state, vow, testify. **2.** promise. **3.** curse, imprecate, blaspheme.

sweat, *v.* **1.** perspire. —*n.* **2.** perspiration.

sweeping, *adj.* **1.** broad, wide, extensive, comprehensive, wholesale, vast. **2.** exaggerated, overstated, extravagant, unqualified, hasty.
Ant. narrow; qualified.

sweet, *adj.* **1.** sugary, honeyed, syrupy, saccharine. **2.** fresh, pure, clean, new. **3.** musical, melodious, mellifluous, harmonious, tuneful, in tune, dulcet, tuneful, mellow. **4.** fragrant, redolent, aromatic, perfumed, scented. **5.** pleasing, pleasant, agreeable, pleasurable, enjoyable, delightful, charming, lovable, kind, amiable, gracious, engaging, winning, winsome, attractive, gentle. **6.** dear, beloved, precious. **7.** manageable, tractable, easy-going.
Ant. sour, bitter.

swell, *v.* **1.** inflate, dilate, distend, grow, expand, blow up. **2.** bulge, protrude. **3.** grow, increase, augment, enlarge. **4.** arise, grow, well up, glow, warm, thrill, heave, expand. **5.** bloat, strut, swagger. —*n.* **6.** bulkiness, distention, inflation, swelling. **7.** bulge, protuberance, augmentation, growth. **8.** wave, sea, billow. **9.** (*slang*) fop, dandy, coxcomb, popinjay, blade, buck. —*adj.* (*slang*) **10.** stylish, elegant, fashionable, grand. **11.** grand, fine, first-rate.
Ant. decrease, diminish.

swerve, *v.* deviate, diverge, depart.

swift, *adj.* **1.** speedy, quick, fleet, rapid, fast, expeditious. **2.** quick, prompt, ready, eager, alert, zealous. —*n.* **3.** swallow.
Ant. slow, slothful.

swindle, *v.* **1.** cheat, cozen, defraud, dupe, trick, gull, victimize, deceive, con. —*n.* **2.** fraud, trickery, confidence game, thimblerig, shell game, deception, knavery.

swindler, *n.* confidence man, cheat, deceiver, charlatan, mountebank, rogue, rascal, knave, sharper, trickster, impostor.

swing, *v.* **1.** sway, oscillate, rock, wave, vibrate. **2.** suspend, hang. —*n.* **3.** sway, vibration, oscillation. **4.** freedom, margin, range, scope, play, sweep. **5.** jazz, ragtime.

sybarite, *n.* voluptuary, epicurean, sensualist.

sycophant, *n.* flatterer, toady, fawner, parasite, boot-licker, yes-man.

sylph, *n.* salamander, undine, nymph, gnome.

sympathetic, *adj.* **1.** sympathizing, compassionate, commiserating, kind, tender, affectionate. **2.** congenial, attached, affected *or* touched by.
Ant. unsympathetic.

synopsis, *n.* compendium, condensation, summary,

brief, digest, epitome, abstract, abridgment, précis, outline, syllabus.

system, *n.* **1.** assemblage, combination, complex, correlation. **2.** plan, scheme, procedure, arrangement, classification. **3.** world, universe, cosmos. **4.** taxonomy, order.

T

taboo, *adj.* **1.** forbidden, interdicted, prohibited, banned, sacred, unclean. —*n.* **2.** prohibition, interdiction, exclusion, ostracism.
Ant. allowed, sanctioned, approved; permission, approval.

tacit, *adj.* silent, unexpressed, unspoken, unsaid, implied, implicit, understood, inferred.
Ant. expressed.

taciturn, *adj.* silent, reserved, uncommunicative, reticent, quiet.
Ant. voluble, talkative.

tactful, *adj.* diplomatic, adroit, skillful, clever, perceptive, sensitive.
Ant. tactless, maladroit.

tactics, *n.* strategy, generalship, maneuvering; maneuvers, procedure.

taint, *n.* **1.** fault, defect, blemish, spot, stain, blot, flaw. **2.** infection, contamination, corruption, defilement. **3.** dishonor, discredit, disgrace. —*v.* **4.** infect, contaminate, defile, poison, corrupt, pollute. **5.** sully, tarnish, blemish, stain, blot.

take, *v.* **1.** get, acquire, procure, obtain, secure. **2.** seize, catch, capture, grasp. **3.** grasp, grip, embrace. **4.** receive, accept. **5.** pick, select, choose, elect. **6.** subtract, deduct. **7.** carry, convey, transfer. **8.** conduct, escort, lead. **9.** obtain, exact, demand. **10.** occupy, use up, consume. **11.** attract, hold, draw. **12.** captivate, charm, delight, attract, interest, engage, bewitch, fascinate, allure, enchant. **13.** assume, adopt, accept. **14.** ascertain, determine, fix. **15.** experience, feel, perceive. **16.** regard, consider, suppose, assume, presume, hold. **17.** perform, discharge, assume, adopt, appropriate. **18.** grasp, apprehend, comprehend, understand. **19.** do, perform, execute. **20.** suffer, undergo, experience, bear, stand, tolerate, submit to, endure. **21.** employ, use, make use of. **22.** require, need, demand. **23.** deceive, cheat, trick, defraud. **24.** catch, engage, fix.
Ant. give.

tale, *n.* **1.** story, narrative, fairy tale, account, fiction. **2.** lie, fib, falsehood, fable.

talent, *n.* ability, aptitude, capacity, capability, gift, genius, faculty, forte.
Ant. inability, incapability, weakness.

talk, *v.* **1.** speak, converse. **2.** consult, confer, discuss; gossip. **3.** chatter, prattle, prate. **4.** communicate. **5.** utter, speak, mention. —*n.* **6.** speech, talking, conversation, colloquy, discourse, dialogue, chat, communication, parley, conference, confabulation. **7.** report, rumor, gossip, bruit. **8.** prattle, empty words, words. **9.** language, dialect, lingo.

talkative, *adj.* garrulous, loquacious, wordy, verbose, prolix, long-drawn.
Ant. taciturn, silent.

tall, *adj.* high, elevated, towering, lofty.
Ant. short.

tame, *adj.* **1.** domesticated, mild, docile, gentle. **2.** gentle, fearless. **3.** tractable, docile, submissive, meek, subdued, crushed, suppressed. **4.** dull, insipid, unanimated, spiritless, flat, empty, vapid, vacuous, jejune, prosaic, boring, uninteresting, tedious. **5.** spiritless, cowardly, pusillanimous, dastardly. **6.** cultivated. —*v.* **7.** domesticate, break, subdue, make tractable. **8.** soften, tone down, calm, repress, subjugate, enslave.
Ant. wild.

tamper, *v.* **1.** meddle, interfere, damage, misuse, alter. **2.** bribe, suborn, seduce, lead astray, corrupt.
Ant. neglect, ignore.

tangible, *adj.* **1.** touchable, discernible, material, substantial, palpable, corporeal. **2.** real, actual, genuine, certain, open, plain, positive, obvious, evident, in evidence, perceptible. **3.** definite, specific, ineluctable.
Ant. intangible; unreal, imperceptible.

tantalize, *v.* torment, tease, torture, irritate, vex, provoke.

tantamount, *adj.* equal, equivalent.
Ant. unequal.

tar, *n.* **1.** pitch, creosote, asphalt. **2.** sailor, seaman, seafaring man, gob, mariner, swabby, seafarer.

tardy, *adj.* **1.** late, behindhand, slack, dilatory, slow, backward. **2.** slow, sluggish; reluctant.
Ant. early, punctual.

tarnish, *v.* **1.** dull, discolor. **2.** sully, stain, taint, blemish, soil. —*n.* **3.** stain, blot, blemish, taint.
Ant. brighten.

tarry, *v.* **1.** remain, stay, sojourn, rest, lodge, stop, abide. **2.** delay, linger, loiter; wait.
Ant. leave, depart.

task, *n.* duty, job, assignment, work, labor, drudgery, toil.

taste, *v.* **1.** try, sip, savor. **2.** undergo, experience, feel. **3.** smack, savor. —*n.* **4.** sensation, flavor, savor, scent. **5.** morsel, bit, sip. **6.** relish, liking, fondness, predilection, disposition, partiality, preference, predisposition. **7.** discernment, perception, sense, judgment. **8.** manner, style, character.

tasteless, *adj.* insipid, flat; dull, uninteresting.
Ant. tasteful; interesting.

taunt, *v.* **1.** reproach, insult, censure, upbraid, sneer at, flout, revile. **2.** ridicule, mock, jeer, scoff at, make fun of, twit, provoke. —*n.* **3.** gibe, jeer, sarcasm, scorn, contumely, reproach, challenge, scoff, derision, insult, reproach, censure, ridicule.

tavern, *n.* **1.** bar, cafe; pub. **2.** inn, hotel, public house, hostelry.

tawdry, *adj.* cheap, gaudy, showy, ostentatious, flashy, meretricious.
Ant. expensive, elegant.

teach, *v.* instruct, educate, inform, enlighten, discipline, train, drill, tutor, school, indoctrinate.
Ant. learn.

teacher, *n.* instructor, tutor, lecturer, professor, don.
Ant. student, pupil.

tear, *n.* **1.** (*plural*) grief, sorrow, regret, affliction, misery. **2.** rip, rent, fissure. **3.** rage, passion, flurry, outburst. —*v.* **4.** pull apart, rend, rip, sunder, sever. **5.** distress, shatter, afflict, affect. **6.** rend, split, divide. **7.** cut, lacerate, wound, injure, mangle.
Ant. joy, laughter.

tease, *v.* **1.** worry, irritate, bother, trouble, provoke, disturb, annoy, rail at, vex, plague, molest, harry, harass, chafe, hector. **2.** separate, comb, card, shred. **3.** raise a nap, teasel, dress.
Ant. calm, assuage, mollify; unite; smooth.

tedious, *adj.* long, tiresome, irksome, wearisome, prolix, labored, wearing, exhausting, tiring, fatiguing, monotonous, dull, boring.
Ant. interesting.

teem, *v.* **1.** abound, swarm, be prolific *or* fertile. **2.** empty, pour out, discharge.

tell, *v.* **1.** narrate, relate, give an account of, recount, describe, report. **2.** communicate, make known, apprise, acquaint, inform, teach, impart, explain. **3.** announce, proclaim, publish, publicize. **4.** utter, express, word, mouth, mention, speak. **5.** reveal, divulge, disclose, betray, declare; acknowledge, own, confess. **6.** say, make plain. **7.** discern, identify, describe, distinguish, discover, make out. **8.** bid, order, command, urge. **9.** mention, enumerate, count, reckon, number, compute, calculate. **10.** operate, have force *or* effect.

temper, *n.* **1.** temperament, constitution, make-up, nature. **2.** disposition, mood, humor. **3.** passion, irritation, anger, resentment. **4.** calmness, aloofness, moderation, coolness, equanimity, tranquillity, composure. **5.** hardness, elasticity. —*v.* **6.** moderate, mitigate, assuage, mollify, tone down, soften, soothe, calm, pacify, tranquilize, restrain. **7.** suit, adapt, fit, accommodate, adjust. **8.** moisten, mix, blend, work, knead. **9.** modify, qualify.

temperament, *n.* disposition, make-up, temper, constitution, nature.

temperamental, *adj.* moody, irritable, sensitive,

hypersensitive, touchy, testy, hot-tempered, bad-tempered, short-tempered.
Ant. serene, composed.

temperate, *adj.* moderate, self-restrained, continent; sober, calm, cool, detached, dispassionate.
Ant. intemperate, immoderate.

tempestuous, *adj.* turbulent, tumultuous, violent, stormy, impetuous.
Ant. peaceful, pacific, serene, calm.

temporary, *adj.* transient, transitory, impermanent, discontinuous, fleeting, passing, evanescent, short-lived, ephemeral.
Ant. permanent, infinite.

tempt, *v.* **1.** induce, persuade, entice, allure, seduce, attract, lead astray, invite, inveigle, decoy, lure. **2.** provoke, test, try, prove.

tempting, *adj.* enticing, inviting, seductive, attractive, alluring.
Ant. repulsive, repellent.

tenacious, *adj.* **1.** retentive. **2.** pertinacious, persistent, stubborn, obstinate, opinionated, sure, positive, certain. **3.** adhesive, sticky, viscous, glutinous. **4.** cohesive, clinging, tough.
Ant. unsure, uncertain.

tenacity, *n.* perseverance, persistency, pertinacity, obstinacy.
Ant. transitoriness.

tendency, *n.* direction, trend, disposition, predisposition, proneness, proclivity, inclination, leaning, bias, prejudice, drift, bent; movement.
Ant. failure, disinclination.

tender, *adj.* **1.** soft, delicate. **2.** weak, delicate, feeble. **3.** young, immature, youthful. **4.** gentle, delicate, soft, lenient, mild. **5.** soft-hearted, sympathetic, tender-hearted, compassionate, pitiful, kind, merciful, affectionate. **6.** affectionate, loving, sentimental, amatory. **7.** considerate, careful, chary, reluctant. **8.** acute, painful, sore, sensitive. **9.** fragile, breakable, frangible, friable. **10.** ticklish, delicate, sensitive. **—*v.*** **11.** offer, proffer, present. **—*n.*** **12.** offer, offering, proposal, proffer. **13.** dinghy, skiff, rowboat, lifeboat, motorboat, boat, pinnace, gig. **14.** coal car, coaler.
Ant. coarse, rough; strong; mature, adult; merciless, ruthless; apathetic; inconsiderate; tough; accept.

tenet, *n.* belief, principle, doctrine, dogma, opinion, notion, position, creed.

tense, *adj.* **1.** tight, taut, stretched, rigid, strained. **2.** nervous, neurotic, excited, strained.
Ant. lax; relaxed.

tentative, *adj.* experimental, trial, probationary, indefinite.
Ant. definite, confirmed.

tenuous, *adj.* **1.** thin, slender, small, attenuated, minute. **2.** rare, thin, rarefied. **3.** unimportant,

insignificant, trivial, trifling, nugatory, unsubstantial.
Ant. thick; substantial, significant.

termagant, *n.* shrew, maenad, bacchante, virago, nag, beldam, Xantippe, vixen.

terminate, *v.* **1.** end, finish, conclude, close, complete. **2.** bound, limit. **3.** issue, result, turn out, eventuate, prove.
Ant. begin, open.

terrestrial, *adj.* earthly, mundane, worldly, terrene.
Ant. celestial.

terrible, *adj.* **1.** dreadful, awful, fearful, frightful, appalling, dire, horrible, horrifying, terrifying, terrific, horrendous, horrid, gruesome, hideous, monstrous. **2.** distressing, severe, extreme, excessive.
Ant. delightful, pleasant; moderate.

terror, *n.* horror, fear, panic, fright, alarm, dismay, consternation.
Ant. security, calm.

terrorize, *v.* dominate, coerce, intimidate.
Ant. ameliorate, mollify.

terse, *adj.* brief, concise, pithy, neat, compact, succinct, curt, sententious, concentrated.
Ant. attenuated.

test, *n.* **1.** trial, proof, assay. **2.** examination, quiz, exam. **—***v.* **3.** try, essay, prove, examine; refine, assay.

testimony, *n.* evidence, deposition, attestation, declaration, affirmation, corroboration.

testy, *adj.* irritable, impatient, touchy, tetchy, petulant, edgy, short-tempered, peevish, vexatious, choleric, snappish, waspish, splenetic, cross, cranky, irascible, fretful.
Ant. composed, calm.

thankful, *adj.* grateful, indebted, beholden, obliged.
Ant. thankless, ungrateful.

thaw, *v.* melt, liquefy, dissolve; warm.
Ant. freeze, solidify, sublimate, cool.

theme, *n.* **1.** subject, topic, thesis, point, text. **2.** composition, essay, paper. **3.** motif, thread, tenor, idea; trend.

theory, *n.* **1.** assumption, hypothesis, rationale, explanation, system, conjecture, guess, plan, scheme, proposal. **2.** view, contemplation, conception.

therefore, *adv.* hence, whence, wherefore, accordingly, consequently, so, then.

thersitical, *adj.* scurrilous, foul-mouthed, abusive, vindictive, impudent.
Ant. honorable, polite, discreet.

thesaurus, *n.* storehouse, repository, treasury; dictionary, encyclopedia.

thick-skinned, *adj.* pachydermatous; insensitive, dull, obtuse, callous.
Ant. thin-skinned, sensitive.

thief, *n.* **1.** robber; pickpocket, mugger. **2.** burglar, cracksman, second-story man, house-breaker, safe-cracker.

thin, *adj.* **1.** slim, slender, lean, skinny, poor, lank, gaunt, scrawny, emaciated. **2.** sparse, scanty, meager. **3.** fluid, rare, rarefied, tenuous. **4.** unsubstantial, slight, flimsy. **5.** transparent, weak. **6.** faint, slight, poor, feeble. **—***v.* **7.** rarefy, dilute, reduce, diminish.
Ant. thick, fat, obese; abundant; substantial; opaque, strong; increase.

think, *v.* **1.** conceive, imagine, picture. **2.** meditate, ponder, consider, regard, suppose, look upon, judge, deem, esteem, count, account. **3.** bear in mind, recollect, recall, remember. **4.** intend, mean, design, purpose. **5.** believe, suppose. **6.** anticipate, expect. **7.** cogitate, meditate, reflect, muse, ponder, ruminate, contemplate.

thirst, *n.* desire, craving, eagerness, hankering, yearning, hunger, appetite.
Ant. distaste, apathy.

thorough, *adj.* complete, entire, thoroughgoing, unqualified, perfect, done, finished, completed, total.
Ant. incomplete, unfinished.

thought, *n.* **1.** concept, conception, opinion, judgment, belief, idea, notion, tenet, conviction, speculation, consideration, contemplation. **2.** meditation, reflection, musing, cogitation, thinking. **3.** intention, design, purpose, intent. **4.** anticipation, expectation. **5.** consideration, attention, care, regard. **6.** trifle, mote.

thoughtful, *adj.* **1.** contemplative, meditative, reflective, pensive, deliberative. **2.** careful, heedful, mindful, regardful, considerate, attentive, discreet, prudent, wary, circumspect.
Ant. thoughtless.

thoughtless, *adj.* unthinking, careless, heedless, inattentive, inconsiderate, negligent, neglectful, remiss, unmindful, unobservant, unwatchful, reckless, flighty, scatter-brained, light-headed, giddy.
Ant. thoughtful.

thrash, *v.* beat, defeat, punish, flog, wallop, maul, drub.

threaten, *v.* menace, endanger, indicate, presage, impend, portend, augur, forebode, foreshadow, prognosticate.
Ant. protect, defend.

thrifty, *adj.* **1.** frugal, provident, economical, sparing, saving. **2.** thriving, prosperous, successful. **3.** growing, flourishing, vigorous.
Ant. wasteful, prodigal, improvident; poor, unsuccessful; stunted.

thrive, *v.* prosper, succeed, flourish, increase, advance, luxuriate.
Ant. languish, die.

throng, *n.* **1.** multitude, crowd, assemblage, swarm, horde, host. —*v.* **2.** swarm, assemble, crowd, press, jostle; herd.

throw, *v.* **1.** project, propel, cast, hurl, pitch, toss, fling, launch, send, let fly. —*n.* **2.** cast, fling. **3.** venture, chance. **4.** scarf, boa, stole. **5.** blanket, afghan, robe.

thrust, *v.* **1.** push, force, shove, drive. **2.** stab, pierce, puncture, penetrate. —*n.* **3.** lunge, stab, push, drive, tilt, shove.

thwart, *v.* **1.** frustrate, baffle, oppose, prevent, hinder, obstruct, defeat. —*n.* **2.** seat. —*adj.* **3.** cross, transverse. **4.** adverse, unfavorable.
Ant. favor, encourage, support, help.

tidy, *adj.* neat, trim, orderly.
Ant. messy, sloppy, untidy.

tie, *v.* **1.** bind, fasten. **2.** knot. **3.** fasten, join, unite, connect, link, knit, yoke, lock. **4.** confine, restrict, limit, obligate, constrain. **5.** equal. —*n.* **6.** cord, string, rope, band, ligature. **7.** necktie, cravat. **8.** knot; link, connection, bond.
Ant. loose, loosen, release.

time, *n.* **1.** duration. **2.** period, interval, term, spell, span, space. **3.** epoch, era, period, season, age, date. **4.** tempo, rhythm, measure. —*v.* **5.** regulate, gauge.

timely, *adj.* seasonable, opportune, well-timed, prompt, punctual.
Ant. untimely, inappropriate, inopportune.

timid, *adj.* fearful, shy, diffident, bashful, retiring, coy, blushing, shrinking, timorous, fainthearted, tremulous, cowardly, dastardly, pusillanimous.
Ant. bold, fearless, intrepid.

tint, *n.* **1.** color, hue, tinge, dye, stain, tincture; rinse; pastel. —*v.* **2.** color, tinge, stain.

tirade, *n.* denunciation, outburst, harangue, declamation.

tire, *v.* **1.** exhaust, weary, fatigue, jade. **2.** exasperate, bore, weary, irk.
Ant. innerve.

tired, *adj.* exhausted, fatigued, weary, wearied, enervated.
Ant. energetic, fiery, tireless.

tireless, *adj.* untiring, indefatigable, energetic, active.
Ant. tired, tiresome.

tiresome, *adj.* **1.** wearisome, tedious, dull, fatiguing, humdrum. **2.** annoying, vexatious.
Ant. interesting, enchanting.

title, *n.* **1.** name, designation, epithet, appellation, denomination, cognomen. **2.** championship. **3.** right, claim. —*v.* **4.** designate, entitle, denominate, term, call, style.

toady, *n.* sycophant, fawner, flatterer, yes-man.

toil, *n.* **1.** work, labor, effort, drudgery, exertion, travail, pains. —*v.* **2.** labor, work, strive, moil, exert.
Ant. indolence, sloth.

tolerance, *n.* **1.** toleration, patience, sufferance, forbearance, endurance. **2.** liberality, catholicity, im-

partiality, magnanimity, open-mindedness. **3.** allowance, variation.
Ant. intolerance.

tool, *n.* instrument, implement, utensil, contrivance, device.

top, *n.* **1.** apex, zenith, acme, peak, summit, pinnacle, vertex, culmination. **2.** best, chief. —*adj.* **3.** highest, uppermost, upper, greatest. **4.** foremost, chief, principal. —*v.* **5.** surpass, excel, outdo. **6.** crop, prune, lop.
Ant. bottom, foot; worst; lowest; least.

topic, *n.* subject, theme, thesis, subject-matter.

torment, *v.* **1.** afflict, pain, rack, torture, harass, harry, hector, vex, annoy, irritate, agonize, distress, excruciate. **2.** plague, worry, annoy, pester, tease, provoke, needle, nettle, trouble, tantalize, fret. —*n.* **3.** agony, torture, misery, distress, anguish.
Ant. please.

torpid, *adj.* **1.** inactive, sluggish, slow, dull, apathetic, lethargic, motionless, inert, indolent. **2.** dormant, hibernating, estivating.
Ant. active, energetic.

torrent, *n.* stream, flow, downpour.
Ant. drop, drip, dribble.

torrid, *adj.* **1.** hot, tropical, burning, scorching, fiery, parching. **2.** ardent, passionate.
Ant. arctic, frigid, cold; dispassionate, cool.

tortuous, *adj.* **1.** twisted, crooked, winding, curved, twisting, bent, sinuous, serpentine, sinuate. **2.** evasive, roundabout, circuitous, indirect, deceitful, ambiguous, crooked, dishonest.
Ant. straight.

torture, *n.*, *v.* torment.

toss, *v.*, *n.* throw.

total, *adj.* **1.** whole, entire, complete, finished, final, full, absolute, utter, unqualified. —*n.* **2.** sum, whole, entirety, totality, aggregate, gross. —*v.* **3.** add up, amount to.

totter, *v.* **1.** stagger, falter, reel. **2.** sway, rock, waver. **3.** shake, tremble, oscillate, quiver.

touch, *v.* **1.** handle, feel. **2.** tap, pat, strike, hit. **3.** come up to, attain, reach, arrive at. **4.** modify, improve. **5.** play, perform. **6.** treat, affect, impress, move, strike, stir, melt, soften. **7.** deal with, treat. **8.** pertain *or* relate to, concern, regard, affect. —*n.* **9.** contact; contiguity. **10.** stroke, pat, tap, blow. **11.** hint, trace, suggestion. **12.** characteristic, trait, style. **13.** quality, kind.

tough, *adj.* **1.** firm, strong, hard, hardy. **2.** sturdy, hardy, durable. **3.** hardened, incorrigible, troublesome, inflexible, rigid. **4.** vigorous, severe, violent.
Ant. weak, feeble, sickly; flexible, soft; slight.

tour, *v.* **1.** travel, visit. —*n.* **2.** excursion, trip, journey, expedition.

towering, *adj.* tall, lofty, high, great, elevated.
Ant. short, low.

town, *n.* city, metropolis, borough, community, village, burgh, dorp, thorp, hamlet.
Ant. country.

toxin, *n.* poison, venom, virus.
Ant. serum, antitoxin.

trace, *n.* **1.** vestige, mark, sign, track, spoor, footprint, trail, record. **2.** mark, indication, evidence. **3.** hint, suggestion, touch, taste, soupçon. —*v.* **4.** track, follow, trail. **5.** ascertain, find out, discover. **6.** draw, delineate, outline, diagram. **7.** copy.
Ant. abundance, plethora.

tract, *n.* **1.** stretch, extent, district, territory, region. **2.** space, period. **3.** treatise, pamphlet, essay, sermon, homily, dissertation, disquisition.

tractable, *adj.* docile, malleable, manageable, willing, governable.
Ant. intractable.

trade, *n.* **1.** commerce, traffic, business, dealing, exchange, barter. **2.** purchase, sale, exchange, swap. **3.** occupation, vocation, metier, livelihood, living, employment, pursuit, business, profession, craft, calling, avocation. —*v.* **4.** barter, traffic *or* deal in, exchange. **5.** traffic, barter, interchange, bargain, deal.

traduce, *v.* slander, calumniate, malign, defame, vilify, abuse, revile, asperse, depreciate, blemish, decry, disparage.
Ant. praise, honor.

traffic, *n., v.* trade.

tragic, *adj.* mournful, melancholy, pathetic, distressing, pitiful, calamitous, sorrowful, disastrous, fatal, dreadful.
Ant. comic.

trail, *v.* **1.** drag, draw. **2.** track, trace, hunt down. —*n.* **3.** path, track; scent, spoor.

transact, *v.* carry on, enact, conclude, settle, perform, manage, negotiate, conduct.

transform, *v.* change, alter, metamorphose, convert, transfigure, transmute.
Ant. retain.

transgress, *v.* **1.** violate, infringe, break, contravene, disobey, infringe. **2.** offend, sin, err, trespass.
Ant. obey.

transient, *adj.* transitory, temporary, fleeting, passing, flitting, flying, brief, fugitive.
Ant. permanent.

transitory, *adj.* transient.
Ant. permanent.

translation, *n.* paraphrase, version, interpretation, rendering, treatment.

translucent, *adj.* semitransparent, translucid; transparent.
Ant. opaque, dense, solid.

transmit, *v.* send, forward, dispatch, convey, transport, carry, transfer, bear, remit.

transparent, *adj.* **1.** transpicuous, diaphanous, clear,

pellucid, lucid, limpid, crystalline; translucent. **2.** open, frank, candid. **3.** manifest, obvious.
Ant. opaque; clandestine, secretive; concealed;

transport, *v.* **1.** carry, convey, transport. **2.** banish, exile. **—*n.*** **3.** conveyance, transportation. **4.** freighter, troopship, tanker, oiler. **5.** joy, bliss, rapture, ecstasy, happiness.

trap, *n.* **1.** pitfall, snare, springe. **2.** ambush, pitfall, artifice, stratagem. **—*v.*** **3.** ensnare, entrap, springe. **4.** ambush.

traverse, *v.* **1.** go counter to, obstruct, thwart, frustrate, contravene. **2.** contradict, deny. **3.** pass *or* go across, cross, cross over. **—*n.*** **4.** obstruction, bar, obstacle. **5.** crosspiece, crossbar, barrier, railing, lattice, screen. **—*adj.*** **6.** transverse, cross.
Ant. encourage.

travesty, *n., v.* burlesque, parody, lampoon, caricature, take-off.

treacherous, *adj.* **1.** traitorous, unfaithful, faithless, untrustworthy, treasonable, treasonous, perfidious, disloyal. **2.** deceptive, unreliable, insidious, recreant, deceitful. **3.** unstable, insecure.
Ant. faithful, trustworthy, loyal; reliable; stable, secure.

treachery, *n.* betrayal, treason, disloyalty, faithlessness, perfidy.
Ant. loyalty, fealty.

treason, *n.* sedition, disloyalty, treachery, disaffection, lese majesty.
Ant. loyalty, allegiance.

treasure, *n.* **1.** wealth, riches, hoard, funds; valuables, jewels. **—*v.*** **2.** lay away, store, stock, husband, save, garner. **3.** prize, cherish.

treat, *v.* **1.** act *or* behave toward. **2.** look upon, consider, regard, deal with. **3.** discuss, deal with, handle. **4.** entertain, regale, feast. **5.** negotiate, settle, bargain, come to terms. **—*n.*** **6.** feast, fête, entertainment, banquet.

tremble, *v.* **1.** shake, quiver, quaver, quake, shiver, shudder. **2.** vibrate, oscillate, totter. **—*n.*** **3.** trembling, shaking, quivering.

tremendous, *adj.* **1.** huge, gigantic, colossal. **2.** dreadful, awful, horrid, horrendous, terrible, terrific, terrifying, horrifying, appalling.
Ant. small, tiny, microscopic.

tremor, *n.* **1.** trembling, shaking, vibration, oscillation, shivering, quivering, quaking. **2.** quake, earthquake, temblor.

tremulous, *adj.* **1.** fearful, timorous, timid, frightened, afraid. **2.** vibratory, vibrating, quivering, shaking, trembling, shivering.
Ant. fearless, intrepid; solid, firm.

trenchant, *adj.* **1.** incisive, keen, sharp, cutting, biting, sarcastic, sardonic, acute, pointed, caustic, piquant. **2.** thoroughgoing, vigorous, effective.
Ant. weak, mollifying; ineffective.

trend, *n.* **1.** course, drift, tendency, direction, inclination. **—***v.* **2.** tend, extend, stretch, run, incline.

trespass, *n.* **1.** invasion, encroachment, intrusion, infringement. **2.** offense, sin, wrong, transgression, crime, misdemeanor, misdeed, error, fault. **—***v.* **3.** encroach, infringe, intrude, invade. **4.** transgress, offend, sin.

trial, *n.* **1.** test, proof, experiment, examination, testing. **2.** attempt, effort, endeavor, struggle, essay. **3.** test, assay, criterion, proof, touchstone, standard. **4.** probation. **5.** affliction, suffering, tribulation, distress, sorrow, grief, trouble, misery, woe, hardship.

trick, *n.* **1.** device, expedient, artifice, wile, stratagem, ruse, deception, fraud, trickery, cheating, deceit, duplicity. **2.** semblance, appearance. **3.** prank, joke, practical joke. **4.** shift, dodge, swindle, maneuver, hoax, confidence game. **5.** jugglery, sleight-of-hand, legerdemain, prestidigitation. **—***v.* **6.** cheat, swindle, beguile, dupe, fool, deceive, defraud, delude, cozen. **7.** dress, array, deck.

trickery, *n.* artifice, trick, stratagem, fraud, deception, deceit, chicanery, knavery.
Ant. honesty.

trifling, *adj.* **1.** trivial, insignificant, unimportant, petty, paltry, negligible, nugatory, slight, worthless, piddling, immaterial. **2.** frivolous, shallow, light, empty.
Ant. important, significant, worthy; profound.

trim, *v.* **1.** reduce, pare, clip, prune, shave, shear, cut, lop, curtail. **2.** modify, adjust, prepare, arrange. **3.** dress, array, deck, bedeck, ornament, decorate, adorn, embellish, garnish, trick out. **—***n.* **4.** condition, order, case, plight, situation, state. **5.** dress, array, equipment, gear, trappings, trimmings. **6.** trimming, embellishment, decoration; cutting, clipping, priming, reduction. **—***adj.* **7.** neat, smart, compact, tidy, well-ordered, ordered. **8.** prepared, well-equipped.
Ant. augment, increase.

trip, *n.* **1.** journey, voyage, excursion, pilgrimage, travel, tour, jaunt, junket. **2.** stumble, misstep. **3.** slip, mistake, error, blunder, erratum, lapse, oversight, miss. **—***v.* **4.** stumble. **5.** bungle, blunder, err, slip, miss, overlook. **6.** hop, skip, dance. **7.** tip, tilt.

trite, *adj.* commonplace, ordinary, common, hackneyed, stereotyped, stale.
Ant. original, uncommon, unusual, extraordinary.

triumph, *n.* **1.** victory, conquest, success. **2.** joy, exultation, ecstasy, jubilation, celebration. **—***v.* **3.** win, succeed, prevail. **4.** rejoice, exult, celebrate. **5.** glory, be elated *or* glad, rejoice.
Ant. defeat, loss.

trivial, *adj.* trifling, petty, unimportant, insignificant, nugatory, paltry, slight, immaterial, frivolous, small.
Ant. important, significant, material.

troop, *n.* **1.** assemblage, crowd, band, squad, party, body, unit, company, group, troupe. **2.** herd, flock, swarm, throng. **—***v.* **3.** gather, flock together, swarm, throng, collect. **4.** associate, consort. **5.** assemble, group, convene.

trouble, *v.* **1.** disturb, distress, worry, concern, agitate, upset, disorder, disarrange, confuse, derange. **2.** inconvenience, put out, discommode, incommode. **3.** annoy, vex, bother, irritate, irk, pester, plague, fret, torment, torture, harry, hector, harass, badger, disquiet, molest, perturb. **—***n.* **4.** molestation, harassment, annoyance, difficulty, embarrassment. **5.** misery, distress, affliction, concern, worry, grief, agitation, care, suffering, calamity, dolor, adversity, tribulation, trial, misfortune, woe, pain, sorrow. **6.** disturbance, disorder. **7.** inconvenience, exertion, pains, effort.
Ant. calm, mollify; convenience, encourage, accommodate; happiness, fortune.

troublesome, *adj.* **1.** annoying, vexatious, perplexing, galling, harassing. **2.** laborious, difficult, arduous, hard, burdensome, wearisome.
Ant. simple, easy; trouble-free.

troupe, *n.* troop.

truculent, *adj.* fierce, brutal, savage, harsh, threatening, bullying, overbearing, ferocious, cruel, malevolent.
Ant. affable, amiable.

trudge, *v.* walk, pace, tramp, plod.

true, *adj.* **1.** factual, actual, real, authentic, genuine, veracious, truthful, veritable. **2.** sincere, honest, honorable, just, faithful, equitable, fair. **3.** loyal, faithful, trusty, trustworthy, stanch, constant, steady, steadfast, unwavering, unfaltering. **4.** accurate, exact, faithful, correct, precise; agreeing. **5.** right, proper. **6.** legitimate, rightful. **7.** reliable, sure, unfailing, persevering. **—***adv.* **8.** truly, truthfully. **9.** exactly, accurately, precisely. **—***v.* **10.** shape, adjust, place.
Ant. untrue.

trust, *n.* **1.** reliance, confidence, assurance, security, certainty, belief, faith. **2.** expectation, hope, faith. **3.** credit. **4.** obligation, responsibility, charge. **5.** commitment, office, duty, charge. **—***v.* **6.** rely on, confide in, have confidence in, depend upon. **7.** believe, credit. **8.** expect, hope. **9.** entrust, commit, consign.
Ant. mistrust, distrust.

trustworthy, *adj.* reliable, true, honest, honorable, faithful, stanch, loyal, steadfast, steady, straightforward.

truth, *n.* **1.** fact, reality, verity, veracity. **2.** genuineness, reality, actuality. **3.** honesty, uprightness, integrity, sincerity, candor, frankness, openness, ingenuousness, probity, fidelity, virtue. **4.** accuracy, precision, exactness, nicety.

Ant. lie, fiction, fabrication, untruth; fraudulence; dishonesty; inaccuracy.

try, *v.* **1.** attempt, essay, endeavor, strive, put forth effort. **2.** test, prove, examine, investigate. **3.** melt, render; extract, refine, distill.

tryst, *n.* appointment, meeting, rendezvous, assignation.

tumid, *adj.* **1.** swollen, distended, dilated, enlarged, turgid. **2.** pompous, turgid, bombastic, inflated, grandiloquent, grandiose, rhetorical, declamatory.
Ant. deflated, self-effacing.

tumult, *n.* **1.** commotion, disturbance, disorder, turbulence, uproar, hubbub, fracas, agitation, affray, melee; riot, outbreak, uprising, revolt, revolution, mutiny. **2.** agitation, perturbation, excitement, ferment.
Ant. peace, order; calm, serenity.

tumultuous, *adj.* **1.** uproarious, turbulent, riotous, violent. **2.** noisy, disorderly, irregular, boisterous, obstreperous. **3.** disturbed, agitated, unquiet, restive, restless, nervous, uneasy.
Ant. calm, peaceful, pacific; regular, orderly; quiet, restful.

tuneful, *adj.* musical, melodious, harmonious, dulcet, sweet.
Ant. discordant, sour, flat.

turgid, *adj.* **1.** swollen, distended, tumid. **2.** pompous, bombastic.
Ant. humble.

turmoil, *n.* commotion, disturbance, tumult, agitation, disquiet, turbulence, confusion, disorder, bustle, trouble, uproar.
Ant. quiet, serenity, order, peace.

turn, *v.* **1.** rotate, spin, revolve. **2.** change, reverse, divert, deflect, transfer. **3.** change, alter, metamorphose, transmute, transform, convert. **4.** direct, aim. **5.** shape, form, fashion, mold. **6.** send, drive. **7.** curve, bend, twist. **8.** disturb, derange, infuriate, infatuate, distract. **9.** sour, ferment. **—*n.* 10.** rotation, spin, gyration, revolution. **11.** change, reversal. **12.** direction, drift, trend. **13.** change, deviation, twist, bend, turning, vicissitude, variation. **14.** shape, form, mold, cast, fashion, manner. **15.** inclination, bent, tendency, aptitude, talent, proclivity, propensity. **16.** need, exigency, requirement, necessity.

tussle, *v.* **1.** struggle, fight, wrestle, scuffle. **—*n.* 2.** struggle, fight, scuffle, conflict.

twist, *v.* **1.** intertwine, braid, plait. **2.** combine, associate. **3.** contort, distort. **4.** change, alter, pervert. **5.** wind, coil, curve, bend, roll. **6.** writhe, squirm, wriggle. **7.** turn, spin, rotate, revolve. **—*n.* 8.** curve, bend, turn. **9.** turning, turn, rotation, rotating, spin. **10.** spiral, helix, coil. **11.** turn, bent, bias, proclivity, propensity. **12.** torsion, torque.

twit, *v.* **1.** taunt, gibe at, banter, tease. **2.** deride, reproach, upbraid.

type, *n.* **1.** kind, sort, class, classification, group, family, genus, phylum, form, stamp. **2.** sample, specimen, example, representative, prototype, pattern, model, exemplar, original, archetype. **3.** form, character, stamp. **4.** image, figure, device, sign, symbol.

tyrannical, *adj.* arbitrary, despotic, dictatorial, cruel, harsh, severe, oppressive, unjust, imperious, domineering, inhuman.
Ant. judicious, unbiased, just, humane.

tyrant, *n.* despot, autocrat, dictator, oppressor.
Ant. slave, serf.

tyro, *n.* beginner, neophyte, novice, greenhorn; learner, student.
Ant. expert.

U

ubiquitous, *adj.* omnipresent, being everywhere, present.
Ant. absent, missing.

ugly, *adj.* **1.** repulsive, offensive, displeasing, ill-favored, hard-featured, unlovely, unsightly, homely. **2.** revolting, terrible, base, vile, monstrous, corrupt, heinous, amoral. **3.** disagreeable, unpleasant, objectionable. **4.** troublesome, disadvantageous, threatening, dangerous, ominous. **5.** rough, stormy, tempestuous. **6.** surly, spiteful, ill-natured, quarrelsome, vicious, bad-tempered.
Ant. beautiful.

ultimate, *adj.* final, decisive, last, extreme, furthest, farthest, remotest.
Ant. prime, primary.

umbrage, *n.* offense, pique, resentment, displeasure, grudge.
Ant. pleasure.

umpire, *n.* **1.** referee, arbitrator, arbiter, judge. —*v.* **2.** arbitrate, referee, judge; decide, settle.

unaccountable, *adj.* **1.** unanswerable, irresponsible. **2.** inexplicable, inscrutable, strange, unexplainable, incomprehensible, unintelligible.
Ant. accountable.

unaccustomed, *adj.* **1.** unusual, unfamiliar, new. **2.** unused.
Ant. accustomed.

unaffected, *adj.* **1.** sincere, genuine, honest, real, unfeigned, natural, plain, naive, simple, guileless, artless. **2.** unmoved, untouched, unimpressed, unstirred.
Ant. affected.

unanimity, *n.* accord, agreement, unanimousness, harmony, unity, unison, concert.
Ant. discord, disagreement.

unapt, *adj.* **1.** unfitted, unsuited, unsuitable, unfit, inappropriate, inapplicable, irrelevant. **2.** unlikely, indisposed. **3.** slow, inapt, unskillful, inept, incompetent, unqualified.
Ant. apt.

unassuming, *adj.* modest, unpretending, unpretentious, humble, unostentatious.
Ant. immodest, pretentious.

unbearable, *adj.* unendurable, intolerable, insufferable, insupportable.
Ant. bearable.

unbecoming, *adj.* **1.** inappropriate, unsuited, unapt, unsuitable, unfitted, unfit. **2.** unseemly, improper, indecent.
Ant. becoming, appropriate; seemly, proper.

unbiased, *adj.* fair, equitable, impartial, tolerant, unprejudiced, neutral, disinterested, uninterested.
Ant. biased, prejudiced.

unbounded, *adj.* **1.** unlimited, boundless, limitless, immense, vast, infinite, immeasurable, endless, interminable, illimitable. **2.** unrestrained, unconfined, unfettered, unchained, uncontrolled, unbridled, immoderate.
Ant. bounded, limited; restrained.

unbroken, *adj.* **1.** whole, intact, complete, entire. **2.** uninterrupted, continuous, deep, sound, fast, profound, undisturbed. **3.** undisturbed, unimpaired.
Ant. broken, incomplete; interrupted, discontinuous; impaired.

unburden, *v.* **1.** disburden, unload, relieve. **2.** disclose, reveal; confess.
Ant. burden.

uncalled-for, *adj.* unnecessary, improper, unwarranted.
Ant. necessary, essential, proper.

uncanny, *adj.* strange, preternatural, supernatural, weird, odd.
Ant. common, usual, natural.

uncertain, *adj.* **1.** insecure, precarious, unsure, doubtful, unpredictable, problematical, unstable, unreliable, unsafe, fallible, perilous, dangerous. **2.** unassured, undecided, indeterminate, undetermined, unfixed, unsettled, indefinite, ambiguous, questionable, dubious. **3.** doubtful, vague, indistinct. **4.** undependable, changeable, variable, capricious, unsteady, irregular, fitful, desultory, chance.
Ant. certain.

uncivil, *adj.* **1.** ill-mannered, unmannerly, rude, impolite, discourteous, disrespectful, uncouth, boorish, brusque, curt, impudent. **2.** uncivilized.
Ant. civil.

unclean, *adj.* **1.** dirty, soiled, filthy, nasty, foul. **2.** evil, vile, base, impure, unvirtuous, unchaste, sinful, corrupt, polluted.
Ant. clean.

uncomfortable, *adj.* **1.** disquieting, discomforting. **2.** uneasy, ill at ease, unhappy, miserable, cheerless.
Ant. comfortable.

uncommon, *adj.* unusual, rare, scarce, infrequent, odd, singular, strange, peculiar, remarkable, queer, extraordinary, exceptional.
Ant. common.

uncommunicative, *adj.* reserved, taciturn, close-mouthed, reticent.
Ant. communicative, talkative, voluble.

uncompromising, *adj.* unyielding, inflexible, rigid, firm, steadfast, obstinate.
Ant. compromising, yielding, flexible.

unconcern, *n.* indifference, nonchalance, insouciance.
Ant. concern.

unconditional, *adj.* unrestricted, absolute, complete, unqualified, unconditioned, unreserved, categorical.
Ant. conditional, restricted, qualified.

unconscionable, *adj.* **1.** unscrupulous, shady, dishonest, unlawful. **2.** unreasonable, excessive, extravagant, exorbitant.
Ant. scrupulous; reasonable.

uncouth, *adj.* **1.** awkward, clumsy, unmannerly, discourteous, rude, ill-mannered, uncivil. **2.** unusual, strange, odd, unknown, unfamiliar.
Ant. courteous; natural, usual.

uncover, *v.* lay bare, disclose, reveal, expose, open, strip.
Ant. cover, conceal.

undaunted, *adj.* undiscouraged, fearless, brave, intrepid, undismayed.
Ant. daunted, discouraged.

undeniable, *adj.* **1.** irrefutable, indisputable, indubitable, incontrovertible, incontestable, unquestionable; obvious, evident, clear, certain, sure, unimpeachable, unassailable. **2.** good, unexceptionable.
Ant. doubtful, dubitable, questionable; poor.

undergo, *v.* experience, suffer, bear, tolerate, sustain, endure.
Ant. avoid.

underhand, *adj.* secret, stealthy, sly, crafty, dishonorable, clandestine, surreptitious.
Ant. open, candid.

understand, *v.* **1.** perceive, grasp, realize, comprehend, interpret, conceive, know, see, apprehend, discern. **2.** learn, hear. **3.** accept, believe.
Ant. misunderstand.

undertow, *n.* underset, undercurrent, riptide, crosscurrent.

undine, *n.* sprite, water nymph, sylph.

undying, *adj.* immortal, deathless, unending, eternal, everlasting permanent.
Ant. dying, mortal, temporary.

unearthly, *adj.* weird, ultramundane, supernatural, preternatural, ghostly, spectral, unnatural, strange.
Ant. earthly, terrestrial.

unuducated, *adj.* untutored, unschooled, unenlightened, uninstructed, uncultivated, untaught, uninformed, unlettered, illiterate, ignorant.
Ant. cultivated, cultured, literate.

unemployed, *adj.* unoccupied, idle, at liberty, jobless, between engagements.
Ant. employed, occupied.

unequaled, *adj.* unparalleled, matchless, unmatched, unrivaled, peerless, inimitable, incomparable.
Ant. parallel, rival, comparable.

unequivocal, *adj.* clear, plain, simple, direct, unambiguous, certain, obvious, evident, incontestable, absolute, explicit, unmistakable.
Ant. equivocal, ambiguous.

unerring, *adj.* unfailing, right, correct, exact, precise, sure, infallible, certain, accurate, definite.
Ant. errant, failing, fallible.

unessential, *adj.* nonessential, unimportant, dispensable, immaterial, unnecessary.
Ant. essential.

unexpected, *adj.* unforeseen, unanticipated, sudden, abrupt; surprising.
Ant. expected, foreseen, anticipated, gradual.

unfair, *adj.* biased, partial, prejudiced, unjust, inequitable.
Ant. fair.

unfaithful, *adj.* **1.** false, disloyal, perfidious, faithless, treacherous, traitorous, deceitful, recreant, untrustworthy. **2.** dishonest, crooked, unlawful. **3.** inaccurate, inexact, imprecise. **4.** fickle, untrue, inconstant; adulterous.
Ant. faithful.

unfavorable, *adj.* disadvantageous, unpropitious, adverse, inimical.
Ant. favorable.

unfeeling, *adj.* insensible, insensate, numb, callous, unsympathetic, hard, hard-hearted.
Ant. feeling, sympathetic.

unfit, *adj.* **1.** unfitted, unsuited, unsuitable, inappropriate, inapt, unapt. **2.** unqualified, incompetent, incapable. —*v.* **3.** disqualify.
Ant. fit.

unfortunate, *adj.* unlucky, unhappy, luckless, unsuccessful, hapless, star-crossed, ill-starred.
Ant. fortunate.

unfriendly, *adj.* inimical, unkindly, hostile, unkind.
Ant. friendly.

unfruitful, *adj.* unproductive, barren, sterile, fruitless.
Ant. fruitful.

ungainly, *adj.* awkward, clumsy, ungraceful, uncouth.
Ant. graceful.

ungodly, *adj.* irreligious, impious, sinful, piacular, profane, wicked, depraved, polluted, corrupted, base, vile, evil.
Ant. godly.

unguarded, *adj.* **1.** unprotected, undefended, open, naked, defenseless. **2.** incautious, imprudent, thoughtless, careless.
Ant. guarded, protected; cautious, careful.

unhappy, *adj.* **1.** sad, miserable, wretched, sorrowful, downcast, cheerless, disconsolate, inconsolable, distressed, afflicted. **2.** unlucky, unfortunate, hapless. **3.** unfavorable, inauspicious, unpropitious. **4.** infelicitous, inappropriate, inapt, unapt.
Ant. happy.

unhealthful, *adj.* **1.** insalubrious, unwholesome, unhealthy, noxious, poisonous, harmful. **2.** ill, unhealthy, sick.
Ant. healthy, healthful, hale, hearty.

unhealthy, *adj.* **1.** sickly, delicate, frail, weak, feeble, enfeebled, ill, diseased, afflicted. **2.** unwholesome, unhealthful, unsanitary, unhygienic, insalubrious, deleterious, poisonous, noxious.
Ant. healthy.

uniform, *adj.* **1.** invariable, unchanging, unwavering, unvarying, unvaried, unchanged, constant, regular. **2.** undiversified, unvariegated, dun, solid, plain. **3.** regular, even. **4.** consistent, regular, constant. **5.** agreeing, alike, similar. —*n.* **6.** livery.
Ant. irregular, wavering; diversified; uneven; inconsistent.

unimpeachable, *adj.* irreproachable, unassailable, blameless, unexceptionable.
Ant. reproachable, censurable.

unimportant, *adj.* trivial, trifling, paltry, nugatory, secondary, insignificant, petty, slight.
Ant. important.

uninterested, *adj.* indifferent, unconcerned.
Ant. interested.

union, *n.* **1.** junction, combination, unity, coalition. **2.** society, association, league, confederacy, alliance. **3.** marriage, matrimony, wedlock. **4.** brotherhood.
Ant. separation, fissure.

unique, *adj.* **1.** sole, only, single. **2.** unequaled, alone, peerless. **3.** rare, unusual, singular, odd, peculiar, strange, uncommon.
Ant. common, usual.

unite, *v.* **1.** join, combine, incorporate, connect, conjoin, couple, link, yoke, associate. **2.** combine, amalgamate, compound, blend, coalesce, fuse, weld, consolidate. **3.** marry, wed.
Ant. separate, sever.

unity, *n.* **1.** oneness, union, singleness, singularity, individuality. **2.** concord, harmony, agreement, unison, concert, unanimity, uniformity.
Ant. disunity; disharmony.

universal, *adj.* **1.** general, whole, total, entire; ecumenical. —*n.* **2.** concept.
Ant. local; special.

unjust, *adj.* **1.** inequitable, partial, unfair, prejudiced,

biased. **2.** undeserved, unjustified, unjustifiable, unmerited.
Ant. just.

unkind, *adj.* harsh, cruel, unmerciful, unfeeling, distressing.
Ant. kind.

unlawful, *adj.* illegal, illicit, illegitimate; bastard, spurious, natural.
Ant. lawful, legal.

unlike, *adj.* different, dissimilar, diverse, variant, heterogeneous.
Ant. like.

unlimited, *adj.* unrestricted, unconstrained, unrestrained, boundless, unfettered, limitless, unbounded, vast, extensive, infinite.
Ant. limited.

unlucky, *adj.* unfortunate, hapless, ill-fated, unsuccessful, ill-omened.
Ant. lucky.

unmeasured, *adj.* **1.** unlimited, measureless, immense, vast, infinite. **2.** unrestrained, intemperate, unconstrained; unstinting, lavish.
Ant. measured, finite; temperate, constrained.

unmerciful, *adj.* merciless, pitiless, unpitying, relentless, cruel, unsparing; unconscionable.
Ant. merciful.

unmindful, *adj.* heedless, regardless, careless, inattentive, neglectful, negligent, unobservant, forgetful.
Ant. mindful, aware.

unmistakable, *adj.* clear, plain, evident, obvious, palpable, patent.
Ant. unclear, dim.

unmitigated, *adj.* unqualified, absolute, complete, consummate.
Ant. mitigated.

unmixed, *adj.* pure, unalloyed, unmingled, unadulterated.
Ant. mixed, impure, mongrel.

unnatural, *adj.* **1.** affected, forced, strained, out of character. **2.** unusual, strange, abnormal, irregular, anomalous, aberrant. **3.** cruel, evil, inhuman, heartless, hard-hearted, brutal.
Ant. natural; humane.

unnecessary, *adj.* needless, superfluous, *de trop.*
Ant. necessary.

unnerve, *v.* discourage, disarm, shake, fluster, disconcert, upset.
Ant. steel, encourage.

unparalleled, *adj.* matchless, unmatched, unequaled, unrivaled, peerless.
Ant. equaled.

unpleasant, *adj.* unpleasing, disagreeable, unpalatable, unappetizing, offensive, obnoxious, noisome, repulsive, repellent; noxious.
Ant. pleasant.

unpractical, *adj.* impractical, visionary, speculative, theoretical.
Ant. practical.

unprejudiced, *adj.* unbiased, impartial, fair.
Ant. prejudiced, biased.

unprincipled, *adj.* unscrupulous, tricky, shrewd, dishonest, cagey, wicked, bad, evil, amoral.
Ant. principled; scrupulous.

unpretentious, *adj.* modest, unassuming, shy, abashed, bashful, self-effacing, unpretending, retiring, unobtrusive.
Ant. pretentious.

unqualified, *adj.* **1.** unfit, incompetent. **2.** absolute, unmitigated, out-and-out, thorough, complete, direct, unrestricted, downright.
Ant. qualified.

unquestionable, *adj.* indisputable, indubitable, incontrovertible, undeniable, irrefutable, incontestable; unexceptionable.
Ant. questionable.

unquiet, *adj.* restless, restive, turbulent, tumultuous, disturbed, agitated, upset, uneasy, nervous, perturbed, fidgety.
Ant. quiet.

unreal, *adj.* imaginary, artificial, unpractical, visionary, sham, spurious, fictitious, illusive, illusory, vague, theoretical, impractical.
Ant. real.

unreasonable, *adj.* **1.** irrational, senseless, foolish, silly, preposterous, absurd, stupid, nonsensical, idiotic. **2.** immoderate, exorbitant, excessive, unjust, unfair, extravagant.
Ant. reasonable.

unrefined, *adj.* **1.** unpurified, coarse, harsh, crude. **2.** unpolished, uncultured, ill-bred, rude, boorish, vulgar, gross.
Ant. refined.

unrelenting, *adj.* unabating, relentless, unremitting, implacable, inexorable, merciless, unmerciful, ruthless, pitiless, unpitying, uncompassionate, cruel, hard, bitter, harsh, stern, remorseless, austere.
Ant. relenting.

unreserved, *adj.* **1.** full, entire, complete, unlimited. **2.** frank, open, ingenuous, candid, naive, artless, guileless, undesigning, sincere.
Ant. reserved, incomplete; artful.

unruffled, *adj.* smooth, calm, unperturbed, tranquil, serene, collected, imperturbable, cool, composed, peaceful, controlled, undisturbed.
Ant. ruffled.

unruly, *adj.* ungovernable, disobedient, insubordinate, unmanageable, uncontrollable, refractory, stubborn, lawless; turbulent, tumultuous, disorderly, riotous.
Ant. obedient, subordinate.

unsatisfactory, *adj.* disappointing, inadequate, insufficient.
Ant. satisfactory.

unsavory, *adj.* tasteless, insipid; unpleasant, offensive, distasteful.
Ant. savory, tasteful.

unscrupulous, *adj.* unrestrained, unrestricted, conscienceless, unprincipled, unethical.
Ant. scrupulous, restrained.

unseasonable, *adj.* inopportune, ill-timed, untimely, inappropriate.
Ant. seasonable, opportune.

unseat, *v.* displace, depose; throw.
Ant. place.

unseemly, *adj.* unfitting, unbecoming, improper, indecorous, indecent, unbefitting, inappropriate.
Ant. seemly, fitting, becoming.

unsettled, *adj.* unstable, unsteady, shaky, undependable, unsure, unfixed, undetermined, indeterminate, changeable, wavering, vacillating, infirm, fickle, faltering, irresolute.
Ant. settled, stable, steady.

unsightly, *adj.* unpleasant, unattractive, ugly, disagreeable, hideous.
Ant. beautiful.

unskillful, *adj.* untrained, inexpert, awkward, bungling, clumsy, inapt, maladroit.
Ant. skillful.

unsophisticated, *adj.* **1.** simple, artless, ingenuous, guileless, naive. **2.** unadulterated, pure, genuine.
Ant. sophisticated.

unsound, *adj.* **1.** diseased, defective, impaired, decayed, rotten, sickly, sick, ill, infirm, unhealthy, unwholesome. **2.** fallacious, unfounded, invalid, false, erroneous, untenable, faulty. **3.** fragile, breakable, frangible. **4.** unreliable, unsubstantial.
Ant. sound.

unsparing, *adj.* liberal, profuse, generous, lavish, bountiful; unmerciful, merciless, ruthless, pitiless, unsympathetic, severe, unforgiving, harsh, inexorable, unrelenting, relentless, uncompromising.
Ant. illiberal, sparing, penurious.

unspeakable, *adj.* unutterable, inexpressible, ineffable, indescribable.

unstable, *adj.* **1.** infirm, unsteady, precarious. **2.** unsteadfast, inconstant, wavering, vacillating, undecided, unsettled.
Ant. stable.

unsteady, *adj.* **1.** unfixed, infirm, faltering. **2.** fluctuating, wavering, unsettled, vacillating, fickle, changeable, unstable. **3.** irregular, unreliable.
Ant. steady.

unsuitable, *adj.* inappropriate, unfitting, unbefitting, unbecoming.
Ant. suitable.

untangle, *v.* unravel, unsnarl, disentangle.
Ant. tangle, snarl, entangle.
unthinkable, *adj.* inconceivable.
Ant. conceivable.
untidy, *adj.* slovenly, disordered; sloppy.
Ant tidy.
untie, *v.* unfasten, loose, unknot, undo, unbind.
Ant. tie.
untimely, *adj.* unpropitious, unseasonable, inappropriate.
Ant. timely.
untruth, *n.* falsehood, fib, lie, fiction, story, tale, tall tale, fabrication, fable, forgery, invention.
Ant. truth.
unusual, *adj.* uncommon, extraordinary, exceptional, rare, strange, remarkable, singular, curious, queer, odd.
Ant. usual.
unvarnished, *adj.* plain, unembellished, unexaggerated.
Ant. embellished, exaggerated.
unwary, *adj.* incautious, unguarded, imprudent, indiscreet, hasty, careless, rash, heedless, precipitous, headlong.
Ant. wary.
unwholesome, *adj.* unhealthy, insalubrious, unhealthful, deleterious, noxious, noisome, poisonous, baneful, pernicious; corrupt.
Ant. wholesome.
unwieldy, *adj.* bulky, unmanageable, clumsy, ponderous, heavy.
Ant. manageable, light.
unwise, *adj.* foolish, imprudent, injudicious, ill-advised, indiscreet.
Ant. wise.
unwitting, *adj.* unaware, unknowing, unconscious, inadvertent, unintentional, ignorant.
Ant. intentional, aware.
unworthy, *adj.* inadequate, undeserving; worthless, base.
Ant. worthy.
unyielding, *adj.* **1.** inflexible, firm, stanch, steadfast, adamant, resolute, indomitable, pertinacious, determined. **2.** subborn, obstinate, stiff, intractable, perverse, headstrong, willful.
Ant. flexible.
upbraid, *v.* reproach, chide, reprove, blame, censure, condemn.
Ant. praise, laud.
uphold, *v.* **1.** support, sustain, maintain, countenance. **2.** raise, elevate.
Ant. attack.
uppermost, *adj.* highest, topmost, predominant, supreme.
Ant. lowermost, lowest.
upright, *adj.* **1.** erect, vertical, perpendicular, plumb.

2. honest, just, righteous, honorable, straightforward, virtuous, true, good, pure, conscientious. —*n.* **3.** pole, prop, support, pile, pier, column, lally column.
Ant. horizontal, prone.

uprising, *n.* insurrection, revolt, revolution, rebellion.

uproar, *n.* disturbance, tumult, disorder, turbulence, commotion, hubbub, furor, din, clamor, noise; fracas, melee, riot.
Ant. peace.

upset, *v.* **1.** overturn, capsize. **2.** overthrow, defeat, depose, displace. **3.** disturb, derange, unnerve, disconcert, agitate, perturb, fluster. —*n.* **4.** overturn, overthrow, defeat. **5.** nervousness, perturbation, disturbance. **6.** disorder, mess. —*adj.* **7.** overturned, capsized. **8.** disordered, messy; sloppy. **9.** worried, concerned, disconcerted, agitated, disturbed, perturbed, irritated.
Ant. steady, stabilize.

urbane, *adj.* courteous, polite, refined, elegant, polished, smooth, suave.
Ant. discourteous, impolite.

urge, *v.* **1.** push, force, impel, drive. **2.** press, push, hasten. **3.** impel, constrain, move, activate, animate, incite, instigate, goad, stimulate, spur. **4.** induce, persuade, solicit, beg, beseech, importune, entreat, implore. **5.** insist upon, allege, assert, aver, declare, asseverate. **6.** recommend, advocate, advise. —*n.* **7.** impulse, influence, force, drive, push. **8.** reflex.
Ant. deter, discourage.

urgent, *adj.* **1.** pressing, compelling, forcing, driving, imperative, requiring, immediate. **2.** insistent, importunate, earnest, eager.
Ant. unimportant.

use, *v.* **1.** employ, utilize, make use of, apply, avail oneself of. **2.** expend, consume, use up, waste, exhaust. **3.** practice, put to use, exercise. **4.** act *or* behave toward, treat, deal with. **5.** accustom, habituate, familiarize, inure. —*n.* **6.** employment, utilization, application, exercise. **7.** utility, usefulness, service, advantage, profit, benefit, avail. **8.** help, profit, good. **9.** custom, practice, usage, habit. **10.** occasion, need. **11.** treatment, handling.
Ant. disuse.

useful, *adj.* **1.** serviceable, advantageous, profitable, helpful, effectual, effective, efficacious, beneficial, salutary. **2.** practical, practicable, workable.
Ant. useless.

useless, *adj.* **1.** unavailing, futile, inutile, fruitless, vain, ineffectual, profitless, bootless, valueless, worthless, hopeless. **2.** unserviceable, unusable.
Ant. useful.

usual, *adj.* habitual, accustomed, customary; common, ordinary, familiar, prevailing, prevalent, everyday, general, frequent, regular, expected, predictable, settled, constant, fixed.
Ant. unusual.

utilize, *v.* use.

utter, *v.* **1.** express, speak, pronounce, say, voice. **2.** publish, proclaim, announce, promulgate. **3.** circulate. **—***adj.* **4.** complete, total, absolute, unconditional, unqualified, entire.
Ant. partial, incomplete, relative.

V

vacant, *adj.* **1.** empty, void. **2.** devoid *or* destitute of, lacking, wanting. **3.** untenanted, unoccupied, empty. **4.** free, unoccupied, unemployed, leisure, unencumbered. **5.** unthinking, thoughtless. **6.** vacuous, blank, inane.
Ant. full; occupied; encumbered; thoughtful.

vacillate, *v.* **1.** sway, waver, reel, stagger. **2.** fluctuate, waver, hesitate.

vagabond, *adj.* **1.** wandering, nomadic, homeless, vagrant. **2.** good-for-nothing, worthless. **—***n.* **3.** tramp, vagrant, hobo, gypsy, outcast, loafer. **4.** scamp, rascal, knave, idler, vagrant.

vagrant, *adj., n.* vagabond.

vague, *adj.* **1.** indefinite, unspecific, imprecise, obscure, dim, uncertain, unsure, indistinct, undetermined, indeterminate, unsettled. **2.** unclear, unknown, unfixed, lax, loose.
Ant. definite, specific.

vain, *adj.* **1.** useless, hollow, idle, worthless, unimportant, nugatory, trifling, trivial, inefficient, unavailing, unfruitful, futile, vapid. **2.** conceited, egotistical, self-complacent, proud, vainglorious, arrogant, overweening, inflated.
Ant. useful; humble.

vainglory, *n.* **1.** egotism, vanity, conceit. **2.** pomp, show, ostentation.
Ant. humility.

valiant, *adj.* brave, bold, courageous, stout, stouthearted, intrepid.
Ant. cowardly.

valid, *adj.* just, well-founded, sound, substantial, logical, good, cogent, authoritative, effectual, efficient, efficacious, effective, binding, legal.
Ant. invalid, unjust.

valor, *n.* courage, boldness, firmness, bravery, intrepidity, spirit.
Ant. cowardice.

valuable, *adj.* **1.** costly, expensive, rare, precious, dear. **2.** useful, serviceable, important, estimable, worthy.
Ant. worthless.

value, *n.* **1.** worth, merit, desirability, usefulness, utility, importance. **2.** cost, price. **3.** valuation, evaluation, estimation. **4.** force, import, significance. —*v.* **5.** estimate, rate, price, appraise. **6.** regard, esteem, appreciate, prize.

vanish, *v.* **1.** disappear, evanesce. **2.** end, cease, fade. *Ant.* appear; begin.

vanity, *n.* **1.** pride, conceit, self-esteem, egotism, self-complacency, self-admiration. **2.** hollowness, emptiness, sham, unreality, folly, triviality, futility. *Ant.* humility.

vanquish, *v.* conquer, defeat, overcome, overpower, subjugate, suppress, subdue, crush, quell, rout. *Ant.* lose.

vapid, *adj.* **1.** lifeless, dull, flavorless, insipid, flat. **2.** spiritless, unanimated, dull, uninteresting, tedious, tiresome, prosaic. *Ant.* spirited, animated.

variable, *adj.* **1.** changeable, alterable. **2.** inconstant, fickle, vacillating, wavering, fluctuating, unsteady. *Ant.* invariable; constant.

variance, *n.* **1.** divergence, discrepancy, difference. **2.** disagreement, dispute, quarrel, controversy, dissension, discord, strife. *Ant.* invariance, similitude, sameness.

variation, *n.* **1.** change, mutation, vicissitude, alteration, modification. **2.** deviation, divergence, difference, discrepancy; diversity. *Ant.* sameness.

variety, *n.* **1.** diversity, difference, discrepancy, divergence. **2.** diversity, multiplicity. **3.** assortment, collection, group. **4.** kind, sort, class, species. *Ant.* sameness.

various, *adj.* differing, different, divers, distinct, several, many, diverse, sundry, diversified, variegated, varied. *Ant.* same, similar.

vary, *v.* **1.** change, alter, diversify, modify. **2.** transform, metamorphose, transmute, change. **3.** differ, deviate. **4.** alternate.

vast, *adj.* extensive, immense, huge, enormous, gigantic, colossal, measureless, boundless, unlimited, prodigious, stupendous. *Ant.* limited, small.

vault, *n.* **1.** arch, ceiling, roof. **2.** cellar, catacomb, crypt, tomb. **3.** safe, safety deposit box. —*v.* **4.** arch. **5.** leap, spring, jump.

vehemence, *n.* eagerness, impetuosity, verve, fire, ardor, violence, fervor, zeal, passion, enthusiasm, fervency, fury. *Ant.* coolness, apathy, antipathy.

vehement, *adj.* eager, impetuous, impassioned, passionate, violent, ardent, zealous, earnest, fervent, fervid, burning, fiery, afire, ablaze. *Ant.* cool, dispassionate.

velocity, *n.* rapidity, swiftness, quickness, speed, alacrity, celerity.

venal, *adj.* corrupt, bribable, unscrupulous, mercenary, purchasable, sordid.
Ant. pure, scrupulous.
veneration, *n.* respect, reverence, awe.
Ant. disrespect, irreverence.
vengeance, *n.* avenging, revenge, retribution, requital, retaliation.
Ant. forgiveness, pardon.
venial, *adj.* excusable, forgivable, pardonable.
Ant. inexcusable, unforgivable, mortal.
venom, *n.* **1.** poison, virus. **2.** spite, malice, malignity, maliciousness, spitefulness, acrimony, bitterness, acerbity, malevolence, gall, spleen, hate, contempt.
venture, *n.* **1.** hazard, danger, jeopardy, risk, peril. **2.** speculation. *—v.* **3.** endanger, imperil, risk, jeopardize, hazard. **4.** dare, presume, make bold.
venturous, *adj.* **1.** bold, daring, adventurous, venturesome, daring, rash, intrepid, fearless, enterprising. **2.** hazardous, dangerous, risky, perilous.
Ant. fearful, cowardly; secure, safe.
verbal, *adj.* oral, nuncupative, spoken, worded.
Ant. mental, physical.
verge, *n.* **1.** edge, rim, margin, brim, lip. **2.** brink, limit. **3.** belt, strip, border. **4.** room, area, scope. **5.** rod, wand, mace, staff. *—v.* **6.** border, tend, lean, incline.
verse, *n.* **1.** stich. **2.** poetry, meter, poesy, versification, numbers. **3.** stanza, strophe, stave, section.
versed, *adj.* experienced, practiced, skilled.
Ant. inexperienced, unskilled.
version, *n.* **1.** translation, rendering, interpretation. **2.** variant, form, rendition.
vertical, *adj.* upright, plumb, zenithal, erect, perpendicular.
Ant. horizontal.
vestige, *n.* trace, hint, suggestion, mark, evidence, token.
vex, *v.* **1.** irritate, annoy, pester, provoke, anger, irk, fret, nettle. **2.** torment, plague, worry, hector, harry, harass, torture, persecute. **3.** agitate, discuss, debate.
Ant. delight.
vexatious, *adj.* disturbing, annoying, vexing, troublesome, irritating.
Ant. delightful, pleasant.
vexed, *adj.* **1.** disturbed, troubled, annoyed. **2.** disputed, discussed.
Ant. delighted.
vibrant, *adj.* **1.** vibrating, shaking, oscillating; resonant. **2.** pulsating, energetic, powerful, vigorous; exciting, thrilling.
vibrate, *v.* **1.** oscillate; shake, tremble, quiver, shiver. **2.** resound, echo.
vicarious, *adj.* substituted; delegated, deputed.
Ant. real, actual.
vice, *n.* **1.** fault, sin, depravity, iniquity, wickedness,

corruption. **2.** blemish, blot, imperfection, defect.
Ant. virtue.

vicious, *adj.* **1.** immoral, depraved, profligate, sinful, corrupt, bad, abandoned, iniquitous. **2.** reprehensible, blameworthy, censurable, wrong, improper. **3.** spiteful, malignant, malicious, malevolent. **4.** faulty, defective. **5.** ill-tempered, bad-tempered, refractory.
Ant. moral; commendatory; benevolent; temperate.

victimize, *v.* dupe, swindle, cheat, deceive, trick, defraud, cozen, fool, hoodwink, beguile.

victory, *n.* conquest, triumph, success.
Ant. defeat.

vie, *v.* compete, rival, contend, strive.

view, *n.* **1.** sight, vision. **2.** prospect, scene, vista. **3.** aspect, appearance. **4.** contemplation, examination, survey, inspection. **5.** aim, intention, purpose, reason, end, design, intent, object. **6.** consideration, regard. **7.** account, description. **8.** conception, idea, notion, opinion, theory, belief, judgment, estimation, assessment, impression, valuation. **—*v.*** **9.** see, behold, witness, contemplate, regard, look at, survey, inspect, examine.

vigilant, *adj.* attentive, wary, alert, awake, sleepless, watchful.
Ant. inattentive, unwary.

vigorous, *adj.* strong, active, robust, sturdy, sound, healthy, hale, energetic, forcible, powerful, effective, forceful.
Ant. weak, inactive.

vile, *adj.* **1.** wretched, bad; base, low, vicious, evil, depraved, iniquitous. **2.** offensive, obnoxious, objectionable, repulsive, disgusting, despicable, revolting, repellent, nauseous, nauseating. **3.** foul, vulgar, obscene. **4.** poor, wretched, mean, menial, low, degraded, ignominious, contemptible. **5.** valueless, paltry, trivial, trifling, niggling, nugatory.
Ant. good, elevated.

vilify, *v.* defame, traduce, depreciate, slander, disparage, malign, calumniate, revile, abuse, blacken, asperse, slur, decry.
Ant. commend, honor, praise.

village, *n.* town, hamlet, municipality, community.

villain, *n.* scoundrel, cad, bounder, knave, rascal, rapscallion, scamp, rogue, scapegrace, miscreant, reprobate.
Ant. hero, protagonist.

vindicate, *v.* **1.** clear, exonerate. **2.** uphold, justify, maintain, defend, assert, support.
Ant. convict, blame.

vindictive, *adj.* revengeful, vengeful, spiteful, unforgiving, rancorous, unrelenting.
Ant. forgiving.

violation, *n.* **1.** breach, infringement, transgression. **2.** desecration, defilement. **3.** ravishment, rape, defloration, debauchment.
Ant. obedience.

violence, *n.* **1.** injury, wrong, outrage, injustice. **2.** vehemence, impetuosity, fury, intensity, severity, acuteness. **3.** energy, force.

virgin, *n.* **1.** maiden, maid, ingenue. **—***adj.* **2.** pure, unsullied, undefiled, chaste, unpolluted. **3.** unmixed, unalloyed, pure, unadulterated. **4.** untouched, untried, unused, fresh, new, maiden.
Ant. defiled, polluted, impure, unchaste; adulterated.

virile, *adj.* masculine, manly, vigorous, male.
Ant. effeminate.

virtue, *n.* **1.** goodness, uprightness, morality, probity, rectitude, integrity. **2.** chastity, virginity, purity. **3.** justice, prudence, temperance, fortitude; faith, hope, charity. **4.** excellence, merit, quality, asset. **5.** effectiveness, efficacy, force, power, potency.
Ant. vice.

virtuous, *adj.* right, upright, moral, righteous, good, chaste, pure.
Ant. vicious.

virulent, *adj.* **1.** poisonous, malignant, deadly, venomous. **2.** hostile, bitter, acrimonious, acerb, spiteful, vicious.
Ant. harmless.

virus, *n.* poison, venom, toxin.

visage, *n.* **1.** face, countenance, physiognomy. **2.** aspect, appearance.

viscous, *adj.* sticky, adhesive, glutinous, ropy, thick.

visible, *adj.* **1.** perceptible, discernible, open. **2.** understandable, discernible. **3.** apparent, manifest, obvious, evident, open, clear, patent, palpable, conspicuous, observable, unmistakable.
Ant. invisible.

vision, *n.* **1.** sight. **2.** perception, discernment. **3.** view, image, conception, idea, anticipation. **4.** apparition, specter, ghost, phantom, phantasm, illusion, chimera.

visionary, *adj.* **1.** fanciful, unpractical, impractical, impracticable, fancied, unreal, ideal, imaginary, speculative, illusory, chimerical, romantic. **—***n.* **2.** romantic, dreamer, idealist, theorist, enthusiast.
Ant. practical, practicable.

visitor, *n.* caller, guest, visitant.
Ant. host, hostess.

vista, *n.* view.

vital, *adj.* indispensable, essential, necessary, important, critical.
Ant. dispensable, secondary, unimportant.

vitriolic, *adj.* acid, bitter, caustic, scathing.
Ant. bland, mild, sweet.

vituperate, *v.* abuse, revile, objurgate, censure, vilify, reproach, upbraid, berate, scold.
Ant. praise, commend.

vivacious, *adj.* lively, animated, sprightly, spirited, brisk, sportive.
Ant. inanimate, dull, inactive.

vivid, *adj.* **1.** bright, brilliant, intense, clear, lucid.

2. animated, spirited, vivacious, lively, intense. **3.** vigorous, energetic. **4.** picturesque, lifelike, realistic. **5.** perceptible, clear, discernible, apparent. **6.** strong, distinct, striking.
Ant. dull.

vocation, *n.* business, occupation, profession, calling, trade, metier, employment, pursuit.

vociferous, *adj.* clamorous, noisy, loud, obstreperous, uproarious.
Ant. quiet, pacific, peaceful.

vogue, *n.* fashion, style, mode; currency, acceptance, favor, usage, custom, practice.

void, *adj.* **1.** useless, ineffectual, vain, ineffective, nugatory. **2.** empty, devoid, destitute, vacant. **3.** unoccupied, vacated, unfilled. —*n.* **4.** space, vacuum; gap, opening. —*v.* **5.** invalidate, nullify, annul. **6.** empty, discharge, evacuate, vacate, emit.
Ant. useful; full; occupied; validate; fill.

volition, *n.* will, will-power, determination, preference, discretion, choice, option.

voluble, *adj.* fluent, glib, talkative, loquacious.
Ant. taciturn, quiet, silent.

volume, *n.* **1.** book, tome; scroll, manuscript, codex, papyrus. **2.** size, measure, amount, magnitude. **3.** mass, quantity, amount. **4.** loudness, softness.

voluntary, *adj.* **1.** deliberate, considered, purposeful, willful, intentional, intended, designed, planned. **2.** spontaneous, impulsive, free, unforced, natural, unconstrained.
Ant. involuntary.

voluptuous, *adj.* sensual, luxurious, epicurean.
Ant. intellectual.

voracious, *adj.* ravenous, greedy, hungry, rapacious.
Ant. apathetic.

vow, *n., v.* pledge, promise.

voyage, *n.* trip, flight, cruise, sailing.

vulgar, *adj.* **1.** coarse, inelegant, ribald. **2.** underbred, unrefined, boorish, common, mean, ignoble, plebeian, crude, rude. **3.** vernacular, colloquial.
Ant. elegant; refined; standard.

vying, *adj.* competing, competitive.

W

wage, *n.* **1.** (*usually plural*) hire, pay, salary, stipend, earnings, emolument, compensation, remuneration, allowance. **2.** recompense, return, reward. —*v.* **3.** carry on, undertake, engage in.

wager, *n.* **1.** stake, hazard, bet, risk, venture, pledge. —*v.* **2.** stake, bet, hazard, risk, lay a wager.

waggish, *adj.* roguish, jocular, humorous, mischievous, tricky, sportive, merry, jocose, droll, comical, funny.

wagon, *n.* cart, van, truck, dray; lorry, wain; buckboard, dogcart.

wait, *v.* **1.** stay, rest, expect, await, remain, be inactive *or* quiescent, linger, abide, tarry, pause, delay. —*n.* **2.** delay, halt, waiting, tarrying, lingering, pause, stop. **3.** ambushment, ambush.
Ant. proceed.

waive, *v.* **1.** relinquish, forgo, resign, demit, surrender, renounce, give up, remit. **2.** defer, put off *or* aside.
Ant. require, demand.

wake, *v.* **1.** awake, rise, arise, get up. **2.** rouse, waken, arouse, awaken. **3.** stimulate, activate, animate, kindle, provoke, motivate. —*n.* **4.** vigil, deathwatch. **5.** track, path, course, trail.
Ant. sleep.

wakeful, *adj.* **1.** sleepless, awake, insomnious, restless. **2.** watchful, vigilant, wary, alert, observant, on the qui vive.
Ant. sleepy.

waken, *v.* wake.

walk, *v.* **1.** step, stride, stroll, saunter, ambulate, perambulate, promenade, pace, march, tramp, hike, tread. —*n.* **2.** stroll, promenade, march, tramp, hike, constitutional. **3.** gait, pace, step, carriage. **4.** beat, sphere, area, field, course, career; conduct, behavior. **5.** sidewalk, path, lane, passage, footpath, alley, avenue.

wall, *n.* **1.** battlement, breastwork, bulwark, barrier, bunker, rampart, bastion. **2.** barrier, obstruction. **3.** embankment, dike. —*v.* **4.** enclose, shut off, divide, protect; immure.

wallow, *v.* welter, flounder, roll.

wan, *adj.* pale, pallid, sickly, ashen.
Ant. ruddy, robust.

wander, *v.* **1.** ramble, rove, roam, stray, range, stroll, meander, saunter. **2.** move, pass, extend. **3.** deviate, err, go astray, digress, swerve, veer. **4.** rave, be delirious.

wane, *v.* **1.** decrease, decline, diminish, fail, sink. —*n.* **2.** decrease, decline, diminution; failure, decay.
Ant. wax.

want, *v.* **1.** need, desire, wish, require, lack. —*n.* **2.** necessity, need, requirement, desideratum. **3.** lack, dearth, scarcity, scarceness, inadequacy, insufficiency, scantiness, paucity, meagerness, deficiency, defectiveness. **4.** destitution, poverty, privation, penury, indigence, straits.
Ant. relinquish.

wanton, *adj.* **1.** reckless, malicious, unjustifiable, careless, heedless, willful, inconsiderate, groundless. **2.** deliberate, calculated, uncalled-for. **3.** unruly, wild, reckless. **4.** lawless, unbridled, loose, lascivious, lewd, licentious, dissolute, lustful, prurient, lecherous, salacious, incontinent, concupiscent, libidinous. **5.** luxurious, magnificent, elegant, lavish. —*v.* **6.** squander, waste.

Ant. justifiable, careful; lawful, prudish; inelegant; save.

warden, *n.* warder, guardian, guard, custodian, keeper, caretaker, superintendent.

warlike, *adj.* martial, military; bellicose, belligerent, hostile, inimical, unfriendly.
Ant. peaceful.

warm, *adj.* **1.** lukewarm, tepid, heated. **2.** hearty, enthusiastic, emotional, zealous, fervent, fervid, ardent, excited, eager. **3.** cordial, hearty, glowing. **4.** attached, friendly, amiable, amicable, close, intimate. **5.** heated, irritated, annoyed, vexed, angry, irate, furious. **6.** animated, lively, brisk, vigorous, vehement. **7.** strong, fresh. —*v.* **8.** warm up, heat up, heat, make warm. **8.** animate, excite, waken, stir, stir up, rouse, arouse.
Ant. cool.

warn, *v.* **1.** caution, admonish, forewarn. **2.** notify, apprise, inform.

warning, *n.* caution, admonition, advice; omen, sign, augury, presage, portent.

warp, *v.* **1.** bend, twist, turn, contort, distort, spring. **2.** swerve, deviate, **3.** distort, bias, pervert.
Ant. straighten.

warrant, *n.* **1.** authorization, sanction, justification, commission. **2.** pledge, guarantee, assurance, security, surety, warranty. **3.** certificate, license, receipt, commission, permit, voucher, writ, order, chit. —*v.* **4.** authorize, sanction, approve, justify, guarantee, vouch for. **5.** assure, promise, guarantee, secure, affirm, vouch for, attest.

wary, *adj.* alert, cautious, vigilant, careful, circumspect, watchful, scrupulous, discreet.
Ant. unwary.

wash, *v.* **1.** cleanse, clean, lave, launder, scrub, mob, swab, rub. **2.** wet, bedew, moisten. **3.** bathe. —*n.* **4.** washing, ablution, cleansing, bathing. **5.** fen, marsh, bog, swamp, morass, slough.

waspish, *adj.* **1.** resentful, snappish. **2.** irascible, petulant, testy.

waste, *v.* **1.** consume, spend, throw out, expend, squander, misspend, dissipate. **2.** destroy, consume, wear away, erode, eat away, reduce, wear down, emaciate, enfeeble. **3.** lay waste, devastate, ruin, ravage, pillage, plunder, desolate, sack, spoil, despoil. **4.** diminish, dwindle, perish, wane, decay. —*n.* **5.** consumption, expenditure, dissipation, diminution, decline, emaciation, loss, destruction, decay, impairment. **6.** ruin, devastation, spoliation, desolation, plunder, pillage. **7.** desert, wilderness, wild. **8.** refuse, rubbish, trash, garbage. —*adj.* **9.** unused, useless, superfluous, extra, *de trop.* **10.** uninhabited, desert, deserted, wild, desolate, barren. **11.** decayed, ghost; devastated, laid waste, ruined, ravaged, sacked, destroyed. **12.** rejected, refuse.
Ant. save.

watch, *v.* **1.** look, see, observe. **2.** contemplate, regard, mark, view, look upon. **3.** wait for, await, expect. **4.** guard, protect, tend. —*n.* **5.** observation, inspection, attention. **6.** lookout, sentinel, sentry, watchman, guard; vigil, watchfulness, alertness. **7.** timepiece.

watchful, *adj.* vigilant, alert, observant, attentive, heedful, careful, circumspect, cautious, wary, wakeful, awake.
Ant. unwary, inattentive, incautious.

watchword, *n.* **1.** password, countersign, shibboleth. **2.** slogan, motto.

wave, *n.* **1.** ridge, swell, undulation, ripple, breaker, surf, sea. —*v.* **2.** undulate, fluctuate, oscillate; flutter, float, sway, rock.
Ant. hollow.

waver, *v.* **1.** sway, flutter. **2.** flicker, quiver. **3.** shake, tremble, quiver, shiver. **4.** vacillate, fluctuate, alternate, hesitate.

wax, *v.* **1.** increase, extend, grow, lengthen, enlarge, dilate. **2.** grow, become, come *or* get to be.
Ant. wane.

way, *n.* **1.** manner, mode, fashion, method. **2.** habit, custom, usage, practice, wont. **3.** means, course, plan, method, scheme, device. **4.** respect, particular, detail, part. **5.** direction. **6.** passage, progress, extent. **7.** distance, space, interval. **8.** path, course, passage, channel, road, route, track, avenue, highroad, highway, freeway, throughway.

wayward, *adj.* **1.** contrary, headstrong, stubborn, capricious, captious, obstinate, disobedient, unruly, refractory, intractable, willful, perverse. **2.** irregular, unsteady, inconstant, changeable.
Ant. agreeable, obedient, tractable; regular, constant.

weak, *adj.* **1.** fragile, frail, breakable, delicate. **2.** feeble, senile, anile, old, infirm, decrepit, weakly, sickly, unhealthy, unwell, debilitated, invalid. **3.** impotent, ineffectual, ineffective, inefficient, inadequate, inefficacious. **4.** unconvincing, inconclusive, lame, illogical, unsatisfactory, vague. **5.** unintelligent, simple, foolish, stupid, senseless, silly. **6.** irresolute, vacillating, unstable, unsteady, wavering, weak-kneed, fluctuating, undecided. **7.** faint, slight, slender, slim, inconsiderable, flimsy, poor, trifling, trivial. **8.** deficient, wanting, short, lacking, insufficient.
Ant. strong.

weaken, *v.* enfeeble, debilitate, enervate, undermine, sap, exhaust, deplete, diminish, lessen, lower, reduce, impair, minimize, invalidate.
Ant. strengthen.

weakly, *adj.* weak, feeble, sickly.
Ant. strong.

weakness, *n.* **1.** feebleness, fragility. **2.** flaw, defect, fault. **3.** tenderness, liking, inclination.
Ant. strength.

wealth, *n.* **1.** property, riches. **2.** abundance, profusion. **3.** assets, possessions, goods, property. **4.** affluence, opulence, fortune, treasure, funds, cash, pelf.
Ant. poverty.

wealthy, *adj.* **1.** rich, affluent, opulent, prosperous, well-to-do, moneyed. **2.** abundant, ample, copious.
Ant. poor, poverty-stricken; scanty, scarce.

wearisome, *adj.* **1.** fatiguing, tiring. **2.** tiresome, boring, tedious, irksome, monotonous, humdrum, dull ,prosy, prosaic, vexatious, trying.
Ant. energetic; interesting.

weary, *adj.* **1.** exhausted, tired, wearied, fatigued, spent. **2.** impatient, dissatisfied. **3.** tiresome, tedious, irksome, wearisome. **—*v.*** **4.** fatigue, tire, exhaust, tire *or* wear out, jade. **5.** harass, harry, irk.
Ant. energetic; patient; interesting; interest, captivate.

weave, *v.* **1.** interlace, intertwine, braid, plait. **2.** contrive, fabricate, construct, compose. **3.** introduce, insert, intermix, intermingle.

weep, *v.* shed tears, cry, sob, lament, bewail, bemoan.
Ant. laugh, rejoice.

weigh, *v.* consider, balance, ponder, contemplate, study.

weight, *n.* influence, importance, power, moment, efficacy, import, consequence, significance.

weighty, *adj.* **1.** heavy, ponderous. **2.** burdensome, onerous. **3.** important, momentous, significant, serious, grave, consequential.
Ant. light; unimportant, insignificant.

weird, *adj.* eerie, ghostly, unearthly, ultramundane, uncanny, mysterious, unnatural, supernatural, preternatural.
Ant. natural.

welfare, *n.* well-being, prosperity, success, happiness, weal, benefit, profit, advantage.

well, *adv.* **1.** satisfactorily, favorably, advantageously, fortunately, happily. **2.** commendably, meritoriously, excellently. **3.** properly, correctly, skillfully, adeptly, efficiently, accurately. **4.** judiciously, reasonably, suitably, properly. **5.** adequately, sufficiently, satisfactorily. **6.** thoroughly, soundly, abundantly, amply, fully. **7.** considerably, rather, quite, fairly. **8.** personally, intimately. **—*adj.*** **9.** sound, healthy, healthful, hale, hearty. **10.** satisfactory, good, fine. **11.** proper, fitting, suitable, befitting, appropriate. **12.** fortunate, successful, well-off, happy.
Ant. poorly, badly; ill, sick.

wet, *adj.* **1.** soaked, drenched, dampened, moistened. **2.** damp, moist, dank, humid. **3.** humid, misty, drizzling, rainy. **—*n.*** **4.** moisture, wetness, rain, humidity, drizzle, dampness, dankness. **—*v.*** **5.** drench, saturate, soak, ret.
Ant. dry.

whim, *n.* fancy, notion, caprice, whimsy, humor, vagary, quirk, crotchet, chimera.
Ant. consideration.

whimsical, *adj.* capricious, notional, changeable, crotchety, freakish, fanciful, odd, peculiar, curious, singular, queer, quaint.
Ant. considerate.

whine, *v.* complain, grumble; moan, cry.

whip, *v.* **1.** lash, beat; flog, thrash, scourge, beat, switch, punish, flagellate, chastise; castigate. **2.** pull, jerk, snatch, seize, whisk. —*n.* **3.** switch, leash, scourge.

whirl, *v.* **1.** gyrate, pirouette, spin, rotate, revolve, twirl, wheel. —*n.* **2.** rotation, gyration, spin, revolution.

whiten, *v.* blanch, bleach, etiolate.
Ant. blacken, darken.

whole, *adj.* **1.** entire, full, total, undiminished, undivided, integral, complete, unbroken, unimpaired, perfect, uninjured, faultless, undamaged, sound, intact. —*n.* **2.** totality, total, sum, entirety, aggregate, sum total.
Ant. partial; part.

wholesome, *adj.* **1.** salutary, beneficial, helpful, good. **2.** healthful, salubrious, nourishing, nutritious, healthy, salutary, invigorating.
Ant. unwholesome.

wicked, *adj.* evil, bad, immoral, amoral, unprincipled, sinful, piacular, unrighteous, ungodly, godless, impious, profane, blasphemous; profligate, corrupt, depraved, dissolute, heinous, vicious, vile, iniquitous, abandoned, flagitious, nefarious, treacherous, villainous, atrocious.
Ant. good.

wide, *adj.* **1.** broad. **2.** extensive, vast, spacious, ample, comprehensive, large, expanded, distended.
Ant. narrow.

wild, *adj.* **1.** untamed, undomesticated, feral, ferine, savage, unbroken, ferocious. **2.** uncultivated, uninhabited. **3.** uncivilized, barbarous, barbarian. **4.** violent, furious, boisterous, tempestuous, stormy, disorderly, frenzied, turbulent, impetuous. **5.** frantic, mad, distracted, crazy, insane. **6.** enthusiastic, eager, anxious. **7.** excited. **8.** undisciplined, unruly, lawless, turbulent, self-willed, ungoverned, unrestrained, riotous, wayward, outrageous. **9.** unrestrained, unbridled, uncontrolled, untrammeled. **10.** reckless, rash, fantastic, extravagant, impracticable. **11.** queer, grotesque, bizarre, strange, imaginary, fanciful, visionary. **12.** disorderly, disheveled, unkempt. —*n.* **13.** waste, wilderness, desert.
Ant. tame, domesticated.

wilderness, *n.* wild.

wile, *n.* **1.** trick, artifice, stratagem, ruse, deception, contrivance, maneuver, device. **2.** deceit, cunning, trickery, chicanery, fraud, cheating, defrauding, imposture, imposition. —*v.* **3.** beguile, entice, lure.

will, *n.* **1.** determination, resolution, resoluteness, decision, forcefulness. **2.** volition, choice. **3.** wish, desire, pleasure, disposition, inclination. **4.** purpose, determination. **5.** order, direction, command, behest, bidding. —*v.* **6.** decide, decree, determine, direct, command, bid. **7.** bequeath, devise, leave.

willful, *adj.* **1.** willed, voluntary, intentional, volitional. **2.** self-willed, headstrong, perverse, obstinate, intractable, wayward, stubborn, intransigent, persistent, contrary, contumacious, refractory, disagreeable, pig-headed, cantankerous, unruly, inflexible, obdurate, adamant.
Ant. unintentional, involuntary; tractable.

wily, *adj.* crafty, cunning, artful, sly, foxy, tricky, intriguing, arch, designing, deceitful, treacherous, crooked, seditious.
Ant. dull, stupid.

win, *v.* **1.** succeed, advance, win out. **2.** obtain, gain, procure, secure, earn, acquire, achieve, attain, reach. **3.** win over, persuade, convince.
Ant. lose.

wind, *n.* **1.** air, blast, breeze, gust, zephyr, draught. **2.** hint, intimation, suggestion. **3.** vanity, conceitedness, flatulence, emptiness. **4.** winding, bend, turn, curve, twist, twisting. —*v.* **5.** bend, turn, meander, curve, be devious. **6.** coil, twine, twist, encircle, wreathe.

wink, *v.* **1.** blink, nictitate. **2.** twinkle, sparkle.

winning, *adj.* taking, engaging, charming, captivating, attractive, winsome.
Ant. losing, repulsive.

wisdom, *n.* **1.** discretion, judgment, discernment, sense, common sense, sagacity, insight, understanding, prudence. **2.** knowledge, information, learning, sapience, erudition, enlightenment.
Ant. stupidity.

wise, *adj.* **1.** discerning, judicious, sage, sensible, penetrating, sagacious, intelligent, perspicacious, profound, rational, prudent, reasonable. **2.** learned, erudite, schooled. —*n.* **3.** manner, fashion; respect, degree.
Ant. unwise.

wish, *v.* **1.** want, crave, desire, long for; need, lack. **2.** bid, direct, command, order. —*n.* **3.** desire, will, want, inclination.

wit, *n.* **1.** drollery, facetiousness, repartee, humor. **2.** understanding, intelligence, sagacity, wisdom, intellect, mind, sense.

withdraw, *v.* **1.** draw back *or* away, take back, subtract, remove; retract, recall, disavow, recant, revoke, rescind. **2.** depart, retire, retreat, secede.
Ant. advance.

wither, *v.* shrivel, fade, decay, wrinkle, shrink, dry,

decline, wilt, languish, droop, waste, waste away.
Ant. flourish, thrive.

withhold, *v.* hold back, restrain, check, keep back, suppress, repress.
Ant. promote, advance.

withstand, *v.* resist, oppose, confront, face, face up to, hold out against.
Ant. fail.

witness, *v.* **1.** see, perceive, observe, watch, look at, mark, notice, note. **2.** testify, bear witness. —*n.* **3.** beholder, spectator, eyewitness. **4.** testimony, evidence.

witty, *adj.* facetious, droll, humorous, funny, clever, original, sparkling, brilliant, jocose, jocular.
Ant. silly, stupid.

wizard, *n.* enchanter, magician, sorcerer, necromancer, conjurer, charmer, diviner, seer, soothsayer.

woe, *n.* distress, affliction, trouble, sorrow, grief, misery, anguish, tribulation, trial, agony, wretchedness, disconsolateness, depression, melancholy.
Ant. joy, happiness.

woman, *n.* female, lady.
Ant. man.

wonder, *v.* **1.** think, speculate, conjecture, meditate, ponder, question. **2.** marvel, be astonished *or* astounded. —*n.* **3.** surprise, astonishment, amazement, awe, bewilderment, puzzlement; admiration.

wonderful, *adj.* marvelous, extraordinary, remarkable, awesome, startling, wondrous, miraculous, prodigious, astonishing, amazing, astounding, phenomenal, unique, curious, strange, odd, peculiar.
Ant. usual, ordinary, common.

wont, *adj.* **1.** accustomed, used, habituated, wonted. —*n.* **2.** custom, habit, practice, use.
Ant. unaccustomed.

word, *n.* **1.** expression, utterance; assertion, affirmation, declaration, statement, asseveration. **2.** warrant, assurance, promise, pledge. **3.** intelligence, tidings, news, report, account, advice, information. **4.** signal, catchword, password, watchword, shibboleth, countersign. **5.** order, command, bidding. —*v.* **6.** express, style, phrase.

wording, *n.* diction, phrasing, expressing.

work, *n.* **1.** exertion, labor, toil, drudgery, moil. **2.** undertaking, task, enterprise, project, responsibility. **3.** employment, industry, occupation, business, profession, trade, calling, vocation, metier. **4.** deed, performance, fruit, fruition, feat, achievement. —*v.* **5.** labor, toil, moil, drudge. **6.** act, operate. **7.** operate, use, manipulate, manage, handle. **8.** bring about, perform, produce, cause, do, execute, finish, effect, originate, accomplish, achieve. **9.** make, fashion, execute, finish. **10.** move, persuade, influence.
Ant. leisure, indolence, idleness, sloth.

worldly, *adj.* **1.** secular, earthly, mundane, temporal,

terrestrial, common. **2.** mundane, urbane, cosmopolitan, suave.
Ant. spiritual; naive.

worry, *v.* **1.** fret, torment oneself, chafe, be troubled *or* vexed, fidget. **2.** trouble, torment, annoy, plague, pester, bother, vex, tease, harry, hector, harass, molest, persecute, badger, irritate, disquiet, disturb. —*n.* **3.** uneasiness, anxiety, apprehension, solicitude, concern, disquiet, fear, misgiving, care.

worship, *n.* **1.** reverence, homage, adoration, honor. **2.** regard, idolizing, idolatry, deification. —*v.* **3.** revere, respect, venerate, reverence, honor, glorify, adore. **4.** adore, adulate, idolize, deify, love, like.
Ant. detest.

worth, *adj.* **1.** deserving, meriting, justifying. —*n.* **2.** usefulness, value, importance, merit, worthiness, credit, excellence.
Ant. uselessness.

worthy, *adj.* commendable, meritorious, worthwhile, deserving, estimable, excellent, exemplary, righteous, upright, honest.
Ant. unworthy.

wound, *n.* **1.** injury, hurt, cut, stab, laceration, lesion, damage. **2.** harm, insult, pain, grief, anguish. —*v.* **3.** injure, hurt, harm, damage, cut, stab, lacerate.

wrath, *n.* anger, ire, rage, resentment, indignation, dudgeon, irritation, fury, choler, exasperation, passion.
Ant. equanimity, pleasure, delight.

wrathful, *adj.* angry, ireful, irate, furious, enraged, raging, incensed, resentful, indignant.
Ant. equable, pleased.

wreck, *n.* **1.** ruin, destruction, devastation, desolation. **2.** shipwreck. —*v.* **3.** shipwreck, spoil, destroy, devastate, ruin, shatter.
Ant. create.

wrest, *v.* extract, take.
Ant. give, yield.

wretched, *adj.* **1.** miserable, pitiable, dejected, distressed, woeful, afflicted, woebegone, forlorn, unhappy, depressed. **2.** sorry, miserable, despicable, mean, base, vile, bad, contemptible, poor, pitiful, worthless.
Ant. happy.

wrong, *adj.* **1.** bad, evil, wicked, sinful, immoral, piacular, iniquitous, reprehensible, unjust, crooked, dishonest. **2.** erroneous, inaccurate, incorrect, false, untrue, mistaken. **3.** improper, inappropriate, unfit, unsuitable. **4.** awry, amiss, out of order. —*n.* **5.** evil, wickedness, misdoing, misdeed, sin, vice, immorality, iniquity. —*v.* **6.** injure, harm, maltreat, abuse, oppress, cheat, defraud, dishonor.
Ant. right.

wry, *adj.* **1.** bent, twisted, crooked, distorted, awry, askew. **2.** devious, misdirected, perverted.
Ant. straight; pointed.

xanthous, *adj.* **1.** yellow. **2.** Mongolian.
x-ray, *v.* **1.** roentgenize. **—***n.* **2.** roentgenogram.
xylograph, *n.* wood engraving.
xyloid, *adj.* woodlike, ligneous.

Y

yawn, *v.* **1.** gape. **—***n.* **2.** opening, space, chasm.
yearning, *n.* longing, craving, desire.
yield, *v.* **1.** give forth, produce, furnish, supply, render, bear, impart, afford, bestow. **2.** give up, cede, surrender, submit, give way, concede, relinquish, abandon, abdicate, resign, waive, forgo. **3.** relax, bend, bow. **—***n.* **4.** produce, harvest, fruit, crop.
young, *adj.* **1.** youthful, juvenile, immature. **—***n.* **2.** offspring.
Ant. old, ancient; progenitors, parents.
youngster, *n.* youth, lad, stripling, child, boy.
Ant. oldster.
youth, *n.* **1.** youngness, minority, adolescence, teens, immaturity. **2.** young man, youngster, teen-ager, adolescent, stripling, lad, boy, juvenile.
Ant. maturity; man, adult.
youthful, *adj.* young.
Ant. old.
Yule, *n.* Christmas, Christmastide.

Z

zeal, *n.* ardor, enthusiasm, diligence, eagerness, fervor, desire, endeavor, fervency, warmth, earnestness, intensity, intenseness, passion, spirit.
Ant. apathy, coolness.
zealot, *n.* bigot, fanatic, maniac.
zealous, *adj.* ardent, enthusiastic, eager, earnest, fervid, fervent, warm, intense, passionate, spirited.
Ant. apathetic, uninterested, dispassionate, cool.
zephyr, *n.* breeze.
zest, *n.* piquancy, interest, charm; relish, gusto, heartiness, enjoyment, spice, tang.
Ant. dullness.
zone, *n.* **1.** belt, tract, area, region, district, section, girth. **2.** region, climate, clime: Torrid Zone; North and South Temperate Zone; North and South Frigid Zone. **—***v.* **3.** encircle, gird, girdle, band.
zymosis, *n.* fermentation; germination; decomposition; decay.